P9-CWE-980

Jennifer

Thousands of luscious tidbits of useless information are crammed into the pages of this intriguing volume.

Here, in kaleidoscopic array, are hundreds of facts to marvel about which you never knew before. None of this information will make a difference in your life, but each one of these morsels will provide great entertainment.

Who knows, the very next dinner party may offer the perfect opportunity for the "Did you know that..." gambit.

Profusely larded with humorous cartoons.

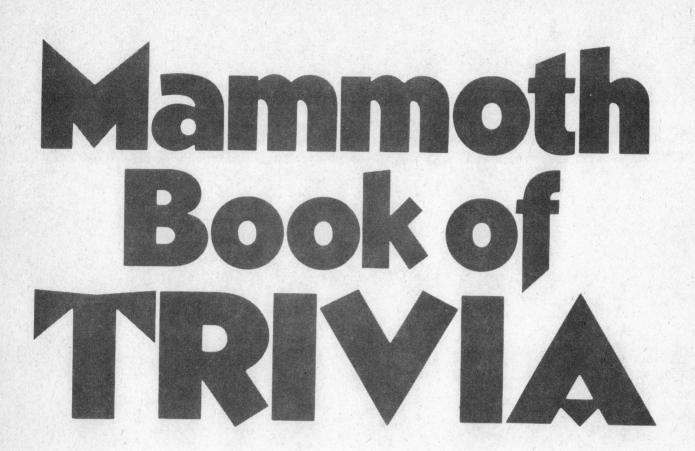

Mammoth Book of TRIVIA

JAMES MEYERS

A HART BOOK

A & W VISUAL LIBRARY • NEW YORK

COPYRIGHT © 1979 BY HART ASSOCIATES

ALL RIGHTS RESERVED. NO PART OF THIS WORK MAY BE
REPRODUCED OR TRANSFERRED IN ANY FORM OR BY ANY MEANS.
ELECTRONIC OR MECHANICAL, INCLUDING
PHOTOCOPYING, RECORDING, OR ANY INFORMATION
STORAGE AND RETRIEVAL SYSTEM, WITHOUT THE PERMISSION
IN WRITING FROM THE PUBLISHER.

PUBLISHED BY
A & W PUBLISHERS, INC.
95 MADISON AVENUE
NEW YORK, NEW YORK 10016

ISBN: 0-89104-164-8

PRINTED IN THE UNITED STATES OF AMERICA

INDEX
starts on page 429

Bulls cannot "see red." Bulls can see no colors at all; in fact, they are thought to be completely color-blind.

Heavy Hail

Most hailstones measure from a half-inch to two inches in diameter, but significantly larger ice balls have been known to plummet to earth. You can be thankful you were not in the vicinity of Coffeyville, Kansas, on September 3, 1970. On that day, a hailstone seven-and-a-half inches in diameter, weighing 1.67 pounds, dropped from the skies—but landed harmlessly.

Giant hailstones that landed on the Russian village of Kostov in July, 1923, were not so benign. Many cattle were killed by the ice balls, many of which weighed over a pound, and 23 people perished trying to save their battered livestock.

And in 1888, a hailstorm in Moradabad, India, took an estimated 246 lives!

What's more popular in the United States, butter or margarine? The average American consumes a little more than 11 pounds of margarine each year, compared to just under five pounds of butter.

The pulse of the average adult is usually around 70 or 80 beats per minute. The heart of a small songbird can beat over a thousand times per minute.

Our planet is getting crowded, and so is the space around us. There are now over 4,000 satellites and discarded rocket or satellite parts orbiting the earth! More than half were launched by the United States.

Have you ever seen the cryptic words ETAOIN SHRDLU at the top of a paragraph in a newspaper? No, they are not scrambled words. The keyboard of a standard linotype machine contains the letters of ETAOIN on its left-hand column, and the letters of SHRDLU on the next column from the left. To test his linotype machine, a typesetter often runs his fingers down the two left-hand keyboard columns. That the strange words appear at times in newspapers is the fault of the proofreader, not the typesetter.

Incidentally, the "words" ETAOIN SHRDLU contain the first 12 letters of the alphabet in order of the frequency with which they are used in English.

The game of croquet evolved from the medieval French game of *paille-maille*. In England, the old game was called "pall-mall," and London's famed Pall Mall owes its name to a pall-mall alley that once occupied the site.

Although the English pronounce the name of the Pall Mall the same as we pronounce the world "pell-mell," the latter does not owe its origin to either the game of *paille-maille*, or the Pall Mall in London. The word instead is derived from a French term meaning "in disorder."

Noah's ark must have been roomy indeed. There are presently some three *million* species of animals on earth. Of these, only a few thousand are mammals.

Although "sideburns" do indeed grow on the side of the face, the origin of the term has nothing to do with their location. Sideburns is a corruption of "burnsides," a term taken from the name of a Civil War general who sported the facial growth, Ambrose Burnside.

To escape its many enemies, a flying fish shoots out of the water and glides as far as 500 feet on its greatly enlarged fins. Some of the most powerful of flying fish can even jump over the deck of a small ship.

Botanists in the seventeenth century were fascinated by a strange fungal growth that much resembles a small bird's nest with a clutch of tiny eggs. This fungus, *Cyathus striatus*, was thought by some to actually contain eggs. Others thought the egglike lumps inside the cup of the plant were seeds. Still others claimed to have seen these lumps give birth to live birds!

Of course, none of these claims were true. The spongy lumps within the acorn-sized cups are actually spore sacs, filled with thousands of tiny spores. The plant's resemblance to a bird's nest appears to be completely incidental: the fungus derives no benefit from its inadvertent mimicry.

The city of Troy described by Homer in *The Iliad* was located not in Greece, but in present-day Turkey. When the supposed site of the ancient city was excavated late in the nineteenth century, nine cities were found, one on top of the other. The sixth city to be built on the site is thought to be Homer's Troy.

For a few centuries after their invention in the thirteenth century, eyeglasses were regarded as a sign of respect, suggesting learning and importance. Contemporary paintings often depicted saints wearing spectacles. A portrait of St. Jerome, painted in 1480 by Domenico Ghirlandajo, showed a pair of spectacles dangling from the saint's desk, though Jerome died a thousand years earlier. So St. Jerome later became the patron saint of the spectacles maker's guild.

Among the many misconceptions the Greek philosopher Aristotle entertained was the belief that men have more teeth than women. And Aristotle was married twice!

In the days of ancient Greece, an hour was defined as one-twelfth of the day. But the day was measured from sunrise to sunset. Thus, the daytime hour was longer in summer than in winter!

French Cut-Off

Parisian flophouses of the nineteenth century offered their more indigent guests a place at the "two-penny leanover," a long bench with a rope stretched in front of it which the sleeper could lean over during his sit-up slumber. In the morning, an inaptly named "valet" rudely awoke the guests by cutting the rope.

In France, the king's bed, known as the "Bed of State," was treated with a reverence that sometimes surpassed that afforded the throne itself. Persons entering the king's chamber were expected to genuflect in front of the bed, even if the king was not in the room.

In 1931, the government of the Netherlands hired Mynheer Verhaat, a self-styled rain-maker, to scatter super-cooled ice crystals into a bank of clouds in an attempt to produce rain. A fleet of army planes was placed at Verhaat's disposal, and the upper atmosphere duly sprinkled with ice dust. When the rain-making was over, all that had been soaked was the taxpayer.

Perhaps Verhaat had the last laugh. The date of his rain-making fiasco? April 1—April Fool's Day.

Cleopatra, the queen who ruled Egypt during the first century B.C., was not Egyptian. She and the other seven women who ruled under the name of Cleopatra were of Macedonian ancestry, descendants of a general who served Alexander the Great and founded the Ptolemaic dynasty.

Cleopatra was a name assumed by all the Ptolemaic queens of Egypt, after the first queen of that name. The name of Julius Caesar's mistress was actually Auletes.

The great cities of the ancient world probably appear larger in legend and lore than they were in actuality. Historians estimate that the cities of Babylon, Nineveh, Athens, Carthage, and Alexandria at their height harbored from 250,000 to 500,000 people, while Imperial Rome had a population of less than a million. Columbus, Ohio, a moderately sized city by modern standards, has a population of over 500,000.

A medieval superstition holds that to remove a wart, simply cut an onion in half, rub the exposed inner flesh against the wart, tie the onion back together, and bury it. When the onion has decomposed, the wart will have disappeared.

Deep-Sea Flying

Where can a plane fly further below sea level than some submarines can dive? At the Dead Sea, of course. The shore of the Dead Sea, the deepest land depression on earth, lies about 1,300 feet below sea level, on the border between Israel and Jordan. Thus, a plane flying just above the surface of the sea would be much further below sea level than a submarine operating at a depth of 1,000 feet!

Although the Dead Sea receives some six million tons of water each day from the Jordan River, the surface level of the salt lake remains virtually constant due to the high rate of evaporation in the desert area. Due to climatic changes, however, the sea has begun to rise slowly over recent decades, rising 20 feet since the 1880's.

One reason for the preponderance of spectator games in ancient Rome was the simple fact that most Romans had a good deal of time on their hands. Today, the average person works from 230 to 240 days a year. The ancient Romans, due to the availability of free or low-cost grain provided by the government, worked on the average about 205 days a year. Of the remaining 160 days, as many as 93 each year were devoted to spectacles such as chariot races, plays, and gladiatorial games.

The winter of 1933 found the city of Damascus, Syria, as dry as a bone. A conclave of Moslem religious leaders met to decide why the faithful's prayers for rain were unanswered. The holy council finally determined that the drought was due to the up-and-down movements of the yo-yos that were then the rage among the city's children. The impious instruments were ordered seized immediately.

You may scoff—but it rained the following day!

An English jury list surviving from 1658, which was compiled in a Puritan district, includes the baptismal names Be-thankful, Live-in-peace, Goodgift, Joy-from-above, Faint-not, More-fruit, Accepted, Stand-fast-on-high, Called, Return, Search-the-Scriptures, and Weep-not, as well as the names Earth Adams, Meek Brewer, Be-courteous Cole, and Kill-sin Pimple.

In 1935, the Illinois State Legislature passed a bill designating "the American language" as the official tongue of that state. "English" was outlawed.

You may soon be able to discard the magazine rack in your bathroom. A company in West Germany now manufactures rolls of toilet paper with English lessons printed on the paper.

The longest fight in the history of boxing took place in New Orleans on April 6-7, 1893. Andy Bowen and Jack Burke fought for 110 rounds—seven hours and 19 minutes—only to have the referee break up the fight and declare it "no contest."

Cubic zirconia gems, man-made byproducts of laser technology, can reportedly pass as diamonds to almost any eye—and cost but $12 a carat!

In September, 1938, a tremendous hurricane struck New England and parts of Long Island, killing 600 people, destroying 275 million trees, downing 20,000 miles of electric wires, damaging 26,000 automobiles, and demolishing hundreds of homes. Near Madison, Connecticut, a two-story house was blown a half-mile by the storm and came to rest *upside down.* Oddly enough, not a single window pane was broken!

John Kemble, a noted English actor of the early nineteenth century, devised a rather ingenious method for erasing a debt. Saddled with a bill for room and board that he could not pay, the actor spun a top around his room over the head of his sick landlord. Much to Kemble's delight, he was promptly evicted.

A Costly Comma

In 1872, Congress passed and the President signed a Tariff Act listing among non-taxable items "fruit-plants, tropical and semi-tropical for the purpose of propagation and cultivation. . ." At least, that's what the lawmakers *thought* the law read. Actually, a typist had inadvertently inserted a comma instead of a hyphen after "fruit," with the result that "fruit, plants, tropical and semi-tropical. . ." became exempt from import taxes instead of the intended "fruit-plants."

A harmless error? Keen-eyed lawyers spotted the mistake, sued the Treasury Department for tariff refunds in behalf of a group of fruit importers, and won over $3,000,000 as a settlement. The attorneys then used the cash to finance the construction of the Culver Line railroad in Brooklyn, New York, that later became part of New York City's rapid transit system. Thus, a misplaced comma financed a railroad!

Time on My Hands!

Have you ever wondered what kind of individual spends his time toiling over the construction of crossword puzzles? Well, of 100 regular contributors to two New York puzzle magazines, 25 are currently in prison.

The bidet, that peculiarly Gallic instrument for feminine hygiene, made its first appearance during the early eighteenth century. The device, first mentioned in 1710, must have been unfamiliar to many Frenchmen in 1739, when a dealer offered a bidet as a "porcelain violin-case with four legs."

The Ritz Carlton Hotel in New York was originally equipped with bidets, but the hotel was forced to remove them after a flood of complaints from outraged Puritanical guests.

The easternmost part of Brazil is actually half the distance from Africa as it is from the United States. Traveling due north from Natal, Brazil, you would reach a point in the North Atlantic Ocean only a few hundred miles west of the Azores—far closer to Europe than to North America!

Today, the words "housewife" and "hussy" are almost mutually exclusive. But around 1800, the word "housewife" carried such derogatory connotations that it spawned the shorter "hussy," with its present meaning.

The literary achievements of English poet Percy Bysshe Shelley seem all the more remarkable when you remember that the poet died at the age of 29. And Shelley's contemporary, the poet John Keats, died a year before Shelley—at the age of 25!

Kleenex tissues were originally manufactured as gas mask filters during World War I.

About one-third of the 18 million volumes in the Library of Congress, the world's largest book and manuscript depository, are too brittle to be handled.

The Bill for Biking

The most important bicycle race in the world today is the annual Tour de France. Begun in 1903, the race is now one of Europe's major sporting events. Originally 3,560 miles long, the present course stretches about 2,780 miles through France, Spain, Switzerland, Italy, and Belgium. An estimated 15 million people in France alone turn out to watch the bikers as they wend their way over hill and dale and climb over mountain passes as high as 8,000 feet. In some towns, petty criminals are released from jail for the day so that they can take in the spectacle.

One observer has calculated that if one-third of all Frenchmen lose one-third of a day's work due to the race, the Tour de France takes a toll of close to two billion dollars on the French economy!

The grebe, the mute swan, some ducks, and the loon have a special way of caring for their young. Very often, especially at the first sign of danger, the crested grebe sinks until its back is level with the surface of the water. Its young climb onto its back. Then the parent grebe rises to its swimming position, and with strong strokes carries them across the water to safety.

The tiny nation of Andorra, nestled among the Pyrenees Mountains between France and Spain, has enjoyed independence—with a few interruptions—since the days of Charlemagne, early in the ninth century. What language predominates in the 188-square-mile republic? French? Spanish? Neither—Catalan, a Romance dialect spoken in the area of Barcelona, Spain, is the official language of Andorra.

A jogger, burning off about 100 calories per mile, would have to jog a mile a day for a year to shed ten pounds.

Incidentally, you would burn off about 100 calories in an hour of card playing.

Mexico, currently the nation with the highest official murder rate, averages about 46 homicides for each 100,000 persons annually. But during a recent year, Soweto, the large black township outside Johannesburg, South Africa, was the scene of 877 murders and culpable homicides—giving the township a murder rate of 97 per 100,000 persons each year!

In addition, Soweto reported 1,336 rapes and 8,239 grievous assaults during the same year, for a total of 1,161 serious offenses per 100,000 persons. One out of every 43 of Soweto's 900,000 persons was either the perpetrator or victim of a serious crime that year. And South African officials estimate that, if all crimes in Soweto were reported, the figures could be as much as 50 percent higher!

If you really want to see time fly, you might take advantage of an unusual trip offered by an Alaskan airline. The journey includes a flight that circles the North Pole, crossing all of the world's 24 time zones within one hour!

Bamboo is the world's largest grass plant, belonging to the same plant family as the grass on our front lawn. Some species of bamboo grow in tufts to a height of 100 feet. And the Molocca bamboo can grow two feet in just 24 hours.

The Prussian monarch Frederick the Great, an avid coffee drinker, sometimes had his java prepared with champagne rather than water.

Meet the Press is the longest-running television show still on the air. The Sunday interview program was first aired on November 20, 1947, and is now over three decades old.

Twopenny Dam

On August 17, 1958, a severe earthquake in western Montana caused a great landslide from a nearby mountain to fall into the Madison River upstream from Ennis, Montana, completely blocking the flow of the river. An estimated 43 million cubic yards of rock and earth crashed from the mountainside into the valley, forming a dam 300 feet high and more than a half mile long. The Madison River soon backed up behind the barrier, forming a lake seven miles long.

At first, engineers thought that the dam would wash away. But by cutting a spillway channel through the rock and earth dam, they lowered the level of the lake 50 feet and shortened the length of the lake to about four miles, greatly reducing the water pressure on the natural dam. A dam of this size would cost about $50 million and take months or even years to construct—but the earthquake accomplished the feat in a few seconds. The lake behind the dam is today named, appropriately enough, Earthquake Lake.

Silhouettes and Shadows

The form of pictorial art known as the silhouette dates back to stone-age man, who traced the outline of a person's shadow on the wall of his cave, then filled it in with colored pigments. The ancient Greeks also traced shadows to draw profile portraits.

Profile portraiture became popular in Europe in the 17th century, when artists used a candle or lamp to cast their subject's shadow against a wall or screen. When paper came into abundant supply, artists began to cut out their profile portraits from black paper and mount them on light-colored backing. This kind of silhouette construction was all the rage in Europe around the middle of the 18th century.

The term we use to refer to these outline drawings comes from Etienne de Silhoette, the French finance minister in 1759. Silhoette instituted a series of new taxes that were particularly odious to the wealthy, and attempted to cut back the expenditures of the royal household. He was forced to resign after only a few months in office, but his name was applied to a new kind of men's pocketless trousers, and *a la Silhoette* came to mean "on the cheap" in reference to his parsimonious fiscal policy.

Partly because cut-out paper portraits were considered art "on the cheap," and partly because Silhoette himself produced paper profiles as a hobby, these black outline drawings soon came to be known as "silhouettes."

As an art form, silhouettes go back to ancient times—to the black figures that adorn Etruscan and other Greek pottery. But the great era of silhouette art dates from the final decades of the 18th century. During that period, the new interest in the science of physiognomy developed by Lavater and the general revival of interest in classical art combined to make silhouettes a dominant art form, supplanting miniature painting in France and Germany. Silhouettes also became popular in England and America, and their popularity continues.

Brussels' best-known statue is "le Manikin Pis," a 20-inch figure of a boy responding to Nature's call, that has stood in the heart of the city for 500 years. During this time, personages such as Louis XV and Napoleon have presented the bronze lad with many medals, swords, and fancy uniforms which he has worn on appropriate occasions. Among the costumes have been the dress of a Belgian Grenadier, a French Chevalier, a British Master of Hounds, a Chinese Manchu, an Indian Chief, and an American G.I.

Captain Allardyce Barclay of Ury, Scotland, once walked 1,000 miles in 1,000 hours to settle a bet.

The record for non-stop piano playing is 44 days, set by Heinz Arntz in 1967. Except for two hours of sleep each day, the 67-year-old Arntz played continually for 1,056 hours. During his stint, which began in Germany, Arntz was carried in a van to a seaport and traveled from Germany to the United States on a steamship, finishing his performance at Roosevelt, Long Island.

The early kings of France stuck three hairs plucked from their beards in the seal of official papers to lend the documents greater sanction.

Of all symbols appearing on the flags of the world, the star is by far the most common. Forty-one flags have this symbol in one form or another. The second most popular symbol, the crescent, appears on only nine flags.

Just Desserts

The first commercially-made ice cream in the United States was sold by a Mr. Hall in New York City in 1786. The first ice cream soda was reputedly concocted by a Robert Green of Philadelphia, who, in 1874, added ice cream to plain soda water. But credit for the first ice cream cone goes to a young ice cream salesman at the 1904 Louisiana Purchase Exposition in St. Louis—or rather, to his date. The salesman, Charles E. Menches, gave an ice cream sandwich and a bouquet of flowers to the young lady he was escorting, and she rolled one of the layers of the sandwich into a cone to hold the flowers, thus founding an American institution.

There are more than 3,000 varieties of tea. Like wines, teas take their names from the districts where they are grown, such as Darjeeling, Assam, Ceylon, etc.

One Type of Speedster

The record for rapid typing is held by Albert Tagora of Paterson, New Jersey, who on October 23, 1923, typed an average of 147 words a minute for one full hour. During that stretch, Tagora ran off 8,840 words—for an average of 12½ strokes per second!

Of all common fowl, the duck is the bird that requires the longest cooking.

Platinum is so malleable that a troy ounce of the metal can be stretched into a wire more than 10,000 miles long.

The civilized nation with the longest average life expectancy is Sweden—71.6 years for men, 75.4 years for women. These figures just about match those of the Australian Aborigines.

The most spectacular musical event in the United States occurred at the World Peace Jubilee, held in Boston from June 17 to July 4, 1872, to celebrate the end of the Franco-Prussian War. An orchestra of 2,000 instruments, including a bass drum 25 feet in diameter, was bolstered by a chorus of 20,000. To lead this vast aggregation in a rendition of *The Beautiful Danube*, its composer, Johann Strauss, was brought from Vienna at a cost of $20,000—and in 1872, that was quite a sum.

Fish can be caught in the Sahara Desert. Strangely enough, there are many underground streams in the Sahara—where, by digging through the sand, a desert angler can obtain fresh-water fish.

Birmingham, England—an inland city—has more miles of canals than Venice, the "Queen of the Seas."

You probably know that a female fox is a *vixen*, and a female peacock is a *peahen*, but how about a female aviator? She's called an *aviatrix*. And a female sultan is a *sultana*, a female maharaja is a *maharanee*, a female kaiser is a *kaiserin*, and a female cob (swan) is a *pen*.

The U.S. Army Overland Train, the longest vehicle in the world, is 572 feet long—almost $\frac{1}{10}$ of a mile! The train, which is used to transport rockets or other very long objects, weighs 450 tons, has 54 wheels, 4 engines, and a 7,828-gallon fuel capacity.

Posers

Why do we enjoy puzzles? What's the fun in being stumped, frustrated, maddened? Maybe it's man's love of a challenge, and maybe it's mere masochism. In either case, a good puzzle is hard to resist.

Perhaps the oldest of all puzzles is the riddle, and perhaps the most famous of all riddles is that asked by the Sphinx:

What goes on four legs in the morning,
on two at noon, and on three at night?

Oedipus answered the riddle correctly, and thus became Oedipus Rex. His solution: "Man. In infancy he crawls; in his prime, he walks; and in old age, he leans on a staff."

Another famous riddle is one that is reputed to have stumped Homer. Someone propounded these two lines to the bard:

What we caught we threw away;
What we couldn't catch, we kept.

The answer to this one is fleas.

Another early puzzle which continues to perplex us in its various forms is the labyrinth, an intricate arrangement of chambers and passages designed to befuddle the unfortunate person trying to navigate it. The great labyrinth of ancient times was built by Amenemhet IV of Egypt near Lake Moeris; its purpose is unknown. More renowned was a labyrinth built, according to Greek myth, for King Minos in Crete by Daedalus to house the voracious minotaur.

In comparison, a crossword puzzle or jigsaw may seem pretty tame. But anyone who has been stuck on a real toughie knows what a victim of King Minos must have felt like as he wended his way through the cul-de-sacs of the labyrinth, heading toward his death.

The Miracle, one of the most spectacular dramas ever presented in the United States, required a cast of 700 and a theatre redesigned to resemble a Gothic Cathedral. When the play went on the road, a train of 204 cars was needed to transport the actors and equipment.

The most famous of all golf courses and clubs is the Royal and Ancient of St. Andrews. Founded in 1774, its basic rules were soon accepted throughout the world. After 1888, the year when the St. Andrews Golf Club of Westchester County, New York, was founded, the game gained in popularity in the United States.

Speed Demon— 19th-Century Style

Chicagoans were out in force on Thanksgiving Day, 1895. They came to see a new-fangled contraption called an automobile. A few of the gasoline-powered horseless carriages were going to race.

The route lay from the heart of Chicago to a nearby suburb and back. The road measured exactly 54.36 miles. The winner would have to cover that terrific distance without breaking down.

J. Frank Duryea busted the tape seven hours and 17 minutes after the start of the race. He had covered the distance at an average speed of 7.5 miles an hour!

The crowd went wild!

What really revolutionized weaponry was the invention of gunpowder, usually attributed to the Chinese firecracker-makers of the 9th century. Gunpowder was introduced into Europe in the 1300s. Field artillery and cannons were first used by the Dutch.

The first advertised radio broadcast was transmitted from Brant Rock, Massachusetts, on Christmas Eve of 1906 by Professor Reginald Aubrey Fessenden. But the first radio station with a regular broadcasting schedule— KDKA of Pittsburgh, Pennsylvania—did not come on the scene until 1920. Today, there are more than 4,370 AM stations and 2,350 FM stations broadcasting in the United States.

In medieval France, King Philip Augustus decreed that the points on his subjects' shoes should be between six and twelve inches, depending upon their station—the longer the point, the higher the rank.

It has been calculated that in the last 3,500 years there have been only 230 years of peace throughout the civilized world.

A Bolt from the Blue

The intense heat of lightning is sometimes responsible for odd accidents. One lady's earring was melted by lightning, and another bolt soldered all the links in a one-yard chain. The U.S. National Safety Council's Report for 1943 told of a soldier being welded into his sleeping bag when the zipper was struck by lightning. The startled soldier had to be cut loose.

The dog who is reputed to have lived the longest was a black Labrador named "Adjutant," who died on November 30, 1963, at the age of 27 years and three months.

Weather or Not

The first thermometers, devised independently by Galileo and Sanctorius at the turn of the 17th century, consisted essentially of a bulb atop a stem which descended into a liquid. Heating or cooling the bulb affected the height of the column of liquid in the tube, which was marked by a scale.

About a hundred years later, in 1714, Fahrenheit of Danzig invented the mercury thermometer to measure heat. The thermometer of Reaumur, invented about 15 years later, used alcohol to measure cold. Mercury was not feasible for this thermometer because mercury solidifies at -39°C.

The centigrade thermometer, created by Celsius in 1742, is used primarily in laboratory work. It has the computational advantage of a 100-degree range between the freezing point and the boiling point.

In 1918, at Bahia Feliz, Chile, rain fell on all but 18 days of the year. And on those 18 it drizzled!

Rum, obtained from fermented sugarcane or fermented molasses, is produced primarily in the Caribbean. Different varieties derive from Puerto Rico, Cuba, Jamaica, and Mexico.

When a Manchurian child is ready to learn how to walk, his parents often embroider a cat's head, whiskers and all, on the toes of his shoes. The parents hope that this will make their child as sure-footed as the cat.

Dave White's round at the Winchester Country Club started fine, but he blew up on the fifth hole and took a horrifying 13! Then the Massachusetts pro settled down with a vengeance. He shot 10 straight birdies to salvage a par round of 72.

The fattest man on record was Robert Earl Hughes, who bequeathed over 1,000 pounds of adipose tissue to posterity when he died of uremia in 1958, in Bremen, Indiana. The heaviest woman, Mrs. Percy Pearl Washington, came 150 pounds short of Hughes' record. She weighed about 880 pounds at her death, in 1972, in Milwaukee.

Missouri and Tennessee both touch on eight other states.

A Stroke of Luck

William Northmore, an inveterate gambler from Okehampton, England, lost his entire fortune of $850,000 on the turn of one card. The townspeople of Okehampton felt so sorry for Northmore that they elected him to Parliament in 1714, and in every election thereafter until his death.

A Breach of Fashion

Until the time of the French Revolution, most men wore knee breeches rather than trousers. But in 1789, supporters of the Revolution separated themselves from the royalists by adopting trousers. Accordingly, they were know as the *sans-culottes* ("without breeches").

In token of their sympathy with the French rebels, many ordinary Americans sported trousers between 1790 and 1800. But it was not until a decade or so later that trousers substituted for breeches on formal occasions. The first President who habitually dressed in long trousers was James Madison.

You've certainly heard of the 4-H Club, but did you know what the four H's stand for? Head, Heart, Health, and Hands.

No Soap

The ancients are believed to have washed themselves with ashes and water, which was followed by an application of oil or grease to relieve the irritation caused by the ashes. The first mention of soap, as we know it today, was made in the first century A.D. by Pliny, who wrote that some Germanic tribes washed their hair with a mixture of tallow and ashes of wood.

Subsequently, soap became popular in Rome, but fell into decline when the Roman Empire fell in 476. Some 300 years later, soap was "re-discovered" by the Italians.

Oddly enough, soap did not reach France until the early 13th century. For many years, the English—like the French—favored perfumes as a means of, if not keeping themselves clean, at least seeming to. But by the 17th century, soap became common in England, and in its North American colonies as well. In colonial America and Canada, many housewives made their own soap from waste animal fats and lye.

Although soap may be made of many substances, all methods of manufacture are based on the same principle. Fats and oils are heated, an alkali introduced, and the mixture stirred. When salt is added, the brew forms a curd which floats to the top. This curd is the soap. To produce a purer soap, the curds may be washed with a salt solution and allowed to settle. The upper layer thus formed is the pure soap, which is then churned, perfumed, colored, poured into huge frames, cut, shaped, and stamped.

The world's record for non-stop see-sawing is 101 hours, set by two California boys in 1964.

A tiny tropical fish called the anableps has eyes that work just like a pair of bifocals. The upper half of each eye is focused for water-surface vision, the lower half for underwater sight.

Gasoline has no definite freezing point. Ordinary gas will solidify only under temperatures of between 180 and 240 degrees below zero—a temperature which has never been reached on this planet outside the laboratory.

Slumberland

How much sleep does one need? Answer: Anywhere from five to ten hours. Science has come up with no explanation as to why one individual requires more sleep than another. An infant sleeps most of the day because he is growing at a faster pace than at any other period in his life.

As we age, the quality of our sleep tends to gradually deteriorate. The sleep of older people is sometimes so fragmented that it is little more than a series of catnaps. Winston Churchill managed to turn his handicap into an advantage. He took short snoozes throughout the day to rejuvenate himself; and he insisted that his daily nap in the afternoon turned one day, in effect, into two. Still, medical evidence suggests that sustained sleep is more helpful; "to sleep like a baby" is an apt description of ideal slumber.

However, not even the sleep of infants is always tranquil. In the 1950s, psychologists Eugene Aserinsky and Nathaniel Kleitman observed a regular pattern in the sleep of infants: intervals of quiet slumber alternated with periods of body activity. Extending their discovery to a study of adult sleep, these scientists noticed recurring periods of rapid eye movements *(REMs)* beneath the closed lid, alternating with periods of peaceful sleep. These REMs, the psychologists learned, signaled the onset of dreams.

The Geodesic Dome is the only man-made object that becomes structurally stronger as it increases in size.

America's Favorite Hymns

Of the estimated 400,000 Christian hymns that have been published, fewer than 500 are in common use, and only 150 of them are well known by churchgoers. To determine their popularity in this country, a poll was made, not long ago, which disclosed that four hymns alone constituted the first choice of 20,384 of the 30,000 churchgoers questioned. And the relative popularity of these four outstanding favorites is shown by the following figures: For every 100 persons whose first choice was *Abide With Me*, the hymn that led, 75 preferred *Nearer My God to Thee*, 57 preferred *Lead, Kindly Light*, and 47 preferred *Rock of Ages*.

The largest mushroom farm in the world is located near West Winfield, Pennsylvania, in an old limestone mine. The farm produces about 14 million pounds of mushrooms each year.

The term "limited" when used to refer to an express train does not, as often supposed, refer to the limited number of stops the express will make. Instead, it originates from the practice of running special fast trains with limited seating space.

When the Wright Brothers made aviation history at Kitty Hawk, North Carolina, their initial 12-second flight spanned a distance shorter than the wingspan of a Boeing 747 jumbo jet—which measures 195.7 feet from tip to tip.

It is commonly thought that an intestinal parasite, like a tapeworm, produces an insatiable appetite in its host. Actually, the amount of food necessary to maintain a parasite of this type is almost infinitesimal.

It Never Rains, It Pours

New York City, with an average annual rainfall of 43 inches, is pretty bad. Foggy London has only 25, and sunny Los Angeles gets by with 15. Bergen, Norway, seems wet indeed with 73 inches. But Bergen is dry as a desert compared with Cherrapungi, India, which has an annual downpour of 432 inches, or 36 feet!

The elephant is the only animal with four knees.

When you're stuck on a crowded highway it may seem as if everyone and his brother owned a car. Actually, more than half of the people in the world still rely on their own or their animals' muscles not only for transportation, but for all their other power as well.

The hummingbird is the only bird that can fly backwards or hover in the same spot like a helicopter.

All in the Family

Ch'in Shih Hwang-ti, the Emperor who constructed the Great Wall of China, possessed an immediate family numbering in the thousands. According to some ancient records, the Emperor had more than 13,000 wives—one for each of the days he reigned! Ts'in Shih housed his huge family in an imperial palace said to have contained more than 10,000 rooms. And the Emperor ordered that his entire family be buried with his body after he died.

Apparently, the Emperor's wishes were not carried out, for after his death in 210 B.C., his eldest son had to go to the trouble of beheading 12 brothers, ten sisters, and all other relatives who might covet his crown.

The largest shark in the world, the *Rhincodon typus*, or whale shark, can grow to a length of 50 feet, and specimens 70 feet long have been reported. But there's no need to fear the jaws of this mammoth creature—the whale shark eats plankton.

In an average year in the United States, one teenage girl in every 50 gives birth to an illegitimate child. About half of the over 400,000 illegitimate children born in this country each year are born to girls age 15 to 19, including over 10,000 born to girls under 15 years old.

Women 40 years of age or older give birth to about 2,300 illegitimate children each year.

A titmouse is not a mouse, but a small bird. A ladybird is not a bird, but a beetle. A silverfish is not a fish, but an insect. And a guinea pig is not a pig, but a rodent—and it doesn't come from Guinea, either!

The forerunners of the game of horseshoe pitching are over 2,000 years old. The game of quoits, played with rings instead of horseshoes, goes back to the days of ancient Greece, and was played by English peasants throughout the Middle Ages. When some peasants couldn't find the time to fashion quoit rings, they substituted ordinary horseshoes—and that's how our game of horseshoe pitching was born.

If you fancy yourself a nifty horseshoe pitcher, you might want to try your hand at matching the current world's record for consecutive ringers—72!

The Ross Ice Shelf, a floating ice sheet attached to the continent of Antarctica, covers as much territory as the entire country of France! The ice sheet, from 500 to 1,200 or more feet thick, reaches to within 300 miles of the South Pole.

Our number system uses a set of numerals commonly referred to in the West as "Arabic numerals." These numbers were devised not by the Arabs, but by scholars in India. It was the Arabs, however, who introduced the numbers to Europe.

Astronomers have estimated that stars range in size from bodies 2,000 times as large as the sun to others as small as the moon.

There is no "weather" in the stratosphere. This region of the atmosphere, which begins about six miles above the earth, is above the clouds and the weather changes we experience occur only below. Blizzards and rainstorms do not occur in the stratosphere, where it is still, quiet, and bitterly cold—often more than 100 degrees below zero!

The expression "breed like flies" is quite apt. If all the descendants of a single pair of flies survived, they would number over 335 *trillion* at the end of one summer.

A Peasant a Day

Otto of Bavaria went to his grave firmly convinced he'd murdered hundreds of innocent peasants. In 1886, the line of succession to the Bavarian crown left Otto as the nominal king, but the Prince never assumed the throne. He'd been declared insane and locked in a room by his family for the previous 14 years. There the Mad Prince carried on a spirited repartee with the ghosts that lived in his dresser drawer, and indulged a singularly gruesome belief: The murder of a peasant a day would keep the doctor away.

Each day, one of Otto's guards would load the Prince's gun with blanks while another guard donned peasant garb and strolled in a field beside Otto's window. The Prince would appear in the window, take aim, and fire—and the "peasant" would obligingly fall dead at the sound of the shot.

A mathematician once computed the number of permutations possible with a standard 11-by-11-square crossword puzzle—that is, given 122 squares and a 26-letter alphabet, how many different puzzles could be constructed? The answer was found to be 24,873 plus 222 zeroes. That's higher than the number of seconds that have elapsed since the beginning of the universe!

Lobsters were once so plentiful near Plymouth, Massachusetts, and other parts of New England that they were gathered for use as fertilizer when washed ashore during a storm.

In 1817, an Englishman named Ashford accused a gentleman of murdering Ashford's sister. The accused, Thornton, challenged Ashford to decide the case in battle, and appeared in full armor, with a lance and a sword, to settle the matter. Ashford, naturally, did not appear for the combat.

Thornton then claimed he had won the case—and he was right. Parliament had neglected to officially abolish the medieval custom of trial by battle!

The word "idiot," far from a complimentary term today, is derived from a Greek word that originally meant merely a private citizen or layman. Thus, all men not in public office were "idiots." Today, we tend to regard the converse as more apt.

Pool Shark

In 1956, the great pocket billiards champion Willie Mosconi won a tournament match against Jimmy Moore by running the entire game—150 balls—in one inning. Moore played a safety shot on the break, and never got to shoot again.

The skillful Mosconi once ran 526 balls in a row—a world's record—and won the world's championship in 1953 by running the game in only two innings.

Otto Witte impersonated a king and fooled an entire country

In 1913, Albanian revolutionaries threw off the yoke of the Ottoman Empire and established their nation as an independent state. For a nominal ruler, the little Moslem nation on the Adriatic naturally looked to Turkey, and chose Prince Helim Eddine.

The capital city of Durazzo was decorated colorfully and the people crowded together to welcome the prince's carriage. The first to emerge was a seven-foot man in an ornate military costume, with a saber at his side and a fez atop his head. "Stand back," he cried. "Make way for the new Prince of Albania!" The second man out of the carriage was not so tall, but exceedingly broad in the chest and shoulders.

After these two, the Prince stepped forward, to the cheers of the masses. After a few words of greeting, Helim Eddine offered his first official decree: that he was now a citizen of Albania, not Turkey, and that there would be a week of general celebration and an amnesty for all prisoners. The people responded wildly to this magnanimous gesture. The new nation had a new national hero.

That night, at a feast, Helim Eddine was presented with a 25-woman harem. As befit a Moslem ruler, he gratefully accepted this gift. The next day, he further endeared himself to the natives of Durazzo by appointing the city's councilmen to be his cabinet. The councilmen were so honored that they moved to promote the Prince to King. The Prince graciously acceded to their wishes, suggesting that as King he be known as King Otto. This

puzzled the cabinet members, since Otto was a distinctly non-Moslem name. Nevertheless, they had no reason to stand in his way.

It was not until the fifth day of King Otto's reign that the general gaiety waned. A wire arrived in the prime minister's office. It was signed by the real Eddine who was still in Turkey, and who was quite puzzled by reports that he had arrived in Durazzo.

The picture started to become clear. The prime minister rushed to the imperial chambers, but "King Otto" and his two aides-de-camp were gone.

A long investigation into the matter revealed that King Otto was, in fact, one Otto Witte, a circus performer. His two aides had been the circus giant and the circus strong man.

Albania had lost a king, but Otto Witte had enjoyed the best four days of his life.

The body of the average adult contains 2,800 square inches of skin, making the skin the largest single organ in the human body.

What does it mean when the weatherman says that one inch of rain fell in your area yesterday? For instance—say one inch of rain fell on one acre of ground. Since an acre equals 43,560 square feet, a rainfall of one inch over this area would produce 6,272,640 cubic inches of water, or 3,630 cubic feet of water. A cubic foot of water weighs about 62.4 pounds, the exact weight varying with the water's density. Therefore, one inch of rain over one acre of surface would equal 226,512 pounds, or better than 113 tons of liquid.

Nicotine Nostalgia

Originally raised in Virginia, *rustica* tobacco is now grown chiefly in Turkey. American cigarette manufacturing dates from the Civil War period. During that era, Greek and Turkish tobacconists in New York City hand-rolled the expensive tobaccos then popular among the carriage trade: Havana, Turkish, Perique, Cavendish, Persian, Cut Navy, Latakia, and St. James. By the 1880s, natural leaf cigarettes, such as Bull Durham, began to dominate the market. The hoi polloi could buy a pack of smokes for a nickel.

Fatima, Sweet Caporal, Vanity Fair, Between the Acts, Melachrino, Murad, Wings, Spud—do these names ring a bell? Well, some of them are still around, but most of them are only nostalgic memories to veteran smokers.

The smallest of all birds is the bee hummingbird which is about 2¼" long, most of that length being the beak. It takes 18 of these creatures to tip the scale of one ounce.

What could be drier than a desert? Answer: The town of Arica, on the border between Chile and Peru. With a population of 14,000 inhabitants, Arica receives a mere .02 inches of rain per year. This is all the more remarkable because Arica is situated on the Pacific Ocean. To give you an idea of how dry this town is, the rainfall of Arizona—the driest of the 50 American states—is almost 400 times as heavy.

In 1871, a book entitled *Rosicrucian Dream Book* was published in Boston, containing the solutions to over 3,000 different dream symbols in alphabetical order. According to this work, a dream about potatoes indicates that someone is trying to poison the minds of those who would do you good. And camels in a dream mean that one's beloved is far better than he or she looks.

A baby rattlesnake at birth has the same amount of poisonous venom as a full-grown rattler.

Ocean waves are sometimes 80 feet high. Most so-called mountainous waves are only 30 to 40 feet high, and no ocean wave is higher than 100 feet from trough to crest. The highest wave ever scientifically measured was 80 feet tall. But mariners are sure some waves are as high as a ten-story building.

Just in case you were wondering—the first Eskimo Bible was printed in Copenhagen in 1744.

A French magazine conducted a survey to investigate sexual behavior in France. If the responses of those interviewed are to be believed, the average Frenchman sleeps with 11.8 women in his life, while the average Frenchwoman shares her bed with only 1.8 men.

Magnificent Microcosm

Franklin H. Avers of Portage, Wisconsin, made a miniature electric village, which enacts the activities of an average midwestern town from late afternoon to sunrise. This model is mounted on a 5' by 12' stage. As the five-foot curtain opens on the scene, a breeze wafts the scent of flowers out toward the audience and flutters a flag in the park. A motorboat passes a sailboat on the lake, an automobile drives up to a house and honks its horn, and a plane glides in and lands noisily. The sun becomes reddish and finally disappears behind the mountain. Cattle moo, cowbells jingle, the moon appears, stars twinkle. A train pulls into the station, and all is still for a moment to signal the passing of several hours. As the day begins to break, a rooster on a fence crows, the flag is raised, a plane roars, the curtain closes, and the five-minute performance is over.

The longest poem ever penned by one man is the *Shah Namah*, written by the Persian poet Firdausi in the 10th century. The poem, known as "The Book of Kings," is 2,804 pages long, and its 120,000 lines fill nine good-sized volumes. Firdausi worked on the poem for 35 years.

There is one family of birds whose young can fly immediately after being hatched. These birds are the mound builders, natives of Australia and some South Sea Islands, which emerge from the shell fully feathered.

Is a Spice an Herb?

What is a spice? According to Christopher Morley, *spice* might be the plural of "spouse." According to Webster, a spice is an aromatic vegetable such as pepper, cinnamon, nutmeg, mace, allspice, ginger, cloves, or such, used to season food and to flavor sauces and pickles.

An herb, on the other hand, is defined as "a seed plant which does not develop a woody tissue as that of a shrub or tree, but is more or less soft or succulent." An herb may be used for medicinal purposes; or because of its scent or flavor, for culinary purposes.

There is but a thin line of distinction between an herb and a spice.

In ancient times, spices were used for incense, for embalming preservatives, as ointments, as perfumes, as antidotes against poisons, as cosmetics, and for medicinal use.

In One End, Out the Other

Each day the average person consumes, in one form or another, about three quarts of water. This liquid is released in urine at the rate of about 1/40 ounce per minute, for a total output of 1½ quarts of urine a day.

If the earth were reduced to the size and weight of a ping-pong ball, and the sun shrunk accordingly, Old Sol would still be over 12 feet in diameter and weigh 6,000 pounds. And the sun is one of the smaller stars in our galaxy.

The longest national anthem is that of Greece, which contains 158 verses. The shortest are those of Japan, Jordan, and San Marino, each of which contains but four lines. And the anthems of Bahrain and Qatar contain no words at all.

A Carload of Firsts

Gottlieb Daimler, a compatriot of Carl Benz, independently arrived at his own version of the internal-combustion engine that Benz had developed. Although the two never met, the firms which succeeded their enterprises merged and formed the present Mercedes-Benz company.

Perhaps the first truly practical gasoline-powered automobile was the Panhard, designed, in 1894, by a Frenchman named Krebs. The French had begun to produce autos a few years earlier, after Levassor purchased the French rights to Daimler's engine of 1887.

In the United States, several inventors get high marks for pioneering efforts in the field. Among them were the Duryea brothers, who won the first automobile race in America in 1895. One year earlier, an American named Elwood Haynes had gained the patent for a gasoline-powered car that was developed at the Apperson wagon works in Kokomo, Indiana. The first car manufactured in Detroit was made by Charles King in 1896. By 1898, there were no fewer than 50 automobile manufacturers in the United States.

Contrary to almost everyone's belief, the Pilgrims did not land at Plymouth Rock when they first arrived in America. The *Mayflower* first touched land at the tip of Cape Cod on November 11, 1620, and did not reach Plymouth Rock until the following December 21. The legend of the Pilgrims and Plymouth Rock originated in the 1740s.

Although the whale weighs over a hundred tons and the mouse tips the scales at only a few ounces, they develop from eggs of approximately the same size.

The world's largest rodent is the capybara, also called the carpincho or water hog. A native of tropical South America, it can attain a length of 3½ to 4½ feet and a weight of 150 pounds.

The Niftiest Natator

When Johnny Weissmuller retired from amateur competition in 1929, he could have taught Tarzan himself how to swim.

The handsome swimmer won his first National Championship in 1921. From then on, Johnny made records in every free-style distance from 100 yards to 880 yards and even held the world's record for the 150-yard backstroke.

His mark of 51 seconds flat for the 100 yards stayed on the record books for 17 years!

The face is sometimes dubbed the *mug* owing to the 18th-century practice of carving grotesque human faces on the outside of drinking mugs.

A Welsh rabbit has nothing to do with bunnies. It's a dish made with cheese and beer.

Portuguese explorers journeying to South America brought along convicts on their ships, who were cast ashore in unfamiliar areas to discover if the local natives were cannibals.

The loveable koala bear is a finicky eater. He'll touch nothing but eucalyptus leaves.

Faster Than a Speeding Bullet

A movie camera has been developed for taking pictures of objects traveling at extremely high speeds. If the camera—which takes 11,000,000 pictures a second—photographed a bullet traveling at the speed of 1,900 miles per hour, three minutes of normal-speed projection would be required to show just one foot of the bullet's travel.

Top Dog

The greatest racing dog in history was Mick the Miller, a greyhound owned by an Irish priest named Father Brophy. Mick flashed sensational speed on the English tracks, and the Father was offered $4,000 for the beast. He accepted on condition that he receive the Derby purse if the dog won the classic. The Miller came through, winning $50,000.

In his three-year career on English soil, Mick never lost a race.

The Hindus of India are said to play more varieties of musical instruments than are found in all other countries combined. The Hindus have several thousand instruments, for virtually all of their early instruments remain in use. In fact, their most popular instrument is still the seven-stringed vina, which was invented more than 1,200 years ago.

Soda water was invented by a Philadelphia resident, Townsend Speakman, in 1807. He later added fruit juices to make the water more palatable.

Have you ever tried to figure out what bodies of water the expression *seven seas* refers to? Don't waste your time. The *seven seas* is a figurative term meaning all the waters of the earth. The expression appears in the ancient literature of the Hindus, Chinese, and Persians, as well as in Western cultures.

When in 1608, Thomas Coryat, an Englishman who had visited Italy, introduced the Italian custom of eating with a dinner fork, everyone thought the idea was an insult to human dignity. But little by little, of course, this affront became standard practice.

The 18th-century Italian Cardinal Mezzofanti spoke 53 languages fluently, another 61 tongues almost as well, and understood 72 more dialects, for a total of 186 languages and dialects. Yet the Cardinal never left Italy in his entire life.

Sic Transit Records

Helene Madison held 16 swimming records at one time. At the end of 1932, the 6-foot, 18-year-old blonde from Seattle, Washington, held every important free-style swimming record. She had smothered all Olympic competition.

She was the first woman to swim 100 yards in one minute flat. Tank experts predicted that her records would last for generations. Today, not a single one of Helene's marks stands.

Blow, Winds, Blow!

And t'is, an ill wind that blows no good. This is certainly true for artists, who discover all kinds of possibilities in depicting the winds.

Here are drawings in varied styles and moods, each a remarkable conception.

A drawing from Judge *shows effects of the wind on a flapper of the 1920s*

"Wind in the Trees," a drawing by a Russian artist which appeared in Art of the Book, *published in Moscow in 1971*

A drawing depicting the awful blasts of England as they appeared to an English cartoonist in Punch

A concept of the winds drawn by Dorothy Braby, circa 1950, New York

A drawing by the great satirist, Grandville, which first appeared in Un Autre Monde, *published in Paris in 1844.*

The Comic Almanac *was published by Chato & Windus of London during the 1850s. This is a drawing which appeared in that notable magazine.*

In 1195, the Sultan of Marrakesh, Morocco, ordered that 960 sacks of musk be added to the mortar for a minaret he was building to commemorate a military victory. That minaret still stands, and the fragrance of the musk can be perceived today.

A Fish Story

The largest fish ever caught by any method was a 17-foot-long, 4,500-pound white shark, harpooned by Frank Mundus off Montauk Point, Long Island, New York in 1964.

The largest fish ever caught by rod and reel was a white shark measuring 16 feet 10 inches long and weighing 2,664 pounds. It was brought in by Alf Dean at Denial Bay, near Ceduna, South Australia, on April 21, 1959.

Talk about slow basketball games! Until 1937, the referee had to throw up a jump ball after every basket!

Chinese women, as well as the men, enjoy smoking a pipe. Their pipes are extremely delicate and unusually decorated. Cigarettes, on the other hand, which caught on only in the Chinese metropolises before the advent of Mao, are less common in China today than they were 25 years ago.

For many years, the tobacco habit was bitterly opposed by the English crown and the English church. In his *Counterblast to Tobacco*, King James I described smoking as "a custom loathsome to the eye, hateful to the nose, harmful to the brain, dangerous to the lungs, and in the black stinking fume thereof nearest resembling the horrible Stygian smoke of the pit that is bottomless."

Adolf Keifer won more than 2,000 swimming races. He won his first U.S. championship in 1935, when he was 16 years old. For eight years thereafter, the great backstroker was undefeated, and won 24 indoor and outdoor championships.

In 1946, at the time of his retirement from amateur competition, Keifer held every backstroke record in the books. In a brilliant athletic career, Keifer had lost only two races out of more than 2,000!

A Bird's-eye View

The bird on the wing is a symbol of man's aspiration to be more than man, to soar above the natural world. The combination of grace and power epitomized by a bird in flight is both nature's pride and man's joy.

The bird's evolutionary progenitor was the reptile, and several birds—such as the ostrich, the penguin, and the kiwi—remain bound to earth. As the bird moved up the evolutionary scale, it developed many fantastic traits. For example, a bird can focus its eyes more quickly than any other living creature. Its sight is astonishingly keen; so is its sense of hearing; its smell, however, is poor.

For the tea ships of 1610, sailing from the Orient to Europe was perilous. The seas swarmed with pirates and cutthroats; there were few charts to show reefs and rocks; and the frail vessels were often sunk by storms. In 1618, another method of transportation was tried—tea was brought by camel caravan from China across the deserts and mountains of Asia to Eastern Europe. The journey took 18 months.

Al Capone's business card described him as a "secondhand furniture dealer." Capone grossed about $105 million in 1927.

If you think Adelle Davis brewed up a storm over nutrition, you should have been around when Sylvester Graham, the father of the graham cracker, was stirring up the country with his lectures and books in the 1830s-1840s. He antagonized thousands by opposing such standard commodities as tea, coffee, tobacco, liquor, meat, corsets, and featherbeds. He also persuaded thousands to follow his diet, which included bread made of coarse flour, since known as Graham flour. The number of Grahamites became so great that, to accommodate them, scores of Graham boarding houses were established, and restaurants set apart special Graham tables.

A flying honeybee beats its wings 250 times a second; the housefly, 190 times a second.

Metric Measure

The two systems of measurement now in use are the Metric and the English system. Oddly enough, the English have recently converted to the metric system.

The meter is defined in terms of light-waves. According to this definition, one meter is equivalent to 1,533,164.12 wave lengths of the red light emitted by cadmium.

An angry llama will spit in his antagonist's face.

Pianoforte comes from two Italian words: *piano* which means soft, and *forte* which means loud. So pianoforte actually means "soft-loud." The piano, which is what most of us call a pianoforte, was the first keyboard instrument ever invented which could play both soft and loud.

Solace for Southpaws

There are no records of the exact beginning of discrimination against lefthanders, but as far back as Rome, right was right; which means to say that *dexter* from which comes our word *dextrous* or *handy*, means right in Latin. But how did the Romans designate the other side? Anything that was left was *sinistra* (sinister). Even the Old English, who gave us the word *left*, used it to mean *weak*. Now is that fair?

Fighting a ratio of five righthanders for every lefthander, lefthanders have risen to the challenge. Da Vinci worked with his left hand. A study of Einstein's brainwaves indicated that his right hemisphere—the side responsible for the responses on the left side of the body—was more highly developed than his left.

The nations of Iceland, Costa Rica, and Liechtenstein have no armed forces.

The rarest and most valuable button in the world is the "Morse" or "Cope" button, a magnificent work of art fashioned by Benvenuto Cellini in 1530 for Pope Clement VI. A large, round, and flat button measuring six inches in diameter, it is made of gold and encrusted with gems. Over the beautiful diamond at the center is an image of God the Father. According to his *Autobiography*, Cellini worked 18 months on this one button and employed a staff of 10 artisans to help him.

Before a baby bird is hatched, it has a temporary tooth that enables it to break out of the egg. Full grown, a bird may have a beak strong enough to crack seeds, or long enough to snap up little creatures from the bottom of a stream.

Diamonds Are Forever?

Whether true beauty lies without or within, a jewel is a rare and a precious thing. The most precious stone today is the ruby, which after 1955 became increasingly rare as supplies from Ceylon and Burma dwindled. Carat for carat (one carat equals 200 milligrams), a flawless natural ruby of good color is more valuable than a diamond. An excellent six-carat ruby, for instance, recently brought $30,000 on the open market.

If rubies have topped diamonds in the gem hierarchy, diamonds nevertheless remain a girl's best friend. The diamond is the most durable of all gems—90 times harder than the next hardest mineral, corundum. Commercially, the diamond is used to cut other stones.

If heated sufficiently, diamonds will burn. Although an ordinary fire will not ignite them, a blow torch will do the job easily. Diamonds are not affected until the temperature reaches from 1,400 to 1,607 degrees Fahrenheit, depending on the diamond's hardness. Such high temperatures are not common in ordinary fires, but they were achieved in the great 1906 fire which destroyed San Francisco.

For almost 200 years, a festival called the Fiesta of the Radishes has been held each December 23 in Oaxaca, Mexico. During the festival, immense radishes are sold, and native artists carve them into many shapes—fantastic figures of men and animals. Prizes are awarded for the best and most imaginative shapes.

The parents of the famous sculptor, Sir Jacob Epstein, were religious people. His mother, who took the religious injunction "Thou shalt not create graven images" quite seriously, dumped a pile of her young son's works into the trash can. These would have been worth a pretty penny today.

The world's largest gem reposes not in a wealthy dowager's vault but in a glass case on the fifth floor of the American Museum of Natural History in New York City. A topaz of 1.38 million carats, taken from Brazil's Minas Geraes, it weighs 596 pounds. It is rather dull-looking, and few of the visitors who make it up to the fifth floor pay this huge gem any mind.

Shake, Rattle, and Roll

There's a certain art in even such a seemingly simple activity as shaking fruit from a tree. In general, a hard, slow shake is preferable to a quick, short motion. But for each fruit there's a specific frequency that's best. Plums, for example, will fall about three times as freely if the plum tree is shaken 400 times a minute, two inches per shake, than they would at 1,100 times a minute, one inch per shake. Cherries respond most favorably to 1,200 short shakes per minute, while apple trees are most generous when shaken 400 times per minute.

Elektro, the mechanical man, was made by the Westinghouse Company, and first exhibited in New York City during the World's Fair of 1939-40. The seven-foot, 260-pound robot was set in motion by vibrations of the human voice. He could walk, smoke, count on his fingers up to 10, tell whether an object held before him was red or green, and perform 20 or so other feats. Elektro's electrical system contained 24,900 miles of wire, or enough to encircle the globe.

The first portable timepiece was made in Nuremberg in 1504 by Peter Henlein. Because of their shape and heft, these early watches were called "Nuremberg live eggs." The first wrist-watch appeared as early as 1790. It was made by Jacquet-Droz and Leschot of Geneva.

Lightning Strikes Twice?

Contrary to folk wisdom, lightning does strike twice in the same place, and may even strike as many as ten times in a single spot! Successive photographs of lightning flashes have been taken by engineers of the General Electric Company during electrical storms in the Berkshire Mountains of Massachusetts.

One can get an appreciable shock from an ordinary electric socket in a house wired at a voltage of 115. A single flash of lightning has been estimated to carry a charge of 100 million volts.

The heaviest weight ever lifted by a human being is 6,270 pounds, accomplished by Paul Anderson at Toccoa, Georgia, in 1957. The 5-foot, 10-inch strongman, using his back, lifted a table loaded with a lead-filled safe and heavy auto parts. The weight of the objects equalled that of a 33-man college football team!

The smallest breed of dog extant is the Chihuahua. At maturity, this Mexican wonder generally weighs somewhere between two and four pounds, but some Chihuahuas tip the scales at no more than a pound.

Steam Heat

Automobile enthusiasts were aghast. The world's speed record was held, not by one of their pet gasoline-powered cars, but by an automobile with a steam engine in its nose. And the honor of being first to travel faster than two miles a minute had gone to this traitorous device.

It happened in January, 1906, when the Frenchman Marriott took his steam-powered Stanley to Daytona Beach, Florida. On the sands outside Ormond, Marriott sped over a measured mile at a rate of 121.52 miles per hour!

Not until 1908 did the gasoline engine return unto its own. Then a huge Fiat named *Mephistopheles* zoomed to a new record, searing the cinders at the rate of 121.64 m.p.h.

The greatest single rainfall fell in the Philippines. In 1911, from July 14 to July 17, the floodgates of heaven opened wide over Baguio, and down gushed a record 88 inches of rain—or more than *seven feet of water!*

Anyone can swim or float more eaily in salt water than in fresh water because salt water is heavier, and thus has greater buoyancy. There is so much salt in the Great Salt Lake of Utah, that one cannot sink or completely submerge oneself in it. Nevertheless, an inexperienced swimmer can drown if he panics and loses his balance. Although his body will float on the surface, the brine will suffocate him.

To Play's the Thing

Sports have existed since the day that primitive man could take a slight breather from the serious business of self-preservation.

In addition to the use of language, it is play that distinguishes the lower orders of living things from higher ones. The animals that display the least amount of playfulness are those most bound by the instinctual functioning. The higher we go on the evolutionary scale, the more playful the species— witness the dolphin and the human child.

What distinguishes sports from other playful pastimes is that, whether engaged in by an individual or a group, conformity to agreed-upon, prescribed rules is required.

Stone arrowheads uncovered by archaelogists indicate that archery was a hunting skill way back in primordial days. This activity became transformed into an organized sport in the 3rd century, when contests among archers became popular.

Sports are of interest to both men and women—to people of all ages. All over the world, artists have translated the excitement of athletic contests. Here are some of the most fascinating graphic interpretations of the 19th and early 20th centuries.

Bizarre Magazine *was published during the 1960s in* Paris. *This drawing graced its pages.*

Racing as depicted in the Police Gazette.

In the famous fight between Sullivan and Kilrain, Sullivan lands his right in the 15th round—smack on Kilrain's jaw. This is how the artist of Police Gazette *saw the action.*

Tennis played on ice was the subject of this drawing in Punch in 1876.

Un Autre Monde, *published in Paris in 1844, was the work of Grandville.*
This caricature of horse and jockey was one of the drawings that made Grandville famous.

From the noted humorous publication, Life, *which flourished in the early 1920s.*

Scenes of lawn tennis among the upper echelon of American society as depicted in Frank Leslie's Popular Magazine, *published in New York during the 1880s.*

Two scullers, as they appeared in a French magazine of the day.

In 1893, on Thanksgiving Day, Yale defeated Princeton in football. The captains of the teams and some of the action were depicted in the Police Gazette.

Some of the oldsters are trying this monstrous game of football. Here's how the artist of Life Magazine saw it.

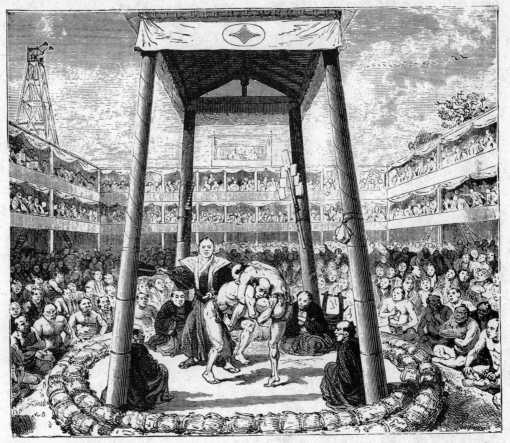

From Voyages and Travels, *a book published by E.W. Walker & Co. of Boston around the turn of the century.*

The Police Gazette *was practically standard equipment in every barber shop during the late 1800s. This magazine featured sports pictures. This drawing of the Kilrain-Sullivan fight of 1889 shows some of the action. Kilrain claimed that Sullivan fouled him in the third round.*

A Lacrosse scene, as depicted in Harper's Magazine.

Lady fencer, from a French magazine of the 1890s.

In the early part of the 20th century, Simplicissimus, a magazine of humor published in Munich, was the outstanding German publication in the field. This drawing of a man skating appeared in 1913.

From Punch *of 1879.*

Drawing by the great French satirist Grandville, which first appeared in a book entitled Petites Miseres de la Vie Humaine. *This drawing was published in Paris by Fournier in 1843.*

Water, Water Everywhere

On November 23, 1942, the S.S. Lomond, an English merchant vessel, was torpedoed in the South Atlantic. The explosion killed all but one man—25-year-old Poon Lim. After being catapulted off the deck by the blast, Lim grabbed hold of a drifting life raft and began one of the most extraordinary feats of survival in history. Lim spent 133 days on the exposed raft before being rescued, catching fish and sea gulls for his meals.

Modern timepieces are electric, self-winding, magnetic, solar-cell-powered, etc. The most accurate time-measuring device of all is the system of twin atomic hydrogen masers installed at the U.S. Naval Research Laboratory in 1964. It is accurate to within one second per 1,700,000 years.

One of the strangest land vehicles ever devised was the marsh buggy, an enormous four-wheeled contraption designed by the Gulf Oil Company to traverse the treacherous Louisiana bayous in search of mineral deposits. Looking like a giant's roller skate, the marsh buggy had wheels 10 feet tall mounted on an ordinary automobile frame.

Cycling Circuit

The most ambitious cycling venture ever attempted by man was undertaken by Thomas Stevens in 1884. Leaving California in April, the young San Franciscan crossed the United States on his bike, sailed for Europe, resumed his bicycle travel across Europe and Asia, and sailed across the Pacific, arriving back in San Francisco less than three years after he had set off. Stevens had actually ridden around the world on a bicycle!

Johann Heinrich Karl Thieme, of Aldenburg, Germany, dug an estimated 23,311 graves during his 50-year career as grave digger. In 1826, Thieme's understudy had to dig his master's grave.

The Equine Imposter

In the early 1900s, a vaudeville act called *Han, the Educated Horse* captivated Europe with a nag whose specialty was solving arithmetic problems. After the horse's trainer had written a question on the blackboard, the animal would tap out the answer with his feet, indicating 23, for instance, by tapping twice with his left foot and then three times with his right. Actually, the horse had been trained to respond to signals from its trainer which were so slight that they remained imperceptible for years.

One day in July, 1940, John V. Sigmund waded into the Mississippi River at St. Louis and started swimming south. When his friends pulled him out of the drink, a little above Memphis, Sigmund had covered 292 miles. He had been swimming continuously for 89 hours and 42 minutes!

Terns migrate halfway around the world twice each year. They summer in the Arctic, then in the autumn move south to the Antarctic region—a trip of some 11,000 miles. The next spring, they trek back to the Arctic!

An old Scottish custom held that a casket should be carried out of a house not through the door, but through an opening made in the side of the house and walled up immediately after the casket's departure. The belief was that a ghost could reenter a house only through the opening through which he had left it.

Pandora's Box

There was a time when jewelry boxes were equipped with devices that killed anyone who attempted to open them without knowing the secret. One such case, sold at auction in New York several years ago, stood about 14 inches high by 20 inches wide and 10 inches deep. It had a bottom lock for the box, and a top lock for the protective mechanisms. If the top lock was opened when the case was opened, four doors instantly flew open, a pistol sprang into position behind each door, and all four pistols fired automatically.

Between 1881 and 1889, a French company attempting to construct a canal across the isthmus of Panama lost $325 million and 20,000 men before going bankrupt.

The record for the most strikes in a row in a sanctioned bowling match is 29. That's two-and-a-half perfect games!

Rain keeps the earth dry. It is the rain process that takes the moisture out of the air and gathers it into concentrated rain clouds. Were it not for this, moisture would condense on every solid surface; and all humanity, bathed in tepid, humid perspiration, would slide over the damp and slippery earth, like life prisoners in a steam bath!

The most widely spoken language on earth is Chinese, with 750 million speakers. English is spoken by 300 million. Russian, Spanish, Hindi, Bengali, Arabic, Japanese, German, and Portuguese complete the top ten, in that order.

During the mid-1700s, two thirds of all tea drunk in England was smuggled into the country to avoid the high import tax.

Model Tea

In 2737 B.C., says Chinese legend, leaves from a wild tea bush fell by chance into the Emperor Shen Nung's boiling drinking water. "What a delightful flavor!" said the wise Emperor, drinking the world's first cup of tea.

The Chinese poet, Lu-Yu, published the first book about tea in 780 A.D. Wait until the water boils, he tells us, and when the bubbles resemble crystal beads rolling in a fountain, it is time to pour the water over the tea leaves.

No birds now on earth have teeth.

Back in 1927, Lawrence Grant and Dr. Munro MacLennan began a chess match at Glasgow University. The game has still not ended. The pair make one move every Christmas, and they expect a result this decade.

The micropantograph—a device used to cut extremely small markings on calibrated instruments—is capable of producing writing—legible under a microscope—on the scale of 32,000,000 words to a square inch. That's about as many words as there are in 250 300-page novels!

The record distance for spitting a watermelon seed is 38 feet, 8¾ inches, achieved by Lee Roberts of Rio, Wisconsin, in 1972.

Did you ever wonder what the *T* in the expression *to fit to a T* stands for? Well, the *T* refers to the T-square, an instrument used by mechanics and carpenters, which fits exactly to the surfaces of a wooden board or block. *To fit to a T* means to fit perfectly.

The largest lake in the world is not called a lake, but is misnamed the Caspian Sea. Lying between Asia and Europe, it covers an area of over 43,000 square miles, and it is about four and one-half times as large as the second largest lake, Superior.

Handy Andes

Tourists huffing and puffing in the cold, rarified air of the Andes Mountains often wonder how the Andean Indians can live comfortably at altitudes of up to 17,000 feet. What these tourists don't realize is that the Andean Indians are much better suited to the rigors of this climate than are other men. The lungs of these mountain inhabitants are larger, and their veins contain about two quarts more blood than those of sea-level dwellers. The Indians' slower-beating hearts are about one-fifth larger than ours, their arms and legs are shorter, and their eyes are covered with a fold of skin to keep the eyeball from freezing.

Until 1869, coffee was the chief crop of Ceylon (now Sri Lanka). In that year, a terrible blight attacked the Ceylonese coffee trees and soon killed them all. The planters decided to start again with tea. Today, tea is the principal crop of that island.

The tallest dog extant is the Irish Wolfhound "Broadbridge Michael." Owned by a woman in Kent, England, it measures 39½ inches at the shoulder.

Because the tuna needs a continual flow of water across its gills in order to breathe, the fish would suffocate if it ever stopped swimming.

Unhappy Firsts

The first automobile accident in the United States occurred in New York City on May 30, 1896, when a car driven by a Massachusetts man collided with a bicycle rider. The bicyclist was injured, and the driver was forced to spend the night in jail awaiting the hospital report.

The first person to die as a result of a car accident was Henry H. Bliss, a 68-year-old real estate broker, who was run over as he alit from a New York City streetcar on September 13, 1899. The driver of the car was arrested.

In ancient times, demand for the dye of royal purple—derived from particular shellfish and used to color the togas of the Romans—was so great that it stimulated the exploration that helped Rome build its great empire.

Whiskey is obtained through the distillation of the fermented mash of grain. It is then aged in wood. Whiskey is produced principally in the United States, Canada, Scotland, and Ireland. Scotch whiskey gets its distinctive smoky flavor due to the use of peat in drying the barley malt and also through the quality of Scotch water.

The earth does not revolve around the sun once every 365 days. Rather, it takes our planet 365 days, 5 hours, 48 minutes, and 46 seconds to make the circuit. The extra time is accounted for by the addition of an extra day once every four years—except those years divisible by 100 but not by 400.

A Ticklish Situation

One of the oldest—and strangest—methods of fishing is practiced by the Maoris of New Zealand. The Maori fishermen wade out into the clear stream or lake, moving very quietly so as not to create ripples. Here fish swim in and out of clumps of rock or coral, sometimes stopping for a quick nap. Half of the fish may be hidden by the rock, but the rest of the fish juts out into view.

Wading up behind the fish, the silent Maori will reach down and tickle the fish's sides. In trying to wriggle away, the fish backs out of his hiding place and lands right in the fisherman's hands. The stealthy tickler must be very adept to hold on to his slippery supper.

In 1869, Charles Elmer Hires opened a drug store in Philadelphia and placed a sign over his fountains which read "Hires Root Beer—5¢," thus taking the honor of manufacturing and selling the first root beer in the United States. Seven years later, Hires started the national root beer business which still bears his name.

King Augustus III of Poland boasted a wardrobe that was probably unmatched in all history. The monarch, who died in 1764, filled two entire halls with his clothes, and for each of his many costumes he had a special watch, snuffbox, cane, sword, and wig. Augustus consulted a book in which his outfits were reproduced in miniature to choose his royal apparel for the day.

In her lifetime, one termite queen can produce over 500 million children.

According to Hoyle

Edmond Hoyle has been credited with formulating the rules to many popular games, but actually Hoyle wrote only two books on card playing. Furthermore, Hoyle never heard of most of the games for which he is supposed to have formulated the rules. Among them is poker, which was not invented until almost 100 years after Hoyle's death.

An adult flatfish—a large group of fish that includes the flounder, halibut, and sole—has both eyes on the same side of its head.

What a world we live in! Howard Cosell broadcasts an amateur boxing match in Havana, Cuba, which is about 90 miles away from Florida. But the broadcast is sent via satellite some 93,000 miles around the world, and this method of transmission winds up more expeditious than sending the impulses directly from Cuba to the United States.

The route taken is to the Russian satellite, *Molniya*, and from thence to West Germany, and still on to an American satellite which propels the impulses to the American continent.

Stamps of the South

Among the rare and valuable American postage stamps in existence today, are those issued by the Confererate States of America during the Civil War.

Shortly after the Southern states seceded from the Union in 1861, the postmasters in various southern cities found it impossible to do business without stamps of some kind. The use of Federal stamps was, of course, taboo. So, the postmasters of many cities and town began issuing their own stamps. Still extant are postage stamps issued by the postmasters in such places as Greenville, Alabama, Ringgold, Georgia, and Petersburg, Virginia.

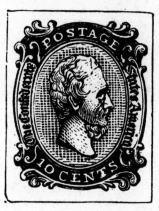

Lat in 1861, the Confederacy issued its first regular series of postage stamps, with three values: two, five, and 10 cents. The 1861 series was replaced by another in 1863.

The earlier stamps issued by local postmasters are rarer, and therefore more valuable, than the regular Confederate series. As early as the 1890s, some of these stamps were selling for as much as $750.

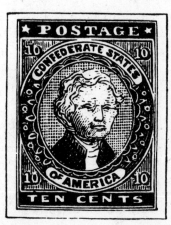

Postage stamps of the Confederacy used throughout the South during the War of the Secession.

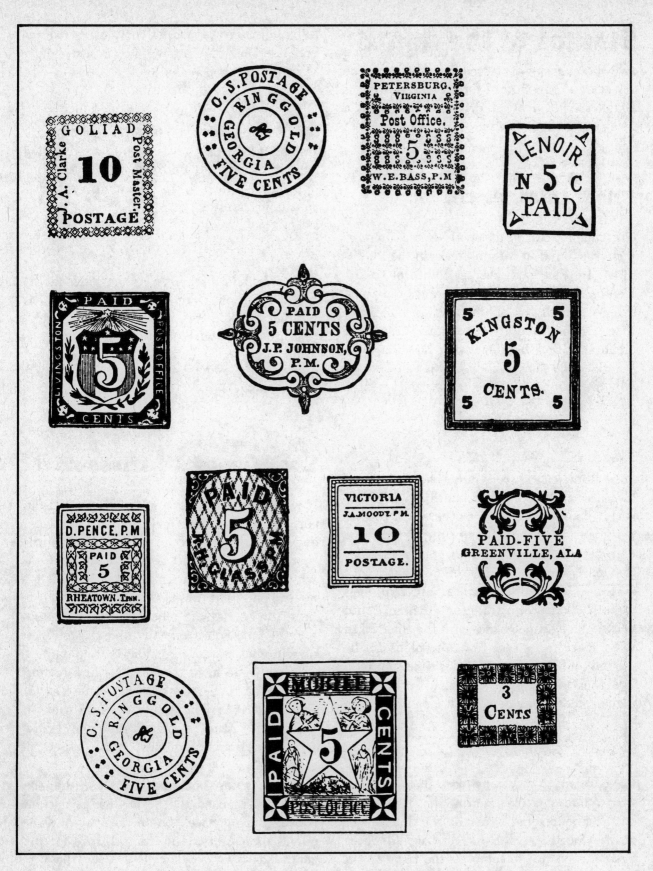

Postage stamps issued by different localities of the Southern States during the War of the Secession.

A leaping flea accelerates from a standstill to a speed of three feet per second in less than two-thousandths of a second, subjecting the insect to a gravitational force of 150G. This is roughly equivalent to driving a car into a brick wall at 200 m.p.h.

The Puniest Pisces

The smallest fish in the world is the *Pandaka pygmea*, found in certain creeks in the Philippines. It reaches an average width of six-sixteenths of an inch, and an average length of seven-sixteenths of an inch. It is no bigger than an ant, and it is probably the tiniest creature with a backbone that has ever been isolated. The slender body of this fish is virtually transparent and the only clearly visible features are its comparatively large eyes.

An altimeter, as you might have guessed, measures altitude. Used primarily in airplanes and balloons, the device is generally a type of barometer. But the altimeter differs from the barometer in that it can indicate the distance that one is above the surface of the ground.

Some altimeters, such as an airplane's terrain-clearance indicator, utilize radio waves. The altimeter measures the time taken for a wave to be sent from the plane to the ground and back, converts this time into feet, and thus indicates the distance between the plane and the ground.

If you were to place one grain of rice on the first square of a chessboard, then two grains on the second square, four on the third, eight on the fourth, and so on, you would never have enough rice to complete the task. To fill the last square you would need 2^{63} grains of rice—enough rice to bury the population of Richmond.

Dolphins are the world's most uneasy sleepers. They nap only a few hours at a stretch—with one eye open at all times!

In 1864, in response to an outcry against trains, the British government passed a law which limited steam-driven vehicles to a speed of 4 m.p.h. in the country and 2 m.p.h. in the city.

The left bank of a river is the bank to the left of a person looking *downstream*, and has nothing at all to do with the right-left relationship of the two banks on a map. Thus, St. Louis is on the right bank of the Mississippi, and Manhattan Island forms part of the left bank of the Hudson.

The Way of All Whiskers

It was, of course, the hippies who started the current style of long hair, beard, whiskers, and sideburns—more properly called burnsides, after the Union general A.E. Burnside who sported this particular brand of hirsute adornment. The hippies, and their forerunners, the beats, who rebelled against the foppery of fancy duds and the time-wastefulness of trimming away the indicia of manliness, can be said to have become a social force just around the time Jack Kerouac wrote *On the Road* in 1957. The hippy paean struck its high note with the presentation of "Hair," which celebrated the most visible aspect of hippiness.

Yet it is now being bruited about that the beard has reached the heyday of its current vogue, and may well be on the way out—or off, as the case may be. Indeed, love for the beard has been very fickle. During the first part of this century—between 1910 and 1960—facial foliage in the United States was indeed a rarity.

The keenest sense of smell exhibited in all nature is that of the male silkworm moth. It can detect the sex signals of a female 6.8 miles away!

Fishy Business

Try as you might, you won't find the word *sardine* on any list of fish species, for strictly speaking, there is no such thing as a sardine. What we eat as sardines are actually any of a number of small, thin-boned fish, usually herring or pilchards, that are suitable for packing in oil. Conceivably, a can of sardines may contain fish of a number of different species.

From India, nutmegs and cloves, native to the Moluccas—the Spice Islands—were introduced into China. A tradition has come down to us that in the 3rd century B.C., the courtiers of the royal court were required to carry cloves in their mouths in order to sweeten their breath when addressing the emperor.

The producers of the 1947 spectacular *Caesar and Cleopatra* were perfectionists indeed. For a moonlight scene beside the Sphinx, a set was designed which showed hundreds of stars in the sky in the exact position they occupied over the Egyptian desert in the year 45 B.C.

If upon their arrival in Bethlehem the Three Wise Men had invested one dollar at four percent interest, their account would now be worth a quantity of gold 100,000 times the size of the earth!

Here's one for Western fans: a 10-gallon hat actually holds ¾ of a gallon.

A Journey to Dreamland

Dreams are similar to hallucinations in that they are not usually caused by sense impressions. To be sure, a toothache or indigestion may affect the form of the dream, but it will not determine the content of the dream. While the duration of a dream is a matter of dispute among scientists, many believe that even the most image-crowded dream lasts but a few seconds. All dreams occur in living color.

What gives the dream its restorative power? Little is known for certain about the dream world, but Freud believed that dreams provide a safety valve for suppressed desires, and that dreams actually protect sleep by draining off the emotional turmoil that would otherwise cause a person to wake up.

So many of us have so much trouble getting to sleep in the first place that nearly half a billion dollars are spent annually in the United States on sleeping pills.

An Apollo spacecraft develops more power on lift-off than all the automobiles in England put together.

The longest street in the world that runs through the same city is Figueroa Street, in Los Angeles, which runs north and south through the city for a distance of 30 miles.

The Sears, Roebuck Company is the largest retailing company in the United States. In 1973, Sears totaled over $10 billion in sales—almost twice as much as its nearest competitor for top honors, the Atlantic and Pacific Tea Company (A & P).

I'll Take Mine Black, Please

Surprisingly enough, coffee, which accounts for a staggering $2 billion a year in international trade, didn't reach Brazil until a mere 250 years ago. The coffee tree, indigenous only to Arabia and Ethiopia, was supposedly discovered by goats. They ate the wild-growing berries and began to cavort in the fields, convincing their goatherd to join them in a cup.

The Arabs were cultivating the plant as early as 600 A.D., and used the berries as medicine. It wasn't until the 13th century that it was discovered how to brew coffee into a beverage. For the next 400 years, the Arabs jealously guarded the coffee trade, exercising a monopoly by forbidding the export of fertile seeds on pain of death.

But at about the year 1700, Dutch traders managed to smuggle out some plants, sending the embezzled botanica to the island of Java, where the growth became so prolific, the island's name became synonymous with the brew.

The largest crabs in the world—which live off the coast of Japan—stand three feet high and often weigh as much as 30 pounds.

The term *drawing room* has nothing to do with sketching. The word *drawing* is actually a shortening of *withdrawing*—for this was the room to which guests "withdrew."

Smoking Out the Smokers

These days, pipes, cigars, and cigarillos are taking an increasing share of the tobacco sales, while the popularity of non-filter cigarettes has declined precipitously in recent years. Yet the Surgeon General's report on the hazards of smoking has hardly meant the last gasp for filtered cigarettes. More filtered cigarettes are now sold each year than the year before. Demon nicotine seems to have secured a niche in the American way of life.

And, by the way, it was Europe—not the United States—that developed the filter cigarette. America only lays claim to the invention of the smoker's cough.

If you tried to pay the month's rent or your bus fare with cigarettes, people would laugh at you. But in pre-Revolutionary America, tobacco was acceptable legal tender in several Southern colonies. Virginia even enacted a law that taxes should be payed in tobacco.

Snow is not frozen rain. Snowflakes change directly from water vapor into snow, without going through an intermediary stage as rain.

An ostrich cannot fly, but the 400-pound bird can outrun many racehorses.

What're the odds against a coin coming up heads fifty times in a row? Well, according to one calculation, a million men would each have to toss a coin ten times every minute for 40 hours a week in order to achieve an occurrence of 50 straight heads just once in nine centuries.

Who Put the "Green" in Greenland?

There is very little green in Greenland, for the island is covered with ice and snow for most of the year. According to legend, the misnomer was given to the land by the Scandinavian explorer Eric the Red in an attempt to induce followers to settle on the barren island.

Koreans believe that snake meat is healthful. In Seoul, some 600 restaurants serve only a snake soup, called "baim tang." About 30,000 snakes a day are consumed.

Scraping Bottom

The brilliant pink flamingo goes to the unappetizing bottoms of lakes and bogs for its meals. Standing in fairly shallow water, it plunges its head and long neck straight down into the mud so that it seems to be standing on its head.

With the upper part of its beak, the flamingo scoops up the mud. Then it strains the mud through its specially built, immovable lower beak. What's left—small mollusks and other little creatures—it eats.

The flag of Denmark is the oldest unchanged national flag in existence, dating back to the 13th century.

The world's tiniest plant seeds are those of the *Epiphytic* orchid. They come 35,000,000 to the ounce!

The flea is the world's champion high jumper. This mighty mite can accomplish a leap 80 times its own height and 150 times its length. If a man could do the same, he would be capable of leaping over a building 50 stories high and three football fields long.

The United States produces more than twice as many cars each year as babies.

About 525 songs and instrumental pieces were written about Abraham Lincoln, the largest number ever produced in honor of a secular individual. Approximately 450 of these compositions were published between his campaign in 1860 and his assassination in 1865. They comprise campaign and nomination selections, presidential hymns, emancipation songs, and minstrel and comic pieces. The other 75 consist of some 50 funeral marches and 25 memorial pieces.

The guards at the jail in Alamos, Mexico, may well be the most vigilant in the world. Regulations at Alamos provide that a guard must serve out the sentence of any prisoner who escapes while he is on duty.

Few professional performers have heard of an amateur comedy called *Aaron Slick from Punkin Crick*. But this 1919 play has been put on by small-town dramatic clubs in more than 25,000 communities and has been seen by over 10,000,000 people.

The anglerfish catches its prey with luminous bait

Miles below the surface of the ocean, where pressure is a thousand times greater than at sea level and no glimmer of light pierces the cold darkness, creatures take on appearances more bizarre than the strangest land animals. One of the oddest of all deep-sea creatures is the female anglerfish, a large, grotesque fish that uses a luminous appendage to catch her prey.

Affixed to the top of the anglerfish's body is a thin strand of flesh, up to four inches long, that floats in the water like a fishing line. The strand is tipped with a wad of fleshy bait that glows in the inky blackness of the deep. Smaller fish attracted to the dangling light are quickly gobbled up by the waiting angler as they approach.

The glow of the angler's lure is due to a phenomenon known as bioluminescence, which also accounts for the firefly's glow. A chemical reaction takes place at the end of the angler's lure—as well as in any of the other luminous appendages the fish may have on her body—which releases radiant energy in the form of a glow.

This luminous property belongs only to the female angler. The male is much smaller, and completely parasitic to the female. Early in its life, the male bites into the skin of a female and hangs on. The site selected appears to be haphazard, and occasionally more than one male becomes affixed to a female. Soon the lips and tongue of the male fuse with the flesh of its host, and the blood-streams of the two creatures connect. Almost all the organs of the male then degenerate, except the reproductive organs, and the male gets its nourishment directly from the blood of the female!

It has been suggested that this unusual relationship has evolved because anglerfish are slow-moving, live in almost total darkness, and are solitary, so that their chances of finding a mate would otherwise be remote.

The first explosion of an atomic bomb took place on July 16, 1945, in a desert area near Alamogordo, New Mexico. This was only 21 days before a similar device was detonated over Hiroshima, Japan.

Tea Formation

Tea is grown on large estates of from 300 to 3,000 acres. The best teas grow at high altitudes, sometimes at over 6,000 feet. Many of these estates in India, Ceylon, and Indonesia are completely self-contained. They provide fully equipped factories, storehouses, housing for both manager and the native workers, and even schools for the children. Large estates have their own hospitals with native doctors in charge.

New tea seedlings are carefully planted by native workers three to five feet apart in the rich, tropical soil. Fern leaves are then spread over the plantings to protect the young growth from the sun's fierce, withering heat. The soil where the tea plants grow is kept well cultivated. Hand labor and oxen are widely used, but many of the modern estates have up-to-date cultivation equipment. Chemical ferilizers are used extensively.

If left to nature, the tea plant would grow into a tree 30 feet high. The cultivated plant, however, is kept pruned to a height of three or four feet. This provides delicate growth of leaf and makes plucking easy. Usually five years must pass before a tea plant is ready for plucking. A native girl can pluck as much as 40 pounds of leaf a day.

The fresh green leaves are brought to withering lofts and spread evenly on racks. Here, currents of warm, dry air remove a great deal of the moisture from the leaves. This process takes from 12 to 24 hours. The limp, withered leaves are rolled in special machines. This breaks up the cells and hastens fermentation of the leaves. In the process, the leaves change color, and give out the fragrant aroma we associate with tea.

Double Your Pleasure

Norman L. Manley stepped to the seventh tee at the Del Valle Country Club course at Saugus, California. The date was September 2, 1964. He hit a prodigious drive, and the ball bounced unerringly to the green and into the cup. He had scored an ace, one of the longest ones on record. But the best was yet to come. On the very next hole, the 290-yard eighth, Manley, bubbling with excitement and confidence, hit another mammoth drive. As if directed by radar, that ball landed smack in the hole! Manley had hit two holes-in-one, back to back, scoring six strokes under par for the pair.

The highest tides anywhere in the world are to be found in the Bay of Fundy, which separates New Brunswick from Nova Scotia. At the head of the bay, a few times each year, the tides rush in and out at a rate of 10 feet an hour—an incredible 60 feet from highest to lowest tide. The tide moves nearly as fast as the water rises in a bathtub with both taps opened full, and the rise of the tide goes on for six hours, twice a day. At no time is the water in the bay still.

A seven-inch North African ostrich egg takes 40 minutes to boil.

The Pentagon is one of the largest office buildings in the world, with a total floor area of 6½ million square feet. Yet no two offices in the building are more than 1,800 feet—or six minutes walking time—distant from each other.

The Rain in Spain

Sometimes, in Europe, the rain is red. The so-called "blood rains" of Europe used to plunge the people of that continent into a frenzy. The scientific cause of the phenomenon was not known, and the pinkish rain was thought to be diluted blood.

There are still "blood rains" at odd intervals in Italy, southern France, and southeastern Europe. It seems that storms lift reddish desert dust from the Sahara, and blow billions of these particles across the Mediterranean into the cloudbanks above Europe. Then they are washed down as red rain.

The circumference of the earth is about 42 miles greater around the equator than it is around the poles.

There are approximately two and one-half times as many cattle in Argentina as there are people.

Mary Mallon, known as "Typhoid Mary," was blamed for spreading typhoid to at least 1,300 people in New York City in 1903 alone. Despite her illness, Miss Mallon refused to stop working and often obtained jobs—under assumed names—that involved the handling of food. To prevent further contamination of the populace, "Typhoid Mary" was placed in permanent detention in 1915 and remained there until her death in 1938.

Ounce for ounce, the tiny shrew is the most ferocious of all mammals. This tiny creature kills and eats twice its weight in food every day.

Scientists at the U.S. Air Force Missile Development Center at Holloman, New Mexico, constructed a train that traveled so fast that no human could ride in it. The rocket-powered sled attained a speed of 3,090 m.p.h. on a 6.62-mile-long rail track.

That St. Patrick drove all snakes from Ireland is certainly a legend, but the truth is there are no native snakes on the island. Other islands without native serpents include Crete, New Zealand, Malta, Iceland, and Hawaii.

On July 26, 1955, Ted Allen set a world's record for horseshoe pitching by throwing 72 consecutive ringers.

A Gift of Gulls

The pioneer people of Salt Lake City, Utah, had watched the summer sun of 1884 bring forth a good crop. They needed the food to get through the coming winter. But out of nowhere an all-consuming mass of crickets swept across the fields. The pioneers fought them in every way they knew, but the crickets kept on eating.

Suddenly, a flock of seagulls arrived to feast on the crickets, gorging themselves until all the marauders were consumed. Fortunately, enough of the crop was left to sustain the people through the winter.

The people of Salt Lake erected a monument to their unexpected saviors and passed a law prohibiting anyone from killing a seagull.

The state with the youngest legal marriage age is New Hampshire, which permits a female with parental consent to marry at 13. Five states—Alabama, New York, South Carolina, Texas, and Utah—permit a female to marry at age 14. The youngest age at which a male may marry is 14, permissable only in New Hampshire.

A chameleon's tongue is as long as its body.

The Netherlands—about 13,000 square miles in area—uses as much fertilizer in a year as the whole of South America, which has an area of almost 7 million square miles.

Casting Lots

The dice game of Craps was introduced to America in 1813 by Bernard de Mandeville, who had seen a variation of the game played in France. De Mandeville brought the game to New Orleans, where it became popular among the Creole population. The nickname for a Creole was "Johnny Crapaud," and thus the game became known as "Crapaud's game," later shortened to "Craps."

De Mandeville himself was not lucky in the game, however, and was forced to sell a good deal of his property in New Orleans to pay his gambling debts.

A camel can go without water for almost a week, and without food for much longer.

A person with ordinary vision can distinguish about 150 different colors. An expertly trained eye can distinguish more than 100,000 colors, tints, and shades.

The record for cornhusking is 46.71 bushels in 80 minutes, set by Irving Bauman in 1940.

The first municipal fire department in the United States was organized in 1659 by Peter Stuyvesant, governor of New Amsterdam. Stuyvesant distributed 250 leather buckets and a supply of hooks and ladders to his firemen and levied a tax of one guilder per chimney to maintain the department. The fire alarm was sounded by the twirling of a rattle, giving the department the nickname of "Rattle Watch."

If at First You Don't Succeed . . .

The bridge that spans the Narrows Strait near Tacoma, Washington, is actually the second bridge built on that spot. A 2,800-foot suspension bridge constructed there in 1940 blew apart in gale winds a few months after completion.

One of the earliest recorded rail excursions was an 1840s day trip from London to Cornwall to view the public hangings in Bodmin jail.

Due to the shower of meteoric material, chiefly dust, falling from the sky, the weight of the earth increases by about 100,000 pounds each year.

The longest golf hole in the world is the 17th hole at the Black Mountain Golf Club in North Carolina. It measures 745 yards, and is a par 6.

The Millionaire Racehorse

The greatest racehorse in American history was undoubtedly Man o' War. Bought at auction for $5,000 in 1918, the phenomenal speedster went on to win 20 of the 21 races in which he was entered, earning close to $2,000,000 in purses and stud fees. So certain was Man o' War's victory, that on some occasions the odds in his favor approached 1-to-100!

In addition to his race-course earnings, the remarkable stud sired 383 sons and daughters, who won a total of $3,500,000 in purses.

Man o' War was the first animal whose obituary and biography appeared in the list of celebrities compiled by the major press associations. The horse also had the largest personal guest book on record, with the names of 2,000,000 people who visited him in retirement. When Man o' War died in 1947, his funeral was attended by 2,500 admirers.

The longest recorded drive of a badminton bird is 79 feet, 8½ inches, achieved by Frank Rugani in California on February 29, 1964.

Mercury, the planet closest to the sun, is thought, by most people, to be extremely hot. Actually, at all times half of the planet is extraordinarily cold, with temperatures in the neighborhood of -250 degrees. The side of Mercury facing the sun, however, is broiling hot—temperatures there approach 700 degrees.

If all space between atomic particles were eliminated, matter in the resultant state—called the neutron state—would be so dense that one cubic inch would weigh about 1,800 million tons.

In 1965, a New Zealand resident produced the longest loaf of bread ever baked—20 feet, 5 inches long. The loaf weighed 50 pounds.

Tommy Woods, working for his college's radio station in Wayne, New Jersey, disc-jockeyed for 272 hours without a break in 1972—that's 11 full days!

The social weaver bird of Africa really deserves its name. As many as 90 couples may join to build a huge community nest. A favorite location is a big acacia tree. After the nest is built, each pair of weavers goes to work fashioning its own individual chamber inside the large structure—a bird version of the modern apartment house.

A Close Shave

Peter the Great, Czar of Russia from 1682 until 1725, wanted his countrymen to adopt Western customs and dress. To discourage the growth of beards, which were then unfashionable in Europe, the Czar first levied a tax on all beards, and later decreed that men wearing beards would be shaved by force with a blunt razor, or would have their whiskers removed one by one with a set of pincers. On one occasion, Peter personally cut off the beards of his noblemen.

Paint It Black

Dark clothes will help you keep warm in winter, for black absorbs the heat of the winter sun. On a chilly day, a thermometer registering 10 degrees will shoot up to 60 degrees if painted black.

The Swiss explorer A. de Quervain, who crossed Greenland in 1912, cleverly utilized this principle to eliminate one of the hardships of Arctic travel. Obtaining and storing drinking water is one of the greatest problems facing humans in the Arctic region, where in winter the temperature rarely rises above the freezing point. It's not particularly healthy to chew on ice for weeks on end. De Quervain stored his water in a waterproof black cloth sack attached to the side of his sled on which the sun was shining. Even though the temperature of the air around him was below freezing, the temperature inside the black sack was found to be about 80 degrees. Snow could be readily melted inside the bag, and drinkable water stored in abundance.

Beginning around the age of 30, a person loses about 100,000 neurons, or brain cells, each day. But there's no danger of your brain ever "burning out"—a human brain contains some *ten trillion* neurons!

The Hindu temple of Siva at Madura, India, is adorned with an estimated one million intricately-molded idols. Actually, legend claims that ther are more than 30 million idols on the temple. To count them would take years.

The oldest surviving European document written on paper, a deed of King Roger of Sicily, dates from the year 1102.

Hippocrates, the "Father of Medicine," is to some extent a mythical figure. Although a Greek physician named Hippocrates did practice in the fifth century B.C., almost nothing is known of the man. The group of medical works known as *The Hippocratic Collection* was almost certainly composed by a number of physicians and writers.

During the construction of the Hoover Dam, concrete had to be poured *continually* for two years.

Not all insects taste with their mouths. Insects such as the butterfly and the housefly do have tongues for licking and sucking food, but they also carry taste organs on their feet which are especially sensitive to sugar.

Minutiae

The smallest flowering plants in the world are Wolffia and Wolffiella which make up the green film seen on fresh-water ponds. These flowering plants, known as the duckweed, run from 1/30 to 1/50 of an inch in diameter. The duckweed is but one seventy-millionth the size of the mammoth *Amorphophallus titanum*, the world's largest flower.

Would you guess that the Canary Islands were so named because of the now familiar yellow finches that thrive there? Well, the islands actually owe their name to dogs! When the Romans first came upon the islands, they found a large number of wild dogs, and called the islands *Insulae Canariae*, or "islands of the dogs." Not until much later were the beautiful finches of the islands named "canaries."

When George Washington Carver began his work with the peanut in the 1890s, the goober was not even recognized as a crop in this country. By 1940, the peanut was the sixth leading crop in America, and the largest crop in the South after cotton.

To build up a market for peanuts, Carver developed no fewer than 301 separate products from the peanut plant, including twine, dye, oil, cheese, ink, soap, and cosmetics. And in his spare time, Carver found over 100 uses for the sweet potato!

At the entrance to some bridges you might see the notice: "Break Step." What does it mean? It's a warning that soldiers crossing the bridge should not march in step.

If the vibrations caused by a marching troop happened to equal the "natural period of vibration" of the bridge, the repeated force of the marching steps could build up and cause the bridge to sway and shatter. Thus, a bridge that could easily support the weight of a thousand soldiers might well collapse if the men marched in step.

Wheel 'em Away!

In 1975, two men held up a doughnut shop in Sepulveda, California, and made off with $125 aboard most unusual vehicles—skateboards!

The world's largest airline is state-owned Aeroflot of the U.S.S.R., with some 1,300 craft and 400,000 employees. The largest commercial carrier in the world is United Air Lines, with about 365 craft. But surprisingly, private planes in the United States carry about 50 times as many passengers per year as all American-owned scheduled airlines combined!

Quaking with Fear

In 1886, an earthquake shook Charleston, South Carolina, toppling 1,400 chimneys to the ground in 70 seconds. No buildings in the city were entirely demolished, but more than 50 people died, and damage was estimated at 5 million dollars. The quake was felt as far away as Bermuda.

The greatest earthquakes to strike the United States centered around New Madrid, Missouri, in 1811-1812. The three quakes were felt as far away as Canada, and toppled chimneys in Cincinnati, Ohio—400 miles away!

And in 1935, three earthquakes and almost continual earth tremors kept the residents of Helena, Montana, shaking for a full year—in more ways than one.

The largest jigsaw puzzle in the world, made in 1954, measured 15 feet by 10 feet and contained over 10,000 pieces.

One evening in 1913, a 125-pound boxer named Preston Brown stepped into the ring at the Broadway Athletic Club in Philadelphia, and announced that he would take on all comers that night. Six ring-wise professional fighters arose from the ranks—all bigger than Brown.

One by one, the six tough boxers climbed through the ropes, and one by one their seconds had to carry them away. Brown knocked out five of the six—in early rounds, no less. The sixth challenger lost on a decision.

A spider's web is so lightweight that if one ounce of the material were stretched into a thin strand, it could reach across the Atlantic Ocean.

During the Civil War, the Union Army lost more men as a result of disease than it lost in battle. The same was true of the American armed forces serving in the Spanish-American War and World War I. In the Mexican War, the United States suffered 1,733 battle deaths—and lost 11,550 men to "other causes."

Well over a thousand persons each day commit suicide worldwide, including about 70 Americans. Hungary can—well, boast the highest annual rate, about 37 suicides per 100,000 persons.

Firearms and explosives rank first overall as the preferred method of suicide in the United States, followed closely by poisoning. Poisoning is the preferred method worldwide, though hanging, strangulation, and suffocation rank first among males.

On June 13, 1948, a Los Angeles resident named Jack O'Leary caught a fit of hiccoughs. It was not until June 1,1956—about 160 million hiccoughs later—that the fit ended. During that time, the unfortunate Mr. O'Leary lost 64 pounds, and received through the mail over 60,000 suggested cures for hiccoughs.

Livy relates that when the barbarians overran the Golden City, a Roman senator sat still, unmoved at everything, until a Goth touched his beard—then he struck, although he died for the blow.

Pint-sized Pauline

Many people have laid claim to the title of "world's smallest adult human," but only one justly deserved that title. In 1876, Pauline Musters was born in Holland to normal-size parents. At birth, she measured 12 inches, against the normal baby's 20 to 22 inches. Throughout the rest of her life, Pauline grew only 11 inches!

When appearing in public exhibitions, Pauline was billed at 19 inches. But shortly before she died in New York City at age 19, she was measured at 23.2 inches—making her the smallest mature human on record. Her feet never measured more than four inches in length.

Flavored spirits, including gin, aquavit, absinthe, and zubrovka, are produced by redistilling alcohol with a flavoring agent. Juniper is used to flavor gin; caraway seeds to flavor aquavit.

Samuel Morse, the inventor of the telegraph, did not turn his hand to invention until he was over 40 years old. Before beginning work on the telegraph in 1832, Morse was a painter, and served as the first President of the National Academy of Design. He still held that post when the first telegraph message was sent from Baltimore, Maryland, to Washington, D.C. in 1844.

William Frederick Cody, better known as "Buffalo Bill," was well deserving of his nickname. When Cody was 21 years old, he was hired as a buffalo hunter by a firm supplying food to workers laying tracks for the Kansas Pacific Railroad. Using a 50-calibre Springfield rifle, "Buffalo Bill" earned his nickname by slaying—by his own count—4,280 buffalo in a period of 17 months.

Pierre Auguste Renoir, one of the great masters of the Impressionist school of painting, was partly disabled by arthritis and gout during the later years of his life. Yet he never ceased to paint. During his last years, Renoir often could not hold his paint brushes, and instead had to work with the brushes strapped to his wrist.

Another French artist saw the aged Renoir working one day and asked: "Why do any more? Why torture yourself?"

Renoir's reply was: "The pain passes but the beauty remains."

Forgetful Fiddler

Trains and cabs must be the greatest repositories for "left objects." Every once in a while something of real value is forgotten by a passenger. Every once in a rarer while, the story has a happy ending.

On February 25, 1979 Alexander Schneider left his violin in a New York taxicab. This extraordinary instrument is a Guarnerius, estimated to be worth $250,000. You can well imagine Mr. Schneider's distress. Picture his glee when the instrument was returned to him. The two men who found it in the cab are band musicians and say they will share the $13,500 reward offered by the insurance company with the other members of their band.

Popcorn is actually an Indian invention. The first Americans to enjoy popcorn were the colonists who attended the first Thanksgiving dinner, on February 22, 1630.

The creature with the longest recorded life span is—no, not the tortoise or parrot—but the lake sturgeon. One of these fish reportedly attained the age of 152 years!

Coffee became widely popular in London during the 17th century. The first coffee house opened its doors in 1652. Soon coffee houses became the centers of political, social, literary, and business life in the city. In America, the first popular coffee houses opened as early as the 1680s—and the *Mayflower* listed among its cargo a mortar and pestle to be used for grinding coffee beans.

The first air-conditioned office building in the United States was the Milam building in San Antonio, Texas, which was completed in 1928. The 21-story structure was the first office building in the world to be built with air-conditioning as a part of the original construction.

Against All Odds

Lightning can play some funny tricks. In Lapleux, France, lightning struck a sheepfold. It killed every black sheep, but left all the white sheep unharmed.

A bolt of lightning set fire to a building, then hit a nearby fire-alarm box and summoned the firemen to put out the fire.

A seven-year-old boy was sitting in a cart underneath a tree during a thunderstorm. Lightning hit the tree and leapt to the cart, removing three sides of it—leaving the boy stunned, but unharmed.

A park ranger in Virginia was struck by lightning six times over a 34-year period—and survived all six bolts!

And lightning not only *can* strike twice in the same place, it frequently *does*.

Marsupials

Of course, you know what a marsupial is—a mammal that carries its young in a natural pouch on its stomach. The kangaroo comes immediately into mind, and so does Australia.

But there are many other marsupials in addition to the kangaroo, and not all are indigenous to Australia or to the adjacent islands. The opossum, for example, lives right here in North America.

All marsupials do have one thing in common: the extraordinary way in which they bear their young. Baby marsupials are incompletely developed, and very small—a newborn kangaroo may be only an inch long! The young nurse for several months within their mother's pouch, or marsupium, to complete their development.

The Australian marsupials were virtually unknown until Captain James Cook visited Australia in 1770. When Cook saw his first kangaroo, he thought he'd found a gigantic leaping rodent. We now know that the marsupials form their own order within the mammal family, an order that includes some of the most unusual looking creatures on earth.

BANDICOOT *This rabbitlike marsupial spends most of the day inside his burrow, emerging at night to feed on worms and insects. Bandicoots are fairly pugnacious, and fight by leaping into the air and striking at each other with their hind feet. There are about a dozen species, all native to Austrailia and adjacent islands.*

OPOSSUM *The most familiar American marsupial, the opossum, has given his name to the defensive ploy of playing dead when threatened by a predator—though a number of other animals similarly "play possum." This cowardly creature, one of the most prolific of mammals, bears two or three litters each year, with as many as 18 bee-sized babies in each litter.*

KOALA *This small Australian native looks just like a toy teddy bear. But he gets his name from an aboriginal term meaning "no water," for this cute creature never drinks water in his entire life. He's a fussy eater, though: A koala will eat only the leaves of the eucalyptus tree, and spends almost all his time in one of these trees, munching on the leaves.*

WALLABY *The wallaby is more closely related to the kangaroo than any of the other marsupials. In fact, many of the larger wallabies are commonly called kangaroos or bush kangaroos in their homeland, Australia. The smaller wallabies are about the size of a rabbit. They spend their days in rock crevices, and feed on grass at night.*

MARMOSET *A close relative of the opossum found in South and Central America.*

TASMANIAN DEVIL *This strong, carnivorous marsupial has proved a devil to many Australian sheep and poultry farmers. About the size of a badger, with large, powerful jaws, the Tasmanian devil spends his days in his burrow, and comes out at night to hunt.*

WOMBAT *Often called "native badgers" because of their strength and burrowing abilities, wombats are closely related to another Australian marsupial, the koala. This shy, gentle herbivore can grow up to three feet in length.*

Cheers!

The Italians are currently the reigning world champions in the per capita consumption of wine. The average Italian consumes about 30 gallons of *vino* each year, about three gallons more than his French counterpart. Portugal ranks third in wine drinking, at about 21 gallons per person, while Argentina and Spain round out the top five.

The people of the Soviet Union apparently enjoy making wine far more than they do drinking it. The U.S.S.R. ranks fourth in wine production after France, Italy, and Spain, though it places a mere 19th among wine consumers. The United States, which ranks a distant 31st in wine consumption at just 1.7 gallons per person, nevertheless stands as the sixth leading wine producer, with Argentina number five.

Americans do somewhat better at beer consumption—the 21-gallon per person annual figure makes the United States the 13th leading consumer of the foamy brew. West Germany is the leader at about 40 gallons per person yearly, while Czechoslovakia and Australia follow. But in beer production, the United States is far and away number one. American breweries turn out close to four-and-a-half billion gallons each year, almost double the figure for the second-ranking nation, West Germany.

At the other end of the scale, the people of Iceland and Israel rank as the premier tee-totalers among all alcohol-consuming nations.

Disneyland in Japan? Don't be surprised if Mickey Mouse and friends turn up in the Land of the Rising Sun by the middle of the 1980s. Present plans call for a 204-acre Disneyland amusement park near Tokyo.

The Vatican Library contains writing materials from pre-Columbian Peru and Mexico that were made from human skin.

George Washington had no children. His wife bore four children during her earlier marriage to Daniel Custis, two of whom died in infancy. Only one of the other two children lived long enough to have children of his own.

Incidentally, when George Washington married Martha, she was considered to be the richest widow in Virginia, having inherited an estate of 17,000 acres from Custis, along with 300 slaves. Washington himself had 49 slaves when he married.

Don't bother looking for a rainbow during the next noontime sun shower. A rainbow can be seen only in the morning, late afternoon, or night, when the sun is at a certain distance above the horizon.

In regard to the world fuel supply, the birth of an American child has the same effect as the birth of eight children anywhere else in the world. For the average American uses eight times as much fuel energy as the average person outside of the United States.

In the early 1950s, an estimated one-quarter of all the males in Tibet were Buddhist monks.

One of the most closely guarded prisons in the world is the Sante prison in Paris, France. Only six inmates have escaped from the Sante since its completion in 1867. One of the escapees, a French politician, Leon Daudet, actually walked out the front door of the prison in 1927. Daudet hoaxed the warden by having a friend telephone and say that Daudet had received a government pardon. The unsuspicious jailor never thought to check up on the call, and Daudet was immediately released.

The average human body contains some seven trillion living cells, 45 miles of nerves, and an amazing 70,000 miles of blood vessels. Those vessels contain about 30 trillion red blood cells, of which 15 million are replaced each second.

A Deadly Hand

In poker, a pair of aces along with another pair is a reasonably good hand. But if the aces are matched with a pair of eights, the hand is considered unlucky by some poker buffs.

The superstition dates back to 1876, when "Wild Bill" Hickok of old Western fame was shot dead by Jack McCall during a poker game in a Deadwood, South Dakota saloon. As Wild Bill fell dead, his last poker hand was exposed to view—a pair of aces and a pair of eights. Ever since, those two pairs have been known as the "dead man's hand."

More people choke to death in this country than you might imagine. Choking is now the fifth leading cause of accidental death in the United States. Two-thirds of these choking victims are under four years old. And the most common culprit? The toothpick!

The average American woman now buys about five pairs of shoes each year, and the average man, about two pairs. As a rule, men's shoes last longer and remain in fashion longer than women's footwear.

You shouldn't be surprised to learn that a majority of the Swiss cheese consumed in the United States is made domestically, and not imported from Switzerland. More surprising, for sure, is that of the Swiss cheese that is imported by the United States, more comes from Finland, Norway, and Austria than the nation for which the cheese was named.

An orange tree brought to France in 1421 may have been the most productive single tree on record. The tree, known as the "Constable Tree," bore its last fruit in 1894—473 years after it reached Europe!

About ten percent of the earth's land surface is covered by glaciers. The ice sheets cover about 5.8 million square miles—an area the size of South America!

The Himalayan nation of Bhutan has an estimated population of 1.1 million people. Estimated, indeed—no census has ever been taken in Bhutan!

Art theft has lost a good deal of its glamor and intrigue—it's simply too common today to arouse great interest. In a recent year, there were a reported 33,000 art thefts around the world, including close to 10,000 in the United States. After narcotics smuggling, art theft has become the second most common international crime.

The Inca Indians, who built a massive empire in South America before Columbus sailed for the New World, did not have an alphabet or a written language.

Masterstroke

Out at the Inverness Golf Club in Toledo, Ohio, they still call the seventh hole "Ted Ray's Hole." It is so named in honor of the great Britisher who won the U.S. Open there in 1920.

The hole itself is a 320-yard dogleg which can be straightened out to 290 yards—*if* you clear the forest between the tee and the cup.

Four times in the U.S. Open, Ted Ray cleared those woods: twice, he got directly on the green; once, he landed in a trap beside the green; and once, he came to rest on the fairway at the edge of the green.

The British pro scored four birdie 3's at this tough hole—and he won the championship by a single stroke!

Seals sometimes swim 6,000 miles over a period of eight months without once touching land.

In 1952, the first train to run without motormen or conductors was placed into service in New York City, between Times Square and Grand Central Station. Nevertheless, a motorman was present in the car—although he did not perform any duties—because of labor demands by the Transit Workers' Union.

A heavy dew is actually the portent of good weather. On cloudless nights the earth loses its heat more rapidly, and a heavier dew results.

The Straight and Narrow

The Green Lantern in Amsterdam bills itself as the "narrowest restaurant in the world." Its frontage measures just over four feet, and nowhere inside is the inn more than 20 feet wide. Nevertheless, the Green Lantern can accommodate 85 guests.

The narrow frontage is a relic of the times when an Amsterdam homeowner was taxed according to the width of his facade, which prompted the Dutch to build their houses as narrow as possible.

A massive mosaic in the Roman Catholic National Shrine in Washington, D.C. called *The Immaculate Conception*, stands 10 feet high and contains 35,000 pieces of stone. The selecting and inlaying of the stone required 25 man-years of labor.

The longest section of straight railroad track in the world stretches across the Nullarbor Plain in Australia. For 328 miles this track does not take the slightest curve.

Steam Takes the Cake

Believe it or not, the first automobile race ever held was won by a car that was powered by a steam engine. On June 22, 1894, Paris was bubbling with excitement as 20 horseless carriages lined up for the 80-mile race from Paris to Rouen and back again to the big town.

Could these new-fangled things run at all? And if they did, would they prove as fleet and as durable as a few changes of horses?

Less than five hours later, a De Dion Bouton lumbered down the boulevards of gay Paree. The steamer had covered the distance at the dare-devil rate of 17 miles per hour.

The Australian walking fish occasionally leaves the water and climbs a tree to enjoy a snack of insects.

Seventeen harvest mice have a combined weight close to that of a 150-pound man. The mice, however, need about 17 times as much food a day as does the man.

The movie *Sleep* by Andy Warhol, the longest non-talking film ever made, consists solely of a man sleeping for eight hours.

In the middle of the 14th century, in Spain, there arose a vogue of wearing false beards. In the morning, a grandee dandy would drape his chin in a crimson beard; in the evening, he serenaded his senorita in an adjustable, long, black hanging. Soon the country resembled a huge masquerade party. No one knew who was who. Creditors could not catch up with debtors. The police arrested the innocent while villains hid behind hair. Wives were conjugal with the wrong husbands, whereupon the price of horsehair skyrocketed. King Peter of Aragon had to end the farce by forbidding the wearing of false beards.

An otter is quick enough to dodge a rifle bullet.

The oldest alcoholic beverage we know of is mead, a wine made from honey. The sweet drink is stored in wooden casks, and must be left to mature for up to five years.

Mead is the national drink of Poland. The stiff attitude the Poles displayed while enjoying their mead prompted Napoleon to tell his troops to "drink, but in the Polish fashion."

The Long and the Short of It

The longest name of any city or town in the world belongs to the Welsh city of Llanfairpwllgwynggyllgogerychwyrndrobwell-Llantysiliogogogoch. Compare that to the French village of Y, or the Norwegian town A.

Dope on Diamonds

The largest diamond ever found was the 1½-pound Cullinan diamond, unearthed in South Africa in 1905. Other notable diamonds: the Koh-i-noor, now among the British crown jewels; the Hope diamond, the largest known blue in existence; the Star of Africa No. 1, cut from the Cullinan; the Tiffany, an orange-yellow diamond; and the Dresden, a greenish diamond.

The green variety of beryl is known as emerald; the blue is aquamarine. Highly prized in antiquity, the emerald was a particular favorite in pre-Columbian Mexico and Peru. An 11,000-carat emerald was reportedly found in South Africa in 1956.

Sapphire is a variety of transparent blue corundum. It is mined primarily in Asia and Australia, though some sapphires are to be found in Montana. The "Black Star Sapphire of Queensland" is the largest cut gem-quality sapphire.

The crawling fish of Asia can live for a week out of water. In fact, this fish will instinctively leave a stream that is going dry and head for the nearest water, often traversing a mile or more of dry land.

Flight of Fancy

The world record for altitude by a model aircraft is 26,929 feet by Maynard L. Hill, of the United States, on September 6, 1970, using a radio-controlled model. The speed record is 213.71 m.p.h. by V. Goukoune and V. Myakinin with a motor piston radio-controlled model at Klementyeva, U.S.S.R. on September 21, 1971.

Nicholas Joseph Cugnot of France is credited with the invention of the first automobile. Cugnot built himself a steam-powered tricycle in 1769, which attained a speed of 2 m.p.h. while carrying four people.

The largest cigar ever made—now on display in the Bunde Tobacco and Cigar Museum in Germany—is 170 centimeters (about 67 inches) long and 67 centimeters in circumference. The giant cigar would take about 600 hours to smoke.

My Kingdom for a Book

Joao de Barros, a 16th-century Portuguese writer, once received an entire province for writing a book. As a young man of 20, Barros composed a chivalric romance entitled *Cronica do Clarimundo*, and dedicated it to Prince John of Portugal. When the Prince later became King John III, he gave the writer the vast province of Maranhao as a reward for his work.

Maranhao, in the Portuguese South American colony of Brazil, then comprised some 177,000 square miles—five times the area of Portugal itself!

Joan of Arc was only 17 years old when she led the French army to victory against the English at Orleans. But Joan actually was not French! Her birthplace, the village of Domremy, lay within an independent duchy allied with the duchy of Lorraine. Lorraine warred frequently with France until it became part of the French kingdom in 1776.

Elderly people are less likely to die in the months preceding their birthdays than in the months that follow. The death rate among the elderly is lowest in the two months before the month of birth, and peaks in the month following the birthday.

The Himalaya-Karakoram Range, which stretches across the borders of China, India, and Nepal, contains almost all of the world's 60 highest mountain peaks.

Most people know that Mount Everest, the most famous Himalayan peak, is the world's tallest mountain. Do you know the name of the world's second highest peak? It's Godwin-Austen, at 28,250 feet, which lies in the Kashmir district of India.

The greatest log-rolling exhibition ever recorded took place in 1900 in Ashland, Wisconsin. Two lumberjacks, Alan Stewart and Joe Oliver, spun a log for three hours and 15 minutes without tumbling into the water.

Captain Courageous

Admiral Horatio Nelson, Britain's greatest naval hero, had but one arm and one eye when he achieved his victory over Napoleon's fleet at the historic Battle of Trafalgar.

In 1793, Nelson lost the use of his right eye during a battle with French forces off the coast of Corsica. Four years later, during a naval engagement with the French in the Canary Islands, Nelson's right arm was so badly mangled that it had to be amputated.

During the Battle of Trafalgar, an enemy sharpshooter's bullet hit Nelson in the spine. He died while the battle raged on, but not before he knew that Britain had won the day. The admiral's last words were: "Thank God I have done my duty."

Sophocles, the great Greek dramatist most noted for his play *Oedipus Rex*, wrote more than a hundred dramas during his long life—and all but seven have perished. Sophocles composed the last surviving work, *Oedipus at Colonus*, when he was close to 90 years old!

Got a Match?

According to one theory, the superstition that "three on a match" is unlucky dates back to the days of trench warfare during World War I. Soldiers believed that by holding a match long enough to light three cigarettes, they were providing the enemy with enough time to aim his shot and perhaps bring down the unlucky matchholder.

In 1644, Peter Stuyvestant, who later became the Dutch colonial governor of New Amsterdam (New York), suffered a leg wound in battle against the Portuguese in the Caribbean. After the leg was amputated in Holland, the Dutch afforded the severed limb a Christian burial and full military honors.

Coca-Cola was originally sold as a patent medicine, for use against headache and hangover. Unlike the early beverage, today's Coke contains almost no cola, and none of the narcotic extract of the coca plant, cocaine.

In 19th-century England, suicide was decreed a crime punishable by death. Despondent Britons who attempted to take their own lives faced the hangman's noose if they failed.

A few years ago, a West German crossword puzzle buff became so frustrated by a particularly difficult crossword that she woke her husband for assistance three times as she battled the poser through the night. The fourth time she woke him, he strangled her to death. A court acquitted the husband on grounds of temporary insanity.

More than a dozen nations have a lower infant mortality rate than the United States. Of the 10 countries with the lowest rates, all but Japan are in Europe, with Sweden the lowest at about 9.5 deaths per thousand births.

A redwood tree can grow to a height of 340 feet—as high as a 30-story building—and a girth of 25 feet. The redwoods are the tallest living things on our planet.

Mozart wrote a symphony when he was only eight years old

Mozart was the greatest musical genius the world has ever known. His accomplishments were so breathtaking that they are hardly believable; yet the amazing facts given here have all been authenticated.

Wolfgang Amadeus Mozart began playing the harpsichord when he was only three. He seemed to learn everything almost instinctively, and never had to be told twice about anything relating to music. In fact, his ear was so sensitive that it could detect an aberration of even an eighth of a note in the tuning of a violin string.

Wolfgang's father used to play in a string quartet. One day, the quartet was playing at the home of the senior Mozart. The second violinist had failed to come, and young Mozart, then five, took the missing musician's place. He had never seen the music before, but he played it as if he had been practicing it for weeks. His father and the other musicians expressed great amazement but the child merely shrugged and said, "Surely you don't have to study and practice to play *second* violin, do you?

Wolfgang started to compose music almost as early in life as he learned to play music. He wrote two minuets for the harpsichord when he was five years old. When he was seven, he wrote a creditable sonata; and, unbelievable as it seems, he was only eight when he wrote a complete symphony.

The elder Mozart knew he had a prodigy on his hands, and he took Wolfgang on a tour of the musical capitals of Europe. The young Mozart played with a mature understanding that electrified the great musicians of Europe. Moreover, the youngster performed feats that were near miracles—tricks of ear and memory that baffled everyone. A melody would be played just once; Mozart would listen and reproduce it faithfully without a flaw. Blindfolded, he would identify all the elements of a chord, no matter on what instrument it was played. He would be given intricate scores to read at sight, and would then play them with a precision that could be equaled only by a first-rate musician who had practiced for hours, or perhaps days.

In Rome, once a year during Holy Week,

the *Miserere* of Gregorio Allegri was performed by the papal choir. The Pope had forbidden its performance anywhere else in the world, and the only copy of the score in existence had been jealously guarded in the papal vaults. A decree issued by the Vatican prohibited anyone from reproducing this holy work in any form. Transgression was to be punished by excommunication.

The *Miserere* was a lengthy, complex contrapuntal composition. Mozart heard it played once. Returning to his room, he transcribed the entire score from memory! The Pope heard about this feat and was so moved by this manifestation of utter genius that instead of anathematizing the boy, he bestowed upon him the Cross of the Order of the Golden Spur.

Before he died in 1791, Wolfgang Amadeus Mozart had produced some 600 operas, operettas, concertos for piano and string quartet, sonatas for the violin, serenades, motets, masses, and many other types of classical music. Perhaps the most astounding fact about this prolific and brilliant production is that Mozart only lived to the age of 35.

The first toll road in the United States, the Little River Turnpike in Virginia, was opened in 1785. Privately owned turnpikes abounded in this country during the early 19th century, beginning with the Lancaster Turnpike in Pennsylvania.

There are only eight places in the United States authorized to display the American flag 24 hours a day. They include Fort McHenry National Monument, in Baltimore, the birthplace of our national anthem; the Washington Monument; Valley Forge National Historic Park; the White House; the site of the Battle of Lexington; the U.S. Marine Corps Memorial in Arlington, Virginia; Flag House Square in Baltimore; and all U.S. Customs Ports of Entry that are open around the clock.

If you want fog, you won't have to journey to London. The foggiest place in the United States, in terms of a single-year average, is Cape Disappointment, Washington, which was shrouded in fog one year for a total of 2,552 hours—that's more than 106 days!

The first bona-fide railroad in this country was the Baltimore & Ohio, which began hauling passengers and freight in 1830. The nation was first crossed with a coast-to-coast line on May 10, 1869.

The ubiquitous beer can made its first appearance in this country in 1935. There are now literally hundreds of different brands of American beer, including the likes of Dutch Treat, Cook's Goldblume, Premium Grain Belt, Fyfe & Drum, Hop'n Gator, Luck, and Short Snorter.

Small "toy" dogs became popular in the British Isles when laws were enacted to control poaching pooches. The 11th-century King Canute, for one, decreed that all dogs kept within 10 miles of the king's forest preserve must have their knee joints cut to hinder them from chasing his game. But exceptions were made for any dog that could fit through a "dog gauge," a ring seven inches wide and five inches high.

The largest commercial elevator on record was constructed to raise and lower a full swimming pool on the stage of the Hippodrome Theater in New York. The device had a capacity of 250,000 pounds—that's equal in weight to 35 hippopotami—and moved at a speed of 12 feet per minute, slower than the most sluggish hippo!

Since meat preservation was a problem before the invention of refrigeration, preserved meat was always popular. In the Middle Ages, sausage makers developed individual formulas for seasoning their products, which frequently took the name of the city where they originated. Genoa salami hails, of course, from Genoa. From Frankfurt came the frankfurter; from Bologna—well, need we say more?

The North Magnetic Pole is commonly located at latitude 71 degrees North, longitude 96 degrees West, in the vicinity of the Boothia Peninsula on the northernmost shore of mainland North America. The South Magnetic Pole, at latitude 73 degrees South, longitude 156 degrees East, is located on the continent of Antarctica. But the exact location of the poles shifts from time to time. And the true magnetic poles are located hundreds of miles away from the "apparent" or compass-indicated poles!

The two favorite plays among amateur dramatic groups in the United States are currently *Ah, Wilderness!* by Eugene O'Neill, and *Barefoot in the Park* by Neil Simon.

In the early days of photography, the long exposure time necessary for an adequate shot required the photographer to attach a head clamp to the person sitting for a portrait to prevent movement and a blurred image. The clamp did much to produce the rigid, artificial facial expressions typical of most early photo portraiture.

According to legend, Henry I of England established the yard as the distance from the point of his nose to the end of his thumb when his arm was outstretched.

Most tennis historians trace the origin of the sport to a 12th and 13th-century French game called *jeu de paume*, "palm game." As you might guess, the sport was played with the palm of the hand, not a racket. The indoor court that came to be used for the game suggests a religious cloister, and the earliest references to the game are usually to be found in ecclesiastical writing, confirming that tennis probably owes its origin to French priests playing handball in a cathedral cloister.

By the way, French king Louis X reportedly died from a chill he received after a heated game of *jeu de paume* at the Vincennes courts.

Life with Father still reigns as the all-time longest-running dramatic production in Broadway history. A number of musicals have surpassed *Life with Father*, but no non-musicals. *Tobacco Road* is second among non-musicals, with 3,182 performances, just 42 less than *Life with Father*.

Dotage

George Bernard Shaw wrote a play at the age of 93. Goethe completed his masterpiece, *Faust*, at the age of 81. W. Somerset Maugham, Leo Tolstoy, and Michelangelo all were working at age 80.

You know those white blobs you see when you close your eyes? These are phosphenes—visual images produced when the retina is stimulated by pressure exerted on the eyeball through closed eyelids.

The pillory, that curiosity of Colonial America used to punish lawbreakers, was not the harmless humiliation most people presume. The pillory victim frequently incurred serious injury, even death, from severe beating inflicted by the citizenry.

Air-conditioning is good business. Tests have shown that absenteeism is less and efficiency far higher in air-conditioned offices and factories.

Key West, Florida, is not the southernmost point in the United States—not since Hawaii became a state, that is. The southernmost point in the nation is now Ka Lae, or South Cape, on the island of Hawaii.

A honeybee can carry a burden 300 times its own weight. To equal this feat a 250-pound man would have to carry a 35-ton truck on his back.

The Whiskerino Club

In 1922, when the city of Sacramento wanted to arrange a celebration commemorating the swashbuckling era of the forty-niners, they passed an ordinance compelling "all male citizens over the age of consent to grow whiskers and thus make the town look like it used to." Loyalty to their fair and sentimental city outweighed gallantry toward their wives and sweethearts; and all the males became so enthusiastic over the idea, they even formed a Whiskerino Club, offering a prize for the longest pair of whiskers. A natty gent, sporting passementerie some 17 feet in length, won the first prize. In keeping with the whole idea, and feeling quite hellish, the Sacramento Club also awarded a prize for "the most impressive cootie garage." There are no further statistics.

Among the unusual names for money throughout the world are: *Rupee* (India); *Cruzeiro* (Brazil); *Kyat* (Burma); *Balboa* (Panama); *Quetzal* (Guatemala); *Bolivar* (Venezuela); *Sucre* (Ecuador); *Gourde* (Haiti); and *Zloty* (Poland).

Chocolate for eating was not perfected until 1876. M.D. Peter of Switzerland turned the trick. Today, Swiss milk chocolate is universally renowned for its flavor, color, and texture. But the most popular eating chocolate in the world is the plain old Hershey Bar, produced in Hershey, Pennsylvania, in the world's largest chocolate factory. The Hershey factory turns out well over 200 million candy bars a year.

Southpaws, Take Heart

Many theories have been advanced to explain the dominance of right-handedness. One of these theories holds that the origin of this phenomenon is physiological, the result of an unequal distribution of the viscera in the abdominal cavity. A more commonly accepted view, however, is that right-handedness is primarily a product of primitive warfare. Early man was engaged in a continual struggle for survival with his fellow man. When called upon to protect himself and his family, he would instinctively protect the vital region around his heart by fending off blows with his left arm, while using his right to strike blows against his adversary. Through a long process of natural selection, those men who had powerful right arms survived to pass their hereditary characteristics on. The natural southpaws who were forced to battle with their right arms fell by the wayside.

The Weight of Responsibility

On May 20 of each year, a ceremony known as the Weighing of the Mayor takes place in High Wycombe, England. Outside the town hall, the mayor, his wife, and a number of minor officials are each placed on the scales and their weights are announced to the assembled populace, along with the weights of the previous year's incumbents.

The record for the most consecutive sit-ups is held by Richard John Knecht, who on December 23, 1972, did 25,222 in 11 hours, 14 minutes. He was eight years old.

The first railroad station in the United States was the Baltimore & Ohio Railroad depot in Baltimore, Maryland. The two-story building, erected in 1830, still stands.

English contains more words than any other language—800,000—but it is doubtful that any individual uses more than 60,000.

A Shocking Tale

When attacking another fish, an electric eel can produce a current of 550 volts—more than four times the current produced by one electric wall outlet. The eel's current is produced by some 8,000 minute storage cells situated along the whole length of its body. The current runs between the eel's head, which is positive in charge, and its tail, which is negative.

Because the eel's vital nervous and swimming organs are electrically insulated by fatty tissue, an eel cannot electrocute another of its species.

Dogs have been known to have litters as large as 23.

The gateway to the fortress of Purandhar, near Poona, India, is built on a foundation of solid gold. The 50,000 gold bricks in the foundation would be worth over $40 million at today's prices.

The Crossing of the Bar

For those who cannot swim the English Channel, there are more ingenious modes of crossing that body of water, and attracting the attendant publicity. For example, one man rowed across the Channel in a coffin, while another man walked across it shod in wooden boots in the shape of flatboats. Still another enterprising individual traversed the Channel in an inflated rubber suit sporting a sail the size of a bath towel.

The Bigger They Come, the Harder They Fall

Although only one foot long, a sea creature known as the urchin fish is capable of killing a 20-foot shark. The urchin fish is often attacked and swallowed by a shark. But once in the belly of the larger fish, the urchin fish blows up its prickly body like an inflated balloon, finally ripping apart the shark's belly and swimming out of the monster's body.

You've often wondered who holds the record for tobacco-juice spitting, right? Well, that noble distinction belongs to one Don Snyder, of Eupora, Mississippi, who in 1975, at the annual classic, spit a wad of tobacco a whopping 31 feet 1 inch.

Talk about your fat cats! The heaviest domestic cat was a feline named Tiger, of Essex, England, who weighed 42 pounds.

From the 11,200-foot peak of Mount Izaru in Costa Rica, you can see both the Atlantic and Pacific Oceans. This is the only point in the Americas from which such a view is possible.

One-Wheel Antics

In 1934, a vaudeville performer named Walter Nilsson pedaled across the United States on an 8½-foot-high unicycle—and never once fell from the bike. Nilsson completed the 3,306-mile trek in just 117 days.

The tallest unicycle was ridden by Carlho Sein Abrahams in Paramaribo, Surinam. It was 45 feet, 10 inches high.

It is illegal in Arizona to kick a mule—and quite foolhardy as well. A mule is not liable to prosecution for a like offense.

In Baltimore, it is a crime to mistreat an oyster.

Despite its nickname, the "Windy City" of Chicago is far from the windiest city in America. That dubious honor belongs to Great Falls, Montana, where the average wind speed is just over 13 miles per hour. Chicago does not even rank in the top ten of windy cities. Boston, Cleveland, Dallas, and Milwaukee must all contend with an average wind speed greater than that of the "Windy City."

You can credit the French monarch Louis XVI for the uniform shape of today's handkerchiefs. At one time, hankies could be bought in almost any size and shape—round, square, oval, or whatever. According to one tale, Queen Marie Antoinette told the king she was tired of seeing handkerchiefs in all kinds of extravagant shapes. The king quickly decreed that "the length of the handkerchief shall equal the width throughout the kingdom." Since French fine-hanky makers dominated the industry for centuries, Louis' dictum became unwritten law throughout Europe.

John Paul Jones, the greatest American naval hero of the Revolutionary War, ended his military career as an admiral in the Russian navy.

In 1788, the Russian Empress Catherine the Great invited Jones to join her Imperial Navy as a rear admiral. Jones accepted the commission, and helped to lead a Russian fleet in a successful campaign against the Turks in the Black Sea.

After his death in 1792, the American hero lay buried in an unmarked grave in France for more than a century. He now lies buried at the U.S. Naval Academy in Annapolis, Maryland.

A single sheet of paper produced in 1830 by the Whitehall Mills in Derbyshire, England, measured four feet in width and *three miles* in length!

Tornadoes have been reported in every state in the continental United States, with the sole exception of Rhode Island. Iowa has reported the greatest number, averaging 15 tornadoes per 50 square miles each year. Texas has suffered the greatest property damage, and Arkansas the most fatalities.

The worst tornado in United States history struck Missouri, Indiana, and Illinois in March, 1925, killing 689 and damaging or destroying an estimated $17 million in property. In 1953, a tornado that hit, oddly enough, Massachusetts took a toll of $52 million in damages and killed 92 people, more than all the tornadoes that struck Iowa in the previous 37 years!

When the headmaster of a high school in Oregon began broadcasting the names of absent students every morning on the radio, truancy at his school dropped by 25 percent.

The first ferris wheel was erected at the 1893 Columbian Exposition in Chicago. Built by George Ferris, the wheel had 36 cars, each capable of holding 60 passengers, and rose to a height of 264 feet.

In a Nutshell

Early American artists were fond of miniature wood carvings, but in some cases they may have carried their craft a bit too far. The Peabody Museum in Salem, Massachusetts, contains a wood carving done in the inside halves of a rosary bead which depicts, in one half, Judgement Day, and in the other, Heaven. The entire scene in each half is less than 2 cubic inches in area, yet includes close to 50 figures—none of which can be seen without a magnifying glass.

The wildcat is the most vicious fighter in the animal kingdom. Asleep, it resembles a gentle housecat—in a fight, it is a furry ball of rage. This spitfire's speed gives it an advantage over most other animals. In one swift leap, it can rip open its enemy's throat with its razor-like teeth.

The term *bootlegger* originated on the Indian reservations of the West. Since it was unlawful to sell alcoholic spirits to the Indians, ingenious peddlers often carried flasks of firewater in their boots to conceal them from government agents.

A corkscrew of recent invention consists of a needle attached to a pellet of carbon-dioxide. The needle pierces the cork, and a pump pushes the CO_2 into the bottle until the pressure inside the bottle ejects the cork. At least, that's the way the device is supposed to work. Frequently, the pressure will explode the bottle itself instead of the cork.

Until the mid-19th century, postage fees in most of Europe and in the United States were paid by the addressee rather than the sender. Junk mail was presumably no problem at the time.

There are an estimated 400 to 500 different names for the cheeses produced around the world, but many of these names are merely different terms for one cheese commonly produced in an area. Actually, there are but 18 or 19 distinct varieties of cheese.

A large Hawaiian fish is called by natives an "O." A much smaller Hawaiian fish is the "homomomonukunukuaguk."

Anteojos is the Spanish word for eyeglasses. Anteojos comes from two Spanish words. *Ante* means "in front of" and *ojos* means "eyes." So *anteojos* means "in front of the eyes," which is exactly where eyeglasses belong.

Willy Ferrero, born in Rome, Italy, in 1907, made musical history only a few years after coming into the world. He conducted an orchestra in Paris when he was only four years old!

Although mechanical refrigeration techniques have been developed only within the last 100 years, ice cream was enjoyed in Italy as early as the sixteenth century—and perhaps even earlier in England. Italian ice cream arrived in France in 1533, along with Catherine de Medici and her retinue of chefs, when the 14-year-old Florentine moved to Paris to marry King Henry II. For many years, the chefs of various French noblemen tried to keep their recipes for ice cream a secret from other chefs—and from their masters, who were frequently astounded by their cooks' talent for serving a cold dessert even in the warmest months.

Roses have been cultivated for so long that it's impossible to determine where or when the flower was first domesticated. No species of purely wild rose remain on earth.

The Whole Story

Next to apple pie, nothing is considered more American than the doughnut. During the two World Wars, special doughnut-making machines went from one battle area to another to provide soldiers with this favorite American treat.

So it may come as quite a surprise to learn that the doughnut is not American. It was brought over from the Netherlands more than 300 years ago by the Dutch colonists, and then became a popular accompaniment to coffee and milk.

An apocryphal tale traces the origin of billiards in England to a 16th-century London pawnbroker named William Kew. The Englishman allegedly took down the three balls identifying his pawnbroker's shop and used a yardstick to push the balls around in the street. Eventually, young canons from nearby St. Paul's Cathedral joined in the game. *Bill's yard-stick* became *billiard stick*, and later, billiard *cue*, from Kew. Of course, the clergymen invented the *cannon* shot.

The American bicycle industry was born in 1877, when Colonel Albert A. Pope of Boston commissioned the Weed Sewing Machine Company to make 50 "Columbia" bikes in a corner of their shop in Hartford, Connecticut. Bicycle manufacture quickly became one of America's leading mass production industries. By 1892, applications for bicycle patents had grown so numerous that the U.S. Patent Office had to establish a special department for cycles and their parts.

In October, 1937, the Russian icebreaker *Sedov* sailed from Murmansk, U.S.S.R. Arctic ice soon closed in around the ship, imprisoning it off the coast of Siberia. The ship drifted with the ice pack for 3,000 miles over Arctic seas until a new Soviet icebreaker came to its rescue, freeing a path to the open sea.

The next time the 15-man crew of the *Sedov* saw Murmansk was in January, 1940—27 months after they embarked!

We have no idea if the crew members were paid overtime.

If you're eagerly awaiting the day when you open an oyster and find a small pearl inside, don't hold your breath. Pearl oysters are found only in tropical waters, and are not considered fit for consumption.

Starfish on the Rampage

The Great Barrier Reef, the largest animal-made structure on earth, may be shrinking. Vast areas of the 1,200-mile-long reef, which was formed by tiny animals called corals, have been damaged—not by oil spills or any other man-made peril, but by a plague of crown of thorns starfish!

The starfish were first reported in large numbers during the 1960s. Since then, they have eaten their way down to the southern end of the reef, which lies off the eastern coast of Australia. Portions of the reef already ravaged by the starfish have begun to grow back, but Australian scientists fear that the hungry echinoderms may start eating their way northward again, devouring the regenerated portions of the reef.

The crown of thorns starfish derive their name from prominent, poisonous spines that cover the upper portion of their body. The starfish, which sport 16 or 17 arms and grow up to 20 inches in diameter, have been found in concentrations of up to 300,000 per square mile.

Some scientists believe the starfish plague may be the result of the activities of shell collectors and spear fishermen, who kill off many of the starfish's normal predators.

Earthquakes have probably killed more than 13 million people over the last 4,000 years. The most deadly quake of all time occurred in 1556, in Shensi Province, China, when some 830,000 people lost their lives!

The worst quake of this century occurred on July 28, 1976, destroying the city of Tangshan in eastern China, and taking a toll of some 700,000 lives. The greatest material damage was caused by the Great Quake in Tokyo and Yokohama, Japan on September 1, 1923. It took 140,000 lives and damaged property valued at an estimated $2.8 billion! The sea bottom in a nearby bay sank close to 1,000 feet—and tossed potatoes right out of the ground!

You might think that Reykjavik, Iceland, which lies almost on the Arctic Circle, is one of the coldest capital cities on earth. Actually, Reykjavik has a warmer mean temperature—29 degrees—than Chicago, Detroit, or Boston during January, Reykjavik's coldest month.

You shiver when you're cold because shivering increases muscular action and thus raises body temperature.

Persons wishing to immigrate to New Zealand must answer a number of questions pertaining to their health, none less weighty than: "Susceptible to bunions?"

As Old As the Hills

Perhaps the oldest living thing on Earth is the Macrozamia tree, which grows in the Tambourine Mountains of Queensland, Australia. Scientists estimate that these trees are anywhere from 12,000 to 15,000 years old—more than six times as old as the giant redwoods of California and Oregon.

Although there is some controversy over the exact age of these palmlike trees—counting their concentric rings is a very difficult task—everyone agrees that the Macrozamia is unequaled in age. The giant bald cypress of Mexico is definitely known to be 4,000 years old, and is far younger than many of the Australian Macrozamias. These trees were old when David and Goliath were boys.

In case you've forgotten: the face of Woodrow Wilson adorns the U.S. Treasury's $100,000 note. And, of course, Salmon Portland Chase appears on the $10,000 bill.

Oh! Oh! The Beautiful Snow!

You may occasionally curse snow for the inconvenience it causes, but no one could find fault with an individual snowflake. Each snowflake that falls to earth has its own unique crystal design, and many of these designs are among the most beautiful symmetrical forms to be found anywhere in nature.

Snowflakes generally assume a hexagonal form, but they're found in a wide range of patterns. The smallest flakes, called "diamond dust," may be just .005 inches in diameter, while others may be several inches across. An average-sized snowflake takes eight to ten minutes to fall to earth from a height of 1,000 feet. Approximately ten inches of snow contain water equal to an inch of rain.

Since 1940, scientists have had a means to produce replicas of snowflakes so that their structure may be studied. A chemical compound is spread over a glass plate on which the flakes settle. As part of the compound evaporates, the snow crystal is left encased in a plastic shell. When the flake melts, the shell remains, forming a perfect replica of the original flake. In all studies of snowflakes, no two flakes with the same crystal design have ever been discovered.

A painting entitled "Late afternoon in winter" which originally appeared in Harper's Magazine

A winter scene in the woods as depicted in a 1800s drawing in Leslie's Magazine

"Travelers in a snowstorm" is the title of this Japanese drawing which first appeared in Harper's Magazine *around 1890*

A *drawing by the great French satirist, Grandville, which appeared in* Un Autre Monde, *published in Paris in 1844*

A *painting by Malcolm C. Salaman in a publication* New Woodcuts, *published in London in 1930*

A drawing of jolly old England during a snowstorm, as seen in the columns of Punch

This winter scene appears in a book entitled "The Book of the Revolution" by Benson J. Lossing, published by Harper's *in 1860.*

A winter scene in Czarist Russia, as depicted by a Soviet artist of the 1970s.

A winter scene of woods covered with snow.
The drawing appeared in the London Illustrated News *of 1886.*

Batman

During the 1930's, Clem Sohn of Lansing, Michigan, justly earned the nickname "Batman." The air-show performer fashioned a set of canvas wings and attached them to his arms, fitted a canvas web between his legs, and then jumped from airplanes at altitudes of up to 20,000 feet! Sohn looked much like the comic strip character Batman as he glided through the air in his wings and goggles, floating downward some three miles and then opening his parachute for the final descent.

Sohn soared through the air with the greatest of ease more than 2,000 times. Then, on April 25, 1937, at Vincennes, France, 100,000 horrified spectators watched as the 26-year-old daredevil's parachute failed to open and he plunged to his death.

The Venus flytrap is actually misnamed, for the plant feeds primarily on ants and not flies. But it can digest any insect, or meat in any form. Flytraps have been known to snare creatures as large as a small frog!

Home, Sweet Homeless

John Howard Payne won lasting fame by writing a single song, the nostalgic *Home, Sweet Home.* Yet Payne virtually never had a home of his own!

Born in New York City in 1791, Payne spent most of his life on the move, homeless and often penniless. An actor, playwright, composer, and for a time, prison inmate, Payne died in Tunis, North Africa, where he was employed by the U.S. consulate. Today, the home in East Hampton, Long Island, where Payne spent part of his childhood, is maintained as a shrine, for the humble cottage is probably the only home, sweet home that Payne ever knew.

King Louis XIV of France owned an estimated 413 beds in his various palaces. A ribald painting called "The Triumph of Venus" originally adorned the king's favorite bed at Versailles, but his second wife, a woman of a more religious bent, had it replaced with "The Sacrifice of Abraham."

A dentifrice currently made in France tints the gums pink to make the teeth look whiter by comparison.

In 1973, a 54-year-old man in Hanover, West Germany, began hiccoughing. Two years and some 36 million hiccoughs later, the distraught German decided to end the hiccoughing bout once and for all, and leapt to his death from a hospital window.

The squirting lapel flower is an old practical joke, but there are many specimens of the plant kingdom that do indeed squirt liquid. Among these is the aptly named squirting cucumber. When the fruit of this Mediterranean plant is ripe, the inner tissue forms a liquid in which the seeds float. The "cucumber" swells with liquid to the bursting point, then explodes and propels the juice and seed mixture through a small hole punched in the end of the fruit. The explosion is powerful enough to propel the seeds as far as 40 feet from the plant!

Hail rarely falls in the winter. Surprisingly, the ice balls will not fall when the ground temperature is below freezing. And hail almost never forms unless a thunderstorm is occuring. Since the conditions which produce thunderstorms rarely occur in winter, hail is generally a summer phenomenon.

The wedding cake of the ancient Greeks was almost always a cheesecake covered with honey. The island of Samos was noted throughout Greece as the home of great cheesecake.

"French" ice cream is definitely different from other varieties in this country, for only ice cream made with eggs can legally be sold as "French."

The Big Shake-up

Seismologists estimate that more than 500,000 earthquakes occur each year, of which about 100,000 can be felt by people in the vicinity of the quake. But only about 1,000 quakes— or .2 percent—cause damage of any kind.

Although the instrument that measures the intensity of earthquakes, the seismograph, was not invented until almost a century later, many scientists believe that the most powerful earthquake of modern times occurred on November 1, 1755, in Lisbon, Portugal. Within six minutes of the main shock, more than 30,000 persons were dead and 12,000 dwellings were destroyed. The fire that followed the quake burned for six days.

The Lisbon quake was so powerful that cities in Morocco, hundreds of miles away, were badly damaged. And lakes in Norway were disturbed—over 2,000 miles from the center of the quake!

Texas has flown the flags of six nations: Spain, France, Mexico, the Republic of Texas, the United States, and the Confederate States of America.

The Republic of Texas, with its famed Lone Star flag, remained an independent nation for nearly a decade before being annexed by the United States in 1845.

The eggplant was once known as the "love apple" in England because it was thought to possess aphrodisiac properties. Botanists in northern Europe dubbed the eggplant *mala insana*, or "mad apple," because they thought that eating the fruit could result in insanity!

Specialists in brolliology—the study of the umbrella, that is—are reluctant to estimate the number of umbrellas in use throughout the world, but the country with the highest per capita use of the gamp is definitely England. As late as 1954, 300,000 umbrellas were produced in the British Isles each month! Today, most umbrellas are imported from Hong Kong and Japan. And close to 75,000 umbrellas are lost each year on the bus and underground system of London alone!

The first house numbers appeared in 1463, on the Pont Notre-Dame in Paris.

Dubious Honor

In April of 1972, a little-known world title was lost at Beaver, Oklahoma. Governor David Hall of that state, who a year earlier had hurled a hand-sized wad of cow dung a whopping 94 feet to win the World Dung-Throwing Championship, managed a throw of only 68 feet and was dethroned by former Governor Dewey Bartlett, who broke all records with a stunning toss of 138 feet.

A Spirited History

The use of liquor is so widespread that almost every country in the world utilizes some native product to make an alcoholic beverage. Asian liquors, distilled from rice, from millet, or from palm sap originated around 400 B.C., and took the names of *sautchoo*, *arrack*, *arika*, and *skhou*. Around the year 300, Ireland brewed up some *usquebaugh* from oat and barley beer. Around the year 900, Italy began distilling grapes to produce brandy. Around 1500, the Scots got the hand of making whiskey from malted barley. In 1750, France distilled cognac from grapes.

A play by Sinclair Lewis entitled *It Can't Happen Here* opened in 21 theatres in 18 cities—on the same night of October 27, 1936.

Chow Hound

A dog may be man's best friend, but that friendship can be pushed beyond its limits. In parts of China, roast dog is considered a gourmet's delight. The Chinese have gone so far as to develop a special breed of dog for the table, a type of chow, with black-haired dogs the most desirable.

Our slang word for food, *chow*, may or may not be linked to the edible dog of China. A Cantonese word pronounced *chow* means "fried." The word appears in the name of America's most popular Chinese dish, chow mein.

A sign painted on a glass window will read differently from outside the store than it will from the inside—with the exception of the sign on the Yreka Bakery, in Yreka, California, which forms a palindrome.

A California law makes it illegal to shoot any game bird or animal from an automobile—except a whale!

A respectable marathon runner today can cover 26 miles over a smoothly paved track in less than two-and-a-half hours, for an average speed of about ten miles per hour.

But in 1764, an English barrister named Foster Powell covered the 50 miles between London and Bath, England, in just seven hours—walking! Although almost the entire route wound over cobblestone and dirt roads, Powell walked at a rate of better than seven miles per hour.

Surprisingly, Jupiter—the largest planet in the solar system—has the shortest day of all the planets. Jupiter completes a rotation on its axis in less than ten earth hours.

The deepest lake in the world is Lake Baykal, in the Soviet Union. At some points it is more than a mile deep.

Although the Romans took baths and had excellent plumbing facilities for hot and cold water more than 2,000 years ago, the habit of bathing died out during the Middle Ages. Baths were usually taken only on a doctor's request. The result was a lack of hygiene that encouraged infection. Even the United States did not get its first bathtub until 1840.

The United States is by far the world's largest importer of spices and herbs. In 1968, this country imported over 150 million pounds of spices, with a value in excess of $60 million.

Many people believe that Charles Lindbergh was the first man to complete a transatlantic airplane flight. Actually, the feat had been accomplished many times before Lindbergh's historic flight in 1927. Eight years earlier, a crew of six U.S. Navy flyers had crossed the Atlantic in a Curtiss hydroplane, landing in the Azores before continuing on to England. Later in the same year, two Englishmen accomplished the first nonstop crossing, traveling from Newfoundland to Ireland in just over 16 hours. Their gear included two stuffed black cats. Including airship crews, Lindbergh was actually the 81st person to fly across the Atlantic Ocean. But he was the first to do it alone.

You won't find many picnic tables in the sandy plateau region of southwestern Africa, but in a pinch you could spread your lunch on top of the *Welwitschia mirabilis* plant. The trunk of this grotesque giant is often six feet in diameter, yet rises just a few inches above the ground, with an almost flat top. This bizarre form give the *Welwitschia* the appearance of a slightly folded round table!

From around the rim of this trunk extend a number of long, leathery leaves that curl like ribbons over the surrounding soil. These leaves can measure as much as 18 feet in length—long enough to be bent over and used as a table cloth!

The Ruwanweli Pagoda in Anuradhapura, Sri Lanka (Ceylon), is built on a 500-square-foot, seven-inch-thick foundation of solid silver.

Over 65 percent of the world's population goes through the day without coming in contact with a newspaper, radio, television, or telephone.

The time required for the earth to orbit the sun—that is, the length of an earth year—increases by about .04 seconds each century.

Georgia, with an area of 58,073 square miles, most nearly approaches the average size of the 48 conterminous states.

Good Things Come in Small Packages

Mrs. Pemberton, a 16th-century painting by Hans Holbein, brought $30,000 in a 1935 auction. The round portrait is only two inches in diameter.

The Egyptian Queen Cleopatra was Greek by ancestry and had not a drop of Egyptian blood in her veins. The famed Queen of the Nile was descended from a line of brother-sister marriages, and she herself married two of her own brothers.

In the Book of Esther, it is stated that when the candidates for the Persian queenship were assembled by King Ahasuerus, they were brought to the royal harem and there treated for "six months with balm and six months with spices."

A tornado that struck St. Louis in 1927 caused $26 million worth of damage in five minutes.

A Colorful Tune

Green with Envy, Purple with Passion, White with Anger, Scarlet with Fever, What Were You Doing in Her Arms Last Night Blues is the title—the longest known title to date—of a tune written by Phillip Springer and Nita Jones in 1961.

When active, the Paricutin volcano in central Mexico could spew 4 million pounds of rock and lava into the air in one minute.

Even when you're standing still, you're actually traveling at incredibly high speeds. The earth is revolving at the speed of 1,000 miles per hour, and orbiting the sun at the speed of 66,700 miles per hour.

There are 156 languages in the world—each of which is spoken by at least one million people.

A mother cod can lay as many as five million eggs at a single spawning—of which only a half dozen usually survive. If all cod eggs produced live fish, there would be no room left in the ocean for water.

The Rinconada Racetrack in Venezuela—called the most luxurious track in the world—has a swimming pool for horses.

Between dawn and dusk an acre of peas can increase in weight by 50 percent, owing to the vegetable's high rate of absorption.

People begin to shrink after the age of 30.

Modern Monickers

If you're thumbing through an old book and come across a reference to a city or nation that you've never heard of, the chances are good that you've merely stumbled onto the old name for a well-known place. Among the more recent place-name changes are:

Old	New
Ceylon	Sri Lanka
Siam	Thailand
Mesopotamia	Iraq
Persia	Iran
Ciudad Trujillo	Santo Domingo
Christiana	Oslo
Stalingrad	Volgograd
St. Petersburg	Leningrad
Gold Coast	Ghana
Belgian Congo	Zaire
Tanganyika	Tanzania
Constantinople	Istanbul
Peiping	Peking
East Pakistan	Bangladesh
Northern Rhodesia	Zambia
Danzig	Gdansk
Batavia	Djakarta

Jealous Genius

Michelangelo—the great Renaissance painter, sculptor, architect, and poet—signed only one of his many works: the *Pieta* in St. Peter's. The artist chiseled his name and birthplace on the figure of Mary after hearing a group of sightseers erroneously attribute the work to another sculptor.

If in 1600, you happened to be walking along a Dutch canal, you might have been surprised to see a two-masted ship bearing down on you. Not in the canal—on the road. There was one such ship that was said to have reached a speed of 20 m.p.h. while carrying 28 fear-stricken passengers. In his notebooks, Leonardo da Vinci had envisioned some sort of self-propelled vehicle; and some Dutchman, quite naturally, had modeled such a vehicle after a sailing vessel.

The trunk of an elephant can hold six quarts of water—enough to wash down the biggest snootful of peanuts.

During the 21-year-plus London run of the Agatha Christie play *The Mousetrap*, wardrobe mistress Maisie Wilmer-Brown ironed her way through 36 miles of shirts.

Around 1850, a chap by the name of Loy, who lived in London, made a most unusual pair of skates. The springs across the instep and across the heel secured the skate to the foot without using screws. The skate was made of satinwood, and enriched by plates of gilded metalwork. A swan's neck was a graceful and appropriate ornament.

On October 8, 1929, a milestone in modern transportation was reached when a newsreel and two cartoons were shown on a Transcontinental Air Transport plane.

A Timely Tale

In the famous cathedral of Notre Dame de Dijon in France, there is the oldest gong clock in the world. Given to the town of Dijon in 1383 by Philip the Hardy, this clock has been keeping abreast of the time ever since. Constructed by Jacques Marc, the clock contains two large bronze figures which have struck the hour every hour for the last 590 years. An ambitious mathematician computed that by January 1, 1950, these bronze figures had struck the clock 32,284,980 times.

Brandy is obtained from wine or the fermented mash of fruit. It is made from grapes, or cherries, or apples, or plums, or apricots, or peaches, or blackberries.

Of the more than 500 elephants that have been exhibited in the United States, only six are known to have been conceived and born here.

As many as 1,652 languages and dialects are spoken by India's 600 million people. Hindi, the official language, is spoken by only 35 percent of the population.

The most common surname in the United States is Smith. Close to 2.5 million Smiths reside here, half a million more than those with the second most common name, Johnson.

Funeral directors in California are offering a new economy deal—for only $25 your ashes will be scattered over the Pacific Ocean from a light aircraft. A certificate will be issued guaranteeing the time at which your ashes were "committed to the elements of the eternal seven seas."

Jeweled Jahangir

Of the many collectors of glittering jewels down through the ages, Emperor Jahangir, the noble ruler of India who died in 1627, is the most noted who ever lived. It is reported that he owned a total of 2,235,600 carats of pearls, 931,500 carats of emeralds, 376,600 carats of rubies, 279,450 carats of diamonds, and 186,300 carats of jade.

For his time, Jahangir was an enlightened monarch. During his reign, architectural masterpieces rose throughout India.

One of the emperor's hobbies was fishing, but Jahangir never killed a fish he caught. Instead, he would place a string of pearls through the fish's gills and throw it back into the water.

If nothing else, the man was extremely vain, for his name itself, Jahangir, means "Conqueror of the World." In addition, he had other glorious titles such as "Possessor of the Planets," "Mirror of the Glories of God," and "King of Increasing Fortune."

The first boardwalk erected in the United States was located in Atlantic City, New Jersey. The eight-foot wide walkway was completed in 1870 and rested directly on top of the sand.

In 1970, a limbo dancer from the West Indies, Theresa Marquis, limboed her way under a bar only six and one half inches above the ground. Try to match that record.

Only eight breeds of purebred dog originated in the United States: the American foxhound, American water spaniel, Boston terrier, Chesapeake Bay retriever, Coonhound, Amertoy, Spitz, and Staffordshire terrier. The British Isles holds the pedigreed pooch title—of the world's 163 recognized breeds, 47 originated there.

The first successful electric elevator was installed in the Demarest Building in New York City, in 1889.

A Shaggy Dog Story

Between 1892 and 1902, a small mongrel named Tim—with a metal collection box attached to his collar—met all incoming trains in London's Paddington Station to beg for coins for the widows' and orphans' fund of a British railroad. When the animal died, his body was placed in a glass case in the station, with a slot for coins so that the dog could continue his work.

Don't ever accuse the chicken of being behind the times. In the 1930s, the average American hen laid 121 eggs a year. Today, a hen donates about 217 eggs to the breakfast tables of America.

Bet you think that Big Ben is a clock in London. This is a popular misapprehension, even in England. Actually, Big Ben is the name of the hour bell in the *Westminster* clock!

The Moscow to Peking run on the Trans-Siberian Railroad is the longest rail journey that can be made without changing trains.

The Whyos, a Brooklyn gang of mobsters who preceded the Five Points gang, issued a printed list for potential clients: "Punching, $2; both eyes blacked, $4; nose and jaw broken, $10; jacked out (stunned with a blackjack), $15; ear chewed off, $15; leg or arm broken, $19; shot in leg, $25; stabbed, $25; doing the big job, $100."

All in a Day's Work

Despite appearances, bees do not wander aimlessly from flower to flower in search of nectar. Many flowers produce nectar at only certain times of the day, and bees follow a timetable which brings them to the right flower at just the right time. A bee's busy day may begin with a dandelion at nine in the morning, continue with a blue cornflower at eleven o'clock, then a red clover at one o'clock, and a viper at about three—for those are the hours at which each of these flowers is most generous with its nectar.

Twelve architects spent most of their lives working on the construction of St. Peter's Church, in Rome. Most of them never lived to see the church completed.

A scientist at the University of Arizona has developed a heat-sensitive instrument for taking temperature readings from distant planets. This device is so sensitive that it could detect a lit match across the breadth of the Pacific Ocean.

The longest man-made object in the world is an oil pipeline which stretches 1,775 miles between Alberta and Ontario, Canada. But an oil pipeline being constructed in the Soviet Union will be 2,860 miles long.

The fastest dog in the world is either the saluki or the greyhound, depending on whom you talk to. The greyhound has been clocked at 41.7 miles per hour.

In 18th-century America, portraitists journeyed from town to town with an assortment of paintings of men and women, complete in every feature except the faces. A person wishing to sit for his portrait simply had to select the body he liked best, and let the artist fill in the missing face and hair.

Protective Custody

A hornbill must find just the right size hole in a tree for a nest. The female slips inside and there lays her eggs.

The male seals off the entrance with mud, leaving only a narrow slit. Inside, the female is both protected and imprisoned while incubating her eggs. She gets food from her mate by sticking her bill out of the slit. When the young are full grown, the seal is broken, and the young leave the home with their mother.

Shampoo, which to us means to wash your hair, comes from the Hindu word *shampu*, which means to press. A good shampoo is one where you press your fingers hard against your scalp, so our word still indicates part of the original Hindu meaning.

Theogenes fought and killed 1,425 opponents

In ancient days, the rulers of Greece and Rome would amuse themselves and their subjects through gladiatorial combats in which men fought to the death for the amusement of the spectators. History records that the greatest of these gladiators was a Greek called Theogenes, a native of Thasos.

Theogenes served a cruel prince named Thesus, who reigned about 900 B.C. Thesus delighted in sadistic spectacles and ordained a combat that was especially vicious. The two contestants—if they can be called such—were placed facing each other, almost nose to nose, each on a flat stone. Both men were strapped into place. Their fists were encased in leather thongs which were studded with small, sharp, metal spikes. At a given signal, they would strike at each other, and the combat would continue, without rest, until one of the contestants had been beaten to death.

During a long career, Theogenes—strong, skillful, and savage—faced 1,425 men and killed every one of them.

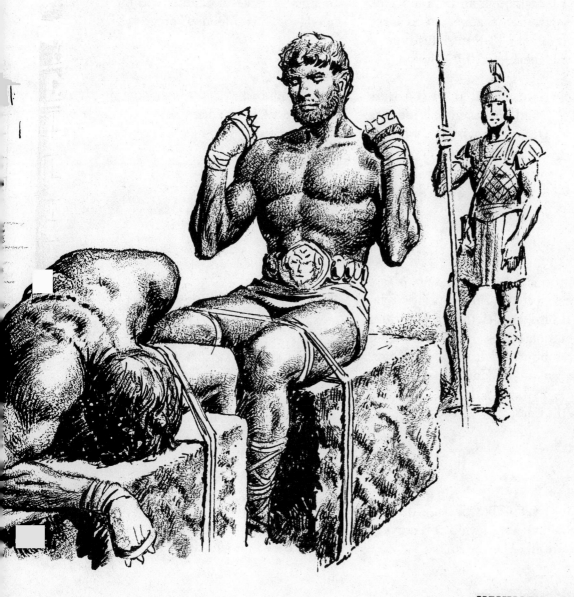

Columbus notwithstanding, the members of the Flat Earth Society refuse to believe that the earth is spherical. As for the evidence supplied by photographs taken from outer space, the Society's president, Charles K. Johnson, of Lancaster, California, discounts them as a gigantic hoax—not to mention the moon landings and other feats of modern science.

The Light Fantastic

The first electric lamp was the arc lamp, developed from the electrochemical principle demonstrated by Humphrey Davy in 1801. In 1879, Cleveland, Ohio, became the first city to use the new carbon-arc street lamps devised by C.F. Brush. Although an impracticable incandescent electric lamp appeared as early as 1858, it was not until 1879 that this type of illumination was perfected by Thomas A. Edison.

Neon lamps were invented by Georges Claude in 1911, and came into wide use within a decade. Different colors could be obtained by using different gases—argon for blue, neon for red, helium for yellow, carbon dioxide for white; and these gases could be mixed to produce virtually any color.

An unusual bird indeed is the hoatzin, a rare South American species with no close relatives. A crested bird smaller than a pheasant, the hoatzin dines on leaves. But the strangest thing about this bird is that the young have claws on their *wings*—in addition to those on their feet. These claws help the baby hoatzins climb about in the trees.

Quito, capital of Ecuador, sits almost directly on top of the equator. But because the city is 9,300 feet above sea level, it enjoys a spring-like climate all year around.

The largest operational telescope in the world is a 236.2-inch reflecting telescope in the Caucasus Mountains of the U.S.S.R. Assembled in October 1970, it is 80 feet long, weighs 935 tons, and contains a mirror which weighs 78 tons by itself. The light-gathering power of this telescope is so great that it can detect the light of a single candle, 15,000 miles away.

The range of this gargantuan instrument encompasses the entire observable universe.

How did the bloodhound get its name? Not, as you might imagine, because of its ability to track down bloodthirsty criminals by scent. Rather, this dog, one of the most gentle and amiable varieties of canine, was the first pedigreed—or "pure blooded" breed of dog.

A human being sheds skin continually, replacing it with an entire new outer layer once every 28 days.

Tequila, indigenous to Mexico, is obtained from the agave plant.

Executive Excursions

The first President to ride in an automobile was Theodore Roosevelt, but he didn't much care for it and seldom allowed the Secret Service chauffeur to take him out for a spin.

The next President, William Howard Taft, made more regular use of his brougham, but he didn't drive the car himself—perhaps because his enormous girth would not allow him to squeeze beneath the steering wheel.

Warren G. Harding was the first man elected President who drove a car himself.

The longest bicycle ever constructed was a tandem bike that could seat 10. The machine was 23 feet long and weighed 305 pounds.

A nation with an amazingly high beer consumption is Belgium. The average Belgian enjoys 30.6 gallons of the frothy nectar each year. In the Northern Territory of Australia, however, beer consumption has been unofficially estimated to be close to 52 gallons per person each year.

Airborne Thievery

The tropical man-of-war, or frigate bird, likes a fish dinner. But it doesn't fish in the way most birds do. Instead, it waits until another bird has done the work. Then it swoops down and beats the bird with its wings. The unlucky bird, trying to defend itself, lets go of the fish. The swift man-of-war dives, snatches the fish, and zooms away.

Sometimes this robber does its own fishing in mid-air above the ocean. It dives down and grabs flying fish when they sail above water.

The term *pekoe* refers only to a size of tea leaf—and not to a type or variety of tea. Other names of sizes are *Orange Pekoe, Souchong, Broken Pekor, Fannings,* and *Dust.*

The longest of all worms is the *Lineus longissimus,* or "living fishing line worm." In 1964, a specimen washed ashore at St. Andrews, Scotland, after a storm. It measured more than 180 feet in length.

Ostriches feed unhatched eggs to their young. Several female ostriches often lay their eggs in a single nest during the mating season. They add a few each day until there is a total of two dozen. Some of these eggs hatch earlier than others. To feed their hungry babies who cannot eat the rough food of the adult ostrich, the parent birds crack open the unhatched eggs and feed them to their youngsters.

Polly Want a Cracker!

The size of a parrot's vocabulary depends upon a variety of factors: the patience and perseverance of the trainer; the age at which the parrot is trained; and of course, the talent of the individual bird. Well-trained birds can accumulate a vocabulary of a few hundred words, but several birds have been taught to utter fairly complex sentences or passages.

There have been fairly reliable reports that a certain parrot was trained to recite the Lord's Prayer entire. According to the United States Biological Survey, there is no reason to doubt the claim on biological grounds.

Vodka is an unaged spirit obtained from potatoes or grain. It is then filtered through vegetable charcoal. In the United States, this process produces a liquid that must be "without distinctive character, aroma, or taste," but which packs quite a noticeable wallop at over 190 proof.

The longest recorded drive of all time is 445 yards, achieved by E.C. Bliss in 1913. Playing on the Old Course at Herne Bay, Kent, England, Bliss—a 12-handicap player—put all of his 182 pounds behind his swing and sent the ball flying over a quarter of a mile. There was a 57-foot drop over the course of the drive. On that particular day, Bliss was blessed with luck, for a registered surveyor was on the scene to accurately measure his shot forthwith.

Time for Tea

It is believed the first shipment of tea to the United States arrived in New Amsterdam about 1650. At the time, tea cost from $30 to $50 a pound, and in addition to making a refreshing drink, the used leaves were sometimes salted and eaten with butter.

Tea traveled with the pioneers who explored and settled our vast land. No wagon train headed West without a good supply of tea on board. Then, as now, it was the drink for people on the go who needed a lift that relaxes and refreshes.

Today, the United States is the second largest consumer of tea in the world, surpassed only by Great Britain. We are the only country that prepares large quantities of tea using three different types: loose, teabags, and instant.

Some cicadas live underground for 17 years, then emerge for a few weeks of sunshine before dying.

The big fish fight, and fight hard, so game fishing is usually considered a man's sport. But on May 6, 1950, Mrs. H.A. Bradley took her boat out to Cape Charles, Virginia, and brought to gaff the largest drum fish ever caught—an 87-pound, 8-ounce giant!

Babies have been known to hiccup several hours before birth. In some instances an unborn baby has cried loudly enough to be heard from 25 feet away.

The Egyptian plover has worked out a mutually satisfactory arrangement with the crocodile: the bird gets food and the crocodile gets service. The plover rides on the crocodile's back and serves as a lookout, emitting shrill cries when danger seems imminent. The plover also digs parasites out of the crocodile's back. When the crocodile finishes its dinner, the big reptile opens up its mouth so that its small helper can hop inside, and pick its teeth clean of uneaten food.

The Western madam known as Diamond-tooth Lil owed her nickname to a gold front tooth studded with a large diamond. Immortalized by Mae West's portrayal in a movie called *Diamond Lil*, the Austrian-born madam accumulated husbands as easily as diamonds—she married eight times without bothering with the formality of a divorce.

The penknife with the greatest number of blades is the Year Knife, made by Joseph Rodgers & Sons, Ltd. of Sheffield, England. Built in 1822 with 1,822 blades, the knife has continued to match the year ever since. The knife will finally run out of space for further blades in the year 2,000.

Itinerant lecturer Walter Stolle had pedaled an estimated 270,000 miles in his lifetime—that's about 11 times around the earth! In his travels, Stolle has pedaled through some 140 nations, and suffered 26 robberies en route.

Gazelles, prairie dogs, wild asses, and many other animals never drink water. They have a special chemical process which transforms a part of their solid food into water.

The Fire Extinguished by an Iceberg

The fateful voyage of the British liner *Titanic* was marred by disaster from the very beginning. As the 46,000-ton vessel left its dock in Southhampton on April 10, 1912, a fire broke out in a bunker. Four days later, when the mammoth liner struck an iceberg and went down in the North Atlantic, the fire was still burning.

The largest clams in the world weigh close to 500 pounds.

You'll need more than a set of strong glasses to read the copy of Omar Khayyam's *Rubaiyat* in the Bodelian Library at Oxford University—you'll need a microscope! This book—the smallest in the world—is only one-quarter inch high and three-sixteenths of an inch wide, and weighs just 1/327 of an ounce.

Beards were once placed under government control in Romania. Whiskers could be worn only if the owner secured an official permit, and paid the appropriate fee.

The invention of the first mechanical clock has been attributed to I'Hsing and Liang Ling-tsan of China, circa 725 A.D.

Tea Lore

The usual tea sold in the supermarket is a blend of 20 to 30 different varieties, each chosen for a certain characteristic—color, flavor, bouquet, body.

There are three different types of tea—black, green, and oolong. All three types come from the same tea bushes. It's how the leaves are processed after they are picked that makes the teas different.

Over 97 percent of all the tea consumed in the United States is black tea. In the processing, the tea is fully fermented.

Green tea is light in color when brewed. In its processing, it is not fermented at all.

Oolong tea is a compromise between black and green tea. It is semi-fermented, so that the leaves turn greenish brown.

At many a fiesta held in rural Mexico, one of the treats enjoyed by the guests is ant candy. This unusual confection consists of the bodies of ants which gather honey from a species of oak leaf. The ants swell enormously until they are about the size of gooseberries. After the ants' legs and heads are removed, their bodies are piled on dishes and served as candy. The taste of these insects is very similar to that of a sweet, juicy fruit.

The next time your day at the beach is ruined by cloudy skies, just remember this: without clouds and the other constituents of the earth's atmosphere, the surface of our planet would reach a temperature of 176 degrees at the equator by day, and -220 degrees at night!

Of all man-made structures on earth, the only one that might conceivably be visible from the moon is the Great Wall of China.

Spilling the Beans

Intent on preserving a monopoly, the Dutch forbade taking coffee seedlings from their East Indian plantations. But a dashing young Brazilian officer won the heart of the wife of the governor of Dutch Guiana, a coffee growing colony in South America, and as a token of her affection, she gave him some of the precious beans and cuttings, anticipating Cole Porter by declaring her love thusly: "Take the beans, for you're the cream in my coffee!"

In the 19th century, students at Cambridge University, England, were not permitted to keep a dog in their rooms. Lord Byron, the famed poet, complied with the rule—he kept a bear instead.

The first building erected by the American Government in Washington, D.C. was the Executive Mansion, designed by James Hoban and modeled after the palace of the Duke of Leinster in Ireland. Construction began in 1792, and the building was first occupied by President John Adams in 1800. The mansion was burned by the British in 1814, but later restored, with all stones painted white to obliterate evidence of the blaze. Since that time, the building has been known as the White House.

The Royal Society for the Prevention of Accidents erected a display stand at the Institute of Personnel Management Conference in Harrowgate, England. It collapsed.

Since their formation 10,000 years ago, the Niagara Falls have eaten their way seven miles upstream. If they continue at that rate, they will disappear into Lake Erie in 22,800 years.

The spoon as we know it today, with its spatulate handle, dates from only the 18th century.

Barnum's Biggest Star

In 1882, Jumbo—the largest elephant ever seen in captivity—was sold by the London Zoo to P.T. Barnum. A loud cry of protest immediately arose from the elephant's English admirers—who included Queen Victoria in their numbers. But the protest was to no avail—the elephant sailed to America with a deluge of gifts sent by his English friends. The gargantuan pachyderm—to which we owe the term "jumbo"—was part of Barnum's circus until the elephant was killed by an express train in Canada in 1885.

Glass, though it feels hard enough to be called a solid, is actually a liquid. If left standing in one position, the particles that make up glass will flow downward.

Since the 19th century, the *Tour d'Argent*—the oldest restaurant in Paris—has given a memento ticket to every diner who orders the specialty of the house, *canard rouennais*. The name and number of the guest is entered in a visitors' book, a unique record which has now reached six figures. Ticket number 112,151 went to President Franklin D. Roosevelt; 203,728 to Marlene Dietrich; and 253,652 to Charlie Chaplin.

Hebrew had been a dead language for 2,300 years before it was revived by the Jews in Israel as their common language. There is no other case in which a dead language has been resurrected.

An age-old myth held that certain precious gems could produce offspring. Pearl divers in Borneo often placed a pair of pearls together in the hope that the two gems would mate and have a family.

An Arboreal Affair

Among the Brahmans of southern India, a younger brother may not marry before an older one. When there is no bride available for the senior brother, he is often married to a tree, which leaves the younger brother free to take a wife. Sometimes the tree marriage takes place at the same time as the regular marriage, in the belief that some evil influence which would otherwise attach to the newly wedded pair will be diverted to the tree.

About 1700, a Swiss inventor mounted a windmill on a wagon. It was hoped that as the windmill wound up a huge spring, the vehicle would lope along under its own power.

Women as young as six and as old as 62 have become mothers, while men as young as 13 and as old as 100 have become fathers.

The fastest train in the world is the Japanese National Railroad's Hikari run, between Kyoto and Nagoya. The Hikari makes the 83-mile trip in only 47 minutes, for an average speed of 106.5 miles per hour.

We are put to no end of trouble by a 10-inch snowfall—traffic is snarled, electricity fails, drains overflow, roofs leak. Imagine how the people of Tamarack, California, must have felt in the winter of 1906-7, when 884 inches of snow fell in one heap. That's 73 feet, a world's record.

A Rude Shock

In 1864, an Australian named Siegfried Marcus was experimenting with the lightbulb, and he wasn't very successful. He ignited a mixture of gasoline and air, believing he would at last be producing illumination. He was right. But he also produced a violent explosion, jolting him into the discovery that his mixture could be a method of powering a vehicle. The drawback, however, was that his contraption required a strong man to lift the rear end of the vehicle while the wheels were being spun to get the engine going. Like almost all inventors, Marcus was a bit crazy; and after 10 years, he lost interest in the automobile, calling it "a senseless waste of time and effort."

By this time, the steam vehicle was already coming under public pressure because of the noise it engendered. Moreover, the steam engine was considered downright dangerous, and so it was common for early motorists to find the roadway blocked with barricades.

Osbaldeston rode horseback for 200 miles in eight hours and 42 minutes.

George Osbaldeston was a 155-pound jockey who operated the Newmarket Inn. He was known as "The Squire." On November 5, 1831, George announced that he would ride horseback for 200 miles in less than 10 hours over a Newmarket track. To back his words, Osbaldeston put up 1,000 guineas in cash, a considerable sum in those days.

The terms of the bet were that the rider could change horses (he would ride one horse for four miles and then switch to another horse), that he could use the same horse two or more times, that all elapsed time—whether used for riding, mounting, or resting—would be counted, and that if a horse failed to last a distance for any cause whatsoever, that would just be too bad—and Osbaldeston would lose.

The race would take place on a set Saturday, regardless of the weather.

Days before the race, Newmarket was crowded with racing fans. On Saturday, November 5, 1831, as per agreement, the ground was measured at Newmarket's Round Course. George would mount at Duke's Stand, where many celebrities had gathered to watch, and he would go the four-mile distance around the track, ending up at Duke's Stand to mount another horse. "The Squire" would do 50 laps.

A fresh lamb-skin-covered saddle would be ready for George every time he arrived for

a new mount. So would refreshments, including porridge, warm jelly, and weak brandy. A change of clothing was also laid out, but Osbaldeston did not require it.

The hazards were many: a lame horse could slow him down; an injured horse could ruin the day; an accident to himself would be the supreme disaster. Thundershowers threatened to turn the track into a quagmire; and in fact, it did rain all day long. But the dauntless jockey, clad in a purple silk jacket and doeskin breeches, was off and running at 7:12 a.m. He made it around the first four miles in the good time of nine minutes flat. *Clasher*, his 10th horse, broke down near Duke's Stand, but Osbaldeston nursed it home. His 13th mount, *Coroner*, used for a second time, turned in an 8:40 clocking. His 21st mount, *Fury*, negotiated the track in 8:10. Without question, "The Squire" was running well as the race neared the halfway point.

After a six-minute rest period, on round No. 31, the jockey ran into his first setback. *Ikie Solomons* tripped and threw him, but Osbaldeston held onto the reins and managed to avoid serious mishap. Still, the accident cost him about four minutes' time.

Now the rain began to fall faster. By the 48th round, horse and rider were both mercilessly drenched by a driving torrent. One of "The Squire's" mounts actually did turn around on the track and try to run back to shelter. But George braved on.

As he crossed the finish line, Osbaldeston drew a mighty cheer. He had spent seven hours, 19 minutes, four seconds on his horses, and another one hour, 22 minutes, and 56 seconds mounting and resting. His total elapsed time—eight hours and 42 minutes—was well under the allowed 10 hours of his bet.

However, "The Squire" hadn't had enough. After he rode home on his favorite horse, he penned a letter to the *The Times of London* offering to make the same 200-mile trip in eight hours! There were no takers.

Airships like the blimp and dirigible may not be dead yet. American scientists and industrial executives are now studying the possibility of using these vessels for the hauling of heavy machinery and prefabricated structures. Helicopters can carry no more than a 16-ton load, while the gas-inflated airships could hoist as much as a 60-ton load—at a cost far lower than any other form of transportation!

Despite the fact that the jew's harp has to be held between the teeth and its tone modulated by movements of the mouth, Charles Eulenstein of Germany could play 16 in different keys at one time. The 19th-century virtuoso accomplished this feat by fastening the instruments to a stand on a level with his lips.

The largest litter ever thrown was 23, by a fox-hound called Lena, on February 11, 1945.

The Buddhist saint, Dengyo Daishi, crossed the sea to Japan in 805 A.D. and planted tea seeds in a temple garden. The plants flourished. In 815 A.D., the Japanese Emperor, Saga, was entertained at a monastery. He liked the tea so well he decreed that the plants be cultivated in the provinces near his capital. By the 10th century, Japan was growing her own tea instead of importing it from China.

An inn in Soleure, Switzerland, called the *Krone*, still possesses a bill for 1,417 Swiss francs charged to Napoleon's troops for an opulent meal and other amenities in 1797. Although a lavish feast had been prepared for Napoleon, the General merely drank a glass of water and moved on.

In 1793, a girl in Tourcoing, France, was born with only one eye—in the center of her forehead! Otherwise normal, the girl lived to the age of 15.

Canine Comparisons

Of the many thousands of dogs registered by the American Kennel Club, in 1970, there were only four breeds in which there were less than five dogs registered. It appears that throughout the entire United States, there were only four Sussex Spaniels on record, only three Belgian Malinois, only two Field Spaniels, and only two English Foxhounds.

Compare these, for example, with 61,042 Dachshunds, or with 13,180 Great Danes, or even with 769 Irish Wolfhounds.

Chocolate, the bane of adolescent complexions and bulgy midriffs, is a preparation made from the seeds of the cacao tree. The Aztecs favored a chocolate beverage which they introduced to the Spanish explorers in the 16th century. This beverage found its way to Europe, where it soon became all the rage. Many chocolate shops became centers of political discussion, such as the famous *Cocoa Tree* in London.

A celebrated Chinese artist of the 1920s, Huang Erhnan, painted beautiful designs on silk cloth—with his tongue as a brush.

The day was August 19, 1962. Longview, Texas was agog. Homero Blancas, a 24-year-old graduate of the University of Houston, had just completed the first round of the Premier Invitational Tournament in 55 strokes! His card of 27 for the front nine and 28 for the back was the lowest round of golf ever played on a course measuring more than 5,000 yards.

Not everyone believes that baseball is strictly an American tradition. In 1962, the Russian newspaper *Izvestia* claimed that "Beizbol" was an old Russian game!

The Facts on Fossils

A fossil can be either the actual remains of a plant or an animal, or the imprint of a plant or animal, preserved from prehistoric times by nature. Quick burial in material that excludes bacteria and oxygen prevents decay and permits whole preservation. Preservation for aeons creates fossils. The scientific study of fossils is called paleontology.

Insects that lived millions of years ago are often found in amber. This hard substance was originally a sticky resin which enveloped the insect. Through the years, the fragile tissues of the insect dried, until all that remained was the mold, sometimes so precise scientists can conduct microscopic studies of its structure.

Fossilization is often the result of petrification. Mineral material from underground streams may be deposited in the interstices of bones, shells, or plants, and render the subject more stonelike, thus protecting it from the ravages of time. Over the millennia, the original live material may be replaced entirely by minerals, so that the original structure and appearance are maintained, as in petrified wood. Petrified logs from the Triassic period may be seen in the Petrified Forest of Arizona.

In the 16th century, the Spaniards introduced the musket, a firearm which enabled a marksman to hit a target 400 yards away. The intricate reloading procedure of the musket necessitated the additional defense of a pike. This drawback of the musket led to the invention of the bayonet. Rifles were introduced in the 18th century; and by the 19th century, they became the standard firearm of all infantry.

The nation with the highest reported murder rate is Luxembourg, with 14.4 murders per 100,000 population. The lowest reported rate is that of Norway, 0.1 per 100,000. The United States rate is 8.5.

A Long Talk

At 12:30 p.m. on June 12, 1935, Senator Huey Long of Louisiana began a filibuster in the Senate. When Long finally dropped into his seat from physical exhaustion at 4 a.m. the following day, he had been speaking continually for 15½ hours—the longest speech on record. The speech was 150,000 words long and included such irrelevancies as cooking recipes and humorless anecdotes. Long's marathon monologue filled 100 pages in the *Congressional Record*, and cost the Government $5,000 to print.

There are more individual species of insects on earth than there are men. Each year about 1,000 new species are discovered.

A curlew can fly non-stop for more than 2,000 miles. Most of the bird's flight is over water, so the curlew doesn't have much of a choice about taking a breather. He can't swim!

Your birthday may not be such a special day after all—you share it with at least nine million others.

There are 30 times as many people buried in the earth as there are people now living.

A Pane-ful Story

Glass was made in prehistoric times, and glass-making was already a well-established industry in Egypt by the 16th century B.C. The Romans refined the art of glassmaking to a level unequaled until modern times. They made small windowpanes, hollow ware, and colorful millefiori (thousand flowers) vessels.

After the Crusades, Venice was the leader in making fine glassware for almost four centuries. The city officials tried to monopolize the industry by strictly controlling the glass-workers at Murano. Artisans were severely penalized for betraying the secrets of their art.

France became dominant in the 18th century with the invention of a process for casting glass. French plate glass was used to line the magnificent Galerie des Glaces at Versailles.

The first glass manufactory on this side of the Atlantic was built in 1608.

One inch of rain contains the same amount of water as a ten-inch snowstorm.

Australian aborigines are not in the least ashamed of their nakedness, and don't mind defecating in view of others. But they are quite embarrassed to be seen eating. Think of the problems such mores could create in one of our crowded cities!

One of the most spectacular homing-pigeon flights of all time took place in 1931, when a bird that had been taken from its home in Saigon was released in Arras, France, and found its way over completely unfamiliar territory to its Far-Eastern home. The bird made the trip in just 24 days.

Divorce, Moslem style: According to the laws of Islam, a Moslem husband can divorce any of his four lawful wives by simply saying "I divorce you" three times. Wives do not have the same privilege.

The female cuckoo of Europe searches out the egg-filled nest of some hard-working bird and lays her single egg in that nest. Then the cuckoo picks up one of the eggs of its host, drops that egg on the ground, and flies away, never to return, hoping that the substitution won't be noticed. If the returning mother recognizes the strange egg as an interloper, she jabs a hole in it, and rolls it out of the nest.

For the largest amount of cold cash ever laid out for a piece of diamond jewelry, we must turn to the 69-carat ring bought at a 1969 auction by actor Richard Burton, and presented to his wife, Elizabeth Taylor. The gem set Burton back a neat $1.2 million!

Pitcher Cy Young holds all of the following baseball pitching records: most wins, most complete games, most innings pitched; he ranks fourth in total shutouts, and fourth in strikeouts. One statistic in which Young does not rank among the leaders is bases on balls.

The all-time most generous pitcher in baseball history is Early Wynn, who dished out 1,775 walks during his career.

A Careful Decision

In 1844, when Amos Lovejoy and Francis Pettygrove were laying out a new city in what is now the state of Oregon, they could agree upon everything but the choice of a name for their embryonic town. Lovejoy, a Massachusetts native, opted for Boston; Pettygrove, a former Maine resident, held out for Portland. So, the two men did the sensible thing: they flipped a coin. Pettygrove won—and the city was named Portland forevermore.

The fastest speed at which a giant tortoise can crawl is about five yards a minute. A rabbit can cover the same distance in less than a half-second.

The fattest man who ever lived, Robert Earl Hughes of Fish Hook, Illinois, weighed 1,069 pounds in the last year of his life. Hughes' waist measurement at that time was 124 inches. When he died in 1958, he was buried in a coffin made from a piano case and transported to the cemetery by a moving van.

Of the more than 110 species of mammals that have become extinct in the last 1,900 years, at least 70 percent have died out within the last century. About 600 other mammal species are presently endangered and will also perish unless measures are taken now to preserve them.

The fastest bird alive is called—appropriately enough—the swift. This speedster is capable of speeds of more than 200 miles per hour.

Four men in the history of boxing have been knocked out in only 11 seconds of the first round.

A little-known invention by Thomas A. Edison is a doll that talked, the first ever to do so. Built in 1888, the doll had a small phonograph in its body that enabled it to recite a dozen nursery rhymes. After making several hundred of these dolls, Edison was informed that his company had previously sold the right to manufacture phonograph toys to another firm. Although that firm had never exercised its right, Edison stopped production and had the dolls destroyed. Of the few he saved and presented to friends, only two are believed to be in existence today.

Though the word "pencil" might appear to be a diminutive of "pen," the two words come from entire different roots. "Pen" is derived from the Latin *penna*, "feather," while "pencil" is based on the Latin *penicillus*, "little tail," and was first applied to fine-pointed brushes used for painting.

A Bevy of Terms

The English language was once rich with collective nouns to designate groups of animals. The most colorful terms, some of which are still in use, include: a *cete* of badgers; a *muster* of peacocks; an *exaltation* of larks; a *mute* of hounds; a *nye* of pheasants; a *skein* of ducks; a *pride* of lions; and a *skulk* of foxes.

An English highway that runs from London to Exeter boasts the smallest underpass in the world—a tunnel one foot wide which was constructed to permit badgers to get safely to the other side of the road.

There's One Born Every Minute

In the summer of 1824, two retired New Yorkers, named Lozier and DeVoe, perpetrated a wild hoax on their numerous friends. They convinced a crowd that they had obtained the mayor's approval to saw off Manhattan from the mainland, and *turn the island around!*

The purpose of this grand plan was to keep Manhattan's southern end from sinking into the harbor under the weight of the many new buildings. DeVoe and Lozier started immediately to sign up laborers, and to award contracts for food, equipment, and even for a huge anchor to prevent the island from being swept out to sea. After eight weeks of preparation, all those associated with the project were instructed to meet the following Monday morning so they could proceed to the north end of Manhattan where the work was to begin. As instructed, hundreds of workmen plus scores of contractors arrived at the spot. They waited for hours before they learned that Lozier and DeVoe had, for reasons of health, gone on an extended journey.

The Icelandic language has remained unchanged since the 12th century.

Rag Apple, a Holstein bull belonging to the New York Artificial Breeders Cooperative, is said to have sired over 15,000 offspring in the three years and four months of his service—an average of 87 a week.

Gourmets who savor "authentic" Chinese food may be disheartened to learn that when chop suey was first concocted in New York in 1896, the dish was completely unknown in China. A chef of the Chinese Ambassador Li Hung-Chang devised the dish to appeal to both American and Oriental tastes.

A few years back a woman in Texas loved her dog so much she married him in a standard religious ceremony presided over by a cleric.

The Best-kept Secret

Since the invention of Coca-Cola, only seven men have ever known the formula for the drink. Today, only two are living, and as a precaution these two men never fly in the same airplane.

Incidentally, 90 million bottles of Coke are drunk each day throughout the world.

Among his many claims to fame, Benjamin Franklin can list the honor of being the first spelling reform advocate in the United States. In 1768, Franklin proposed a scheme to reform English spelling with a new alphabet. He advocated dropping the letters *c, j, q, w, x,* and *y,* and substituting six new characters, so that every sound in the language could be expressed with one letter.

In case you've forgotten: Snow White's seven dwarf friends were named Dopey, Grumpy, Sleepy, Happy, Bashful, Sneezy, and Doc.

You complain that you never go anywhere? Well, many small rodents live out their entire existence without ever straying more than 20 feet from the place of their birth. On the other hand, a humpback whale often covers more than 4,000 miles in a single year.

A Car in Every Garage

Preceding Henry Ford by two years, Ransom Olds commercially produced a three-horse-power Oldsmobile. He produced over 400 cars a year before the turn of the century.

Henry Ford's ideas were as brilliant from the standpoint of marketing as they were from the standpoint of mechanics. Ford perceived the need to transform the automobile from a luxury to a necessity by making cars cheap and making them simple to operate. His was a car everyone could afford. In its heydey, the flivver sold for about $400. Ford's concept succeeded beyond his wildest dreams, and the Tin Lizzie transformed the face of America. Its success enabled Ford to retire at an early age, whereupon he took up sailing to avoid the traffic jams he had created.

Among mammals, only men and monkeys are capable of distinguishing colors.

The sun gives the sea its blue color. Actually, pure sea water is colorless. The surface water absorbs all but the blue rays of the sun. But the sea reflects back the blue rays to make the ocean traveler think the water itself is blue.

Assuming that the earth were completely dry, a man walking day and night at a steady pace could circumnavigate the planet in a little less than a year. A tidal wave could accomplish a round trip in just 60 hours; a bullet, in 14 hours; and a beam of light in just one-tenth of a second.

During the 12th century, Sutoku, Emperor of Japan, spent a three-year exile copying the *Lankauarn Sutra*—a Buddhist religious work containing 10,500 words—in his own blood.

The word *ye* in such expressions as "Ye Olde Shoppe" is pronounced like the word *the*. The letter *y* in Anglo-Saxon indicated the same *th* sound apparent in the current spelling.

An Enlightening Account

Man is not a nocturnal creature; his eyes do not adjust to darkness as well as do those of an owl. When early man discovered the secret of fire, he soon thereafter discovered how to brighten his night with a torch or a candle.

The candle probably evolved when a piece of wood, or rush, or cord fell into ignited fat. How astounding it must have been to realize that the foreign body was not immediately consumed.

In the late 18th and early 19th centuries, candles were made of tallow, beeswax, and vegetable wax, such as bayberry. During the past decade, there has been a great revival in candlemaking, especially of the organically scented varieties.

The first lamp was probably a dish which contained oil and a wick. The next development, thought to have originated in Egypt, was the float-wick lamp; here the wick was supported *above* the oil.

Royal Shenanigans

In the long history of royalty, only one king is know to have been crowned *before* he was even born. When the Persian King Hormizd II died in 310, Persian magnates killed his eldest son, blinded the second son, and imprisoned the third. The throne was reserved for the unborn child of one of Hormizd's wives. In anticipation of the baby's birth, the royal symbol of Persian sovereignty was placed on the pillow in the cradle of the baby-to-be. Three days later, Shapur II came into the world—already a king. One can only wonder how the Persians could be so certain that the baby would be male.

Shapur II went on to become one of the greatest monarchs of his dynasty, reigning for 69 years—including the three days in which he lay within his mother's womb.

By law, the term "Roquefort" may be applied only to cheeses ripened in the damp limestone caves near Roquefort in southeastern France. As long ago as 1411, Charles VI decreed that the term could not be applied to "bastard cheeses made in bastard caves.

The United States postal system is now by far the largest, handling close to one-half of the world's volume. Americans presently post some 80 billion items each year, or about 410 for each citizen, spending over 1.5 billion dollars annually in postal fees.

On a clear day, you can see forever from a lookout point near Chattanooga, Tennessee. Seven states are visible from this promontory—Tennessee, Alabama, Georgia, South Carolina, North Carolina, Virginia, and Kentucky.

The average American now sends 20 Christmas cards each year. But many Americans send considerably more. In what was probably the largest outpouring of Christmas-card generosity in history, one Werner Erhard of San Francisco sent 62,824 cards in a single year.

The United Nations Economics Commission of Europe recently estimated that the average ton of refuse discarded by a French household was worth more than $250, most of it in recyclable aluminum. In an effort to cash in on its normally overlooked riches, one French town sold 34,000 tons of recyclable materials over a six-month period.

If you're ever hightailing it from a bear in the woods, don't try the old trick of climbing a tree to escape. Almost all bears can climb trees.

As late as the sixteenth century, many oculists remained skeptical of eyeglasses. In 1583, Dr. Georg Bartisch of Dresden, one of the most famous oculists of his time, advised patients to do without spectacles. "A person sees and recognizes something better when he has nothing in front of his eyes than when he has something there," the doctor reasoned. "It is much better that one should preserve his two eyes than that he should have four."

The city of Newcastle is the center of England's coal-producing region. So, "to carry coals to Newcastle" means to bring things to a place where they already abound. But an American merchant once accomplished the seemingly absurd feat of shipping coals to Newcastle—and made a handsome profit!

Late in the eighteenth century, a coal miner's strike in Newcastle left the people of that city short of fuel. American merchant Timothy Dexter sent a shipload of coal to Newcastle and easily sold his cargo to the fuel-starved people.

During the early 18th century, Europeans began to hide their latrines inside pieces of furniture. A common custom of the time was to cover the lid of a latrine with a pile of dummy books. To correctly identify the apparatus they shielded, the dummy books always bore the title of *Voyage au Pays Bas*—which means *Journey to the Low Country*—or *Mystères de Paris*.

What do the terms jeroboam, rehoboam, methuselah, salmanazar, balthazar, and nebuchadnezzar have in common, aside from the fact that each is the name of an ancient king or patriarch? Well, each term also refers to a champagne bottle of a particular size. The jeroboam, the smallest of the six sizes, contains 104 ounces, twice as many as the magnum. The nebuchadnezzar, the largest, contains 520 ounces, or five gallons. And that's an amount of bubbly fit for any king!

How short was Pepin the Short? The Frankish king, who ruled from 751 to 768, measured just four-and-a-half feet from crown to toe. His sword, when held at his side, stood a foot-and-a-half higher.

A theatre in Manteca, California, erupted in flames shortly after the end of its feature presentation. The film? *The Towering Inferno.*

Big Wheel

The largest wheels of Swiss Cheese, or Emmentaler, can weigh as much as 220 pounds. A giant Swiss wheel can require over a ton of milk!

In medieval England, a criminal was punished less severely if he could read and write. A literate criminal could pass under the jurisdiction of the ecclesiastical courts instead of the civil courts; in the church courts, the death penalty could not be handed out for minor offenses. The opening words of the first verse of Psalm 51, which comprised the reading test given to law-breakers, became known as the "neck-verse," for reasons that should be obvious.

In 1486, a law was enacted in England stipulating that every layman convicted of a felony by an ecclesiastical court should be branded on the thumb. The thumb mark barred the felon from receiving "the benefit of clergy," or trial by church court, a second time.

The game of volleyball is today played around the world, and volleyball competitions have been part of the Olympic Games since 1964. But despite its current global popularity, the game is not an old sport of European vintage. Volleyball was invented in 1895, by a Y.M.C.A. director in Holyoke, Massachusetts. Originally, the game was conceived as a less taxing alternative to the then new game of basketball. By the middle of this century, volleyball was the leading participant sport in the world after golf.

Christopher Columbus, the "Discoverer of America," never reached our country. In all, the explorer made four voyages to the New World. On his first two voyages, he landed on islands in the West Indies; on his third trip, he reached South America; and on his fourth voyage, he landed in Central America. But Columbus never set foot on these United States.

In 1874, the first practical typewriter was placed on sale by E. Remington and Sons. You might imagine that the first Remingtons were scooped up by clever businessmen as fast as they could be manufactured. Not true. Most businessmen couldn't see the advantage of a machine only slightly faster than handwriting that cost, in the words of one, "a thousand times as much as a pen." As late as 1881, Remington was selling only 1,200 machines a year.

Cat on Cue

David Belasco's 1879 play *Hearts of Oak* began with a cat walking out from under an armchair and stretching before a log fire. Theatre-goers were puzzled as to how the animal could be taught such perfect timing. Months later, Belasco revealed that before curtain time each night, the cat was squeezed into a box hidden under the chair and, as the curtain rose, released from its temporary prison by means of an offstage cord. The cat then naturally crawled out and stretched its cramped muscles.

A Corker of a Porker

Despite their undeserved reputation for slovenliness, pigs are among the most intelligent of animals. Scientists in the Soviet Union have taught pigs to respond to up to 44 different commands, and have organized "pig circuses" starring their porcine pupils.

American scientists have been stymied in their attempt to import the umi umi, a tiny pig from French Polynesia, for use in biomedical research. Though the umi umi—whose name means "cuddly" in Polynesian—are said to be perfect for research models, United States regulations prohibit the importation of umi umi from the South Pacific due to a fear that the animals could transmit hoof and mouth disease.

By the way, pigs do not sweat. On hot days, they like to wallow in the mud to lower their skin temperature.

Big Shots

The "Old Faithful" Geyser in Yellowstone National Park, Wyoming, sends forth more than 33 million gallons of water daily, enough to provide for the needs of a city of 300,000 people. The eruptions of Old Faithful, the most frequently erupting geyser in the world, last about five minutes, and occur every hour or so.

The height of Old Faithful's spout rarely exceeds 150 feet. But to see the tallest active geyser on earth, you won't have to go very far from Old Faithful. Among the 3,000 geysers and hot springs in Yellowstone National Park is Steamboat Geyser, which erupts at intervals ranging from five days to ten months and has sent its fiery spray as high as 380 feet!

The word *potpourri*, meaning a mixture or miscellany, originally meant simply a stew. The exact translation of the French *pot pourri* is "putrid pot."

The suit of armor worn by the later medieval knight offered the warrior such complete protection that many battles were fought and won without the loss of a single man. In 1423, when the Milanese defeated the Florentines at Zagonara, only three men died in the fray—and all were killed by drowning in the mud after falling from their horses.

A Surfeit of Smiths

Most Americans are aware that Smith is the most common surname in this country— nearly one in every 100 Americans is named Smith. And with John the most common first name here, there are indeed a great number of John Smiths in the United States. Think of the problem this superabundance of John Smiths causes for official record keepers. The U.S. Veterans Administration alone has had 13,000 John Smiths on its roles at the same time—8,000 with no middle name or initial!

If the amount of soap used is any indication of a nation's cleanliness, the English are the cleanest people in Europe. A recent survey, conducted by a Swiss organization, found that the average Englishman uses 40 ounces of soap each year. Switzerland ranks second with 37 ounces per person, followed by West Germany, France, and the Netherlands.

The four busts of American presidents carved into the side of Mount Rushmore, in South Dakota, average 60 feet from the top of the head to the chin. Abraham Lincoln's mouth alone measures 22 feet in length, and a man could easily stand in Thomas Jefferson's eye. If a full-figure statue of one of the presidents was constructed on the scale of the Mount Rushmore busts, the statue would stand 465 feet tall!

Old Soldiers Never Die...

In 1699, a spirited lad of 15 named Jean Theurel joined the Touraine Regiment to defend France in the war against Holland. The boy proved to be a demon on the battlefield, and soon opted for a career in the military. He distinguished himself in hundreds of battles, and in 1777, Louis XVI promoted him to captain. At the time, the King suggested that since Theurel was then 92, he might contemplate retirement.

But Theurel continued in the active ranks of the French army until Napoleon officially deactivated him in 1802, providing the old warrior with a pension for life. Whether civilian life agreed with the soldier no one can say, but he died in 1807 at the age of 123— having served as a soldier in three centuries!

The first published reference to stamp collecting appeared in 1841, when a woman placed an ad in an English newspaper for cancelled postage stamps she planned to use to wallpaper her dressing room. The mania for stamp collecting spread so quickly in England that by 1842, the magazine *Punch* could declare that stamp collectors "betray more anxiety to treasure the Queens' heads than Henry the Eighth did to get rid of them!"

A Nose for Music

You may have an ear for music, but to master one peculiar native instrument, you'll need a nose for music as well.

The nose-flute is the favorite musical instrument of the Tinguian tribe, who live in the north of Luzon, one of the Philippine Islands. A tribesman plays the flute by blocking up one nostril and expelling air gently through the other. As the flutist breathes into the flute, he moves his fingers over holes in the instrument to produce a tune.

Malaria is the most prevalent infectious disease threatening man. Malarial fever strikes about 300 million people each year throughout the world, resulting in some three million deaths. In India alone, a million deaths a year were attributed to malaria around the middle of this century. In some parts of the world, virtually the entire population is constantly infected with the disease.

Malaria is a worldwide disease, especially prevalent in the tropics. But some tropical areas, such as Hawaii and the Fiji Islands, are malaria-free, due to the absence of the disease-carrying mosquitoes.

A Spooky Hill

Stop your car at the foot of a sloped street in Lake Wales, Florida, set the gears in neutral, release the brake, and watch your car begin to roll—uphill!

The slope, known as Spook Hill, has puzzled tourists and residents alike for many years. Oranges and grapefruits dropped on the street at the foot of the slope roll uphill. Liquid poured on the street seems to flow upwards. Engineers with tripods and levels try to measure the slope, and walk away shaking their heads.

"It's an optical illusion," said a Lake Wales City Manager, but he refused to tell just how the illusion of Spook Hill works.

A 19th-century London tavern owner was frightened one evening by a peculiar whistling sound emanating from his storage cellar. Fearing a thief, he tiptoed into the cellar and began gingerly trying to locate the source of the plaintive wailing. What he found was so remarkable that he invited a number of his usual patrons to a special dinner the following night—when Charles Dickens, William Thackeray, and other London notables were delighted by the performance of a singing oyster!

Apples, Apples Everywhere

Johnny Appleseed was a legendary figure, right? Wrong. Johnny Appleseed indeed lived. His real name was Jonathan Chapman, and he was born in Springfield, Massachusetts. Before he died in 1845, he covered more than 100,000 square miles with apple trees!

As a young man, Johnny set out alone into the unexplored wilderness that is now Ohio, Indiana, and western Pennsylvania, with a sack of apple seeds he'd collected from cider mills in Pennsylvania and New York. Wherever he went he planted apple seeds, so that as the years went by, apple orchards bloomed and provided nourishment to pioneers who settled in or passed through the area. He retraced his paths over and over again to cultivate and prune the trees he'd planted.

Along the way, Johnny drew attention with his eccentric garb—a coffee sack for a shirt and a tin pot for a hat, in which he would cook his meals. The attention was fine with Johnny—he distributed Bibles as well as seeds.

On May 13, 1950, Mrs. Julia St. Clair of Jacksonville, Florida, set out with her son on a leisurely trip to California. There were two things unusual about Mrs. St. Clair's vacation trek, however. First of all, the 49-year-old woman and her son *walked* the 2,500-odd miles to the Golden State, reaching Los Angeles on June 25, 1951, 13 months after leaving Florida. And second, Mrs. St. Clair covered the entire distance *pushing a wheelbarrow*—loaded with 135 pounds of food, clothing, and a cat!

A single galaxy may contain more stars than the number of seconds that have elapsed since animals first appeared on earth.

And the number of galaxies in the universe has been estimated at over ten billion!

Down-at-the-mouth telephone users in New York City no longer have to call a friend to hear a few words of good cheer. On April 1, 1974—approximately, April's Fool's Day—the New York Telephone Company instituted a Dial-a-Joke service, offering a new joke each day for the price of one call. On the average, close to a million calls are received by the Dial-a-Joke number each month, with 3,331,638 calls standing as the record for one month.

Rome XII, Pompeii VI

So football is a relatively new, American game? Actually, games similar to modern football predate the discovery of America!

The ancient Romans played a game called *harpastum* that included many features of modern football and soccer. An inflated animal bladder was probably used for the ball. Here's how a Roman historian described the game: "The players divide themselves into two teams. The ball is placed on a line between them. At the two ends of the field are two other lines, beyond which the two teams strive to carry the ball."

By the eighteenth century, English football was so violent that a French spectator observed: "If Englishmen call this playing, it is impossible to say what they would call fighting."

A Welsh zoologist has been working on a high-protein burger made from rat meat. And other scientists with tainted tastebuds have proposed a burger made from cotton—talk about flannelmouth!

As *red as a lobster* may be a cliche, but uncooked lobsters are actually dark blue or green in color. The lobster turns red or orange only when cooked.

Mozart, perhaps the greatest pure genius the musical world has ever known, played the harpsichord at age three, composed his first minuet at age five, wrote his first sonata at age seven, and his first complete symphony at age eight! Thereafter, Mozart wrote at least one symphony each year, and eventually produced some 600 symphonies, operas, operettas, concertos, string quartets, sonatas, masses, and other classical pieces.

Mozart was fortunate to have begun his composing career at such a young age, for he died at the incredibly young age of 35!

In 1912, George Sewell leapt from an airplane with 12 parachutes harnessed to his body. He opened the first chute, then cut it loose, opened the second chute, and so on, until he'd opened and cut loose 11 parachutes. The 12th chute took him safety to earth.

A Concert of Swine

The musical highlight of the Great Exhibition of 1851, in England, was an instrument called the pigtail organ. The organist of this most unusual instrument had assembled a herd of pigs, each of which had a squeal of a different pitch. The tails of the melodic swine were connected to a system of pincers, which were operated by the keys of the organ. To play the instrument, the organist merely pressed the desired keys and—*viola!*—the pigs squealed out a melody, to the delight of the audience.

The Atlantic Ocean was not named, as some people believe, for the legendary lost continent of Atlantis—in fact, the name Atlantis was taken from the name of the ocean which supposedly surrounded it. The second largest of the world's oceans was actually named after the Greek Titan Atlas, who in mythology was forced to hold up the earth on his shoulders. Early references to Atlas depicted him holding up pillars which supported the sky. These pillars were thought to rest in the sea we now call the Atlantic Ocean.

Since the figure of Atlas supporting the heavens was often used on the frontispiece of a volume of maps, we now use the word *atlas* to refer to any collection of maps.

?:".(;/,'!

In 1802, Timothy Dexter, an eccentric American businessman, published a collection of his philosophical musings, entitled *A Pickle for the Knowing*, that boasted a host of unprecedented spellings and a total absence of punctuation!

In a second edition of the book, Dexter made a concession to traditional grammar and included punctuation. But the periods, commas, and other punctuation marks were all lumped together in an appendix, so that readers could "pepper and salt [the book] as they please."

The mass entertainment spectacles of ancient Rome included not only gladiatorial contests, but fights between animals, or between animals and men. When the Roman consul Pompey opened a new theater in 55 B.C., he christened the structure with a show that cost the lives of 500 lions and perhaps 20 elephants. On the inaugural day of the Roman Colosseum in 80 A.D., some 5,000 animals were slain in the arena.

You say you have temperamental house plants? Well, there's one specimen of the plant kingdom that really seems to be quite nervous. The colocasia, an Asian and Polynesian plant noted for the profuse water discharge of its leaves, actually has shivering fits! These violent tremors occur at erratic intervals, shaking the entire plant. As yet, scientists have offered no satisfactory explanation for these strange seizures.

The tusks of some male African elephants eventually become so heavy that their owners must frequently rest them in the forks of trees. The longest African elephant tusk on record was some 11 feet long.

Heavy Hitter!

Composer/pianist Franz Liszt often attacked his piano so violently that hammers would fly from the carriage and strings snap from the force of his blows. Audiences came to expect such accidents, and felt cheated if Liszt did not break at least one string during a concert performance.

Though a great number of meteorites bombard earth's atmosphere each day, only one person on record has ever been killed by a falling meteorite. It happened in 1887, when a man in India was struck in the head by a falling stone.

The Mightiest Midas

The wealthiest monarch of all time was probably Ashurbanipal, King of Assyria, who amassed a fortune equal to *three trillion* dollars before his death in 625 B.C.

Having inherited riches beyond imagination from kings who preceded him on the Assyrian throne, the king added to his riches by conquering Babylonia and Egypt and seizing vast amounts of gold and jewels. The personal wealth of this potentate was so tremendous that if he were alive today—and felt generous enough—he could pick up the tab for the entire United States federal budget for five straight years, and still have about half of his great fortune left!

What Hit Me?

A big crowd was assembled at the Lewiston, Maine, boxing arena on September 24, 1946, expecting to see a battle royal between Al Coutoure and Ralph Walton. But those spectators who were a few seconds late in taking their seats missed the entire fight. As the bell rang for the first round, Coutoure rushed at Walton and swung his trusty right. Walton caught the punch smack on the chin. Including the ten seconds the referee counted over Walton's prostrate figure, the whole fight took only 10½ seconds!

If you think that fight has to be the shortest on record, think again. On September 2, 1957, the bell for the first round rang in Maestag, Wales, and a Nigerian welterweight named Bob Roberts rushed at his English opponent, Teddy Barker. Roberts swung, Barker ducked and came through with a right counter, catching the overenthusiastic Roberts square on the jaw. The Nigerian collapsed, then staggered to his feet. But the referee stopped the bout and awarded Barker the victory on a TKO (technical knock-out).

The entire fight had lasted just seven seconds!

The fastest regularly produced automobiles now available are the Lamborghini Countach and the Ferrari BB Berlinetta Boxer, both of which can reach speeds of 186 miles per hour.

If price is more important to you than speed, you might want to test-drive a Mercedes 600 Pullman, the most expensive standard car now on the market. One of these six-door beauties will set you back close to $100,000— less your trade-in, of course. And if used cars are your preference, you might be interested in a Rolls-Royce Phantom, once owned by the Queen of the Netherlands, that sold in 1974 for a record $280,000!

The 10 American states west of the Rockies, excluding California (Oregon, Washington, Idaho, Montana, Nevada, Wyoming, Colorado, Utah, Arizona, and New Mexico) have a combined population significantly less than that of California itself. And if all the approximately 15.5 million people living in these 10 states were crammed into Yosemite National Park in California, the park's population density would still be about half that of New York City.

Jumping for Joy

One leap from an airplane is about all anyone but a dedicated skydiver would want—literally—to stomach. But on July 5, 1952, Neil Stewart of Birmingham, Alabama, achieved an unenviable record by jumping from a plane 124 times in a single day!

On his first jump, Stewart's parachute failed to open and he had to use an emergency shute. His wife, observing from *terra firma*, fainted. But even that inauspicious beginning did not deter the Alabama jumper. Though once knocked unconscious by a hard landing, Neil jumped 123 more times from the airplane—including 49 jumps in total darkness!

John Gully boxed his way from prison to Parliament

One day in 1805, Henry Pierce, heavyweight boxing champion of England, came to a debtors' prison to entertain the inmates. For Pierce's victim, the warden chose John Gully. To the warden's surprise, and the howling cheers of his fellow convicts, Gully battered Pierce all around the ring.

The taverns soon were bubbling with the story of Gully's victory. A group of gamblers determined to pay off Gully's debts, and get him out of prison. To repay the gamblers, Gully agreed to fight exhibition bouts for them.

And Gully really fought. He fought so well that he soon amassed sufficient winnings to buy himself out of the clutches of the gamblers.

From 1806 on, Gully managed himself. He signed for an official championship bout with Henry Pierce, and lost the fight in the 59th round. But after that single defeat, he never was beaten again. When Pierce retired in 1807, John Gully was acclaimed heavyweight champion of England.

Unlike many prize fighters, Gully saved his money and knew when it was time to quit. He left the boxing ring, and invested his savings in horse racing. Two of his horses won the famous English Derby.

And then John Gully took a real jump—all the way from the race track to politics. In 1832, he was elected to the House of Commons. Thereafter, he served several terms in Parliament.

When he died in 1863, at the great age of 90, Gully left a substantial fortune and a fine country estate.

And it all began with a roundhouse right...

An Unabandoned Ship

A drowning swimmer is supposedly done for when he goes down for the third time. Before the Dutch liner *Westerdam* made her first voyage in 1945, she had been sunk three times!

Construction of the boat began in Rotterdam in September, 1939. When the Germans invaded the Netherlands the following year, they seized the ship and set about completing the construction. They had just about finished in 1942, when an Allied bomb sent the *Westerdam* to the bottom for the first time.

German engineers raised the *Westerdam* and began to repair the ship. But Dutch patriots stole aboard, opened the seacocks, and sank her again.

Once more the ship was raised and repaired. This time, Dutch patriots attached explosives to the outside of the hull and sank the ship right next to its pier.

When the war was over, the Dutch raised the *Westerdam* for the last time and rebuilt it as a passenger ship. She was launched in 1945, and became the first passenger vessel to cross the Atlantic after the end of World War II.

Parts of the moon have been more thoroughly explored than some regions on earth. Much of the Amazon Basin and parts of Antarctica, Greenland, and Saudi Arabia have never been explored and mapped by civilized man.

The world's first crossword puzzle appeared in the December 21, 1913 edition of the New York *World*. Devised by editor Arthur Wynne, the crossword contained 32 words, in a diamond-shaped diagram with a diamond-shaped opening in the center, and no black squares. Clues were keyed to the diagram by the number of the last square each corresponding answer filled, as well as by the first, as is the case with today's crosswords.

Aviation pioneer Wilbur Wright wrote that the airplane would make war impossible, since air observation could expose an army's movements. In 1911, the Italians demonstrated the first use of aircraft equipped with bombs during the Italo-Turkish War in North Africa.

Triple Champion

On October 29, 1937, Henry Armstrong became the world's featherweight champion by knocking out Pete Sarron in the sixth round of a title fight. Seven months later, Armstrong took the world's welterweight crown away from Barney Ross in a 15-round decision.

But "Homicide Hank" was still not content. Two-and-a-half months later, on August 7, 1938, Armstrong met the rugged Lou Ambers at Madison Square Garden to fight for the lightweight championship, and won the title on a decision. No one else has ever simultaneously held three world championship titles in boxing!

Horse Sense

A cavalry troop once captured an entire naval fleet. Sound impossible? Well, the capture had nothing to do with the swimming abilities of the cavalry's horses. Here's how it happened:

In the winter of 1794, French General Charles Pichegru, while fighting the British and Austrians, struck deep into the Netherlands. General Pichegru had invaded Holland during the cold weather months because his troops could easily cross rivers and canals frozen over with thick ice. On January 20, 1795, French soldiers entered Amsterdam and learned that the Dutch fleet was frozen solid in the harbor ice. A cavalry troop of French hussars then rode out onto the ice and captured the entire fleet!

São Paulo, Brazil, is the most populous city south of the equator. The São Paulo metropolitan area presently has a population of over nine million. Demographic experts predict that if São Paulo continues to grow at the present rate, the city's metropolitan area will, by the year 2000, top the 25-million mark!

Holy Rollers

Dice are the oldest gaming implements known to man. Before dice became gaming pieces, numbered cubes were used as magical devices for divining the future. The next time you're searching for a word to stump a self-proclaimed vocabulary know-it-all, try *astragalomancy*. That's the practice of divination by means of dice!

Archaeologists have shown that dice predate the written word, and can be found in almost every culture in the world. Excavations in Egypt have turned up stone dice dating from 2,000 B.C. Archaeologists in China have discovered gaming cubes from 600 B.C. that look remarkably similar to the modern thing. And dice especially made for cheating have been found in the tombs of Egypt, the Orient, and the Americas!

It is about ten times as easy to shoot a hole-in-one in golf than it is to roll a perfect 300 game in bowling. The odds against the bowler are about 300,000 to 1, while the golfer "enjoys" odds of 30,000 to 1.

Chew-Chew

No one knows for sure how many people chew gum, but some 35 billion sticks will find their way into American mouths this year. That's about five billion packets, or 25 packets for each man, woman, and child in the United States. At, say, 10 cents a throw, Americans will spend this year some $500 million on gum. And you thought gum-chewing was on the wane?

By the way, studies have shown that the use of gum rises in periods of social tension, and falls in more tranquil times. For instance, the use of gum in this country soared from a per capita 98 sticks in 1939 to 165 sticks by the early 1950s, duplicating a similar rise during World War I. Today's per capita consumption of chewing gum stands at 175 sticks per year. So, as if you needed any further confirmation, the chewing gum barometer suggests that we once again live in troubled times.

Double Trouble

In September, 1951, the people of Bermuda were bracing for a powerful hurricane. As the storm swept to within ten miles of Bermuda's coast, winds bent the island's palm trees to the ground. Large-scale devastation seemed certain.

Then, weather bureau observers realized that there was not one, but two storms approaching the island. An even bigger hurricane was coming up right behind the first. The island appeared doomed.

And then it happened. For the first time in recorded weather bureau history, one storm caught up with another and smashed it. The force of the collision weakened both hurricanes and threw them off course. The storms swerved away from the island and blew out to sea, where they wasted their force on the empty ocean.

Bermuda had been saved from one hurricane by another!

Crazy Cattle

When we hear the word *cattle,* we think of domestic cows, placid and bovine, who hold few charms and have less personality. But, the fact is, that although the term *cattle* refers to domestic animals of the bovine genus, there are many different kinds of cattle. Wild cattle still exist in some parts of the world.

Our word *bovine,* meaning slow, stolid, dull, comes from the Latin word *bos,* meaning ox. The ox is actually a castrated bull, although the term may be loosely appleid to any member of the bovine family. The bison, buffalo, and yak are closely related to the cattle family.

The wild ancestors of today's domesticated cattle were tamed by the men of the Neolithic jage, initially for their milk, and for use as draught animals. The raising of cattle for meat is a relatively recent historic development. Cattle are not native to America; they were brought here by Columbus on his second voyage.

Wealth has often been, and still is in some places, measured by cattle, and the words *chattel* and *capital,* are related to the word *cattle.*

Some of the stranger examples of the species are pictured here.

BISON *The American bison, commonly called the buffalo, once roamed the prairies of North America in the millions. Nearly extinct at the beginning of this century, it is now protected in national parks. The European bison is also much diminished in numbers, but some wild specimens survive in the Caucasus.*

MUSK OX *Herds of 20 to 30 musk oxen can be found in the Arctic regions of North America and in Greenland. The oxen's musky odor—not due to a glandular secretion—can be perceived from 100 yards away. When attacked, a heard of musk oxen forms a circle around their young.*

GAYAL *The gayal is a domesticated ox similar to the gaur, found chiefly in Eastern India.*

ZEBU *The sacred bulls of India belong to this species of ox, also known as the Brahman. The humped zebu is valuable for its milk and its draught work.*

BUFFALO *The Indian buffalo has been domesticated since time immemorial. Its milk is very nourishing. The Cape buffalo of Africa is both intelligent and ferocious.*

TARTARIAN BULL *Many members of the cattle family have a hump on their backs, like this Asian male.*

YAK *This Tibetan native is one of the largest oxen, with long shaggy hair and a bushy tail. The black-and-white domesticated yak provides the only means of transportation for some people in the Kashmir region, as well as in Tibet. The wild yak is black, and stands nearly six feet tall.*

Bizarre Botanica

If you've ever walked into a butcher shop where sausage links and salamis dangled from the ceiling, you have an idea of what it might be like to stand under a spreading sausage tree. Surely one of the oddest looking plants on earth, this African native grows to a height of 30 to 40 feet. Its large hanging flowers bloom at night, giving off a mouselike odor that is appealing to the tree's favorite pollinator, the bat. But it is the fruit that gives this tropical wonder its remarkable appearance, and its name.

Cordlike stalks hanging from the branches end in long, slender fruits which greatly resemble sausages. Some grow in bunches like bananas, others dangle alone at the end of their stalks. These wiener-shaped marvels are usually about one to two feet long, but can grow to three feet and can weigh up to 15 pounds each!

Of all mammals, the greyhound shows the greatest disproportion of the sexes—110 male greyhounds are born for every 100 females.

Like Father, Like Son

In early 18th-century France, the office of Chief Executioner was, like many positions, handed down from father to son. So when Chief Executioner Charles Jean-Baptiste Sanson died in 1726, the job passed to his son Charles. But the young Sanson was unable to lift, much less wield, the heavy executioner's ax—he was but seven years old at the time.

The prepubescent official was forced to employ an assistant, named Prudhomme, to perform the actual decapitations, although Sanson had to be present at every execution. Finally, at age 13, the seasoned Chief Executioner was deemed strong enough to perform the dirty deed himself.

The bow and arrow date from prehistoric times as instruments of survival and weapons of war, but the sport of archery is English in origin. In medieval times, a number of great English military victories were largely due to the skill of English archers, and British monarchs have always encouraged the sport among the populace. Charles II enacted laws in the 17th century to guarantee an ample supply of bows and arrows for all citizens—and other monarchs on occasion forbid the playing of other games, lest they interfere with archery!

Monkey Business

A Southern psychologist installed two chimpanzees in adjoining cages, and tried to determine how quickly they could distinguish between two different-colored coins. One cage contained a slot machine that dispensed water only after the insertion of a white coin; the other cage contained a machine that dispensed food and worked only with a black coin. On the first day, each chimp was given a bagful of mixed coins, and soon learned which coins worked his machine.

A few days later, the chimp with the water dispenser was deprived of water for 24 hours, and the one with the food dispenser was deprived of food for 24 hours. Then the thirsty monkey was given food coins, and the hungry one water coins. Instead of being baffled by the ploy, the chimps reached through the bars of their cages and exchanged coins with each other.

Bolts from the Blue

How frequently does lightning occur? Worldwide, over 100 lightning flashes occur each *second!* In the United States alone, about 400 persons are killed and 1,000 injured by lightning each year. But lightning takes its biggest toll on trees. Each year, about 7,000 forest fires in the United States are caused by lightning, resulting in the destruction of perhaps millions of trees.

Still, your chances of being struck by lightning in your lifetime have been estimated to be more than a million to one. A morbid fear of lightning, called keraunophobia, is thus quite without foundation—and quite useless. For if you see the lightning, it missed you; and if it does strike you, you won't know it!

The sound of the bagpipe may immediately conjure up the image of Scotsmen in kilts, but the instrument actually predates the Scottish nation. Instruments identical to the bagpipe were played in ancient Persia, Egypt, Chaldea, and Greece. Roman soldiers played the bagpipe as they marched to far corners of the Empire. It was the Romans, in fact, who first brought bagpipes to the British Isles.

In a sense, the French were the first to depend upon airmail postal delivery for any length of time. During the siege of Paris in the Franco-Prussian War of the 1870s, mail was sent out of the capital by balloon, along with hundreds of homing pigeons. Return letters were photo-reduced to one four- thousandth of their original size, then delivered to the capital by pigeon. Thirty-five pigeons carried the identical 30,000-message mail cannisters so that at least one was certain to survive Prussian pigeon snipers. In Paris, the messages were enlarged on a projection screen, copied by clerks, and delivered to addressees within the city.

Contrary to popular opinion, a lightning bolt does not move at the speed of light. Most downward bolts do not reach speeds over 1,000 miles per second, though the upward return stroke that follows most downward bolts can reach speeds of up to 87,000 miles per second, nearly half the speed of light.

The common length of a lightning bolt is about half a mile, although bolts may be as short as 300 feet or as long as five miles. In rare instances, a lightning bolt may stretch up to 20 miles. No matter the length, a single flash of lightning can carry as much as 100 million volts of electricity.

Proud Parents

Carlo Buonaparte was born in 1746, in Corsica, an island in the Mediterranean Sea. There he struggled all his life, and was never more than a poor clerk in the royal district court. Yet his children lived in glittering palaces and ruled over millions of people, occupying the thrones of seven different countries!

In all, Carlo Buonaparte was the father of one emperor, three kings, a queen, and two duchesses. Of all his sons and daughters, only one—Lucien—did not become a sovereign, though he received the title of Prince of Canino. Carlo's other celebrated children included Joseph, King of Naples and then of Spain; Louis, King of Holland; Jerome, King of Westphalia; Maria Caroline, Queen of Naples; Marie Pauline, Duchess of Guastalla; and Marianne Elisa, Grand Duchess of Tuscany. Of course, it was Carlo's most famous son, Napoleon Bonaparte, Emperor of France, who placed his brothers and sisters on their thrones.

Alas, Carlo Buonaparte never lived to see his children ascend their thrones. He died in 1785, when Napoleon was still a teenager. But the mother of all this royalty, Letizia Ramolino, outlived her husband by many years—long enough to see all her royal children dethroned!

Pasta and tomatoes are today regarded as the most essential elements of Italian cuisine, but neither appeared in Italy before the Renaissance. Pasta originated in China, and may have been first brought to Europe by Marco Polo. Tomatoes are natives of tropical America, and did not reach Europe until the 16th century.

String 'Em Up

The term "lynch," used in this country to designate the unlawful execution of an accused person by mob action, may appear to be a time-worn word of old English vintage. Actually, the term is of recent coinage—and owes its origin to a man's name!

Capt. William Lynch, who died in 1820, organized a vigilance committee in Pittsylvania County, Virginia, to apprehend and punish a band of outlaws. Lynch's method of dealing summarily with thugs gave rise to the expression "Lynch's law," which spawned the verb "lynch."

The city of Lynchburg, Virginia, was named after another Lynch, John, the reputed founder.

To facilitate the printing of horse-racing sheets, regulations insist that the name of a race horse may not contain more than 18 letters, hyphens, apostrophes, and spaces.

Nobody's Perfect

A plaque on the par-five ninth hole of a Los Angeles golf course commemorates the achievement of Arnold Palmer in the 1961 Los Angeles Open. No, Arnie didn't score an ace on that hole, or even a triple birdie. He recorded *12 strokes*, including five out-of-bounds shots!

The Louisiana Purchase of 1803, which transferred from France to the United States some 100 million acres, including probably the richest agricultural area in the world, cost this nation just $15 million, not including interest payments. Today, a moderate sized parcel of land in Manhattan may sell for more than that amount!

The longest completed chess match on record, to date, took place in Baku, U.S.S.R., in 1945. The match—which ended in a draw—took 21½ hours and consisted of 171 moves.

Yellow Press

The newspaper comic strip in the United States was born out of the rivalry between two giants of the American press. In 1893, the *New York World* published the first full-color comic page in the nation, depicting a set of humorous characters under the title *Hogan's Alley*. Soon afterward, publisher William Randolph Hearst countered with the first weekly full-color comic supplement, eight pages in the *Morning Journal*.

Hearst's supplement featured *Yellow Kid*, a strip by Richard Outcault, whom Hearst had lured away from the *World*. *Yellow Kid* was the first continuous comic character in the United States, and standardized the use of speech balloons for comic strip dialogue.

Incidentally, the Italian word for comic strip is *fumetto*, "little puff of smoke," so-named after the speech balloon.

You've dreamed of making a fortune and not paying tax on it, right?

In 1971 Frank McNulty bought an Irish Sweepstakes ticket. The horse was Bronze Hill, and he won. Mr. McNulty went to Dublin and collected $128,410 in winnings. He put the money in a bank on the British island of Jersey.

However, the U.S. Revenue Service demanded that Mr. McNulty pay taxes on his winnings. Mr. McNulty refused, saying he had earned and kept the money outside the U.S. So he was charged with income tax evasion, and sentenced. He has spent some four years in jail, but continues to refuse to pay up. Finally, Federal Judge Alfonso Zirpoli has decided that there is no longer any point in keeping McNulty incarcerated. But the chances of his ever enjoying the use of his money are pretty slim—he can't bring it in here, and he will undoubtedly be denied a passport to go there. His winnings are now worth about $140,000, and his tax bill about $70,000. Like the man said: pay the $2!

On July 18, 1938, pilot Douglas "Wrongway" Corrigan took off from New York on a flight to Los Angeles, and the following day earned his nickname by touching down in Dublin, Ireland. Corrigan blamed a mistake in his compass setting for the colossal navigational error.

Going Bananas

The banana is now America's favorite fresh fruit. The apple and orange are consumed here in greater numbers, but both fruits are frequently enjoyed in juices and other processed products. Bananas are almost always eaten fresh. Americans now devour over 12 billion bananas each year—close to 19 pounds per person! Yet virtually no bananas are grown within this country—and the fruit was almost unknown here just a century or so ago!

The game of badminton was named after the country estate of the English Duke of Beaufort, where the game is thought to have been played for the first time in 1873. But similar games were played earlier in India, and badminton itself was probably developed from the old game of battledore and shuttlecock.

The battledore, the "racket" used to strike the shuttlecock in the early game, probably derived its name from a club used by launderers to beat or smooth clothes.

In 1878, the first American badminton club was formed in New York City, but its charter curiously limited play to men and "good-looking single women."

Maria Gilbert was acclaimed one of the most beautiful women in the world—not by her given name, but as dancer Lola Montez. Other renowned performers who have come to fame under pseudonyms are: John Barrymore (John Blythe); Dave Evans (Frances Octavia Smith); Gypsy Rose Lee (Rose Louise Hovick); Carole Lombard (Jane Alice Peters); Soupy Sales (Milton Hines); and Margot Fonteyn (Margaret Hookham).

High-Rise

The apartment building is not an innovation of the modern era. Large apartment dwellings are actually as old as the hills—the Hills of Rome, that is. As early as the first century B.C., many Roman apartment buildings—called *insulae*, or "islands"—rose to a height of five stories. And they might have risen higher, for the Emperor Augustus set a limit of 70 feet on the height of apartment buildings in the Imperial City, for safety reasons.

In today's tall residences, apartments on the upper floors are deemed the most desirable. But in Rome, the lower floors were preferred. Water supply and sanitation pipes usually did not reach above the first floor.

Blondin crossed over Niagara Falls on a tightrope—while pushing a wheelbarrow

Jean François Grandet, who performed under the name of Blondin because of his flowing blond hair, was the daredevil supreme. In 1859, he had a three-inch rope strung 1,1000 feet across Niagara Falls, 160 feet above the raging waters. Balancing himself with a 40-foot pole, the intrepid Frenchman pedaled

When this was done, Blondin would continue to the other side in inky blackness.

over the Falls on a bicycle. Scorning death, he once walked over the tightrope blindfolded. On another day, he pushed a wheelbarrow across the Falls on the tightrope.

On one occasion, he announced he was going to carry a man across the chasm piggyback style. One hundred thousand curious Americans and Canadians came to Niagara to see that one. The only person he could get to do the stunt with him was his manager, who trembled so violently that Blondin vowed never to do a stunt with a human again.

Always dreaming up new ways to astound the spectators, Blondin would turn somersaults on the rope. He would also have a man below the falls shoot bullets through a hat he held up as a target. The acrobat even cooked and ate an egg prepared on a frying pan heated on a stove which he had carried out to the middle of the rope himself!

One of his most fantastic feats was to walk halfway out on the brightly lighted rope after dark, and then order the light put out.

On September 8, 1860, the Prince of Wales, who was touring North America, showed up in Canada to watch Blondin's final performance over the Falls. And what a show Blondin gave him!

Blondin attached short stilts to his legs; on each stilt, there was a hook which went around the rope. Halfway across the gorge, Blondin swung by the hooks head-down from the rope. Scores of men and women fainted, believing that he had lost his balance, fallen, and was going to plunge to his death. But Blondin had planned it all as a show-stopper. Hanging by the hooks, he swung gaily in his perilous position, and then nonchalantly got up and continued on to the Canadian shore.

You can't have George Washington to dinner, but you can have dinner in George, Washington. The town of George, which was home for 273 persons at the time of the 1970 census, honors its namesake every July Fourth with a mammoth 1,200-pound cherry pie.

Even that pie might look like a mere fruit tart compared to the largest cherry pie on record, a six-ton pastry colossus baked in Charlevoix, Michigan, to mark the 1976 Bicentennial.

An age-old belief holds that the easiest way to assure a rainy day is to leave your umbrella at home. Robert Louis Stevenson seemed aware of this peculiar meteorological wisdom when he wrote: "There is no act in meteorology better established . . . than that the carriage of the umbrella produces dessication of the air; while if it be left at home, aqueous vapor is largely produced, and is soon deposited in the form of rain."

Eureka!

In 214 B.C., a powerful Roman force attacked the city of Syracuse, the home of Archimedes, the great mathematician and astronomer. To hold off the Roman legions, the Greek inventor devised one ingenious weapon after another. Among these weapons was the catapult, which sent a ton of stones flying as far as 600 feet.

But Archimedes' most ingenious contraption was an arrangement of mirrors that directed the concentrated rays of the sun on the Roman ships and set them ablaze.

The noted authors who often worked in bed include Cicero, Horace, Milton, Voltaire, Jonathan Swift, Alexander Pope, Mark Twain, and Marcel Proust. British writer Max Beerbohm once declared that his ideal of happiness was "a four-poster in a field of poppies."

Silver Wares

In the late eighth century, Charlemagne sanctioned the abandonment of the gold standard in Western Europe, and established a monetary system based on silver. A silver penny, or *denarius*, was the basic unit, with 240 pennies to a pound of silver. The words *livre*, *lira*, and *pound*, as used in British currency, date from this era. The Pound Sterling was originally 240 sterlings, or silver pennies, and literally weighed one pound.

Gold came back into use during the 13th and 14th centuries, with the *florin*, from Florence, among the more important coins. But the older silver system remained in use, so that, through the Renaissance, two basic monetary systems were current in most of Europe. Financial calculation was indeed a laborious job.

The peak year for American newspapers—in terms of sheer numbers—was 1916, when 2,461 dailies were published across the nation. By 1944, consolidation and bankruptcy had brought that figure down to 1,744.

American advertisers now spend well over two *billion* dollars each year on television commercials—not including the cost of making the ads themselves. How much money is that? Well, in a recent year, the nations of Ecuador, Sri Lanka, and Kenya each had a Gross National Product of less than three billion dollars.

There was not a single grapefruit growing on the mainland of North America until early in the 19th century. Today, the state of Florida produces 70 percent of all the world's grapefruits.

European governments have always found playing cards an ideal subject for heavy taxation. England began taxing card imports in 1615. By 1628, the tax on each deck had risen to a then exorbitant half-crown. Taxes on playing cards once became so high in Austria that card makers began selling oversized decks that could be gradually trimmed as their edges became worn, thus lasting two or three times as long as a regular deck.

Spuds, a la France

France was the last European nation to accept the potato. A soldier who had spent considerable time in Germany returned to his homeland to convince fellow Frenchmen that the potato was both edible and delicious, despite medical advice that the vegetable was "toxic and the cause of many illnesses."

Since then, the French have contributed many dishes to the world of potato cookery. One of those dishes, the heralded *pomme soufflées*, has been attributed to a number of chefs.

According to one tale, a 19th-century French chef was charged with preparing a banquet to celebrate the opening of a new railroad line. While preparing the repast at one of the new stations, the chef was notified that the train carrying a coachload of dignitaries to the banquet would be delayed. So he took his half-cooked french fries out of the oil and began preparing a fresh batch. Then he was notified that the train was pulling into the station, on time after all. Frantic, the chef plunged the half-cooked potatoes back into the fat, and the soggy fries puffed into crisp ovals—*pommes soufflées!*

Uncurrent Currency

In the early days of our nation, English, French, and Spanish monies all circulated through the American colonies, with a concomitant confusion of trade. In 1785, the dollar was adopted by Congress as a unit of exchange, and the decimal system as the method of reckoning. The U.S. monetary system was established in 1792; the first mint began operation in Philadelphia the following year.

Many coins and bill denominations have come and gone since then. Among the coins no longer in use are the half-cent, the two-cent, the three-cent, the 20-cent, and the silver half-dime. The nickel was not introduced until 1886. Today, gold coins are no longer minted, and you may be surprised to learn that no bills larger than $100 are now placed in circulation.

In the 15th century, Portuguese seamen bound for the East Indies brought along umbrellas as fit gifts for native royalty. Upon landing on a strange island, the seamen immediately opened an umbrella over their captain's head, to demonstrate his authority.

Early this century, the so-called "Indian Whiskey" illegally peddled on Indian Reservations often contained plugs of tobacco to make the Indians sick. The Indians, whiskey salesmen claimed, thought an alcoholic beverage that didn't make them sick was inferior. Much of the Indian Whiskey also contained red pepper for "bite," soap for "head," and strychnine for "kick."

There is now about one car in this country for every two persons. In contrast, only one person in every 14,500 owns a car in China.

Texans in a spinach-growing area in the eastern part of the state have erected a statue of Popeye in tribute to his appetite for the vegetable.

Easy Money

Henry Ford began his motor company in 1903 with capital of only $28,000, 12 workers, and a plant only 50 feet wide. Additional funds were supplied by the Dodge brothers, themselves auto manufacturers. The Dodges' initial $20,000 investment was eventually worth $25 million.

In 1908, preparation for the Model T's production brought Ford so close to bankruptcy that he had to borrow $100 from a colleague's sister to pay for the car's launch. That $100 was eventually worth $260,000 to the generous donor!

The push-button elevator, introduced in 1894, was both more reliable and cheaper to operate than the hand-operated manned elevators you can still find in the moldiest of city buildings. Automatic leveling, which brings the car to rest precisely at floor level, made its debut in 1915, but the cry of "watch your step" will live on forever. By the middle of this century, automation had rendered the elevator operator nearly extinct.

For $350, a New York chocolatier will shape a bust of your head from solid chocolate.

In the early 1950s, the average American family paid about 11 percent of its income in taxes. By the mid-70s, the same family paid twice as much in taxes—about 23 percent of its income.

A controversy once arose in Wisconsin when a mailman refused to handle a particularly pungent shipment of Limburger cheese, claiming that the smell made him ill. A court decision upheld the right of cheese makers to ship their odoriferous product in the U.S. mails.

Some of the major American motion-picture studios now produce as few as a half-dozen or so films each year. In the Hollywood heyday of 1939, all the film companies in this country together turned out an average of two films per *day*!

The first commercial telephone switchboard appeared in 1878 in New Haven, Connecticut, linking just 21 phones. The first telephone directory was in the hands of New Haven phone users in 1878—listing only 50 names. And the first pay telephone reared its coin-snatching head in 1889, in Hartford, Connecticut.

Peanut Odyssey

Although many Americans might guess that the peanut was originally an African product, the peanut is, in fact, a native of tropical South America. Spanish conquistadores exploring the New World found South American Indians eating what many called *cacohuate*, or "earth cocoa."

The goober was gradually transplanted in West Africa as a food and fodder crop. Subsequently, slave traders found that the peanut could provide cheap, nutritious food for Africans being carried across the ocean on slave ships. Eventually, some African peanuts were brought to Virginia and planted for livestock fodder. Thus, the peanut made two transatlantic journeys before becoming a North American crop.

The card game poker became popular in the United States in the 19th century, especially among gold-digging forty-niners. The game was actually based on an older Spanish game called *primero* that included elements of betting and bluffing just like the modern game. According to Shakespeare, Henry VIII played *primero* the night Queen Elizabeth was born. The term "poker" comes to us from the German *pochen*, "to brag" or "to knock," or from a similar German game called *pochspiel*.

The well-known Saratoga potato chips were invented, not surprisingly, in Saratoga, New York, when a guesthouse chef, appropriately named George Crumb, lost his patience with a guest who insisted on thin french fries. Crumb cut a potato into paper-thin slices, dropped them in oil, and—presto!—another American institution was founded.

Packing Them In

The World Championship Sardine Packing Contest is held every year in Rockland, Maine. To pack a sardine, one must pick it up, deftly snip off its head and tail with razor-sharp scissors, and place it neatly in an open sardine can. The all-time record for sardine-packing is held by Mrs. Patricia Havener of Waldoboro, Maine, who in 1971 packed 450 sardines into 90 cans in just 10 minutes.

The vanilla plant is a climbing orchid that attaches itself to trees with aerial rootlets, though the plant does possess ordinary soil roots. Vanilla is unique among the some 20,000 species of orchid known throughout the world, for it is the only orchid that produces a commercially useful commodity.

An airplane once crashed into a New York office building and struck directly into the elevator shaft, destroying the cables. The car plunged 17 floots—but the buffer, a safety device at the bottom of the shaft, saved the life of the elevator's lone passenger!

Since at least the 14th century, the English cutlery industry has been centered around the city of Sheffield. It was 19th-century Sheffield cutlerers who began fitting pocketknives with various other tools, among them buttonhooks, files, leather borers, tweezers, gimlets, saws, and implements curiously known as "castrating blades." One interesting Sheffield creation sported both a pistol and a dagger.

Shepherds and farmers have been fooled by a monstrous fungus known as the giant puffball. This mushroom-like plant is so large that a specimen growing in the grass of a pasture can, from a distance, be mistaken for a reclining sheep!

The giant puffball is a white, globular-shaped fungus that grows on the ground with no visible stalk. In shape and size it most resembles a human brain; in fact, the puffball is also called the *Tête de Mort*, or Death's Head. But specimens have been found that were close to four feet long and weighed well over 20 pounds.

Incidentally, despite its name the *Tête de Mort* is quite edible. A large specimen could feed an entire family.

When the first mail steamer from the East Coast arrived in San Francisco in 1848, the entire crew deserted to join the burgeoning California gold rush.

The Biggest Bloom

If you were to come upon a krubi during a visit to a botanical garden, you might think you were viewing a plant specimen from Jonathan Swift's land of the Brobdingnagians. This flower, a relative of the popular philodendron, is so gigantic that even if you were to stand on another person's shoulder, you would barely be able to reach the top!

The krubi grows in the jungles of Sumatra, a large Indonesian island. Specimens of the krubi have been found to reach the height of 15 feet. The leaves of a well-grown specimen, when unfolded, can cover an area 45 feet in circumference.

But the krubi cannot be termed the largest flower in the world, for it is a collection of flowers simulating a single giant flower.

Talk about big spenders! An Indian maharajah who stayed at the Savoy Hotel in London, one of the world's costliest, took 35 rooms, kept 20 limousines at his disposal, and ordered 3,000 fresh roses daily!

In the years immediately following the Wright Brothers' first airplane flight, most magazine and journal editors regarded the Wrights' story as so much science fiction, refusing to believe that a man had actually flown at Kitty Hawk. Amazingly enough, the first eyewitness account of a Wright Brothers' flight was published in a magazine called *Gleanings in Bee Culture*, after its editor witnessed a flight of the Wrights' second machine, *Flyer II*.

Great Guns

The invention of firearms in the 14th century did not immediately spell the doom of the armored knight. Most early hand guns were not powerful enough to pierce armor. The crossbow remained in common use until the 16th century, and armor makers continued to flourish into the 17th century.

But early cannons, or "thunder guns," were powerful enough to demolish castle walls, and therefore helped bring about the end of the feudal society in which the armored knight reigned supreme.

A French hotel catering to English-speaking guests once had eggs billed on its menu as "extract of fowl." They were offered both "peached" and "sunside up."

Basque farmers in the Pyrenees Mountains use flying saucers to catch pigeons! The bird-catchers wait in mountainside perches for flocks of migrating pigeons, then sail saucer-shaped paddles called *zimbelas* just ahead of the flock. The birds mistake the *zimbelas* for hawks and dive toward earth, only to be caught in huge nets stretched across the valley below. The Basques then ship the pigeons to markets in France, where the birds are considered a delicacy.

The papyrus reed, or *biblos*, was cultivated in the Nile Delta at least as early as 3,500 B.C. Egypt supplied papyrus for the entire ancient world, for the *biblos* has never been grown in any quantity outside that country. Egyptian papyrus was so vital to the Roman Empire that a papyrus crop failure during the reign of Tiberius nearly brought all official and commercial business in Rome to a complete halt.

Bathing, Roman Style

During Imperial times, the Roman's bathing ritual consisted of a series of baths, each taken in a different room of the massive public baths. The bather began in the undressing room, then moved to another room where he was anointed with oil, then to the gym for exercise. After the gym came the *calidarium*, or hot bath; then the steam room; then the *tepidarium*, or lukewarm bath; and finally, the *frigidarium*, or cold bath, which was usually a sort of swimming pool. Sounds much like our modern health spa, doesn't it?

The Roman baths were open continually, except for religious holidays and times of national crisis. Customarily, a Roman would bathe before the principal meal of the day, but some of the more idle—and cleaner—citizens went through the entire bathing ritual as many as six or seven times a day!

The lobster and related shellfish are, in a manner of speaking, "insects of the sea." Lobsters are Anthropods, a phylum which includes the insects, and crustaceans, a class that also includes shrimps and crabs. Crustaceans, like insects, have a horny exoskeleton, jointed appendages, and segmented bodies. In short, if a lobster a half-inch long were crawling across your wall, you'd probably swat it.

Some of the plants that provide man with food can be poisonous if other parts of the plant are eaten. You may love cherries, but don't eat the cherry tree's foliage—it's toxic enough to kill. Enjoy rhubarb pie, but don't munch on the leaf blades, or it could be your last meal. The leaves of the elderberry plant are poisonous—and so are the foliage and acorns of the oak. And that rhododendron that might be flourishing in your home will spell doom for anyone who nibbles on it.

The ancient city of Babylon's most important street, often called the Processional Way, was actually named "The Street on Which May No Enemy Ever Tread." Alas, many a foe came to tread on Main Street, Babylon, before the city was razed to the ground.

In 1960, the *Journal of the American Medical Association* reported that a patient checking into a hospital for a swollen ankle had been found to have swallowed 258 items—including a 3-pound piece of metal, 26 keys, 39 nail files, and 88 assorted coins.

Many Americans who commute to and from work by automobile must drive for over an hour in each direction. If we take eight hours as the time the average American passes in slumber, we can say that many persons in this country spend up to 15 percent of their waking hours in the confines of their home-away-from-home, the automobile!

Early this century, Philadelphia Athletics owner Connie Mack awarded pitcher Rube Waddell a contract stipulating that Waddell's battery mate, Ossie Shreck, could not eat crackers in bed when the pair shared a room on the road. In those days, players had to share not only a hotel room when traveling, but the same bed as well!

Progress is not always without its drawbacks. In 1879, when the first electric arc lights to be used in America for public street lighting were installed in Cleveland, Ohio, many women of that city bitterly complained that the "dazzling white light" showed their complexions to disadvantage.

Still Good!

Prohibition made the sale, manufacture, or transportation of alcoholic beverages illegal in this country. Evidently the news never made it through the bureaucratic labyrinth of Washington, D.C.; for during Prohibition, the U.S. Department of Agriculture continued to distribute pamphlets explaining how to make alcohol from apples, bananas, pumpkins, and other fruits.

The word "daisy" comes from two Anglo-Saxon words meaning "day's eye," since the yellow center of the flower reminded the Anglo-Saxons of the sun. "Dandelion," meanwhile, comes from the French *dent-de-lion*, meaning "tooth of the lion." The French thought the jagged leaves of the flower resembled the teeth of a wild animal.

The average Englishman enjoys 2,000 cups of tea each year—that's almost six cups per day!

Three presidents of the United States—Thomas Jefferson, John Adams, and James Monroe—died on July Fourth. Jefferson and Adams died on the very same day, in 1826.

If you were standing on Pluto, the most distant planet in our solar system, the sun would appear no larger or brighter in the sky than the brightest star does in our sky.

The wood sorrel, a flowering plant widely distributed throughout the North temperate regions, will droop heavily if a leaf is touched—or even breathed upon. What is amazing about the wood sorrel is that an impulse is transmitted almost immediately throughout the plant from the one touched leaf. Thus, if one raindrop falls on one leaf, the plant will fold and droop at once. Experiments have shown that the wood sorrel is so sensitive that it will fold up and droop even at the vibration of approaching footsteps!

Billowing Beacon

The volcano Stromboli, which lies on a small island off the north coast of Sicily, has been erupting fire and smoke throughout recorded history—and remains one of the most active volcanoes in the world. Sailors call Stromboli "The Lighthouse of the Mediterranean," for the glow of red-hot lava on its slopes can be seen at night from miles away.

Stromboli rises 3,000 feet above the Mediterranean. Since the water surrounding the cone is 7,000 feet deep, Stromboli actually rises to a height of 10,000 feet from its base on the sea floor.

Although gas and lava continually pour from its crater, Stromboli never erupts violently. People live without fear around the base of this smoke-belching giant.

A number of noted golfers staying at the Savoy Hotel in London practiced their skills by driving golf balls off the hotel roof onto a barge floating nearby in the Thames.

Like many scientists of genius, Albert Einstein sometimes let his mind wander from the mundane concerns of everyday life—in short, he was absent-minded. Once he received a $1,000 check from a philanthropic institution, and promptly slipped it into a book to mark his place. Soon later, he lost the book.

Car Fare

The United States has been the leader in automobile production for most of this century. Over a million cars were produced here in 1916, and over three million in 1924, when there were some 15 million cars registered in America. In 1952, about four million American passenger cars rolled off the line, 10 times the number produced by the second-ranking nation, Great Britain. At the time, there was a car on the road here for every 3.5 persons, compared to, for example, one car per 564 persons in Japan. The second-ranking nation in car use was, surprisingly, New Zealand, with six persons for each car.

American domination of the automobile market has slipped somewhat in recent years, yet the United States still ranks first in total production, with 6.7 million passenger cars turned out in 1975. Japan ranked second that year with 4.5 million cars, followed by West Germany and France with just under three million each.

On January 30, 1934, the people of Birmingham, Alabama sent President Franklin D. Roosevelt a birthday telegram a quarter-mile long. The wire contained 41,000 names, required 19 hours to transmit, and cost $421.

It wasn't until 1930 that the U.S. Customs Department lifted its bans on certain works by Balzac, Rabelais, and Daniel Defoe. The *Confessions* of Jean-Jacques Rousseau were banned by Customs in 1929. Some of the works of Ovid and Aristophanes were also banned for a time in this country.

In 1927, Lenin's *The State and Revolution* was seized by officials in Boston and declared "obscene."

The Big Bang

The eruption of Mt. Vesuvius in the year 79, which destroyed the Roman cities of Pompeii and Herculaneum, was by far the most well known eruption of that volcano—but by no means the most destructive. An estimated 2,000 people perished in the destruction of Pompeii and neighboring towns. But on December 16, 1631, Vesuvius again erupted, sending volcanic dust as far away as Constantinople and killing 18,000 people in the vicinity of the volcano.

The eruption of 79 was not the only disaster to befall the inhabitants of Pompeii, either. In 63, a violent earthquake destroyed most of the city, including many of the large public buildings. The Pompeiians were still engaged in rebuilding from that cataclysm when the entire city was destroyed by the great eruption of Vesuvius in 79.

Although large-scale excavation of the site was not begun until 1763, the survivors of the 79 eruption began to dig through the volcanic ash covering the city almost immediately after the eruption. Many objects of value were recovered—including the marble slabs used to face the large public buildings.

Many an ambitious American has moved to Washington, D.C., to seek opportunity. Far fewer have moved to Opportunity, Washington, for the same reason.

The Suez Canal is not the first man-made waterway to connect the Mediterranean with the Red Sea. In the sixth century B.C., the Egyptian Pharoah Nikau II began the construction of a canal between a branch of the Nile and the Red Sea. Some historians believe that Nikau did not construct the canal, but merely restored a canal built perhaps as early as 2000 B.C. In any case, Nikau's project was abandoned when an oracle predicted that the canal would soon be in the hands of a "foreigner."

The prophet was right: In 525 B.C., the Persians conquered Egypt. But that "foreigner"—the Persian King Darius—completed the canal project. The canal remained in use until the eighth century. After that, the Mediterranean and the Red Sea were without a link until 1869.

Upside Down Luck

Rarity usually determines the worth of a postage stamp to a collector, and stamps with printing errors regularly bring high prices. In 1918, William Robey of Washington, D.C., bought a sheet of nondescript 24-cent airmail stamps at a local post office and discovered that all 100 stamps in the sheet contained an illustration of an airplane—upside down! Robey quickly sold the sheet, which cost him $24, for $15,000.

But Robey was a bit hasty in his sale. The sheet was soon sold again, this time for $20,000. In the 1940s, just four of the stamps brought $23,000 at auction. And today, single stamps from Robey's topsy-turvy sheet are catalogued at over $5,000 each!

Iron money was used for a time in ancient Sparta. According to some accounts, Spartan monarchs cleverly minted coins so large they could barely be carried—to prevent citizens from leaving the country.

The Japanese learned billiards when they captured Singapore from the British during World War II. Shorter in stature than the British, the Japanese found the billiard tables too high for comfortable play. So they cut off six inches from each table leg, and took to billiards with a passion. During the 1960s, close to 9,000 new billiard parlors were built in Japan each year!

A Clutch Victory

Stanislaus Cygamiewicz was a Polish wrestler well known during the early years of this century by his ring name, Zbysco. A hulking, muscular man of 260 pounds, he was also a lawyer, poet, musician, and linguist who conversed in 11 languages. But Zbysco used few of his intellectual abilities in a wrestling match fought at Petrograd, Russia, toward the end of World War I. On the outcome of the match depended the wrestler's very life.

Shortly before the match with Russian sports hero Alex Aberg, Zbysco was arrested by Russian authorities as a spy for Austria, with whom Russian was then at war. Though there was no evidence to prove his guilt, Zbysco was threatened with execution—unless he beat Aberg.

On the night of the match, the sports arena was filled with Russian soldiers shouting support for Aberg. A loss meant certain death for Zbysco. And if he won, he knew he could be killed just as easily by the antagonistic crowd. For two hours and 43 minutes, the two wrestlers fought furiously. At last, the Polish wrestler overcame his powerful opponent, pinning him flat on his back.

Just as the angry crowd seemed ready to attack him, Zbysco received his prize, a bag of gold pieces. Quickly opening the bag, the wrestler threw the gold pieces into the audience. A near riot followed as the spectators fought to pick up the coins. In the confusion, Zbysco slipped out of the ring, into a waiting car, and off toward a friendly border.

The ancient Greeks and Romans were heavy gamers, favoring dice of bone or ivory and occasionally of semiprecious stone. Even Plato was not wont to take the art lightly, writing that "nobody can become a skilled dice-player if he has not devoted himself to it from his childhood, but only plays for pleasure."

The Spanish owe the name of their nation to the Carthaginians of the sixth century B.C., who gave the land the romantic name of *Spania*, or "land of rabbits."

Westward Ho!

If you've ever wondered what it might have been like to trek across America via covered wagon, the way many of our ancestors did, it's not too late to find out firsthand. For less than $100 per person, a North Dakota travel service will take you and your party on a 120-mile trip across the state by horse and wagon.

Travelers on the wagon train eat the same food as early American settlers, and sleep on the ground in a tent or sleeping bag. No radios, flashlights, or other 20th-century conveniences are permitted. Travelers are expected to help cut wood, build fires, feed the horses, and assist in many of the other tasks our forefathers performed during their westward journeys in the 19th century. And to enhance the historic atmosphere of the trek, each traveler is asked to dress in an outfit appropriate to the period!

Armored Resistance

Imagine spending 24 hours a day for seven years dressed in the same suit of clothes. Then try to imagine spending that time inside a heavy suit of armor!

In 1315, a French nobleman, Enguerrand de Marigny, was executed as an evil magician. The nobleman's godson, Enguerrand de St. Cloud, protested in vain that de Marigny had been innocent. He swore that both he and his horse would remain clad in full armor until the King of France himself admitted that the nobleman's godfather had been condemned unjustly.

Seven long years passed. Finally, the French king proclaimed that Enguerrand de Marigny had been innocent. In 1322, Marigny's godson at last removed his heavy steel armor.

Most modern chewing gums contain 20 percent chicle—derived from the sap of the sapodilla tree—60 percent sugar, 19 percent corn syrup, and one percent flavoring. Gumdrops are made not from chicle, but from gum arabic, a substance obtained from exudations of certain types of acacia tree.

Gum makers are presently working on such earth-shattering innovations as a bubble gum whose bubbles glow in the dark!

The dog may have been the first animal domesticated by man. The fossil jaws and teeth of a domesticated dog, discovered in a cave in Iraq, have been found to be about 14,000 years old. These animals, descended from tamed wolves, are thought to have been used by early man as hunting aids, watchdogs, or both.

The oldest known agricultural animals are sheeps and goats, which were first domesticated about 10,000 years ago. Domesticated plants, such as cereal grains, date back only about 9,500 years.

Misogynist's Delight

The Monks' Republic on Mount Athos, Greece, is probably the only land where the female of any species—including *homo sapiens*—is unwelcome.

Athos is a 40-mile-long peninsula jutting out into the Aegean Sea. The peninsula is ruled not by the Greek government, but by an assembly of 20 members, one from each of the 20 Greek Orthodox monasteries that cluster on and around Mount Athos, which rises 6,000 feet above the rocky promontory. Under a constitution that dates from 1045, women and female animals are excluded from the sacred mountain and its monasteries.

In the last nine centuries, only one woman has been known to set foot on Athos. She was the wife of a British minister in Constantinople during the Crimean War, and was permitted to land as a favor to her husband. Hens and female cats are now permitted on the peninsula, but members of the more conservative communities still bar all female animals.

Mihailo Tolotos, a member of one of the monasteries who died in 1938, is perhaps the only man never to have laid eyes on a woman. Mihailo's mother died when he was born, and the infant was taken to the monastery the following day. Tolotos spent the rest of his life among the monks, completely isolated from females of any species—with the possible exception of female insects that dared to stray into the monastery.

The wife of English King Richard I (Richard the Lion-hearted) never set foot on English soil. Queen Berengaria married the King in 1191, while he and his troops were in Cyprus during the Third Crusade. The Queen spent the rest of her life in Palestine, Italy, and France.

Richard himself saw little of his English domain. In all, the King spent only about six months of his 10-year reign in England.

A Fateful Whistle

In 1786, a 22-year-old French nobleman, Marquis de Pelier, was arrested by the police of King Louis XVI, and promptly locked in solitary confinement. His crime—whistling at the king's wife, Queen Marie Antoinette!

Over the next 50 years, the French monarchy gave way to the Revolution and the First Republic, then the Napoleonic Empire, then the Bourbon Restoration. But the marquis remained in prison for his petty offense. In 1836, after a half-century behind bars, the marquis was finally released, 72 years old and broken in health.

By that time, the woman at whom the unfortunate Frenchman was accused of whistling had been dead for 43 years.

Red Light, Green Light

You may think that the familiar red-green traffic signal is a product of the automotive age, but in fact the world's first traffic signal was installed outside the British Houses of Parliament, London, in 1868—decades before the invention of the automobile. With two semaphore arms—like the railroad signal of the day—and red and green gas lamps for use at night, the device was employed to ensure the safe passage of pedestrians across a busy intersection. Unfortunately, the signal blew up after a short period of use, killing a policeman.

The modern traffic light did not appear until 1914, when a red-green signal was installed on Euclid Avenue, Cleveland.

Chalking Up a Sale

Early in the 19th century, billiards players roughened the leather tips of their cue sticks by rubbing them against a whitewashed ceiling. Then an Englishman named Jack Carr discovered that chalk was a perfect abrasive. Carr toured Europe and demonstrated a billards dexterity previously unknown, using his chalked cue tip to put spin on the ball. Thus, the *masse* shot entered billiards, and the word "English" entered our language, referring to backspin placed on any kind of ball.

Carr peddled a "special formula twisting chalk" that he credited for his great skill, but actually Carr's magic substance was chalk, pure and simple.

A Cheese Story

In 1892, a cheese-maker named Emil Frey set out to duplicate a certain German cheese at a plant in Monroe, New York. Instead, he produced an entirely new cheese. Frey named it after a choral group he belonged to in New York City: Liederkranz, or "wreath of songs."

In 1929, the Borden Company took over production of Liederkranz, and shortly after decided to move the cheese factory to Van Wert, Ohio. In an attempt to duplicate the environment for Liederkranz production as closely as possible, Borden moved every last piece of cheese-making apparatus to Ohio, and continued to use precisely the same ingredients. But the Ohio Liederkranz simply did not taste the same as the New York variety.

Finally, the cheese makers brought a quantity of old Liederkranz made in the New York plant to the new facility, and smeared the cheese over the tile walls of the plant. Thereafter, the Ohio Liederkranz was virtually identical to the New York product. Why? The cheese makers had at first neglected to take into account the effects of airborne bacteria on the final product—bacteria growing on the cheese-smeared walls!

In 1905, when an American businessman gave a birthday party at the posh Savoy Hotel in London, the hotel flooded its forecourt and floated a silk-lined gondola for the two dozen guests. A hundred white doves flew above the Venetian mock-up, and swans floated in the water. A baby elephant brought in the five-foot-high birthday cake.

The party turned out to be less than festive for some of the participants, however. A chemical placed in the water to color it blue killed the swans!

For a time, bicycle racing outdrew all sports in this country, including baseball. As late as the 1950s, bicycle racing as a gambling sport was the rage in Japan, topping all other forms of entertainment, including the movies.

Crippled by Crime

During the gold rush years of the 1890s, Cripple Creek, Colorado was one of the most populous American cities west of the Mississippi River, and unquestionably the most infamous. At its peak, Cripple Creek could boast over 70 saloons, plus an untold number of dance halls, opium dens, gambling parlors, and brothels. At one point there was a prostitute in town for every hundred residents. City fathers grew rich by collecting a monthly tax of six dollars from each shady lady; madams were assessed $16.

A local paper blamed the high incidence of violence in the town on the "potency of good Bourbon at high altitudes." But Julian Street, a famed writer of the time, was less charitable, publishing a scathing indictment of the city's depravity in a national magazine. Angry city fathers retaliated by changing the name of Myers Avenue, the red-light district's main drag, to—yes, Julian Street!

Once a city of 50,000, Cripple Creek now has a population of less than 500.

Full Household

Two women: Mrs. Fyodor Vassilet of Russia and Mrs. Bernard Scheinberg of Austria, gave birth to 69 children apiece.

Mrs. Vassilet achieved her prodigious total of 69 in 27 confinements. She gave birth to four sets of quadruplets, seven sets of triplets, and 16 pairs of twins. If you add up these figures, you'll see that not one confinement produced a single birth. Mrs. Vassilet enjoyed considerable renown, and appeared at the court of Czar Alexander II. She died in 1872.

Mrs. Scheinberg's story is remarkably similar to that of Mrs. Vassilet. She, too, gave birth in 27 confinements; none of these produced less than two children; and miraculously, she likewise gave birth to four sets of quadruplets, seven sets of triplets, and 16 pairs of twins!

When Mrs. Scheinberg died at the age of 56 in 1911, her husband Bernard remarried, and had 18 children by his second wife. Bernard Scheinberg had sired a grand total of 87 progeny.

The first sidewalk in the United States was laid in 1657 on a New York thoroughfare called—what else?—Stone Street.

The animal that takes the longest time to make its debut is the elephant. Its gestation period is 645 days or more than 21 months.

Stand-ins

An old Chinese law permitted a substitute to die for a convicted murderer. A condemned man with enough money could often find a replacement to suffer decapitation for him, with the payment going to the substitute's family.

The saguaro, the giant of the cactus family, is one of the slowest-growing specimens in the plant kingdom. The central stem of this desert titan grows less than one inch during the first ten years of the plant's life, and does not produce a branch until the stem is about 16 feet high. Later, the spiny succulent grows about an inch each year, and can eventually reach a height of 50 feet.

Flowers do not appear until the plant is 50 to 75 years old. The largest saguaro specimens are close to 200 years old, and weigh over ten tons!

Amphibious Assault

It sometimes rains frogs. Scientists explain the phenomenon of raining frogs in this way: Spawn are sucked up from rivers and lakes into the atmosphere by whirlwinds. The lightweight embryos are carried through the air for great distances. The spawn hatch en route. When the wind is spent, the animals drop to the earth!

Coffee is regularly consumed by about one-third of the world's population, and consumption continues to rise steadily. At the turn of the century, world imports totaled about one million tons. But by 1950, that figure had doubled. Today, the total stands at about three-and-a-half million tons—making coffee the second largest item of international commerce after petroleum!

The first night game in baseball history was played on June 2, 1883, at League Park in Fort Wayne, Indiana. The game pitted a boys club team against the Quincey professionals and was witnessed by 2,000 spectators. The field was illuminated by 17 lights of 4,000 candlepower each.

Could you imagine a water lily whose pads are large enough to support the weight of a man? You'll find such an aquatic giant—it's called the Victorian water lily—in the Amazon region of South America. The round, padlike leaves of this jungle monster are sometimes over six feet in diameter. The English explorers who discovered and named the plant reported that it could safely support the weight of three men without being submerged!

Sixteenth-century spectacles makers scratched a number on each lens they made to indicate the age of the person they thought the lens would suit. A person seeking eyeglasses stopped by a spectacles maker's shop and sampled his wares until he found a pair of specs that seemed appropriate. It wasn't until the eighteenth century that lenses were identified by their radius of curvature.

Although the first 10 amendments to the United States Constitution, known as the Bill of Rights, were submitted to the states for ratification in 1789, they were not ratified by Connecticut, Massachusetts, and Georgia until 1939—150 years later.

About 22 billion gallons of sewage are produced in this country each day—about 100 gallons per person!

The point of zero degrees latitude and zero degrees longitude lies in the Gulf of Guinea off the western coast of Africa. The closest land to this point is in Ghana, and the capital of that nation—Accra—is the nearest town.

Low-down on the Atlantic

The greatest mountain range lies under the sea. This is known as the Dolphin Rise and extends from the Arctic to the Antarctic. Mountain tops are so high that at points they rise above the ocean's surface. We know some of these points as the Azore Islands and the Canary Islands. The deepest valleys between these mountains are, in some places, more than five miles below the surface of the ocean. If Mt. McKinley, Alaska, the highest mountain in North America, were dropped into such a spot, it would be completely submerged!

A Trick Up His Sleeve

Why do men have buttons on their coat sleeves? Well, there's no functional reason for their existence, only a historic one. Frederick the Great of Prussia was greatly put out by the grimy sleeves of his soldiers' uniforms. He inquired why the sleeves were so much dirtier than the rest of the uniform, and was told that the soldiers were in the habit of wiping the perspiration on their faces on their sleeves. To stop the practice, Frederick ordered that buttons be put on the top side of all army men's sleeves. The unmindful soldier would recieve a nasty scratch on his face the next time he used his sleeve as a towel.

Eventually, the buttons found their way onto civilian sleeves—but on the lower side of the sleeve. Today, to be in vogue, men must make the weighty decision of whether to adorn their sleeves with one, two, three, or four buttons.

The famed Battle or New Orleans, won by Andrew Jackson and his troops over the British during the War of 1812, was fought on January 8, 1815—15 days *after* the war had ended. A treaty ending the conflict has been signed in Europe, but the news failed to reach either Jackson or the British troops before the battle. And Jackson's superiors in Washington were unaware of both the battle *and* the treaty!

Atypical Type

If you're a practitioner of the "hunt-and-peck" school of typing, you may be encouraged by the development of the Dvorak keyboard, patented in 1936. The Dvorak keyboard is arranged so that the letters most common in English are most easily and comfortably reached by the touch typist. The Dvorak keyboard looks much like the universal keyboard, with three rows of letter keys. But on the Dvorak, 70 percent of all letters in almost any given passage can be found in the middle row, with the most common letters placed under the strongest fingers.

Proponents of the new system claim that the increased speed of the Dvorak methods and the lessening of typist fatigue could result in a savings of $20 million a year in business expenses throughout the country.

The father of the modern comic strip was Rodolphe Topffer, an early 19th-century Swiss illustrator and schoolmaster. Topffer observed that more people can read pictures than can read words—hardly a deduction worthy of Dick Tracy. He went on to produce picture-story books and collections of small drawings that were the forerunners of the modern newspaper strip. Topffer also put out collections of his drawings in oblong albums of about 100 pages. These were the precursors of the comic book.

To many minds, the tulip and the windmill are virtually synonymous with the Netherlands. Most historians would agree that the windmill in Europe made its first appearance in the Low Countries, sometime before the 12th century. But you may be surprised to learn that the tulip is not a native of Holland, and was totally unknown in that country until the 16th century.

The tulip is actually a native of the western Mediterranean and the steppes of Central Asia, and some species can be found growing wild in northern Africa, southern Europe, and Japan. The empire of the Ottoman Turks once included much of the tulip's natural habitat, and it was through Turkey that most tulips reached western Europe and the Netherlands.

The word "booze" does not, as widely believed, come from a liquor bottler named E.C. Booz. The word is quite old, originating perhaps from the Dutch word *buyzen*, "to tipple," or the Middle English *bouse*, "to drink deep."

The Birth of the Burger

The hamburger is a more recent invention that the frankfurter. During the Middle Ages, traveling merchants from Hamburg learned from the Tartars of the Baltic lands how to scrape raw meat and season it with salt, pepper, and onion juice for what came to be known as "Tartar steak." Many restaurants still serve a similar dish known as *steak tartare*.

No one knows the name of the first cook to shape scraped or chopped beef into a patty and broil it, but we do know that the first hamburgers were browned on the outside and almost raw inside. The English and Irish were the first to cook their beef patties well-done throughout.

Some botanists believe the cabbage is the most ancient vegetable still grown today. Cabbage is now the fourth-leading vegetable consumed in the United States, after potatoes, lettuce, and tomatoes. About two billion pounds of cabbage are marketed annually in this country—almost ten pounds per person.

A Seedy Shave

In Panama, a Guaymi Indian need never buy a razor. When he wants a shave, he just wanders to the edge of a grassy field and pulls one of the thick, high stalks. He removes one of the oatlike seeds that grow in bunches on each stalk. On the sides of each of these seeds are two slender blades that are as sharp as glass.

Holding the seed firmly by its tough filaments, the Guaymi draws it across his face, and off go his whiskers. He couldn't get a cleaner shave in a barber shop.

Though New York's subway is today the world's most famous—or infamous—it was not, as many people believe, the first ever constructed. Actually, it was the sixth to begin operation, and the second in this country.

New York's first subway line was completed in 1904. By that time, an underground transit system had been in operation in London for 41 years!

The first American subway was constructed in Boston, and opened in 1897.

The word "tobacco" comes from the Indian word for the tube of the calumet, or peace pipe, not from their name for the plant. When East Coast Indians introduced smoking to the Europeans, they presented their pipe and repeated the word *tobacco* to urge the stranger to put the calumet tube in his lips. The Europeans naturally assumed the Indians were referring to the substance they were smoking, and the leaf was forever after known as tobacco.

Incidentally, no instance has ever been recorded of an Indian violating the peace-pipe compact.

In Anglo-Saxon wedding ceremonies, shoes were as indispensable as the wedding ring is today. Instead of exchanging rings with her betrothed, the bride customarily passed her shoes to her husband, who then tapped her on the head with a shoe.

Noah's Art

The most important milestone in American lexicography came in 1828, when Noah Webster of New Haven published his masterpiece, *An American Dictionary of the English Language*, with about 70,000 entries. Webster's work was the first American dictionary to gain wide acceptance in both the United States and England.

You may be confused by the plethora of dictionaries on the market bearing the name "Webster's." The fact is, none of these books—or at least, very few—are directly derived from the work of Noah Webster. The word "Webster's" has become merely an identifying title, like the word "dictionary" itself, and cannot be copyrighted. Anyone at all can publish a book and call it "Webster's Dictionary," although the G. & C. Merriam Company of Springfield, Massachusetts, claims that their dictionaries are the legitimate successors to Webster's works.

Where Are the Hats of Yesteryear?

Straw boater

An Irish ditty of the 1890s went:

> *Where did you get that hat?*
> *Where did you get that tile?*
> *Where did you get that hat?*
> *Is that the latest style?*

You won't find many of the hats of yesteryear being worn today. The country has almost become hatless, and many women have given up wearing hats, even in the dead of winter. As for men, gone are the days when you'd see the straw boater, the derby, the silk top hat—sometimes called the "stove pipe"—and a score of other headgear.

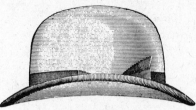

Derby

Lady's cowboy hat, as shown in a Montgomery Ward Catalog *of the 1890s.*

Gorgeous Easter bonnet of the 1880s, as depicted in Leslie's Magazine.

Various caps and head coverings shown in a Montgomery Ward *Catalog of the 1800s.*

So-called sensible hats from France.

A lady's bonnet as shown in
Harper's Magazine.

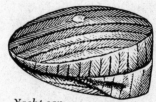

Yacht cap

A hat from Paris, as depicted
in the Illustrated London News.

Silk top hat

Of all nations in the world, New Zealand has the highest rate of calorie consumption per person, as well as the highest rate of protein consumption per person. The world's greatest cereal consumers are the people of Turkey; the greatest potato and root flour consumers are the people of Paraguay; of sugar, Colombia; of alcohol, South Africa.

The first person to go over Niagara Falls in a barrel was Anna Edson Taylor, who on October 24, 1901, took the plunge over Horseshoe Falls in a barrel four-and-a-half feet high and three feet in diameter. The inside of the barrel was filled with cushions, and the passenger was harnessed inside the barrel. It was later discovered that Anna couldn't swim.

As any tailor knows, in about 85 percent of men, the left testicle hangs lower than the right.

An ancient remedy for toothache was to eat a mouse.

On June 6, 1896, George Samuelson and Frank Harpo left New York harbor in an 18-foot rowboat. Fifty-six days later they arrived on the Scilly Islands off the coast of England, thus becoming the first men to row across the Atlantic Ocean—a feat everyone thought was impossible.

When Robert Glen Gibson of Cape Breton, Nova Scotia, came home from his fishing trip on November 1, 1970, an awful lot of people had tuna fish salad. Gibson landed the largest tuna ever caught—a leviathan weighing 1,065 pounds!

A device patented in the United States on May 19, 1896, claimed to "produce dimples on the human body or to nurture and maintain dimples already existing."

The discovery of Lana Turner in a drugstore is well-known, but even in the 18th century, actresses were scouted in unlikely places. For example, Anne Oldfield, the reigning comedienne at London's Drury Lane Theatre, was a drudge in an English tavern when playwright George Farquar overheard her reciting some lines from Beaumont and Fletcher, while she was doing some chores.

The expression *what the dickens* has nothing to do with novelist Charles Dickens. *Dickens*, a euphemism for devil, was used by Shakespeare 200 years before the birth of the Victorian novelist in the play *The Merry Wives of Windsor*, where Mrs. Page exclaims, "I cannot tell what the dickens his name is."

But if he did not leave his own name in our language, Charles Dickens did immortalize a number of his fictional characters as English nouns. We call a miser a *Scrooge*, after the protagonist of *A Christmas Carol*. We call an improvident optimist a *Mickawber*, after the character in *David Copperfield*, who is always confident that "something will turn up." We call a sanctimonious individual a *Pecksniff*, after the clergyman in *Martin Chuzzlewit*. And the adjective *Pickwickian*, so called after the titular hero of *The Pickwick Papers*, denotes a certain wry sense of humor.

Rain never falls on parts of the Sahara Desert. Though clouds pass over these areas, and raindrops actually fall, the water itself never reaches the ground. The sizzling heat of the desert air evaporates the moisture as it falls, changing it back to invisible vapor.

One ostrich—the largest bird now living—weighs as much as 48,000 bee hummingbirds, the smallest birds in the world.

Corn is by far the biggest farm crop in the United States. Over 5 billion bushels of corn were produced in 1972, more than three times the production of the next biggest crop, wheat.

Almost every room of every house in the Sahara city of El Oued, Algeria, is covered with a mud dome.

In 1969, a poll taken in Morocco revealed that only 88 percent of those asked knew that a man had set foot on the moon. Of these, more than half thought the story was a hoax.

The Best of Both Worlds

The Caudron Company of France once devised an airplane-automobile with foldable wings. It was an entirely conventional airplane—except for a small outboard motor mounted on a rear third wheel. In March, 1935, a writer for the *Scientific American* declared that he "saw no reason why some day such a combination should not be practicable for general use." But the "aviocar," as it was called, took a few trial spins down the boulevards of Paris, and that was the end of that.

How did the term *o'clock* originate? Unquestionably, the original form was *of the clock*; *o'clock* is merely a contraction. Many writers of the 16th and 17th centuries said *ten of clock* or *ten a clock*. In the early 18th century, the form *o'clock* began to appear.

A Golfer's Nightmare

Can you believe that a woman golfer—and not a novice either—took 166 strokes on a single hole? Well, it happened. In 1912, in the qualifying round of the Shawnee Invitational for Ladies in Pennsylvania, a poor female—who shall remain nameless—teed off at the 130-yard 16th hole. Her drive flew directly into the Binniekill River. With the ball floating insolently in the water, she set out in a rowboat to continue play, with her husband at the oars. After flailing away for what must have seemed an eternity, she finally drove the ball to dry land. Unfortunately, the ball landed in a dense wood, and again she hacked away for what seemed forever to extricate it from the woods, into the rough, into the sand, into the rough. Before this nightmarish hole was played out, the poor woman had taken 166 strokes, all meticulously recorded by her loving husband.

The longest-named lake in the world is Lake Chargogagogmanchaugagochaubunagungamaug, near Webster, Massachusetts, known locally as Lake Webster. The name, of Indian origin, means: "You fish on your side, we fish on our side, nobody fishes in the middle."

The shortest war on record was fought in 1896 between England and Zanzibar. From the beginning of hostilities to the surrender of Zanzibar by Sultan Said Khalid, there elapsed only 38 minutes.

Airport 1982

The Dallas/Fort Worth Airport in Texas is presently the world's largest airport, extending over nearly 28 square miles—Manhattan island, by contrast, is 22.6 square miles in area. But the Texas facility is likely to enjoy a short reign. When completed, the airport in Montreal, Canada, will cover about 29 square miles. Yet even that airport will be dwarfed by one planned for Jidda, Saudi Arabia.

When completed around 1982, the Jidda facility will sprawl over 41 square miles of desert land outside the Red Sea port. The airport complex will include a commercial terminal, a royal pavilion for the Saudi ruling family and guests, a cargo terminal, an air force base, a hospital, a quarantine area, a hotel, seven mosques, a maintenance plant, housing for airport staff, and a desalination plant.

But the most spectacular feature of the Arabian facility will be an immense haj (pilgrimage) terminal, that will cover 10 million square feet—more space than the two World Trade Center towers in New York combined. Yet the terminal will be open for only one month each year! The facility is designed exclusively to handle the three million Moslems who converge on Jidda during the holy month on their pilgrimage to Mecca, 30 miles away.

The Price of Spice

The ancient Romans used a wide variety of spices and imported them in large quantities. Spices were so valuable during Imperial times that a single sack of peppers could pay a man's ransom. In the fifth century, the Visigoth chieftain Alaric accepted 3,000 pounds of peppers as part of a tribute to lift the siege of Rome.

Even as late as the 15th century, a pound of pepper cost an Englishman about six times the average daily wage of a laborer.

Surprisingly, the United States is the world's largest producer of cheese. The most popular cheese in America is Cheddar, first produced near the English village that bears its name. By law, English Cheddar is no longer permitted in this country. The American product, called Cheddar, American, Monterey, or Jack cheese, accounts for an amazing 85 percent of all the cheese produced in this country.

Danish blue cheese, meanwhile, is the most popular imported cheese in the United States.

The town of Barton, England, contains a most unusual memorial—a monument to a hailstorm. An inscription on the monument commemorates the great hailstorm of July 3, 1883, when pieces of ice five inches in diameter fell from the skies and broke 15 tons of glass in the town. The monument is made from bricks that were being made at the time of the storm, and the bricks retain deep impressions where the mammoth hailstones struck.

Monkey-Shines

You've heard of children being raised by wolves? Well, how about *baboons*?

In 1904, two South African policemen discovered a native boy hopping about on all fours among a group of baboons. He could understand no human words, and would eat nothing but raw vegetables.

After a stay in a mental hospital, the boy worked as a farm laborer, but retained many of his baboonlike mannerisms. When he had learned some English, he described how he and other members of his baboon family had raided ostrich nests and stolen eggs. Though the boy had no recollection of the event, he had obviously been carried away by the apes when he was very young, and raised as one of them.

The eruption of Krakatoa in 1883, the most violent volcanic explosion of modern times, sent volcanic ash up to 50 miles into the atmosphere, where it was carried around the earth many times. The ash cut off the sun's rays to such an extent that the amount of heat reaching the earth in the year following the eruption of Krakatoa was only 87 percent of the normal amount, causing the weather to be unseasonably cold throughout the world. In the New England States, the unusually cold year of 1884 came to be known as "the year without a summer."

Sennacherib, an Assyrian king who ruled around 700 B.C., had little patience with illegal parkers on the main street, or processional way, of his capital city, Nineveh. The king decreed that anyone who parked a vehicle on the street would be put to death, and his body impaled on a stake to serve as a warning to other would-be scofflaws.

Big Baths

The public baths of ancient Rome were the recreational centers of the city, providing not only bathing facilities but gyms, libraries, theaters, gardens, and assembly halls. The Baths of Caracalla, constructed in 217, could accommodate 1,600 bathers in an area of more than a million square feet—an area which included a stadium. Diocletian built baths in the year 302 that were large enough to accommodate 3,200 bathers at one time!

Until the second century, men and women bathed together in Rome. Then emperor Hadrian ordered segregated bathing. However, Hadrian's decree was frequently overlooked during the more decadent eras of the Empire. In most cities outside Rome, men and women used the bathing facilities at different hours, but it was always considered immoral for a woman to bathe at night.

A Real Corker

The current head of a group called the International Correspondents of Corkscrew Addicts has a corkscrew collection that includes over 1,300 specimens, some over 200 years old. Old or rare corkscrews have sold for as much as $400 at auction.

The leek has been the national emblem of Wales since the year 640, when victorious Welsh soldiers pinned leeks to their caps so that they would not inadvertently bludgeon one another instead of the enemy. But some historians discount that tale, pointing instead to a confusion by English writers between the Welsh words for the daffodil, *cenine*, and the leek, *cenin*, for the daffodil was another Welsh national symbol. In any case, the Welsh still pin leeks to their hats on the feast day of St. David, their patron saint.

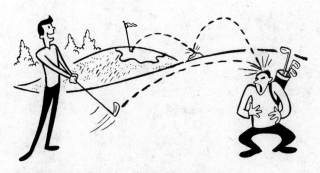

Jones Putts One Over

If you gave Bobby Jones a golfing riddle, he gave you an answer. Long putts are the greatest problem in golf, and Jones showed everybody how to handle them.

In 1928, for 10 consecutive rounds, Jones averaged 30 putts a round.

Confronted with the longest putt in the game—a 120-foot affair on a green at St. Andrews, Scotland—Bobby unsheathed his putter, *Calamity Jane*, and knocked the little white ball into the little green cup for a world's record.

The Mosque of Omar was built to house a rock

The Mosque of Omar in Jerusalem was the first mosque erected with a dome. But this holy structure is more noted for the object it was built to house—a large granite rock sacred to the followers of Islam. Today, the mosque is best known as the Dome of the Rock.

Christians as well as Moslems hold this rock sacred. It is upon this massive stone

that—according to Judeo-Christian tradition—Abraham agreed to sacrifice his son Isaac as proof of his obedience to God. In the 10th century B.C., the Hebrew King Solomon constructed his great temple on this site, with the most sacred area of the temple—the Ark of the Torah—directly over the rock. Solomon's temple was subsequently destroyed by the Babylonians, but another temple was constructed on the site by King Herod. This temple was destroyed by the Romans in 70 A.D.

According to Moslem belief, the prophet Mohammed was carried from Mecca to Jerusalem on a winged horse, and set down atop

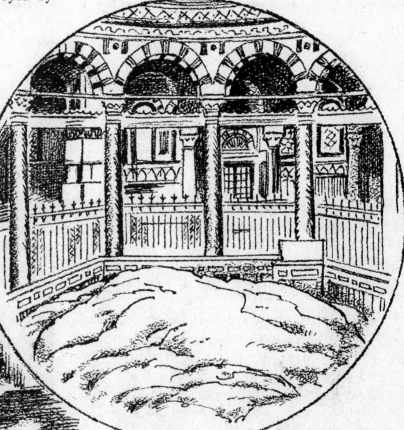

this long-revered rock. Shortly after the Moslems captured the city of Jerusalem in 637, they began to contruct a mosque to enclose the sacred stone, preserving it for the followers of Islam.

This mosque, an eight-sided structure topped by a wooden dome almost 100 feet high, was completed in the year 691 and named for the caliph Omar. The courtyard surrounding the mosque occupies almost ⅙ of the entire area of the old walled city.

The rock itself—a massive chunk of granite 60 feet long and 40 feet wide—contains a number of deep hollows, which Moslems hold to be the footprints of the giant horse that brought Mohammed to the sacred city.

The Empress Josephine of France, the wife of Napoleon, built a huge rose garden at her estate at Malmaison, with over 250 varieties of the flower flourishing—every variety known at the time. The empress often carried in hand a Malmaison rose that she could raise to her lips when smiling, since she was particularly sensitive about her imperfect teeth.

The In-FALL-ible Elevator

Though Elisha Graves Otis is often called the inventor of the elevator, he initially contributed only one major innovation to elevator design. But that innovation was significant enough to make him, in effect, the father of the passenger elevator.

Otis's innovation was a safety device that could stop the fall of the elevator in the event the cable broke. The simple device consisted of two metal hooks and a spring, attached to the cable where it met the platform. If tension in the hoist rope was relaxed—in the event of a cable break, for instance—the hooks immediately sprang to a horizontal position, where their ends would catch in teeth cut into the guide rails and stop the elevator's descent.

Otis demonstrated his invention by holding regular cable-breaking exhibitions at the 1853 Crystal Palace Exposition in New York. Spectators would watch in amazement as Otis climbed on the platform, rose to the top of the shaft, and then cut the cable! His expected fall would be checked by the safety hooks.

The largest pair of shoes ever made—apart from those specially built for elephantiasis sufferers—were a colossal size 42, built for a Florida giant named Harley Davidson. The mammoth clodhoppers measured some 22½ inches in length!

The cocktail party is thought to have originated as an outgrowth of the apéritif hour before dinner. As the "hour" gradually lengthened, a buffet of some kind became necessary to allay the appetites of the imbibers. Psychologists attribute the popularity of the cocktail party, and the before-dinner cocktail itself, to their function as a separation between the working day and the evening relaxation.

Why are gold and silver so appropriate as mediums of exchange? First of all, the metals were always highly prized for their sheen and utility in personal adornment and religious statuary. Gold and silver will neither deteriorate nor rust. And the supply of these metals, while large enough to fill the bill as a medium of exchange, is not so large that the metals become worthless.

The earliest restaurant on record in America appeared in Philadelphia around 1680. By 1955, there were close to 200,000 eating places in the United States—one for every 800 persons—serving over 60 million meals a day with staff of 1.3 million workers. Annual sales totaled about $9 billion, making the restaurant the third largest retail business in this country.

It's been estimated that a New Yorker can dine out every night of his life until age 65 without visiting any establishment twice!

The first application of refrigeration technology to marine food transportation came in 1880, when the steamer *Strathleven* carried a meat cargo from Australia to England. Oddly enough, the meat was meant to be cooled, not frozen—but freezing did take place, and the excellent results led to the subsequent freezing of all meat cargoes.

"**H**ell is others," wrote Jean-Paul Sartre. If you agree, then Reno, Nevada may answer to your idea of Heaven. With just 23 people per square mile, Reno boasts the smallest population density in the United States. Second is Laredo, Texas, with 25 persons per square mile, and third is Greeley, Colorado, with a population of 27 per square mile.

On the other hand, if you have no desire to flee the maddening crowd, you may want to settle in Jersey City, New Jersey. That booming city has the densest population in the country—12,288 per square mile.

From Rags to Riches—and Back

William Crapo Durant, the founder of General Motors, gained control of his first car company, Buick, in 1904, and moved his plant to Flint, Michigan. In 1908, Durant took over the Olds Company. In the following years, Durant continued to absorb ailing car and accessory companies under the corporate umbrella of General Motors. The Cadillac Company—named for Antoine de la Mothe Cadillac, the founder of Detroit—joined GM in 1909. Durant even approached Henry Ford with an offer to join General Motors, but Henry turned him down.

The roller coaster career of W.C. Durant took a turn for the worse shortly after General Motors was formed, and he eventually lost control of the corporation he had founded. Durant's new car firm, the Chevrolet Company, named after a race driver who had designed engines for Durant, was such a success that the new leaders of GM were forced to take Durant, and Chevrolet, into the firm. By 1918, Durant was again at the helm of the corporation. But the founder of what is presently the largest manufacturing corporation in the world, with sales of $35 billion in 1975, declared bankruptcy in 1936, claiming over a million dollars in debts and assets of just $250—the clothes on his back!

The word "cynic" actually comes from *kynos*, the Greek word for dog, and owes its use either to a former dog kennel that served as the first school of the Greek Cynics, or from the uncouth, belligerent manners adopted by adherents of that philosophy. The word "cynosure," in Greek, literally means "dog's tail!"

The largest car ever produced for regular road use was the 1927 "Golden Bugatti," which measured 22 feet from bumper to bumper. Only six of these cars were made, and some of these survive in excellent condition.

An adult African elephant needs 300 lbs. to 400 lbs. of fodder a day.

In ancient Rome, the Emperor Nero had snow transported from nearby mountains to cool his wine cellar, and reportedly concocted some of the first water-ice desserts by mixing snow with honey, juices, and fruit. But the first frozen dessert made from milk didn't reach Europe until the 13th century, when Marco Polo returned from the Orient with a recipe for a milk-ice, presumably similar to sherbet.

Without bacteria, edibles would last almost indefinitely. All food-preservation techniques, then, are designed to kill or limit the growth of bacterial life. For instance, the process of drying works because bacteria cannot grow in the absence of moisture. Cooling does not kill bacteria, but it does stop their growth. Sterilization by heat—cooking—will completely destroy bacterial life, but the effects are temporary. Cooked food will spoil as rapidly as uncooked food if left untreated—or uneaten.

Origin of the Species

Paleontologists believe that the cat family descended from the Miacis, a weasel-like carnivore that lived about 50 million years ago. The Miacis evolved in many directions, one of them producing animals such as the mongoose and the civet that are thought to be ancestors of both the great cats and the smaller felines. Over the ages, the feline species spread to all parts of the earth, with the exception of Australia and a few islands.

The cat family evolved to its present from some seven million years ago, long before most surviving mammals. But the feline was not tamed to any extent until just 5,000 years ago.

The Otis Elevator Company, the world's largest manufacturer of elevators, now installs from 20,000 to 25,000 new elevators and escalators each year, and services an estimated 400,000 Otis elevators functioning around the world.

There are over 200 varieties of sausage made in this country, by some 3,000 individual processors. The frankfurter is by far the most popular. Americans gobble up close to 16 billion wieners each year—about 80 per person!

Dogs skilled at sniffing out caches of concealed drugs are becoming increasingly popular among many police forces. Recently, a Florida policeman demonstrated his dog's sleuthing talents to a group of students. He hid packets of drugs around the room, then loosed his keen-nosed sidekick to find them. The policeman hid 10 packets; the dog brought back 11.

The smallest unit of length measurement in the world is the atto-meter, equivalent to a mere quintillionth of a centimeter. Your pinky is probably about 7,000,000,000,000,-000,000 atto-meters long!

Among the Masai tribesmen of Tanzania, spitting is regarded as an indication of reverence and good will. Newborn children are spat upon by those who wish to endow the child with good luck. Masai will spit at each other when they meet, and spit at each other again to say goodbye. To seal a bargain, two traders will spit at each other.

Wilbert Robinson, manager of the 1920s Brooklyn Dodgers, tried to keep his players on their toes by forming a "Bonehead Club." A player who pulled a "bonehead" play was obliged to pay a fine to the club. Who was the club's first member? Robinson himself earned that honor when he walked up to home plate prior to a game and handed the umpire a laundry slip instead of the line-up card.

A size ten shoe is not ten inches long. So where does the number come from? Believe it or not, it stands for ten barleycorns!

In 1324, English King Edward II decreed that an inch was equal to three average-sized barleycorns laid end to end. The normal shoe was declared to measure 39 barleycorns, and this size was designated with the number 13. Other sizes were graded from this standard, with one barleycorn difference between each successive size.

Zip!

How old is the zipper? Well, the year 1896 saw the first patent for a "slide fastener," a device invented five years earlier by Chicagoan Witcomb Judson as a "clasp locker and unlocker for shoes." The term we use today, "zipper," originally referred only to a boot equipped with a slide fastener.

Judson eventually sold his patent rights to Lewis Walker, who with the aid of a Swede named Gideon Sundback developed the first modern zipper. Zippers began to appear on tobacco pouches, mailbags, and galoshes around 1920; but by and large, the garment industry regarded the zipper as a passing fad. At the time, the only garments fitted with zippers were theatrical costumes for quick-change artists.

The 1930s saw the development of an improved zipper, with the metal teeth cast directly onto the zipper tape fabric. Soon, everyone was using zippers for both fastening and decoration. Zippers with multi-colored teeth were especially popular for a time!

When the Moslem leader Saladin retook Jerusalem from the Crusaders in the 12th century, he refused to enter a mosque until all the walls and objects in the holy place had been purified with rose water. Over 50 camels were required to transport the aromatic cargo from Baghdad to Jerusalem.

When London's second underground railway line opened in 1890, the subway cars that plied the tracks were built without windows. In the opinion of their designers, there was simply nothing to look at in a tunnel!

Taking Measures

Whether or not you've ever been to a race track, you may have wondered exactly what a "*furlong*" is. The term originated with the word "furrow," and at one time was thought to be the length most suitable for a plow furrow. The furlong is now defined as 220 yards.

The world *league* has varied in meaning in different times and countries. In England, the league was equivalent to about three miles. For centuries now, the word has been used chiefly in a figurative sense.

And the *knot* is not a measurement of length, so if you ever hear a sailor say "knots per hour" you'll know he's a landlubber in disguise. The knot is actually a measurement of speed, equivalent to one nautical mile per hour.

Most modern automobile manufacturing plants can turn out 50 to 60 cars per hour. The Chevrolet plant in Lordstown, Ohio, the nation's most modern, can produce over 100 vehicles an hour.

The wide variety of money standards in use in medieval and Renaissance Europe often made business transactions difficult—and made the moneychanger an absolute necessity. Gradually, the moneychanger came to fulfill many of the functions now performed by banks. And with the rise of moneylending and capital accumulation, paper money, otherwise worthless, became reliable as a medium of exchange.

Oh, It's Love That Makes the World Go Round

As one wag has put it, love is a ticklish sensation around the heart that can't be scratched. Artists all over the world have got into the act, and here are some of their effusions.

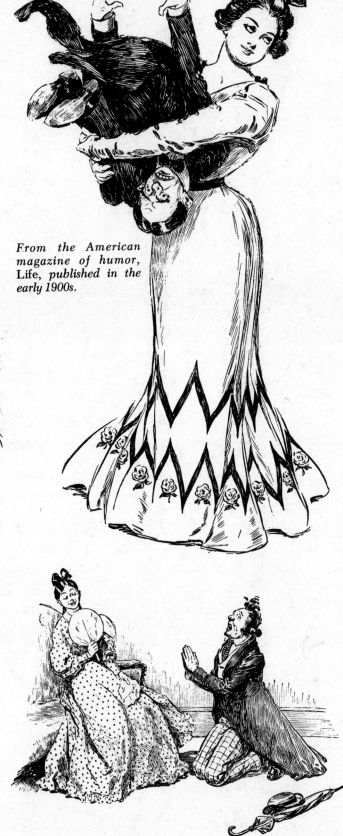

From the American magazine of humor, Life, *published in the early 1900s.*

"Hearts Aflutter," by an artist who drew for Harper's Magazine *in the 1890s.*

From Bab Ballads by the famous W.S. Gilbert, the one who cooperated with Sullivan.

From Life, *American humorous magazine of the early 1900s.*

Drawing by Honore
Daumier, noted
French satirical artist.

"The Attack Direct," drawn by
Ronald Searle, well-known British artist, in 1950 for a book
called The Female Approach.

These drawings are from the world famous English magazine of humor, Punch.

From Art of the Book, *a Russian publication.*

"A Modern Approach" by a Russian artist, contained in Fifty Years of Soviet Art.

Love among the bourgeoisie of the 19th century, according to this artist who drew for Leslie's Magazine.

For economy and ease, you can't beat the food-gathering methods of the Cistercian Monastery in Alcobaca, Portugal. Whenever its cooks want fresh fish, all they do is lower their nets into a branch of the Alcoa River which flows through the heart of their huge kitchen.

The richness of the English language and its genius for particularization are well demonstrated by a look at those words used to identify young animals. For instance, a young frog is called a *polliwog*; a young swan, a *cygnet*; a young hen, a *pullet*; a young oyster, a *set*; a young goose, a *gosling*; and a young swine, a *shoat*.

Three men have been elected to the American Presidency with fewer popular votes than one of their opponents: John Quincy Adams in 1824, Rutherford B. Hayes in 1876, and Benjamin Harrison in 1888. In addition, 12 other men have been elected President without a majority of the popular vote. The last was Richard Nixon, who in 1968 won only 43 percent of the popular vote.

The world's record for chin-ups is 78, set by Anton Lewis in 1913. And the record for one-handed chin-ups, 27, was set by a 38-year-old woman, Lillian Leitzel, in 1918.

Okolehao, an exotic Hawaiian alcoholic beverage, is made out of molasses, Koji rice, and the juice of the Kalo plant.

In 1557, a new English translation of the Bible was printed in Geneva, Switzerland. Though most often known as the Geneva Bible, the book contained one curious translation that earned it another name. Describing Adam and Eve in the Garden of Eden, the Bible tells us that the first man and woman "sewed fig tree leaves together, and made themselves breeches." Thus the Bible came to be known as the "Breeches Bible."

St. Bernard dogs have long been revered for their service in rescuing travelers in snowbound Alpine passes. A gas station owner near Kansas City, Missouri, has found yet another use for the big canine. Each morning, he places the previous day's receipts in a pouch and puts the pouch in the mouth of his St. Bernard, Bourbon. The 150-pound dog then trots down a grassy knoll to a branch of the United Missouri Bank. The trusted messenger has yet to be late—or mugged.

The nation of Iceland has neither trees, snakes, nor railroads—nor any armed forces.

Early this century, the first automobiles to take to the roads in Tennessee frightened horses and people alike—and ran down a few as well. The state passed a law requiring every motorist who planned to drive to warn the public one week in advance by inserting a notice in the newspapers.

Some of today's drivers might do well to give the rest of us similar warning.

Ice skates did not originate in Holland. But roller skates did!

During the time of Louis XIV, it was considered a high honor to be granted an audience with His Majesty while he was heeding the call of nature.

In 1789, there were but 75 post offices and 1,875 miles of post roads in the United States. Today, there are some 40,000 post offices in this country, and the designated post roads exceed *two million* miles in length!

Paris was one of the first cities in Europe to light its streets. During the Middle Ages, each resident of the city was ordered to affix a lit torch to the outside of his house, and later, to keep a lamp in his window through the night.

In fifteenth-century London, citizens were required by law to hang candles outside their homes. But the measure seemed to have been less than effective. In 1679, the Lord Mayor of London wrote that "when night darkened the streets then wandered forth the sons of Belial, flown with insolence and wine." Persons venturing into the night often enlisted the services of paid torch or lantern bearers.

Meteorologists estimate that if all the sparks produced by all the dynamos in the United States were fused together, the result would be but a half-sized lightning flash.

A train doesn't tip over when going around a curve because the rail on the outside of the curve is higher than the rail on the inside of the curve.

Teamwork

The *Pantheon de la Guerre*, a gigantic panorama of the first World War completed in 1918, was the work of 130 individual artists, probably the largest number of artists to work on a single picture. The mammoth work—402 feet long and 45 feet high—contains battlefields, flags, monuments, and the life-sized portraits of 6,000 war heroes.

A modern visitor to a medieval castle might find the garderobes, or latrines, rather cold, bleak places to spend one's precious time. Actually, many garderobes were quite cozy. Some were positioned beside chimney shafts to provide warmth, with wood paneling, matting, or papered walls, and even bookshelves. St. Gregory highly recommended the latrine as a place for reading and serious thought.

The world's record for dashing 100 yards is just about nine seconds. But early this century, American tap dancer Bill Robinson ran the same distance in a time just 4.5 seconds slower than the present record—running backwards!

The most balls a juggler has successfully kept in the air at one time is ten, a feat accomplished by Enrico Rastelli in 1920.

The world's most complete collection of sheet music belongs to the Edwin A. Fleisher Music Collection in Philadelphia. More than 12,000 compositions from nearly 60 countries are included.

The Grand Canal in China, which connects the Yellow and the Yangtze Rivers, is 20 times as long as the Panama Canal—yet the Chinese waterway was built without modern equipment 1,300 years ago!

At noon, on a spring day in Paris in 1910, a truck broke down in the center of the Place de l'Opera. The driver got out, went underneath his vehicle, and emerged a half-hour later, evidently having made the repair. After apologizing to the police for the traffic snarl he had caused, the man drove away. That night he collected several thousand English pounds from friends whom he had bet that he could lie on his back for 30 minutes at the busiest hour in the busiest traffic center in Paris. The man's name was Horace De Vere Cole, England's greatest practical joker of the day.

The most costly punctuation error of all time was committed in November, 1962, when the omission of a hyphen from a set of directions transmitted to a U.S.-Venus space probe rocket resulted in the rocket's destruction.

A microphone placed a few inches away from a toci-toci beetle will not detect the insect's gentle rapping on a stone. Yet a female toci-toci beetle can pick up the vibrations of these mating signals from up to five miles away.

Harrods, a large department store in London, is blessed with three private wells on its Knightsbridge property.

The longest of all worms is the *Lineus longissimus,* or "living fishing line worm." In 1964, a specimen washed ashore at St. Andrews, Scotland, after a storm. It measured more than 180 feet in length.

Any Requests?

An ingenious Californian by the name of Dr. Cecil Nixon constructed a robot in 1940 with uncommon abilities. The doctor, who named his creation Isis, fashioned the instrument in the form of the ancient Egyptian goddess. Isis rested on a couch with a zither on her lap.

The instrument could play any of about 3,000 tunes if asked to do so by anyone within a 12-foot radius. This came about because Isis was constructed so that voice vibrations touched off her complicated mechanism. Isis' right hand picked out the melody on the zither, while her left hand performed the accompaniment.

The machinery inside of Isis included 1,187 wheels and 370 electromagnets. There were numerous other parts. As a crowning touch, Dr. Nixon made Isis react to a warm temperature. When she got hot, she would remove the veil from her face all by herself.

It is not known what has happened to Isis in the 30-odd years since she was built. Apparently, she is not on exhibition anymore.

Domesticated horses have been bred for centuries in almost every country in the world, but of the 38 best-known breeds now in existence, 16 were created in Great Britain. Only four breeds are distinctly American: the Morgan, the Mustang, the American Saddle Horse, and the Hambletonian.

When certain African natives need sutures for first aid, they just dig up a few driver ants and use the insects' huge jaws to clamp together the edges of their wounds.

Locomotive Lore

If railroad trains could be run as efficiently as their model counterparts, rail travel would be significantly improved. The record run by a toy train was achieved at Nuremberg, Germany, in 1971, by a Fleischmann "Black Elephant" HO gauge engine. The tiny workhorse pulled a 62-axle train 1,053 miles over its miniature track without stopping. At scale, this was equivalent to a run of 11,600 miles—more than two round-trips between New York and Los Angeles—at a speed of 123.9 m.p.h. Try to find a train that can match that record!

At any given moment, there are more than 2,000 thunderstorms brewing in the earth's atmosphere.

The world's fastest animal is the cheetah. It has been timed at 70 miles per hour, but many believe that it can do even better over a short haul. Sometimes called the hunting leopard, the cheetah has long been used in India to track down the black buck, the Indian antelope, and other fast game.

The nest of the bald eagle provides a lifelong home for its majestic occupant, and through continual renovation an aerie can weigh over a ton. One eagle's nest at Vermillon, Ohio, measured 12 feet deep and weighed two tons. Try that one in your backyard aviary!

An unconfirmed report to the United States Weather Bureau states that on July 6, 1949, a freak heat wave on the central coast of Portugal resulted in a temperature of 158 degrees, which lasted for two minutes.

Two words in the English language contain the vowels *a, e, i, o, u*, in that order: *abstemious* and *facetious*.

Radio—Alive and Well

Reports of the death of radio are, like those about the death of Mark Twain, greatly exaggerated. More radios were sold in the U.S. in 1971—18,579,000—than in any previous year. And this was more than twice the number of radios sold in 1937, in the "golden age of radio." Today, there are approximately 630 million radios being listened to all over the world. About 354 million of these are in the United States and its possessions—about one-and-a-half sets for every man, woman, and child.

The history of radio begins before Marconi, with the studies of electromagnetic waves conducted by Heinrich Hertz and James Clark Maxwell. But it was Guglielmo Marconi who, in 1895, gave the first demonstration of radio-telegraphy. During the following year, he secured a patent for his system of communication; and in 1901, he accomplished the first transatlantic transmission.

The only gesture man does not share with any other animal is the smile.

Of the 250 known alphabets in the history of language, 50 are still alive today. Half of these are in India.

The duckbill platypus has fangs on its feet

Is it a bird? Well, it lays eggs, and has the bill and webbed feet of a duck. Is it a mammal? Could be. It nurses its young as a dog or cat suckles its offspring. But it burrows tunnels like a rodent. And it has fangs with which it can squirt poisonous venom into an enemy, just like a snake. Then what *is* this strange concoction of a creature? It's a duckbill platypus, one of the oddest specimens in the animal kingdom.

The platypus is usually placed in the mammal family because it nurses its young with milk, but in fact this singular fellow belongs in a class all its own. And the platypus can be found only in that fabulous land of queer and mysterious creatures—Australia.

Since the duckbill lives half in the water and half on land, nature has given it some of the best features of a bird, a reptile, and a mammal. Take the platypus's feet, for instance. Not only are its toes webbed, so that it can swim under water like a turtle or an otter, but it is also equipped with hard, sharp claws for digging tunnels in the mud. And on the inside of each short leg, the platypus has a needle-sharp "fang" made of bone. This dagger is hollow, like a rattlesnake's tooth, and through it the platypus can shoot a deadly poison! If an animal is jabbed with one of these poison needles, he's as good as dead.

Like a duck, a platypus uses its paddlelike snout to poke about in the mud of a river bottom, uncovering worms, snails, and tiny shellfish. Also like a duck, and unlike every other mammal but the spiny anteater, the platypus deposits two crisp white eggs in her tunnel-nest under the river bank, and then sits on them, just like a bird! When the eggs hatch, out pop two peculiar little creatures that look like hairless squirrels.

Naturally, an improbable-looking specimen like the duckbill platypus would be a popular attraction at any zoo. But these crea-

tures have proved very difficult to capture. What is worse, they have not thrived in captivity. If you'd like to catch a glimpse of the strangest of all mammals, you just might have to go to Australia.

Early European lamps were always smoky, because the center of the round wick received too little air for proper combustion. But this drawback was overcome in the 18th century, with the introduction of the flatwick lamp. In that era, the most popular lamp fuel was whale oil; but by the 1840s, kerosene had come to the fore. The kerosene lamp is still in sporadic use today, where gas or electricity are not available.

Aid for the Eyes

If Benjamin Franklin could see his bifocals now, he'd never recognize them. Not the elaborate rhinestone-encrusted variety sported by some vanity fair. For his invention, Ben just stuck two different lenses—one for distance and one for close-up—on top of each other, and went out into the rain to fly his kite.

Half a millennium earlier, Roger Bacon had invented the first pair of spectacles. His discovery of the powers of convex lenses eased the eyestrain of his literate 13th-century contemporaries.

Although reading glasses improved slowly over the centuries, sufferers from astigmatism had to wait until 1827 for Sir George Airy to invent the cylindrical lens. And grapefruit-eaters had to wait until now for a pair of specs fitted with windshield-type wipers.

On September 13, 1922, the thermometers in Azizia, Libya were about ready to burst. On that day, the temperature in the shade soared to 136 degrees Fahrenheit.

The tiniest snow crystal is about 1/500th of an inch in diameter—just a pinpoint. The biggest snowflakes in the world fell in Montana in 1887; they measured 15 inches in diameter and were eight inches thick.

The world's highest free-standing advertising sign beams amid fierce competition in Las Vegas, Nevada, atop the Stardust Hotel. Constructed in 1968, the colossal sign utilizes 25,000 bulbs and 2,500 feet of neon tubing, with individual letters up to 22 feet high.

Diamonds have long been the symbols of undying love. Probably the first suitor to present his fiancee with a diamond ring was Maximilian, Archduke of Austria, in 1477.

The average gem diamond now purchased in the United States weighs a half-carat, and sells for about $250.

One of the men most responsible for the development of the gasoline-powered engine was Carl Benz of Munich, who also supplied one of the first traffic accident statistics. During an exhibition of his 1885 three-wheeled model, he lost control of his car and smashed into a wall. Undaunted, he went on to refine automobile mechanics.

The kiss is not the sole property of the human species, for actions resembling the kiss are found among a great many animals. Birds use their bills in a form of caress. Snails and certain insects caress antennae. And monkeys, of course, are extremely fond of kissing.

A Short Stroll

In 1936, a Norwegian sailor named Mensen Ernst left Constantinople (now Istanbul) on foot and headed east. Crossing mountains, rivers, badlands, and deserts, the 37-year-old Ernst journeyed 2,800 miles to Calcutta—and then turned around and walked back to Constantinople! Ernst made the 5,589-mile round trip in only 59 days.

Shah Jehan, the Indian monarch who built the Taj Mahal, planned to build an identical structure on the bank of the Jumma River opposite the Taj. The second structure was to be built of black marble, to contrast with the white Taj, and would have been connected to the Taj by a silver bridge.

The Biggest Bang

The volcanic eruption on Krakatoa in 1883—the loudest and most powerful explosion in history—sent a massive tidal wave halfway around the world. A Dutch warship in the harbor of Batavia (now Djakarta) was washed ashore by the tremendous wave and left stranded a half mile inland and 30 feet above sea level. The wave—which at some points was 120 feet high—traveled 5,450 miles to South Africa in less than 12 hours.

Eskimo boys of three and four years old may be seen smoking pipes! Little girls are not allowed the privilege. A father is very proud when his son picks up the knack, for smoking is considered a sign of manliness.

The blue whale is the largest and most powerful animal ever to have graced the planet. The largest accurately measured specimen was captured off Scotland in 1926; it measured 109 feet 4¼ inches in length. A whale caught off Argentina five years later is said to have weighed 195 tons.

The first European book mentioning tea was published in Venice in 1559. The first account of tea in English appeared in 1598 in the *Voyages and Travels* of Hugo van Linschooten, a Dutchman who had drunk tea in the far-away, mysterious Orient. Perhaps it was because of him that the Dutch were the first people in Europe to drink tea. During the 1660s, their ships carried most of the leaf to the West. In 1669, the East India Company began transporting tea to England from Java.

Swapping Spouses

The exchanging of wives is still practiced among the Eskimos, sometimes for quite practical reasons. For instance, if a man who is going on a journey has a wife encumbered with a child, he may exchange wives with a friend who is remaining in camp and therefore will not suffer any inconvenience.

Among the Himalayan mountaineers, the exchanging of wives was a common practice when two men became disgusted with their spouses and hoped thereby to effect an improved domestic arrangement.

The sentence believed to be the longest ever to appear in literature is found in Victor Hugo's *Les Misérables*. This sentence contains 823 words, 93 commas, 51 semicolons, and 4 dashes, and occupies almost three full pages.

A Chinese priest in Shanghai reportedly let his fingernails grow for 27 years. The nails reached a length of 22¾ inches.

The silkworm spins a thread 12,000 times as long as its body. That's comparable to a six-foot man spinning a thread 15 miles long.

Milo of Crotona carried an ox across the stadium at Olympia

The greatest wrestler and strongman of the ancient world was a Greek named Milon. He hailed from the southern Italian city of Croton, a Greek colony founded in the 8th century B.C. by settlers from Achaea. He is more commonly known by the Latin form of his name: Milo of Crotona.

Milo was a man of diversified interests and attainments. Skilled as a soldier and singer, he was a favorite disciple of the famous philosopher-mathematician Pythagoras, and he was himself the author of the *Physica*, a book on science and natural history. But above all, Milo was renowned as an athlete. His specialties were wrestling and feats of strength.

Milo won the wrestling championship at each of the six meetings of Olympic Games between 540 and 516 B.C. He was the only man in the history of the ancient Olympics (776 B.C. to A.D. 393) to win so many victories in any sport. Milo's achievement becomes even more impressive when one notes that his active career as a wrestler covered more than 24 years, an extremely long time for an athlete to maintain himself at championship peak.

Milo's amazing feats are recorded in the writings of such reliable ancient historians as Pausanias, Plutarch, and Strabo. According to their reports, Milo's fingers were so powerful that no one could bend them when he extended his hand horizontally. On one occasion, Milo enclosed a tender pomegranate in his mighty fist. Scores of other athletes tried to get it away from him, but none succeeded. When Milo finally opened his hand, there was not the slightest bruise on the fruit.

Milo is best known, however, for a feat he performed on the opening day of one of the meetings of the Olympic Games. Carrying a full-grown ox on his shoulders—the ox must have weighed at least a ton—Milo strolled effortlessly into the stadium at Olympia. Before the amazed eyes of thousands, he carried the ox across the playing field. The story goes on

to say that he slaughtered the ox, which he may have, but the legend that he ate all the meat on that same day seems apocryphal.

Tragically, it was Milo's incredible strength that proved to be his doom. Walking in the wilds one day, Milo chanced upon a tree whose trunk was partially split. Never one to turn away from a challenge, the giant tried to rip the two parts asunder. However, Milo's hand became caught in the tree trunk and, with no companion to free him, Milo was devoured that night by wolves.

The modern copy machine was born on October 22, 1938, when patent lawyer Chester Carlson first demonstrated the principle of electrostatic printing. Carlson brought his invention to more than 50 corporations seeking financial backing—and was turned away from all of them. It wasn't until 1960 that the first Xerox copier reached the market. The Xerox Corporation now claims world-wide revenues of some $5.7 billion a year.

Long Island, New York, is probably the most well-known island in the United States. But there are more than 26,000 other islands, ten acres or larger, within the jurisdiction of the 48 states. Maine alone has more than 1,000 of them. They range in size from Long Island, with an area of 1,401 square miles, and Isle Royale, Michigan, 210 square miles, to Santa Barbara Island, off the coast of California, which has an area of just two square miles.

Winston Churchill, an insomniac, had two beds in his bedroom. When he failed to fall asleep on one, he simply moved to the other.

In the African nation of Upper Volta, only 737 infants of every 1,000 survive. In Sweden, the nation with the lowest infant mortality rate, more than 992 infants in every 1,000 survive. The United States, by the way, ranks 17th on the list of nations with the lowest infant mortality rate.

Horse racing as a sport was popular as long ago as 1400 B.C., in the Hittite culture of Asia Minor. Today, horse racing can be found in almost every country in the world. Horse racing is now the number-one spectator sport in the United States.

A pair of mules cannot mate to produce a young mule. For the most part, mules are sterile. The young must be bred from horses and donkies—usually, a male ass and a mare.

It sounds incredible, but it's true. In the town of Spearfish, South Dakota, the thermometer once soared from four degrees below zero to 45 degrees in the stretch of just two minutes! That's a rise of 49 degrees, or more than 24 degrees per minute!

In Browning, Montana, the temperature once plummetted from 44 degrees to 56 degrees below zero in a 24-hour period. That's a drop of 100 degrees! And in Rapid City, South Dakota, the temperature once dropped from 55 degrees to eight degrees—a total drop of 47 degrees—in just 15 minutes! Now that's rapid!

Actors are notoriously superstitious. One of the more curious theater traditions is that "George Spelvin" is a charmed name, and the alias has been used by thousands of thespians, usually as a second name when the player has two parts in the same production.

The mythical Mr. Spelvin originated on Broadway in 1907, as a member of the cast of *Brewster's Millions*. The cognomen quickly acquired a reputation of being lucky, and it continues to crop up in playbill cast-lists today. Among the variations of the name are Georgette Spelvin, for actresses, and George Spelvin, Jr., for juvenile actors. In 1922, when the Moscow Art Theatre came to New York, one Gregor Spelvanovich was listed in the program!

The first apple orchard in the United States was planted on the slope of what is now Beacon Hill, in Boston, in 1625. By the beginning of this century, over a thousand varieties of apple were being grown in this country.

The idea of execution according to class dates back to ancient Rome, where crucifixion was reserved for slaves and common criminals. Other victims were hurled to their death from the Tarpeian Rocks, or fed to wild animals in the Coliseum.

Crucifixion, by the way, was practiced in Japan as late as the nineteenth century.

There are literally dozens of halls of fame in the United States. The National Baseball Hall of Fame in Cooperstown, New York, and the Professional Football Hall of Fame in Canton, Ohio, might come immediately to mind. But there's also the Weighlifter's Hall of Fame, in York, Pennsylvania; the National Polish-American Sports Hall of Fame, in Detroit; the Amateur Trapshooting Hall of Fame in Vandalia, Ohio; the Circus Hall of Fame in Sarasota, Florida; the International Softball Congress Hall of Fame in Long Beach, California; the National Bowling Museum and Hall of Fame in Milwaukee; the National Cowboy Hall of Fame and Western Heritage Center in Oklahoma City, Oklahoma; and the National Soaring Museum in Elmira, New York.

A of 1978, Elvis Presley has earned more gold records than anyone else in music history. Twenty-one of Elvis' records sold a million or more copies. The Beatles and the Rolling Stones have 20 golden records, Andy Williams has 17, Bob Dylan, 15, and Frank Sinatra, 14.

There are approximately 27 dwarfs for every midget in the world. Midgets, of whom there are about 3,000 alive today, are well-proportioned diminutive individuals, while the more common dwarfs, whose numbers are estimated at 55,000, have normal size heads and torsos on child sized legs.

Would you like to venture a guess as to the largest city in the United States, in total land area? No, it's not New York, nor Los Angeles, nor Chicago. The largest city in the United States is actually Jacksonville, Florida, which comprises some 766 square miles!

No train has ever run over the tracks of the Hampden Railroad, near Belchertown, Mass.

Silent "Talkies"

In 1910, 16 years before the motion-picture industry added sound tracks to films movies were especially made for the deaf in sign language.

In the 1890s, a Le Roy, New York, woman named May Wait concocted a mix of sugar, powdered gelatin, and artificial fruit flavors that she christened Jell-O. Wait's product found its way to few American homes before it was bought by the food tycoon Frank Woodward, who was already marketing a coffee and tea substitute named Grain-O. A genius in packaging, mass marketing, and advertising, Woodward within a few years turned Jell-O into a household word.

By 1925, Jell-O was a big-money industry. In that year, Jell-O joined Postum to form General Foods, today one of the largest corporations in America. Talk about humble beginnings!

The ancient Greeks usually drank their wine diluted with water. Thus, the wine Athenians quaffed during their cocktail hour was probably less than eight percent alcohol, a weak beverage by modern standards. In fact, most of the wine the Greeks and Romans enjoyed would probably taste rather crude to the modern palate. After all, we live in an age when an avid oenologist paid over $14,000 for a single bottle of 1806 Chateau Lafite-Rothschild!

The word "tulip" has a rather odd origin. When the tulip was introduced to Europe, many gardeners saw a resemblance between the flower's shape and Turkish headwear, and dubbed the flower *tulipan*, from *tulbend*, a Turkish word for "turban." From tulipan came the French word *tulipe* and the English "tulip." There is, as you can see, only a whimsical connection between "tulips" and "two lips."

Trifling with Truffles

Hunting for the truffle—a subterranean fungus that is presently the most expensive food in the world—is a difficult, delicate operation. Since the fungus grows underground, it's virtually impossible to tell where a crop of the delicacies might be found. But French and Italian farmers have developed a number of tricks.

Most truffle hunting is carried out with the aid of specially trained pigs, called "rooting hogs." The pigs are excellent at scenting out the truffles, but they present the farmer with additional problems. Once a pig locates a truffle, he's likely to gobble it right up before the farmer can chase him off. Farmers can train pigs to search for truffles in a matter of days—but it may take two or three years to teach them not to eat their find!

The Babylonian Code of Hammurabi, dating from around 1750 B.C., set down regulations for drinking houses. Egyptian doctors frequently prescribed alcohol as a medicine. By studying the remains of the Egyptian and Babylonian cultures, we can conclude that alcoholism has been a problem for well over 4,000 years.

A Quick Game of Chess

Computer chess? Forget it. Since a chess player has about 30 moves to choose from on each turn, and his opponent has about 30 possible answers to each of these 30 moves, then there are roughly 1,000 variations to just one complete move. Each of these complete moves allows another 1,000 potential moves, and so on. Thus, a computer would have to consider about 10^{75} (1 and 75 zeroes) moves to determine the outcome of a short 25-move game. Even if the computer could calculate a million moves each second—far more than is now feasible—it would require 10^{69} seconds to complete the calculations for the game.

How long is that? Well, since the beginning of our solar system, 4.5 billion years ago, only 10^{18} seconds have elapsed.

Undaunted, companies *are* marketing computer chess games.

In Britanny, custom dictates that a young man can express his interest in a favored maiden by offering to carry her umbrella at the fair. Carrying her umbrella along the road is considered a sure sign of engagement.

Paper money is a Chinese invention, dating from the seventh century, although some Chinese historians claim that paper money was actually first printed there in 119 B.C. The first bank notes were not placed in service until 1661, in Sweden.

Wordsworth

"Look it up in the dictionary" is a piece of advice foreign to few ears. But did you realize that until the 18th century speakers of English had no lexicographic authority to consult for the meaning of the thousands of English words now nestled between *aardvark* and *zymurgy*?

English works bearing the title "dictionary" (in its Latin form, *dictionarius*) appeared as early as the 13th century, but these books were intended only as aids to the study of Latin. Other early wordbooks dealt only with troublesome words. It wasn't until 1702 that a book defining words in everyday usage was published in English.

In ancient Greece, aristocratic women owned as many as 20 pairs of shoes, with a style to match every occasion. Slaves were employed solely to carry a supply of their lady's shoes when she left home, assuring that she would be appropriately shod throughout her travels.

Many medieval monasteries were built atop steep cliffs or surrounded by high walls, and some of the more unsociable cloisters depended upon a device known as the basket elevator for entry and exit. The basket elevator was just that—a basket in which the passenger was lifted or lowered by rope along the outside of the monastery walls. Not the most gracious entry, perhaps, but unwanted guests certainly posed little problem.

A popular Mideastern eggplant dish, *Imam Bayaldi*, owes its name to 16th-century Ottoman Turks. According to a legend, a holy man, or Imam, was served a particular eggplant dish by a beautiful woman. When she bent over to present the dish, her veil slipped from her face for a moment. The holy man, captivated by this brief glimpse of her beauty, and overwhelmed by the aroma of the succulent food, simply passed out. The dish was then christened *Imam Bayaldi*—"the priest has fainted."

The expression "raining cats and dogs" has many reputed origins. The most gruesome holds that during the 17th and 18th centuries in England, a heavy cloudburst would fill the gutters with a torrent of refuse not unlikely to include a number of dead dogs and cats. A poem by Jonathan Swift describing a city rainstorm ends with the ones:

> *Drown'd Puppies, stinking Sprats, all drench'd in Mud,*
> *Dead cats and Turnep-tops come tumbling down the Flood.*

The word "unabridged" in a dictionary title does not mean the work contains all the words in the language, but merely that the book includes all entries appearing in earlier editions of the work. No English dictionary but the *Oxford English Dictionary* claims to include anywhere near all the words in the language.

There are three kinds of electric streetcar. One is drawn by cable, another powered by an electrified third rail, and the third is powered by overhead transmission lines, with the car connected to the power lines by a collapsible apparatus called the *trolley*. Strictly speaking, then, only a streetcar powered by overhead lines can be called a "trolley."

The highest valued paper currency ever printed were U.S. gold certificates issued in 1934, worth $100,000. In case you've never seen one, the bill bore the head of President Woodrow Wilson. The highest denomination notes still in circulation are U.S. Federal Reserve Bank notes worth $100,000, but none has been printed since 1944. According to present plans, no further bills over $100 will ever be issued.

The least valuable bill in existence today is the one-cent Hong Kong note, worth just one-fifth of a U.S. penny.

It wasn't until 1836 that scientists found a way of growing vanilla outside Mexico. Charles Morren, a Belgian botanist, discovered that the vanilla plant was pollinated by the Melipone bee, a tiny insect that lives only in Mexico. Thus, the plant could not be naturally pollinated in another country. Morren found a method for artificially pollinating the plant, and vanilla plantations soon began appearing in many of France's colonial possessions.

The water pipe, a popular means of smoking in the Near East for centuries, was probably invented by the Persians for smoking hashish. In a water pipe, smoke is drawn from the bowl into the base, where it is cooled by water vapor and then drawn through the stem. Some Persian men were so partial to the taste of smoke-flavored water that they regularly forced their wives to smoke four or five bowlfuls of tobacco or hashish in succession to produce a well-flavored drink.

The first transatlantic telephone service was inaugurated between New York and London in 1927—with a charge of $75 for the first three minutes. Today, the same call will cost you less than four dollars.

Angostura bitters have been with us since 1824, when a German doctor living in Venezuela prepared them as a tonic for his ailing wife. He reportedly learned the recipe from sailors, who frequently added bitters to rum as a cure for seasickness—and presumably, a host of other ailments. When angostura bitters became part of the Manhattan cocktail, their place behind the bar was established forevermore.

Without doubt, the card game most widely around the world today is contract bridge, a partnership game played by four persons. Bridge is derived from whist, which can be traced back to 1529. Today, bridge is played by over 30 million people in the United States, of whom 200,000 are dues-paying members of the American Contract Bridge League. And it's estimated that over 60 million people play bridge throughout the world!

Fawning over the Feline

The ancient Egyptians tamed a species of wild African cat, *Felis lybica*, an animal about the size of the modern house cat, and put him to work protecting grain supplies from rodents. Egyptian artwork also depicts small cats killing snakes in the royal household. Rodent-hunting cats proved so valuable that the Egyptians considered them representations of the gods.

The Egyptians went so far in their ailurophilia—love of cats—as to embalm cats, as they would a member of the royal household. Thousands of cat mummies have been found in Egyptian ruins—along with even more mouse mummies, presumably entombed to provide food for the resurrected cats. In the 1890s, 180,000 mummified cats found near Cairo were auctioned off in England, where many were used as fuel. The auctioneer used a mummified cat as a gavel to peddle the cats in ton lots.

The first automobile license plates appeared in France in 1893. England's first plate, A1, was purchased in 1903 by Lord Russell, after an overnight wait outside the license bureau office. That plate was reportedly sold to a collector in 1973 for $35,000!

To Golf or Not to Golf

"It looketh like a silly game," quoth King James IV of Scotland in 1491, signing a law that prohibited the playing of golf. "I'll not have our brave boys beating up the pasture with a stick when they could be out a-practicing with the trusty bow-and-arrow!"

"Why do ye not try it yourself, sire?" queried a crafty courier.

"Aye," said the king. "I'll do that. But only to show ye that it be a silly game."

"If your Majesty would borrow my sticks . . . ." volunteered another.

And that's why the law of 1491 was repealed. But you can be sure that the Scots would have continued to play their game, law or no law. Golf is the national game of Scotland, and no land has ever had a fiercer devotion to a sport.

Since the mid-15th century, golf has enjoyed great popularity in Scotland, but the origins of the game probably go back much further in time. The word "golf" is commonly supposed to be an adaptation of the Dutch word *kolf* ("club"), but this is highly uncertain, for there is no record of the Dutch having played a game analogous to the Scots' golf.

Of all the foodstuffs indigenous to the Americans, none is as useful as the potato. Potatoes are easy to cultivate and can be stored for long periods of time. To give you an idea of the fecundity of the potato, in 1968, an English farmer reported that just six seed potatoes had yielded a whopping 1,190 pounds of spuds.

Potatoes are also one of the cheapest and most versatile foods available. Americans now consume some 35 billion pounds of potatoes each year, with the most well-known varieties hailing from Idaho, Maine, and Long Island.

The small fold-up knives we call pocketknives are older than pockets themselves! The metalworkers of ancient Rome produced the first known fold-up knives.

The Roman implements were about three inches long when shut, fashioned without a spring or "nail nick"—the groove used to open the blade. The handles were often elaborately carved. One pocketknife surviving from the first century features an ivory handle skillfully carved into the shape of an armored gladiator. Another Roman knife, now in the British Museum, had the carver's name scratched into the handle.

In 1945, there were but 16,500 television sets in the United States. Today, there are more TV sets than bathtubs in this country. Some 960 TV stations beam their signals at 100 million television sets in 72 million American homes. That's almost one TV set for every two Americans!

In the early decades of this century, many apartments in America were equipped with a bathtub in the kitchen. When European immigrants arrived here, many considered the bathtub an unnecessary luxury, and used the tub as a planter for flowers and vegetables.

Watching the Clouds Sail By

They look so different at different times—and the same cloud looks so different to each one of us.

Today, meteorologists still use a modification of Luke Howard's classification of clouds into four basic types: cirrus, cumulus, stratus, and nimbus.

Each artist will treat a cloud in his own manner. There follows a number of unusual treatments.

"Califlower clouds" as represented in a drawing in the Century Dictionary.

By a Russian painter. Picture appears in Fifty Years of Soviet Art, *published in Moscow.*

By an early German master

*Paul Gustave Dore (1833-1883) was a masterful draftsman, whose book illustrations
are known for their imagination in depicting the weird and the gloomy.*

This drawing first appeared in Modern Pen Drawing, *published in London in 1901 by The Studio.*

Cumulus clouds as shown in a drawing from Leslie's, a famous magazine of the late 1800s

A drawing from the London Illustrated News *which shows the steam tug Resolute of Liverpool in a storm*

Drawing by Grandville, famous French satirist. This drawing first appeared in
Le Magasin Pittoresque

Before this century, the glue needed for gelatin had to be laboriously extracted from meat bones. In the Middle Ages, deer antlers were a popular source of the glue; later, calves' feet and knuckles. Housewives in the 19th century used isinglass, made from the membranes of fish bladders.

Then, in 1890, a Jamestown, New York man named Charles B. Knox was watching his wife make calves'-foot jelly when he decided that a prepackaged, easy-to-use gelatin mix was just what the housewife needed. Knox set out to develop, manufacture, and distribute the granulated gelatin, while his wife invented recipes for the new kitchen staple. Now everyone could make gelatin—in minutes instead of hours.

One of the great musical partnerships was that of Gilbert and Sullivan, librettist and composer respectively of 14 of the most famous and beloved operettas in history. But these men, who made such beautiful music together, cordially detested one another on the personal level, and their collaboration, in the years 1871 to 1896, was conducted almost entirely by mail.

Indeed, three times, the authors of *The Mikado, The Pirates of Penzance,* and other popular light operas swore never to work together again, but after trying unsuccessfully to team up with other individuals, the two enemies found that they could work with no one else.

Tons of Fun

Pierre S. Du Pont loved organ music—and how. Du Pont owned what was probably the largest residential organ ever—a 55-ton Aeolian. The instrument, which required 14 freight cars to ship it to Du Pont's Longwood estate in Pennsylvania, cost close to $300,000, and had 10,000 pipes, one pedal, and four manual keyboards.

Get Them to the Church on Time!

For 33 years—from 1798 to 1828—the streets of Philadelphia were blockaded every Sunday with huge chains. The roadblocks were instituted by the city's clergymen, who objected that the use of the horse and buggy on the Sabbath had caused a marked decline in church attendance.

Opera singer Nellie Melba gave her name to the dessert Peach Melba, but Jenny Lind, "the Swedish nightingale," outdid Miss Melba many times over. During her concert tour in this country during 1850-1852, the Swedish coluratura created a veritable "Lindomania." Thousands of articles were christened after her—these included bonnets, beds, men's pipes, vest buttons, sausages, trout flies, playing cards, wall papers, whiskies, a race horse, and even a clipper ship. This collection of "Lindiana," or products on which Miss Lind's name and picture appear as a trademark, has been preserved by the New York Historical Society in New York City.

The British eat one large loaf of bread each a week; the French and Germans, 1½ large loaves; and the Italians, 2¼ each a week.

The idea of boxing gloves was inspired by the leather covers encasing the spurs of game cocks during training bouts, to prevent the bellicose birds from killing one another before the fight.

Funny Money

Until the seventh or eighth century B.C., money *per se* did not exist. Early man's commerce was built on the barter system, involving a simple exchange of goods.

Among early hunters, tanned hides were useful as a medium of exchange, for everyone could put the hides to use for clothing. Leather money was used in Russia right up until the 17th century, as was tea money in China. Hundreds of other items have served for a time as legal tender, including slaves, tobacco, gunpowder, pig jawbones, and glass beads. Salt once passed for dough in Ethiopia, and skulls were hard cash in Borneo.

Pressing Matters

Close to one-fourth of the newspapers published in the world today are brought out in America—1,768 in 1975—with a total paid circulation of close to 62 million copies daily. But the single newspaper with the largest daily circulation is the Russian *Pravda*, with a reputed circulation of ten million copies. *Pravda* (which means "truth" in Russian) was begun in 1912. After the 1917 revolution, it became the leading organ of the Russian Communist party. *Izvestia*, the official newspaper of the Soviet government, is the second newspaper in the world in terms of circulation, with eight million copies sold per day.

The Japanese daly *Asahi Shimbun* ranks third in circulation, at just over seven million copies per day, and two other Japanese paper claim a circulation in excess of five million. The largest paper in England is now the *London Daily Mirror*, with some four million copies sold per day, and both the *Daily Sun* and the *Daily Express* own circulations close to the three million mark. And the *Evening News*, with an average circulation of over a half-million, is the world's best-selling evening newspaper.

Only a half a dozen men have ever devised a successful alphabet. Of these, perhaps the most famous individual was Sequoya (1770?-1843), a half-Cherokee American Indian who also used the name George Guess. Sequoya, who created the 85 letters of the Cherokee alphabet in 1821, is honored by a statue in the Capitol, in Washington, D.C., and by Sequoia Country, Oklahoma, where his cabin has been preserved as an historical site. But Sequoya's greatest monument are the giant Sequoia trees that bear his name in Sequoia National Park.

The infamous "witch trials," held in Salem, Massachusetts in 1692, were instigated by one man, fire-and-brimstone preacher Cotton Mather. Mather, who lived from 1663 to 1728, claimed to be an authority not only on witches, but on the Devil himself, who, said Mather, spoke impeccable Greek, Latin, and Hebrew, but whose English was oddly accented.

Relics of prehistoric man 20,000 years old include bone needles with eyes and pins with decorated heads. The art of pin-making actually predates agriculture, pottery, and metalworking.

Among the most—literally—colorful freaks traveling with the Barnum circus in the 1870s was a Greek named Georgius Constantine. Constantine was billed as the most-tatooed man in history, and indeed, no one has ever disputed his claim. Not one quarter-inch of Constantine's skin was left bare—even his eyelids and the insides of his ears were tatooed. The lavish ornamentation of Constantine's body—consisting of 388 designs in all—was accomplished by six tatooers over a period of three months.

Call a Club a Club

You must have wondered, at some time or another, how the suit of playing cards called clubs received its name. After all, the spade, heart, and diamond symbols all resemble their namesakes. But the club symbol looks like a clover leaf, certainly not a club.

To explain this anomaly, we'll have to take a look at the evolution of the suit names in various European countries. Playing cards were probably first manufactured in Italy and Spain, during the 14th century. In those countries, decks of the time were divided into four suits: cups, swords, money, and clubs. The Italian deck had a suit of 14 cards (the modern 13 plus the Knight), the Spanish deck had a suit of 13 cards (the Italian deck minus the Queen).

The four suits originally may have denoted the four estates of medieval man. The cup, or chalice, represented the clergy, the ruling class of the day. The sword represented the military class. Money represented the commercial class. And the club, initially a plain piece of wood, represented the peasant agricultural class.

In Germany, the cup became the heart, indicative of courage and the noble virtues of the clergy and ruling class. Swords became acorns, money became bells, and clubs became leaves. Early German decks had no Queen, but two Jacks in each suit.

The French adopted the heart (*coeur*), but substituted the pike (*pique*) for the sword. For money, the French adopted the *carreau*, or paving tile, a symbol of building and the merchant class. And for the club, the French chose the clover leaf (*trefle*), likewise a symbol of agriculture. Cards with the French symbols were easier to produce and read than cards with the larger, more elaborate symbols of the Italian and Spanish decks. And the French were the first to divide the suits into two red suits and two black suits.

The earliest English cardmakers, who worked in the 16th century, used the French deck as their model. The French *coeur* became the English heart, of course. But while the English borrowed the French symbol for the pike, they adopted the Italian word for swords, *spade*. Similarly, they employed the French symbol for the clover leaf, but retained the older Italian and Spanish name, *clubs*. And the word *diamond*, in place of the French word for tile, may have been chosen as a symbol of wealth, since the French *carreau* suit was equivalent to the Italian and Spanish money suit.

Now, the next time you're in the middle of a hot poker game and someone wonders where the club received its name, you'll know the answer.

KING OF SPADES
(French, c. 1490)
In French decks, the King of spades was usually called David, after the Biblical king. The modern French King of spades still shows a harp, since David was a musician as well as a warrior.

QUEEN OF SPADES
(French, 15th century)
In most French decks, the Queen of spades was represented by Pallas, the goddess of war and wisdom. This Queen, however, bears a representation of *La Pucelle*, Joan of Arc.

KING OF CLUBS
(Spanish, c. 1500)
The Spanish and Italian decks were the only early decks containing the clubs suit. Our modern deck has retained the word "clubs," but not the clubs symbol.

KING OF MONEY
(Spanish, c. 1500)
The circular figure in the right-hand corner represents a gold coin. The Spanish called the suit *oros*, or "gold pieces."

TWO OF SWORDS
(Spanish, c. 1500)
The swords suit of the Spanish deck became the French *pique* (pike), and eventually, the English spades.

JACK OF CUPS
(Spanish, 18th century)
In this deck, the court figures of each suit wore the garb of a different period. The cups suit figures wore costumes of the Carlos I period, around 1550.

KNIGHT OF SWORDS
(Spanish, 18th century)
Spanish decks of the period included a King, Knight, and Jack, but no Queen. The swords suit figures in this deck wore clothing from the Roman Empire.

JACK OF SWORDS
(Spanish, 18th century)
The Spanish word for the Jack was *La Sota*, meaning "helper" or "underling." The Jack was always depicted on foot, the Knight always mounted.

FOUR OF CUPS
(Spanish, 1816)
The cups are actually chalices, for the cups suit originally represented the clergy. The inscription contains the manufacturer's name.

KNIGHT OF CLUBS
(Spanish, 18th century)
The clubs suit figures in this deck were depicted in Oriental garb.

KING OF SPADES
(German, 1815)
In this deck, each of the Kings was represented by a general of the armies allied against Napoleonic France. The King of spades bore a representation of the Duke of Wellington.

KING OF CUPS
(Spanish, 20th century)
The number 12 above the cup indicated that the King is the highest ranking member of his 12-card suit. The Spanish deck had no ten; the hierarchy of cards was thus: nine, Jack (10), Knight (11), and King (12).

JACK OF HEARTS
(French, late 18th century)
In this deck from Revolutionary France, the court figures were replaced by republican heroes. The Kings were Voltaire, Moliere, Rousseau, and La Fontaine. This jack bears a representation of the revolutionary soldier, the *sans-culotte*.

QUEEN OF CLUBS
(French, 20th century)
The Queen of clubs usually bore the name Argine, probably an anagram for the Latin *regina*, "queen." This queen may be a portrait of Maria de Medici, wife of Henry IV of France.

FOUR OF MONEY
(Spanish, 20th century)
In the Spanish deck, the four of each suit usually bears a fanciful figure of some kind, such as the unicorn.

JACK OF SPADES
(French, 18th century)
During the 18th century, cardmakers from Lyons often depicted the Jack of spades with a pipe in his mouth, perhaps due to the similarity between the French words *pipes* and *pique*.

JACK OF CLUBS
(Spanish, 20th century)
In Spanish decks, the border of each card was broken in places according to the suit: no breaks for money; one break for cups; two breaks for swords; and three for clubs.

KING OF CLUBS
(French, 17th century)
The King of clubs in most French decks bore the name Lexander, but this one bears the name Artus, for King Arthur of the Round Table.

JACK OF DIAMONDS
(French, 1702)
Jacks of this period were often depicted wearing beards. The inscription at the bottom refers to the cardmaker.

During the 16th century, when heavy silver coins were widely used throughout Europe, Bohemian coins minted in St. Joachimsthal were considered the purest. They therefore formed the standard of excellence. From Joachimsthaler comes the older words *thaler* and *daler*, and of course, the almighty *dollar*.

Gophers love to eat the lead sheath around telephone cables, thereby disrupting transcontinental service.

By the middle of 1942, Nazi Germany and its allies controlled a larger portion of Continental Europe than had ever been held by any single nation in history—including the Roman Empire! At that time, only neutral Switzerland, Spain, Sweden, Portugal, and parts of European Russia remained out of German control.

The U.S. Interstate Highway System is the largest single construction project ever undertaken by man, outstripping even the Pyramids or the Great Wall of China in required funding and man-hours of labor. When complete, the system will include about 42,500 miles of divided highway, accommodating an estimated 25 percent of all traffic in this country. The system was 80 percent complete in the mid-70s.

Merry Old Cole

According to most accounts, the idea of a Christmas greeting card sprang from the brain of Sir Henry Cole, the first director of the Victoria and Albert Museum in London. In 1843, Cole commissioned John Collcott Horsley, a fashionable artist of the time, to design his first card. The artist produced a card consisting of one unfolded sheet, oblong in shape, with a rustic bower forming a frame for three illustrations.

The central scene depicted a typical middle-class Victorian family gathered around a table, drinking to the health of an absent friend—the card's recipient. The card also showed two moralistic scenes, and a banner carrying the greeting "A Merry Christmas and a Happy New Year to you." Christmas cards haven't changed much, have they?

The third-century Roman emperor, Heliogabalus, maintained a fleet of fishing boats exclusively for obtaining eel roe. The captured eels were placed in tugs and fattened on the meat of Christians slain in the Colosseum.

The ancient Romans adopted a form of gold standard for their monetary system, and stored their reserves in the Temple of Juno Moneta. Moneta became the mint, and Juno was regarded as the goddess of money. Such was the origin of that almighty word, *money*.

There were few inventions of the late 19th century that Thomas Edison didn't at least dabble with, and the typewriter was no exception. In fact, Edison constructed the first electric typewriter, which printed letters on a moving roll of paper. Edison's device eventually became the ticker-tape machine.

The nation with the highest per capita phone ownership is the tiny principality of Monaco, with 825 phones per 1,000 persons, compared with about 670 in the United States. The nation with the lowest per capita phone use is the Himalayan kingdom of Bhutan, with just one phone per 2,000 persons!

Circus-goers love the piping melodies of the calliope. The instrument, which consists of steam whistles played by the means of a keyboard, originated in 1855 as an entertainment aboard riverboats. For 20 years, steamboat travelers enjoyed the music of these "floating music boxes." Then steamboats discarded the instruments in favor of other modes of entertainment. But the calliope soon found a home under the Big Top, and still remains the instrument employed by circuses and carnivals.

Cocktail Tales

The origin of the word "cocktail" is uncertain. One claim maintains that it comes from a French drink served in New Orleans in the 1800s, called a *coquetier*, named for the tiny egg-cup in which the drink was usually served to women. Another claim traces the name of the beverage to England, where in the Yorkshire dialect the word "cocktail" referred to foam spilling over a glass of ale.

According to some, the first cocktail in this country was served in a tavern in Elmsford, New York, where cockfights were often held. The story has it that Betsy Flanagan, a barmaid, decorated the bar with the tail feathers of some of the deceased combatants, and inserted one in a mixed drink when an inebriate requested "one of those cocktails." Another story tells us that as a publicity stunt, the proprietor of the tavern regularly inserted the tail feathers of fighting cocks in his mixed drinks, the feathers to be used as swizzle sticks.

Minutiae

The atomic particle known as the *neutrino* is so small that it can penetrate solid matter without once colliding with any of its component atoms. To the neutrino, the spaces between atoms, and between the particles that constitute the atom, are so vast that the neutrino can pass through an atom like a spaceship navigating between stars. Scientists have estimated that a neutrino can pass through 3,500 light-years—one light-year is equivalent to about six trillion miles—of solid lead without being absorbed by any of the lead atoms!

Neutrinos bombard earth continually, but go unnoticed. Each second, billions of these particles pass through your body without interacting with the atoms that comprise it.

The smallest crowd ever to attend a major-league baseball game turned up at the ballpark in Troy, New York, on the last day of the 1881 season. The match between the home team and the Chicago White Stockings was played in a torrential downpour—and witnessed by just 12 die-hard fans!

The library in Alexandria, Egypt, founded in the third century B.C., contained some 750,000 volumes—including a copy of almost every written work in existence at the time. A series of fires and thefts gradually depleted the library. In 646, the volumes that remained were burned by the invading Arabs. Many of the papyrus scrolls were put to the torch to heat the baths of Alexandria!

A poll conducted recently in West Germany revealed that over 20 percent of all German men brush their teeth only on "special occasions."

The *New York Daily News*, founded in 1919 by three Chicago publishers, is the largest newspaper in the United States, selling some two million copies daily. The *Los Angeles Times* is the nation's second best-selling newspaper, with about one million copies sold per day. The *New York Times* follows in the number-three position. Rounding out the top ten are, in order: the *Chicago Tribune*, the *Detroit News*, the *Detroit Free Press*, the *Chicago Sun-Times*, the *Philadelphia Bulletin*, the *New York Post*, and the *Washington Post*.

But the *Wall Street Journal*, published around the nation rather than in one particular city, officially ranks as the number-two American daily, with a circulation of some one-and-a-half million copies.

Before the invention of the printing press, German artists produced woodcuts arranged in panel form like the modern comic strip, dealing chiefly with religious history and current politics. Detective-comic buffs might be amused to learn that German artists began producing crime strips as early as the 16th century. Most strips illustrated heinous crimes and the punishment the perpetrators could expect to receive—in gory detail.

Alcohol is the oldest and most wide-used drug on earth. Primitive man probably discovered the first alcoholic drinks by accident, since any sugar-containing mishmash left exposed to warm air will eventually ferment. Studies of alcohol use among various preiterate societies suggest that alcohol was used by prehistoric man primarily in conjunction with war, religious worship, and various rites of passage—births, marriages, funerals, and feasts.

The ancient Romans ate parsley to prevent drunkenness.

According to some accounts, the expression "to fight like Kilkenny cats" dates back to a rather sadistic custom among Hessian soldiers stationed in Ireland: tying two cats together by the tails and hanging them over a fence or clothesline. One day, the story goes, an officer happened upon a group of soldiers thus occupied. To hide their deed, one soldier cut off the tails of both tormented animals. The officer was then told that the cats had fought so hard that they'd devoured each other, leaving only the tails.

Some inventive individuals have put the familiar bathtub to a rather strange use: bathtub racing. Tubs fitted with outboard motors annually race over a 36-mile course near Vancouver, British Columbia.

Reportedly, the record distance achieved by a hand-propelled bathtub in 24 hours is an impressive 36.6 miles.

As late as 1909, when there were few traffic laws of any kind on the books in this country, driving licenses were required in only 12 American states. And in England, driving tests were not required for would-be drivers until 1935!

The first author to submit a typewritten manuscript was Mark Twain. But there's some disagreement as to which of Twain's manuscripts earned the honor. In his *Autobiography*, Twain maintained that *The Adventures of Tom Sawyer* was the first book he typed. But in a letter to a friend, Twain claimed that the earlier *Life on the Mississippi* was also submitted in typescript. In any case, Twain bought his Remington for $125. Later, when he attempted to give the machine away, he found it extremely difficult to find a taker.

The longest legal prohibition of alcoholic beverages on record is a mere 26 years, in Iceland, from 1908 to 1934. Russia tried to illegalize the grape early this century, but the attempt lasted a mere 10 years. Our own "noble experiment" lasted only 13 years—much too long in the minds of many people.

In 1963, a pair of house cats inherited the entire estate of their owner, a California doctor. The estate turned over to the fortunate felines was valued at $415,000.

The Glasgow, Scotland subway was the second subway in the world to be completed, opening in 1891. The Scottish line, still in operation, runs over a six-and-a-half-mile oval that never reaches the surface. Only one other subway line in the world never reaches daylight: London's Waterloo and City. On both lines, cars have to be lifted by elevator to repair shops and sidings.

Believing in the Wind

Chicago may be the windy city, but it can't compare to Adelie Land, in the Antarctic region. The *average* wind velocity there is 50 miles an hour, and hurricanes of 100 m.p.h. or more are regular occurrences.

The highest wind velocity ever recorded in the United States was 231 m.p.h., on Mount Washington, New Hampshire, in 1934.

The escalator, first developed in 1896, eliminated both the need for an elevator operator and, more important, long waits for an elevator car. Escalators were installed extensively in deep subway stations, transporting a steady stream of riders and thereby eliminating bottlenecks at elevator doors. In fact, the longest stream of escalator in the world can be found in the Leningrad subway, with a vertical rise of 195 feet.

Caffeine is an alkaloid that mildly stimulates cerebral and cardiac activity—in short, it's a pick-me-up. But caffeine's lift is not without its price: caffeine causes gastric acidity and nervousness, as well as heightened cardiac action. But coffee-swillers, take heart. Though theoretically the drug can be fatal in large doses, there is no case on record of a caffeine overdose.

As a food, the peanut is one of the most concentrated sources of nourishment known to man. Pound for pound, the peanut provides more protein, minerals, and vitamins than beef liver, more fat than heavy cream, and—dieters beware—more calories than sugar. Recent experiments in Africa have shown that the discarded shells of the peanut can also be used as animal fodder!

Americans are far from the world's greatest newspaper readers. That honor goes to the Swedes, who pore through about 564 papers for every 1,000 persons. (In the United States, the figure is 300 papers per 1,000 persons.) And the newspaper that comes closest to total national saturation is the *Sunday Post*, published in Glasgow, Scotland and read by about four-and-a-half million people each Sunday—more than 77 percent of all Scots of presumed newspaper-reading age.

Azzar lay on a bed of nails for 25½ hours

The fakirs of the mysterious East claim to have performed fantastic feats of endurance. But many fakirs are no more than common fakers, and upon investigation, it usually turns out that their purported feats took place under circumstances that render their claims dubious.

In Sydney, Australia, there is a fakir who backed up his claims by performing in the presence of newsmen and numerous other spectators, outside Walton's on Park Street, one of Sydney's leading department stores.

On the morning of November 20, 1969, bearded Zjane Azzar, clad only in turban and loincloth, gingerly lowered himself into a prone position on a bed of razor-sharp six-inch nails, spaced two inches apart from each other. Throughout that day, the following night, and into the next morning, Azzar remained on his bed of nails, refreshing himself from time to time by smoking a cigarette or by eating a hamburger and some ice cream. During much of this period, he clearly suffered considerable pain. Once his pulse reading was so weak that the attending nurse had to use hot and cold compresses to revive him, and wanted to call the whole thing off.

Azzar refused. He remained stretched out on his bed of nails for a total of 25½ hours, surpassing all previously recorded feats. As Azzar tried to raise himself at the end of his ordeal, he said, "My body has been dead for fourteen hours," and then fainted. He was later examined by a doctor who found him weak but despite the pattern of deep indentations in his back, the fakir was little damaged physically.

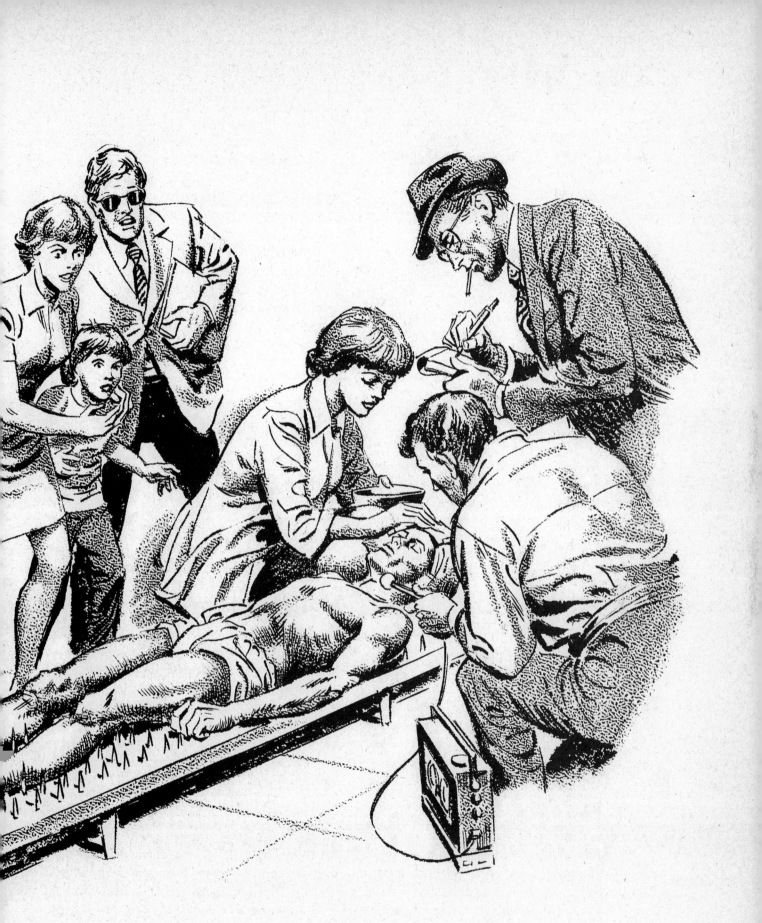

A number of modern baseball players have entered the ranks of the millionaire by playing their favorite game. Baseball's first star, George Wright of the 1869 Cincinnati Red Stockings, batted .518 and hit 59 home runs in 66 games—and received $1,400 for his services!

The Chinese custom of binding women's feet to keep them small is many centuries old. Originally, the practice owed little to pedal aesthetics—bound feet were thought to insure faithfulness, since with such deformed feet the wife would supposedly find it difficult to travel very far on her own.

The most incredible automobile record ever achieved is a matter of opinion. But our vote goes to Charles Creighton and James Hargis, who in 1930, drove a Ford Model A roadster from New York City to Los Angeles *without stopping the engine once!* The two men then promptly drove back to New York, completing the 7,180-mile round-trip in 42 days.

Oh, one more thing: on both coast-to-coast journeys, the car was driven exclusively *in reverse!*

If you think the ribbed, collapsible umbrella was the invention of some clever 18th- or 19th-century Englishman determined to fight back against the soggy weather of London— you're all wet. The fact is, the umbrella is one of the oldest artifacts in man's history, already a familiar item in many cultures by the time man began to write.

The umbrella is so old that historians can't agree on its origin, or decide whether it was first used for protection from the rain or the sun. They do know that it was employed as an item of religious and ceremonial regalia from the earliest days of ancient Egypt.

The word "spa" comes to us from the Belgian town of Spa. A mineral spring discovered in 1326 helped make the town a very fashionable resort during the 18th century. Today, the most famous spas in the world are at Baden-Baden in Germany, Carlsbad in Czechoslovakia, Vichy in France, and Hot Springs in Arkansas.

The rarest coffee in the world is Jamaica Blue Mountain. That particular coffee is sold in only a few stores in the United States. Only 800 bags, or 100,000 pounds, are produced each year.

A Record to Hail

Some hailstones are bigger than baseballs. Most hailstones are the size of small pebbles, but occasionally some fall that are as much as five inches in diameter and weigh more than a pound. On July 16, 1928, in Potter, Nebraska, a huge, single hailstone fell. It tipped the scales at one and one-half pounds—the largest hailstone on record!

In the United States, the chicken is the most populous domesticated animal. About 400 million chickens now roost within the 50 states, compared to about 130 million cattle and calves, 50 million hogs, and 15 million sheep.

The United States leads the world in the annual production of four important minerals—aluminum, coal, copper, and lead. The Soviet Union leads in the production of crude oil and iron ore. Japan is the leading zinc producer, while the small nation of Malaysia leads all countries in the production of tin.

Michaelangelo was not only a painter, sculptor, and architect of genius, but a poet as well. About 300 of his poems survive.

Lightning Letters

What's the fastest typing speed ever recorded? For the top speed ever achieved by a typist, 216 words per minute stands as the record, set by one Stella Pajunas in 1946 on an IBM electric. The record for top speed over an hour of nonstop typing is 149 words per minute, also set on an IBM machine.

Perhaps the most remarkable typing record is held by Albert Tangora, who during a 1923 business show in New York, ran off a total of 8,840 correctly spelled words in one hour of nonstop typing, a rate of 147 words per minute. Incredibly, Tangora achieved his record on a cumbersome old manual typewriter that would seem crude in comparison with modern models. Judges estimated that Tangora executed an average of 12½ strokes per second.

There are now about 1.1 million pedigreed dogs registered in the United States—about one pedigreed pooch for every 200 Americans. The number of mongrels extent is anyone's guess. One knowledgeable estimate puts the total number of dogs in this country at over 40 million.

Americans will spend some one-and-a-half billion dollars this year on pet food, close to four times the sum spent on baby food!

Beginning in England around 1650, the coffee house began taking over many of the social functions formerly provided by the tavern. At first, the coffee houses served only coffee, tea, and chocolate—all new arrivals to Europe. Later, the coffee house provided wine, ale, and occasional hot meals. Another attraction was its supply of gazettes and newsletters regularly kept on hand for coffee swillers on their way to and from work.

The clientele of these establishments evidently was quite varied. An early 18th-century writer noted: "Some shops are a resort for learned scholars and wits; others are the resort of dandies, or of politicians, or again of professional newsmongers, and many are temples of Venus."

The first mention of ice cream in America occurs in 1700, but the dessert was not made here in any quantity until much later in the century. Both George Washington and Thomas Jefferson were known to be ice cream fanciers. Jefferson, who had learned how to make French ice cream during a visit to France, was one of the first rulers to serve the confection at a state dinner. Jefferson once served a dessert of crisp, hot pastry with ice cream in the middle, perhaps the first ice-cream sandwich in America.

Over a thousand years ago, the Mayans and other American Indians chewed gums made from chicle, a substance derived from the sap of the sapodilla tree. The Mexican General Antonio Lopez de Santa Anna—yes, the same Santa Anna of Alamo notoriety—thought that chicle could be used in the manufacture of rubber. So in 1839, he brought some sapodilla sap to the American inventor Thomas Adams. Attempts to manufacture rubber from the tree sap failed, but by the 1870s, Adams's company was marketing the nation's first commercial chicle-based chewing gums.

The most-published Letter to the Editor in history was on the innocuous subject of the difference between centigrade and fahrenheit thermometers. The letter, a reader's inquiry, originally appeared in the Paris edition of the *New York Herald* on December 27, 1899. The next day, due to an editorial slip-up, the letter was reprinted on the editorial page. The *Herald's* publisher, James Gordon Bennet, was so furious about the error, that he ordered the letter to be published in every edition of the paper for the rest of his lifetime, to remind the paper's staff to be more careful. When Bennet died, on May 14, 1918, the letter had been printed more than 6,700 times.

I Left My Heart In Yerba Buena

Originally, San Francisco was named *Yerba Buena*. Other renamings include the giraffe, né *cameleopard*; the elevator, né *vertical railway*; Brazil, né *The Land of the Holy Cross*; Ecuador, né *The Republic of the Sacred Heart*; *The Star-Spangled Banner*, né *The Defense of Fort McHenry*; and the Order of Elks, né *The Jolly Corks*.

Who says an elevator can go only straight up? The Eiffel Tower boasts elevators that move along dizzily inclined tracks, as does the George Washington Masonic Monument in Virginia.

In some modern frankfurter manufacturing plants, computers select raw materials daily and feed them into a continuous hot-dog processing machine, untouched by human hands. Frankfurter production that formerly required nine hours now takes as little as 45 minutes.

The first hotel to employ room service and bellboys was Tremont House, in Boston, Massachusetts, which opened in October 1829. The Tremont, with 180 rooms, was also the largest inn of its day, and the most luxurious. Prior to its construction, American travelers were often forced to share hotel accommodations with as many as five other individuals, usually perfect strangers. Tremont House was the first hotel to guarantee its guest private rooms.

The Spanish forces led by Francisco Pizarro, who conquered the Incas of South America in the 1530s, numbered less than 200 men. The Inca Empire then had a population of over six million!

Where There's Smoke . . .

No one is quite certain that Rodrigo de Jerez of Spain was the first European to smoke tobacco, but he is more often credited with that distinction than anyone else. As the story has it, he learned to smoke from the natives of the West Indies where he landed with Columbus in 1492. When he returned to Spain, he brought a bit of the plant with him, and greatly astonished the populace by his newly acquired habit. His wife denounced him to the Inquisition as a man who "swallows fire, exhales smoke, and is surely possessed by the devil."

Early this century, it was possible to ride by trolley from New York all the way to Boston. Frequent changes of line were necessary to complete the trip, which cost less than four dollars!

The longest continuous streetcar route—gain with frequent changes of line—ran from Freeport, Illinois to Utica, New York, a distance of over 1,000 miles.

The oldest records of Mesopotamia and Egypt show that distinct breeds of domesticated dogs had been developed by the year 3000 B.C., including animals much like the modern greyhound and terrier. The ancient Greeks and Romans kept dogs. The breed classification of the Romans were quite like our own, distinguishing between scent-hunting and sight-hunting dogs, and between *Canes villatici* (housedogs) and *pastorales* (sheep or herding dogs).

Legend has it that cats led to the defeat of the Egyptian army in 525 B.C., through a stratagem of the Persian invader Cambyses. The Persian king placed a row of cats—which the Egyptians considered sacred—in front of his troops, and the Egyptian archers refused to shoot their arrows across the veneated animals.

Before 1848, golf balls were made of leather, stuffed with "as many feathers as a hat will hold." The leather balls were expensive and virtually useless when wet, so the guttie, a ball of sold gutta percha (a rubberlike substance) caught on quickly in the 1850s. Golfers using the guttie noticed that a new ball tended to hook and slice erractically when hit; but old, pockmarked gutties travel-ed straight. So the practice began of manufacturing golf balls with small depres-sions, or dimples, on the outer surface.

Dealt by Whom?

The phrase "New Deal" was invented not by Franklin D. Roosevelt (or his speechwriters) but by Mark Twain. In a letter to the International Mark Twain Society dated December 8, 1933, F.D.R. wrote that he borrowed the title "from that passage in the book *A Connecticut Yankee in King Arthur's Court*, in which the Yankee declares that, in a country where only six people out of a thousand have any voice in the government, what the 944 dupes need is a new deal."

Surprisingly, the eggplant is quite popular in Japan—the fourth most popular "vegetable," in fact, after the sweet potato, radish, and Chinese cabbage.

Why the quotation marks around "vegetable"? Well, the eggplant is botanically a fruit, a member of the nightshade family closely related to the tomato. But eggplants are used almost exclusively as vegetables.

Freak of Fortune

There are many apocryphal tales of miserly millionaires, but the case of John G. Wendel and family is absolutly veracious. Wendel, who died in 1915 at his residence on Fifth Avenue and 39th Street in New York City, was determined that the vast inheritance left to himself and six sisters should not be squan-dered. He never married, and persuaded five of his siters to remain spinsters by virtually imprisoning them in the family manse for 50 years.

So well had Wendel schooled his sisters in parsimony, that when the last of them died, in 1931, it was learned that despite her $1 million estate, the woman had never owned a telephone, an automobile, or electricity, and her wardrobe consisted of one dress, which she had made herself and worn every day for 25 years.

The date of Christ's birth is purely conjectural—there is no historical evidence that Christ was born on December 25. Mention of a December 25 celebration of Christ's birth first appeared around the year 353, but it wasn't until 440—more than four centuries after his actual birth—that the Church proclaimed that day as the official date for the festival.

Conveniently, December 25 already marked a holiday among many Europeans—the celebratory rite of the winter solstice, marking the beginning of lengthening days and the expectation of spring and rebirth. Due to changes in the calendar, Christmas no longer falls exactly on the solstice.

The Creaming of America

Ice cream remained a treat for the rich and regal until 1670, when Paris's first café, the Procope, opened its doors and made the frigid dessert available to the masses for the first time. In America, ice cream remained an expensive dish until the early 19th century, which saw the invention of the insulated icehouse and the hand-crank ice-cream freezer. By the 1820s, the dessert was being sold by street vendors in New York City, who beckoned passersby with shouts of "I scream ice cream."

By the way, beginning in 1921, officials at the Ellis Island immigration station in New York, intent on serving the newcomers a "truly American dish," included ice cream in all meals served at the station.

How much money is there in the world today? It's almost impossible to estimate, since the value of various currencies changes from day to day. But there's an estimated $49.7 billion in gold bullion in the central banks of the world, with the largest single chunk in the Federal Reserve Bank in New York City: $17 billion.

In the 1880s, when inventors on both sides of the Atlantic were tinkering with steam-driven and gasoline-powered automobiles, the general public remained largely unimpressed. A German newspaper, reporting on the work of automotive pioneer Karl Benz, asked the question: "Who is interested in such a contrivance so long as there are horses on sale?"

Over 100 million Americans—virtually half the population—now read one or more comic strips regularly. Surprisingly enough, studies have shown that the more educated a person is, the more likely he is to follow a comic strip. The peak age for Sunday comic strip readers is—no, you'd never guess—30 to 39 years old!

Iced tea was invented in St. Louis, Missouri, at the World's Fair of 1904.

There are many claims for the invention of the ice cream sundae, which emerged during the 1890s. But contemporary laws that forbade the sale of soda on Sunday undoubtedly had a hand in popularizing the dessert. The first sundaes were sold in ice cream parlors only on Sunday, and thus were called "Sundays" or "soda-less sodas." The spelling change to "sundae" was made later by ice cream parlor proprietors eager to see the dish shed its Sunday-only connotation.

Caviar may be everyman's idea of gustatory luxury, but ounce for ounce the acme of epicurean opulence is the peculiar subterranean fungus known as the truffle. Like the mushroom, also a fungus, the truffle has almost no nutritive value. But its taste, aroma, and ability to heavily flavor anything it comes in contact with had made it a prized edible since classical times. The white truffle of the Piedmont district of Italy presently sells for over $200 a pound, making it the most expensive food in the world.

Under the Wire

Alexander Graham Bell is the individual most credited with the invention of the telephone. But Bell was neither the first to conceptualize a voice-transmission device nor the first to design one. He was, quite simply, the first to patent one.

In February, 1876, Bell filed a patent for his invention, "an improvement of the telegraph." Elisha Gray filed a caveat (notice of intent to file a patent) just a *few hours* after Bell applied for his patent. And Thomas Edison had been on the verge of success with his own telephone, when distracted by other work. The stakes? Bell's patent has been called the most valuable ever issued anywhere!

The United States ranks first today among cat-loving nations. There are an estimated 20 to 25 million cats in American households today, but with the inclusion of all alley cats and other strays, the total cat population could well top the 40 million mark, which is the population figure estimated for American dogs.

The cat-care business is now a multi-million-dollar industry in this country, providing cat food and accessories, cat hospitals, kennels, and even kitty cemeteries. Pedigreed cats can sell for over $250.

Proof Positive

Most liquor bottlers indentify the alcoholic content of their product by "proof." The term dates back to the earliest days of liquor distilling when dealers would test the strength of an alcoholic product by soaking gunpowder in the beverage, and then igniting it. Spirits with enough alcohol to permit the ignition of the gunpowder were considered to be 100 proof—the idea being that the gunpowder test was "proof" that the juice was strong.

In England, 100 proof was established as 11 parts of alcohol by volume to ten parts of water. In the United States, the proof figure was set as double the alcoholic percentage. Thus, 86 proof whiskey is 43 percent alcohol, and pure alcohol is 200 proof.

Apple source

The apple, which botanists believe originated in Southwest Asia, has spread through much of Europe before the dawn of recorded history. The Romans knew over two dozen varieties of apple. In the 17th century, an Italian duke gave a banquet that included 56 different kinds of apple!

Today, there are more than 7,000 varieties, only 20 of which are widely cultivated. And of these 20, eight account for 75 percent of all commercial apple production.

You may be surprised to find a 16th-century Dutch painting depicting carrots of a purple or yellow hue. But that's exactly what carrots looked like at that time. The familiar orange carrot did not appear in Europe in any quantity until the 17th century.

Do carrots really improve eyesight? Well, carrots do contain large amounts of Vitamin A, which is essential to good vision. In fact, among all foods carrots rank second after liver in Vitamin A content.

Obstacle Course

The most grueling automobile race on record began on February 12, 1908, when six cars left New York for Paris by way of the United States, Japan, Manchuria, Siberia, Russia, Poland, Germany, and a part of France. The racers—three Frenchmen, a German, an Italian, and an American—found themselves confronted by blizzards, breakdowns, broken bridges, unpassable roads, fuel shortages, and all manner of other obstacles. Nevertheless, three of the cars—all but the French entries—actually completed the run.

The German entry reached Paris on July 26; the American entry on July 30; and the Italian entry six weeks later. The American car was given a 15-day credit for observing the rules of the race, while the German entry was docked 15 days for breaking the rules. Thus, the American car—a Thomas Flyer—was declared the winner. The champion motor car had covered 13,400 land miles in 168 days, the longest run of its kind at that time.

The symbol &, known as the ampersand, and used for the word *and* in hundreds of different languages, was invented by Marius Tiro of Rome in 63 B.C. Actually, the ampersand was one of 5,000 such signs invented by Tiro in the world's first shorthand system, but only the ampersand has survived.

Did you ever wonder why so many Scottish lassies have had masculine-derived first names such as Thomasina, Georgina, or Jamesina? It seems the ancient Scots custom was to give all babies a male Christian name before birth, in the hope that the infant would turn out to be a boy. When a girl was born instead, the family, who had grown used to thinking of the little stranger by the boy's name, simply added the feminine ending *-ina*.

The term *yellow journalism* has nothing to do with the color of the paper on which tabloids are printed, or the valor of their publishers. Rather, this synonym for sensationalist newswriting comes from the world's first comic strip, The *Yellow Kid*, which appeared in a New York newspaper, The *World* in 1894. The comic strip made a big hit with the public, and increased The *World's* circulation considerably. Soon the tabloid was nicknamed "the yellow journal." As The *World* was also notorious for the sensationlist nature of its reportage, the term *yellow journalism* came to mean lurid newspaper-writing, designed to increase mass-circulation.

Holocaust, American-Style

Of all the gratuitous bloodshed of native Americans in this country's history, the worst occurred in November of 1864, at an Indian detention camp in Sand Creek, Colorado. Four hundred members of the Cheyenne and Arapaho tribes had gone to the encampment to await a peace conference with members of the U.S. Department of Indian Affairs, which guaranteed the Indians' safety, and gave them an American flag as a sign of good faith. But on the 29th of November, a famous "Indian Fighter," a colonel in the U.S. army, rode into the village with 900 soldiers, and senselessly slaughtered 300 Indian men, women, and children. A Congressional investigation followed the attack, and the carnage was deemed so appalling that the entire affair was hushed up.

Egyptian mythology held that the visible sky was actually the underbelly of a god stretched from one end of the earth to the other like an immense umbrella. Hence, in contemporary art, priests and pharoahs were often placed in the shade of an umbrella to symbolize royal and religious power.

Bourbon, America's contribution to the world of whiskey, accounted for about one-fourth of all distilled spirits consumed in this country during the 1960s. But that figure has now decreased to about 15 percent, while vodka consumption has doubled over the same period. Vodka-drinking now accounts for about 20 percent of the total American alcohol intake. Consumption of scotch whiskey, meanwhile, has held steady at about 12 percent.

Caviar is the prepared roe, or eggs, of the *acipenser*, a fish found in the Caspian and Black Seas, and the Gironde River in France. At one time, the acipenser could be found in many European rivers, and even in some North American lakes; but since the onset of the industrial age the fish's habitat has been reduced to portions of Russia, Iran, and Rumania. Today, virtually all caviar is produced in those three countries.

The term "sturgeon" is often applied to all kinds of caviar-producing fish. But only one, the Ocietrova, is a true sturgeon.

Stone-Blind

For 92 years, a heated controversy raged about a stone tablet inscribed with hieroglyphics, that was found in Moundsville, West Virginia, in the autumn of 1838. The tablet was found by workmen digging in the Grave Creek Mound, in a chamber containing other prehistoric relics. For the next century, more than 60 linguists examined the hieroglyphic characters on the tablet, and argued as to whether the inscription was Runic, Etruscan, or some other ancient language. The mystery was finally solved in 1930, when an American glanced at the letters from an unusual angle, and was was able to decipher them. The inscription was in English, and read: "Bill Stump's Stone, October, 14, 1838."

In 1976, a mammoth frankfurter was exhibited by a California hotel to celebrate the American Bicentennial . The wiener consisted of 40 pounds of pork and beef, and measured 148 inches in length. To our knowledge, no patriot volunteered to single-handedly devour the dog.

In past times, chefs took pride in constructing elaborate gelatin molds, and no dinner party was complete without at least one jelly construction worthy of the best modern-day wedding-cake baker. In the 19th century, the most popular mold designs were castles and fortresses complete with doors, windows, and crenellated turrets.

The worst inflation in history occurred in Hungary in 1946, when a single gold pengo was valued at 130 trillion paper pengos! A simple purchase might require so many bills that a wheelbarrow was needed for a trip to the store, and notes were issued in denominations as high as 100 trillion pengos.

The inflation rate in Chile, between 1950 and 1973, was an outlandish 423,100 percent—meaning, in American currency, that what could once be bought for one dollar eventually cost $4,232!

The most popular breed in the United States today is the poodle. In 1971, the American Kennel Club had 256,491 poodles on register. Compare this to 11,355 German Shepherds, the next most popular breed.

The Saga of the Streetcar

Today, most people would think of the streetcar as a creature of the big city. True, most American cities have operated trolley systems at one time or another. But before the country was laced with freeways and interstate highways, streetcar travel was the best means of transportation to and from the city, as well as within its boundaries.

With even the fastest modern trains rarely exceeding 60 miles per hour, it now seems hard to believe that the normal operating speed of many interurban streetcar lines was 80 miles per hour. Incredible as it seems, cars of the Crandic Line between Cedar Rapids and Iowa City in Iowa once claimed top speeds of 110 miles per hour!

The production of alcoholic beverages in the United States now stands at over 100 million proof gallons per year, with an estimated half-billion proof gallons in stock. Not bad for a nation in which about one-third of the population are teetotalers.

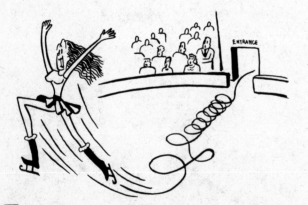

There are now an estimated 20 million ice skaters in the United States, and the U.S. Figure Skating Association can boast over 30,000 of them as its members. In 1950, there were but 120 indoor ice rinks in this country. Today, American ice skating rinks number over a thousand, logging about 20 million admissions annually.

During the 15th century, the English houses of York and Lancaster fought for control of the English crown in a struggle that came to be known as the War of the Roses. The emblem of the house of York was the white rose; of Lancaster, the red rose. Curiously, during a key battle of the war, the Lancastrian forces mistook the star symbol of an ally for the "rose-and-sun" of their enemy, and set upon them in error, costing their side the victory.

The house of Tudor, which took over the English crown after the war, shrewdly combined both red and white roses in its emblem.

Daniel Defoe, best known for his novels, published a weekly newspaper entitled The *Review* between 1704 and 1713. At various times a paid political pamphleteer, a secret agent, and a hack, Defoe was wont to take his political point of view from the highest bidder, and often switched sides when it suited him. The author of *Robinson Crusoe* once edited a Tory newspaper actually sponsored by the Whigs, and a Whig publication sponsored by the Tories—both at the same time!

Brussels sprouts are a member of the cabbage family, with each plant producing a number of small heads instead of one large one. The name comes from—you guessed it—Brussels, Belgium, which is in the area where the sprouts supposedly originated.

Which nation is the leading trading partner of the United States? No, it's not Japan, or West Germany, or the United Kingdom. In fact, the value of the goods we export to and import from those three countries combined is less than the value of the goods exported to and imported from our number one trading partner—Canada.

The A.C. Nielsen Company, the research firm that formulates the Nielsen Ratings of television shows, measures American TV viewing habits by means of small boxes attached to TV sets in 1,170 homes. These 1,170 homes comprise only .0017 percent of all American homes with television—or one in approximately 60,000!

How cool is a cucumber? Scientists claim that the inside of a cuke is precisely 20 degrees cooler than the air on a warm day.

Did you ever wonder why the ace of spades in every pack of playing cards is so distinctive, with the central spade by far the largest symbol in the deck? Well, the ace of spades was the card designated to bear the tax stamp in the days when playing cards were subject to heavy taxation throughout most of Europe. Even today, card makers use the ace of spades to carry their trademark or brand name.

Sundae Supreme

Only in America could you expect to find the largest ice-cream sundae of all times. The 3,956-pound monster, concocted in McLean, Virginia, in 1975, contained 777 gallons of ice cream, six gallons of chocolate syrup, over a gallon of whipped cream, and a case of chocolate sprinkles.

As late as the 1920s, some American dictionaries did not contain the word "hamburger," though most did mention the "Hamburg steak." Today, chopped meat accounts for almost 30 percent of all consumer meat sales. And one hamburger chain, McDonald's, sells over one *billion* burgers every three months!

Golf was being played in the United States at least as early as 1779, when an advertisement for golfing equipment appeared in a New York paper. The game may actually have been enjoyed much earlier here, for upon the death in 1729 of William Burnet, governor of New York and Massachusetts, the Burnet estate listed "nine golf clubs, one iron ditto, and seven dozen balls." There is also evidence of golf in South Carolina and Georgia in the late 18th century. But the game apparently did not catch on here at the time, for almost a century passed before golf was mentioned again in official records.

The familiar Volkswagen "beetle" was first produced in 1938. By the 1950s, Volkswagen was the largest car producer in Europe; and in 1972, the "beetle" surpassed the Ford Model T in total sales for a single model, with over 15 million sold throughout the world.

We think of gelatin basically as a dessert product. But in former times, cooks favored their gelatins with vinegar, wine, almond extract, and other items that produced a tart, rather than a sweet, product. Those cooks hardly had need of a sweet jelly, since the items they glazed were often meats than sweets.

The eggplant is neither oval nor white, and certainly bears no relation to the egg in taste or usage. "Eggplant," then, is a misnomer? Well, almost.

The first eggplants to reach Europe during the Middle Ages were actually a rare white species, with oval fruits that closely resemble a hen's egg. The name "eggplant" was a natural, and stuck to the plant even when the more common purple varieties made their appearance in Europe.

Wild Dogs

The dog has been domesticated by man for so long, and today is such a tame, obedient member of the family, that it's easy to forget that the dog was once a wild animal.

Man began his long and happy relationship with the canine well before recorded history began. Most likely, jackals and primitive dogs, originally independent hunters and scavengers, found it advantageous to follow nomadic human hunters for the bones and food scraps left behind when they broke camp. Gradually, prehistoric man came to realize that the presence of these beasts surrounding the camp at night could benefit him, since the howling canines would warn of the approach of deadly predators.

As the hunter went out of his way to feed his watchdogs, the more dependent upon him they became. Slowly, dog and man began to join forces in hunting, the dog contributing his scent to flushing out game, and man returning the favor by providing dog with a steady diet of meat.

But wild members of the dog family still remain on earth. There follow some of the strange ones of the *Canus familiaris* species.

BRAZILIAN BUSH DOG *This wild creature belongs to a different genus than the dog proper, with one less lower molar than the family pooch.*

COYOTE *The coyote, or prairie wolf, can be found from Alaska to Central America, resting in its burrow by day, hunting and howling by night. The coyote favors small rodents, and eats a good deal of vegetable matter, but his appetite for domestic poultry has made him a menace in many Western states.*

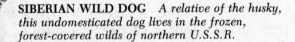

SIBERIAN WILD DOG *A relative of the husky, this undomesticated dog lives in the frozen, forest-covered wilds of northern U.S.S.R.*

JACKAL *Found in Africa, Asia, and parts of Europe, the jackal is not strictly a scavenger. Jackals hunt at night, either alone or in packs, and a group can bring down prey as large as an antelope. When fresh meat is scarce, they feed on carrion, sometimes following a lion or tiger to finish off an animal the cat has killed and left partially uneaten.*

CAPE HUNTING DOG *An African doglike animal resembling a hyena, which hunts its prey in packs.*

DINGO *Also called the war rigal, the dingo is the native wild dog of Australia. Dingoes have interbred with domestic dogs brought by settlers to Australia, and few pure-bred dingoes remain in some areas. But in other regions, the rapid spread of the rabbit, which provides these wild dogs with a staple food supply, has led to a large population of dingoes whose predatory habits threaten sheep farmers.*

To Bathe or Not to Bathe

During the Middle Ages, bathing was considered a sin among some communities, an act of pride and overt concern for the sensual. Among the landed classes, the lack of a need to bathe was considered a sign of wealth and leisure. Many an aristocrat bragged of never having taken a bath. Consequently, the demand for perfume and aromatic oils was very high, and the need for spices helped spur the explorations of the 15th century that led to the discovery of America.

By the way, Queen Elizabeth of England reportedly bathed once a month, "whether she needed it or not."

In the closing days of the 19th century, when automobiles were first being manufactured on a sizable scale, American cities were in dire need of horseless carriages—and horseless streets. Around the turn of the century, New York City's equine helpmates were depositing some two-and-a-half million pounds of manure and 60,000 galls of urine on the streets each day!

The comic strip presently reaches about one-third of humanity each day! In the last 70 years, an estimated eight to 12 million comic strip pictures have been produced throughout the world.

Modern elevators travel at many times the speed of the earliest machines, with express elevators in some taller buildings speeding along at 1,200 feet per minute—fast enough to require machinery to adjust changing air pressures in the car. And newer elevators, such as those in the Sears Tower and the John Hancock Building in Chicago, travel at speeds of up to 1,800 feet per minute!

The first round-the-world telephone conversation took place in 1935. Round the world? Well, the call was placed in New York, routed via San Francisco, Java, Amsterdam, and London, and received in an office only 50 feet from the caller's!

Not surprisingly, there was only one person in the world capable of such telephone extravagance—the president of the American Telephone & Telegraph Corporation.

Though a stilt-walker isn't very speedy, he does get a unique perspective on the world around—and under—him. Hop pickers commonly go about their business on 15-foot stilts, but Albert Yelding ("Harry Sloan") of Great Britain mastered the art of walking on stilts that measured 22 feet from his ankles to the ground.

Indians of the Central United States carved stone pipes with straight or curved stems, and smoked a blend they called *kinnikinnik*, made of tobacco, sumac leaves, and the bark of the willow tree. The Indians, who considered tobacco a sacred herb and regarded smoking as a sacred art, frequently shaped their pipe bowls in the form of animals and other totems. Historians have been unable to explain why some pipes found in the ruins of ancient Indian settlements were carved in the form of elephants and sea cows, two creatures the Indians had presumably never seen.

India, with an area about the size of Argentina, has a larger population than all of the nations of the Western Hemisphere combined.

A total of 96 games separate baseball's best and worst team winning records. In 1906, the Chicago Cubs won 116 games and lost only 36, a record that still stands. Six years earlier, the Cleveland nine established the all-time mark for ineptitude by dropping all but 20 of their 154 games.

Though a native of Mexico and Central America, and a favorite flavoring in Europe and the United States, vanilla is today almost entirely a product of various Indian Ocean islands, where it was brought for plantation cultivation by French colonists. The Malagasy Republic (formerly Madagascar), Reunion, and the Comoro Islands now account for about 75 percent of the world's vanilla supply. Quantities are also produced in Tahiti, Indonesia, Mexico, and the Seychelles Islands.

Underlines

Among all subway systems in operation today, London's is the most extensive, with 252 miles of track and 279 stations. A 600-train fleet with over 4,000 cars carries some 600 million passengers each year, with the one-day record standing at 2,073,134 on VE Day, 1945.

The New York subway system is shorter in track mileage, but far and away the busiest in the world, serving about four-and-a-half million passengers on an average weekday and over two billion a year. This massive system—one of the few to remain in operation around the clock—spans 230 miles, with 462 stations, and its 134 miles of tunnel form the largest underground network in the world.

Strictly speaking, a *penknife* is not the same as a *pocketknife*. A penknife was a specialized pocketknife with one blade opening at each end of the handle. The smaller of the two blades was used to trim and sharpen quill pens.

The Potato Arrives

"Meat and potatoes" are the foundations of most American cooking, and of many European cuisines as well. The spud is so rooted in Western cooking that it's sometimes hard to believe the vegetable was totally unknown in Europe just a few hundred years ago.

In the mid-16th century, Spanish explorers in South America discovered that the Incas ate a white tuber they called "papa." Pedro Cieca, an officer of Juan Pizarro, shipped a load of the spuds back to Spain. Within 20 years of their arrival in Europe, potatoes were being grown, sold, and eaten in Spain.

After Sir Walter Raleigh planted potatoes on his Irish estate, spud farms began to sprout up all around the Emerald Isle. But in England and Scotland, the potato remained unpopular for two centuries—defamed as "Ireland's lazy root."

In Scotland, some Presbyterian clergymen declared that since the potato was not mentioned in the Bible, it could not be fit for human consumption!

Clarence Birdseye, an American, is largely responsible for the development of methods for freezing foods in small packages for the retail trade. The General Foods Corporation introduced the now familiar Birds Eye commercial pack in 1929. Since then, the use of frozen foods has grown with the refrigerator. As early as 1944, Americans were consuming some three billion pounds of frozen meats, vegetables, fruits, fish, and dairy products each year.

If New York has traditionally been the home of baseball champions, Philadelphia is undoubtedly the home of baseball's cellar dwellers. In the National League, the Phillies have ended their season in last place 24 times, while in the American League, the Athletics leased the basement 17 times before moving to Kansas City in 1955. Totaled together, the two teams of the City of Brotherly Love have wound up in last place 41 times!

Truth in Advertising

The whiskey served in the saloons of the Old West was often as coarse as the cowhands and miners who drank it. Most whiskies well deserved the vile names given them—skull varnish, snake water, bug juice, Taos Lightning, and the legendary red-eye.

In the early days of Junction City, Kansas, the Wells Fargo Saloon in that town proudly—and truthfully—boasted "The Worst Liquor, the Poorest Cigars, and a Miserable Billiard Table."

Tulipomania

In the 1630s, a rage of tulip speculation, called tulipomania, gripped much of Holland, and farmers rich and poor began speculating in the tulip trade. Single bulbs of prized varieties sold for as much as $1,000—one particular bulb sold for $4,000, a small fortune at the time. Alas, the tulip rage tapered off within a few years, leaving thousands of Dutchmen penniless. The economic scars of tulipomania were felt in Holland for decades.

Still, the Dutch continued to raise their favorite flower. Today, the Netherlands remains the chief source of tulips bulbs for much of the world, with millions cultivated each year. The total value of Dutch horticulture approaches a quarter-billion dollars annually!

A rather heartwarming tale is told of a San Franciscoan named Joshua Norton, who from 1855 to 1889 "reigned" as emperor of the United States. Calling himself Emperor Norton I, this demented but loveable pauper was humored to an amazing extent by his native city. "Norton I" was invited to attend every municipal function, and a special chair was reserved for him at meetings of the state senate. The transportation lines gave him free life passes, and he dined *gratis* in local restaurants. Newspapers printed Norton's announcements without billing His Royal Highness, and bankers and merchants unblinkingly cashed the old character's checks—which ranged from $1 to $2. Furthermore, the legendary lunatic had no trouble selling his 50-cent bonds to fellow citizens of San Francisco. When Norton died, in 1880, he was given one of the largest and grandest funerals ever held on the West Coast. The obsequies were financed by a club of San Francisco millionaires.

Gas molecules move so quickly that, in one second, a gas molecule will collide with neighboring molecules some five billion times! And in one second. all the molecules in one cubic inch of air will travel a combined distance millions of times as great as the distance between the earth and the sun.

You've heard hunters boast of having killed wild beasts with their bare hands? Well, at least one man actually performed this feat. In 1898, Carl Akeley, an American big-game hunter on safari in British Somaliland, shot and slightly wounded a leopard, but before Akeley could fire a second shot, the animal sprang at him and knocled Akeley's gun to the ground. In the ensuing battle, Akeley was badly scratched and bitten by the ferocious cat, but the hunter managed to strangle the beast before it could kill him.

No one who has carried home a copy of the *New York Sunday Times* could entertain any doubt as to the world's largest newspaper in sheer bulk. The largest *Sunday Times* ever published, on October 17, 1965, consisted of 946 pages in 15 sections, and weighed a whopping seven-and-a-half pounds!

Let's see—if the *Sunday Times* has a circulation of about one-and-a-half million copies, we can calculate that the average issue of that paper comprises a total of some ten million pounds of paper. Now, that's a small forest!

The chemical that gives the skunk his malodorous reputation is called *ethanethiol*, a substance so pungent that less than one ten-trillionth (.000,000,000,000,1) of an ounce can be detected by the human nose.

Americans presently put away about one-and-a-quarter million tons of coffee each year, more than the entire world drank just a half-century ago. Coffee is, to say the least, an institution in this country, with the average American gulping down two-and-a-half cups daily.

But Americans are not the world's heaviest coffee consumers—the average Swede consumes close to 30 pounds of coffee each year.

In 1902, Pittsburgh third baseman Tommy Leach won the National League home-run title by wacking a grand total of six four-baggers. And all six homers were inside-the-park jobs!

So convinced were Americans that it was not in man's power to fly like the birds, that when the Wright brothers announced that they had successfully flown a power-driven airplane at Kitty Hawk, North Carolina, on December 17, 1903, neither the public nor the press believed them. What's more, this skepticism lasted an incredible five years, during which time the Wrights made repeated demonstrations of their airplane, which newspaper editors refused to cover, believing the Wrights to be crackpots or charlatans. The main reason for this editorial cynicism was that three months before the historic flight at Kitty Hawk, an eminent mathematician had "proved" the impossibility of a machine heavier than air ever sustaining flight. Well, the Wright Brothers told their woes, not to the marines, but to the U.S. army, which arranged, in September 1908, for the first formal demonstration of the Wright brothers' plane, at Fort Myer, Virgina. The demonstration was watched by 800 witnesses, finally convincing America that man had indeed conquered the air.

The Japanese traditionally selected their wooden shoes with an ear for the sound made by the wooden blocks, for a discordant pair of shoes was considered the epitome of poor taste.

In a recent year, the average American 15 years of age or older smoked 3,812 cigarettes—that's about a half pack daily for each person, and well over a pack for each smoker. Japan was close behind with 3,270 cigarettes per capita annually, the United Kingdom third with 3,190. Italy was fourth, with West Germany, Denmark, and Sweden rounding out the top seven.

Philip Morris's *Marlboro* remains the world's most popular cigarette, the 136 billion sold annually making the entire earth "Marlboro Country."

Benjamin Franklin was the most versatile man who ever lived

Benjamin Franklin said, "I wish the good Lord had seen fit to make the day twice as long as it is. Perhaps then I cold *really* accomplish something."

Thus spoke this many-sided man who did any number of things—and did them all amazingly well. He was a painter, writer, publisher, scientist, statesman, inventor, businessman, philosopher, and humanitarian.

Franklin's father, a poor Boston candlemaker, hoped to make Benjamin, one of 17 children, a minister. But lack of funds forced young Franklin to leave school at the age of 10. Apprenticed to an older brother, a printer, Benjamin managed to educate himself by giving up meat and using the money saved to buy books. Young Benjamin not only educated himself in such basic subjects as arithmetic and English grammar, but also navigation, algebra, geometry, and philosophy.

In 1723, at the age of 17, Ben left Boston to try his luck in Philadelphia. He arrived in

that colonial town with little money and no friends. Yet within a very few years, Franklin became a famous author and publisher. His sharp wit and common-sense advice, published in his *Pennsylvania Gazette* and *Poor Richard's Almanack*, were known throughout the American colonies.

Marked up to his credit is a series of diverse achievements never equaled in American history. Here are just a few of his accomplishments:

As a scientist and inventor, Franklin:

1. Proved that lightning consisted of electricity.

2. Invented the lightning rod.

3. Invented the Franklin stove, an economical and useful heating device.

4. Invented bifocal glasses.

5. Invented the platform rocking chair.

6. Wrote a scientific essay which for the first time described the existence of the Gulf Stream.

7. Discovered that poorly-aired rooms spread disease.

In the realm of literature, Franklin:

1. Was an original and highly talented writer, whose *Poor Richard's Almanack* and *Autobiography* have assumed a permanent place in the American literary heritage.

2. Founded a popular publication, the *Pennsylvania Gazette*, later to become *The Saturday Evening Post*.

As a humanitarian and tireless contributor to the public welfare, Franklin:

1. Organized the first fire department in Philadelphia.

2. Helped establish the first hospital in America.

3. Founded the first lending library in America.

4. Created the first efficient postal system in America.

5. Founded an academy which later became the University of Pennsylvania.

6. Headed the first society in America to oppose slavery.

7. Established the first American fire insurance company.

8. Founded a club that later became the American Philosophical Society.

Though his accomplishments in any of these fields would have assured Franklin a lasting imprint on American history, it was his role in founding a new nation that gave, Franklin his special place in the hearts of his countrymen. Although he had already attained the advanced age of 70 when the Revolutionary War broke out in 1776, Franklin's guiding hand was felt everywhere during the struggle against the British. As postmaster general of the colonies in rebellion, he contributed his entire salary to help the American wounded. Franklin also took a major part in reorganizing the Continental Army into an efficient fighting force. He helped draft the Declaration of Independence and, as America's envoy to France, did much to forge the alliance that in 1778 brought French aid to the hard-pressed American troops. And it was Franklin's wisdom and gift for compromise that, once the Revolution was won, helped the colonies become a united nation under a federal constitution.

A year before Franklin's death, George Washington wrote the following words to this universally admired American. "If to be venerated for benevolence, if to be admired for talent, if to be esteemed for patriotism, if to be beloved for philanthropy, can gratify the human mind, you must have the pleasing consolation to know you have not lived in vain."

The first "comfort" air-conditioning—designed for people rather than manufactured goods—was installed in 1908, at the Curtis Publishing Company building in Philadelphia.

The Milam Building in San Antonio, Texas, a 21-story structure completed in 1928, was the first office building in the world to be built with air-conditioning as part of its original construction.

Topping Topps

The earliest baseball cards appeared during the 1880s in packets of cigarettes and tobacco. Candy companies began to issue cards in 1913, and bubble gum manufacturers included cards with their product beginning in 1933. The Topps Chewing Gum Company, producers of the familiar Bazooka bubble gum, entered the baseball card field in 1951, and has since become the giant of both the bubble gum and baseball card industries, distributing some 250 million cards each year.

The Topps Company estimates that there are now more than 100,000 serious baseball card collectors in the United States. Enthusiasts will pay surprisingly high sums for a valuable specimen. The largest collection of baseball cards in the world—200,000 cards—belongs to the Metropolitan Museum of Art in New York, and the most prized Topps card in existence is the 1952 Mickey Mantle, valued as high as $100.

The baseball card trade is not without its lighter side. A number of right-handed practical jokers have posed for the Topps photographer wearing a left-handed glove, or vice versa, and more than one player has appeared on a card bearing another player's name. In 1969, California Angels' third baseman Aurelio Rodriquez duped Topps into photographing the team batboy in his place, and thousands of cards bearing the batboy's image over Rodriguez's name were distributed before Topps caught the error.

Halley's Comet appears to viewers on earth once about every 77 years. When Mark Twain was born in 1835, Halley's Comet was shining in the sky. It next appeared in 1910, the year Twain died!

In 1911, an Italian employee of the Louvre in Paris made off with that museum's most famous work, Leonardo da Vinci's *Mona Lisa*. The employee, Vincenzo Peruggia, kept the priceless masterpiece in a trunk for two years before trying to sell it, and was promptly caught when he did. Then, at his trial in Italy, Peruggia maintained that he had stolen the work only to return it to its native land. He was let off with a sentence of 380 days.

Of all the famous generals in United States history, only one ranked first in his graduating class at West Point: Douglas MacArthur. Dwight Eisenhower, Omar Bradley, George Patton, and William Westmoreland all failed to finish within the top 45 students in their graduating classes.

A recent poll conducted in England found that the women most commonly thought of as the most beautiful in the world were Elizabeth Taylor, Sophia Loren, Raquel Welch, Twiggy, and Brigitte Bardot.

When the wife of the Roman Emperor Claudius tried to kill him by serving poisoned mushrooms, Claudius' physician came quickly to the rescue, shoving a feather down the emperor's throat in an attempt to induce vomiting. Claudius choked to death on the feather.

Some historians believe that the feather itself was poisoned.

In 1975, a Canadian named Clinton Shaw set the nonstop roller skating record when he remained atop his wheels for over 183 hours at a California rink. By that time, Shaw had already made his mark as a marathon skater. In 1967, he roller skated across Canada, covering 4,900 miles. Seven years later, he traveled from New York to California on skates in just 78 days, logging up to 106 miles a day!

The donkey's well-earned reputation for stupidity and obstinance is hardly a recent development. The ancient Egyptians used representations of the ass to symbolize an ignorant person, and the Romans considered it a bad omen to run into an ass.

If you're one of those people who doesn't know a filly from a foal, here's a short course in equine terminology. A *stallion* is a male horse above the age of five; a *colt*, a male below five years. A *mare* is a female horse more than five years old, and a *filly* is a younger female. A *foal* is a young horse of either sex.

A *quarter horse* is not a bizarre mixture of horse and another animal, but actually owes its name to its extreme speed over a quarter-mile distance. And *thoroughbred* is not a generic term, like "pedigree," but refers to one breed of horse, developed in England from oriental stock and today is recognized as the acme of equine quality.

There are now 16 metropolitan areas in the United States with a population of over two million. In the last five years, all but four of these areas lost population. The fastest growing area in that period was Miami-Fort Lauderdale, with an annual growth rate of 4.4 percent.

What do Cloudy, Cyclone, Hurricane, Rains, Snow, Tornado, and Frost all have in common, beside the fact that they refer to weather phenomena? Each is the name of a town in the United States!

Proof Positive

On October 6, 1934, the body of a young woman in her early twenties was discovered, riddled with bullets, on a road near Kansas City, Kansas. The victim, who was advertised as a blue-eyed redhead, with freckles and peculiar scars on both ankles, was placed in the local morgue, where 150 persons flocked to "positively" identify the body as someone they knew. The problem was, that among these 150 persons, 26 *different* young women were named as the victim of the crime.

All the identifications were corroborated by at least two—and as many as 18—separate witnesses. The police dutifully investigated every identification. After seven months, all 26 women had been found, alive and well. The victim was finally buried, *unidentified*, having set a record for the greatest number of mistaken identifications in United States history.

"Asparagus" is a second-century Latin word based on the Greek word for "sprout" or "shoot." In 18th-century England, the vegetable was known as "sparagus," "sparage," or "sparagrass," and later as "sparrow-grass."

Mathias won the Olympic decathlon at age 17

No title is held in greater esteem than the Olympic decathlon. The champion in this event is generally regarded as the greatest athlete in the world. There is no doubt that the performances in the 1976 decathlon in Montreal were watched on television by more viewers than any other Olympic event. The decathlon performer must be able to run, to jump, and to throw. He must be able to sprint, and to have sufficient endurance to last a long distance. He must blend agility with strength.

Just a few months before he was tapped to carry the hopes of the United States in the

1948 Olympics in London, 17-year-old Bob Mathias had never touched a javelin. Nor had he ever pole-vaulted. And to top off his inexperience, the 400-meter distance and the 1,500-meter distance were quite unfamiliar. His enthusiastic high school coach suggested to his young charge that he try out for the Olympic team anyhow. The lad weighed 190

pounds, was strong, willing, and was an exceptionally good competitor. Bob Mathias was the cool type. The coach believed that he wouldn't make the team, but that he would gain valuable experience for the next competition, four years later.

However, Mathias exceeded everyone's hopes, including his own. He won the very first decathlon meet he entered, defeating several well-known college stars. Less than a month later, he won the U.S. championship. In a short six weeks, the boy found himself in the international arena in London.

Here Mathias took on the world's best as if he were a veteran. The schoolboy ran the 100 meters in 11.2 seconds; the 400 meters in 51.7 seconds; the rugged 1,500 meters in 5 minutes and 11 seconds; the 110-meter hurdles in 15.7 seconds. He broad-jumped 21 feet 8 inches; high-jumped 6 feet 1¼ inches, and pole-vaulted 11 feet 5½ inches. In the weight events, he threw the javelin 165 feet 1 inch; the shot put, 42 feet 9 inches; and he hurled the discus 144 feet 4 inches. His 7,139 points easily led the field.

When the two-day ordeal ended on August 6, an onlooker asked Bob what he would do to celebrate his victory. "Start shaving, I guess," said Bob.

A pair of sneakers is sold in the United States each year for every two people in the country. Sneaker sales in the United States recently topped an annual mark of 100 million pairs!

The first iron-and-steel skyscraper in the nation was the ten-story Home Insurance Building in Chicago, which was completed in 1885. The first reinforced-concrete skyscraper was built in neither New York nor Chicago—it was the 16-story Ingalls Building in Cincinnati, completed in 1903.

A 1976 poll conducted in England found that the all-time favorite artists of the people polled were Pablo Picasso, Rembrandt, Salvador Dali, and Leonardo da Vinci.

Smash Hit!

The sport of piano smashing has been a popular pastime in the British Isles for some time. In 1968, six Irishmen in Merton, England—well, smashed all previous records in their sport by demolishing an upright pians and passing the pieces of wreckage through a circle nine inches in diameter in just two minutes, 26 seconds.

Comedy of Errors

Records for superlative achievement in baseball are far better known to fans than the all-time marks for ineptitude. Did you know that in 1942, Cub shortstop Lennie Merullo committed four errors—in one inning? Or that the White Sox and Tigers were charged with 18 miscues in a single 1903 game?

How about pitching? In 1936, Philadelphia Athletics hurler Horace Lisenbee surrendered 26 hits during one miserable performance. In 1915, Bruno Haas of that same team yielded 16 bases on balls in one game—plus three wild pitches. In 1949, an assortment of Yankee pitchers gave up 11 walks in a single inning. And in 1883, John Coleman of the Phillies suffered a record 48 losses.

Catchers and batters have gotten into the act, too. In 1954, New York Giant backstop Ray Kaat was charged with four passed balls in one inning. And in 1934, Goose Goslin of the Tigers hit into four consecutive double plays!

Over 50,000 square miles of our nation are now paved over with asphalt and concrete in the form of roads and highways. That's an area close to the size of the state of Wisconsin!

Be sure of your biblical edition before you take the Word as Gospel. In 20 editions of the Christian Bible, published between 1535 and 1823, notable bloopers appeared, causing the bibles to be named for the typographical errors they contained. For example, there is the Adulteror's Bible, in which the seventh commandment (Exodus: 20:14) admonishes the reader: "Thou shalt commit adultery." And there's the Printer's Bible, with a perhaps accidentally-on-purpose boner by some printer's journeyman. Psalm 119:161 reads, "*Printers* (Princes) have persecuted me without cause—"

The average gestation period of a human being is 267 days, which is slightly less than nine months. The elephant, in contrast, has a gestation period of 640 days, the giraffe, 450 days, and the horse, 337 days. At the other end of the scale, the rabbit's gestation period is just 31 days, the hamster's is but 16, and the opossum has a gestation period of only 13 days.

Novel Obituary

The Forsyte Saga, John Galsworthy's *roman fleuve* that recently delighted TV viewers in a BBC adaption, created a great wave in its own day, too. In 1928, *Swan Song,* the sixth book of the series, was published, containing the death of protagonist Soames Forsyte. The character's death so jolted certain London newspaper editors that they published Soames's obituary, under screaming headlines, as front-page news!

According to a poll conducted in England during the early 1970s, Adolf Hitler is the most hated person in history. Among the persons who the poll found to be the most beloved were Winston Churchill, Jesus Christ, and Joan of Arc.

Passengers on the Concorde, the supersonic passenger aircraft, can ride at altitudes of up to 60,000 feet—high enough to view the curvature of the earth!

Aspirin retains its potency no matter how much is taken or for how long—and it's not addictive. But one person in every 500 is allergic to the drug, and adverse reactions can be fatal. People have died from as few as three tablets, or survived as many as 430!

In the manufacture of dice for use in gambling casinos, each spot, or pip, of the dice is drilled precisely 17/1000 of an inch into the face, then filled with paint weighing exactly the same as the plastic removed for the hole. Thus the die remains balanced on all sides.

About 300 comic strips are presently published in American newspapers. *Blondie* alone can be found in about 1,200 papers across the country, and *Dick Tracy* reaches 50 million readers daily in 500 papers. A poll conducted in the 1960s found that the most popular strips countrywide were, in order, *Blondie, Dick Tracy, Little Orphan Annie, Peanuts,* and *Rex Morgan, M.D.*

Care for Caviar?

Until recently, about 35,000 pounds of fresh caviar was consumed yearly in the United States; a current caviar shortage has reduced American consumption to 20,000 pounds. Sixty-five long tons of caviar are imported to the United States from Iran each year, and the total American retail market for caviar is $6 million annually.

Today, you can expect to pay anywhere from four to ten dollars for an ounce of the prized delicacy—and an ounce is considered scarcely a portion. As some connoisseurs have noted, caviar is an acquired taste which, for reasons of the pocketbook, is best not acquired.

If you've ever attended a football game in drizzly weather, and have been annoyed to no end by umbrellas blocking your line of vision, you may find it comforting to know that the Romans had a similar problem at their chariot races. A hot dispute over parasol use was finally decided by Emperor Domitian, in favor of the sunshade.

Almost everyone in the United States has heard of Cadillac, Michigan. But how about Chevrolet, Kentucky? Or Chrysler, Alabama. Or Mercedes, Texas. And let's not forget Pontiac, Michigan, or Vega, Texas. There's a town named Ford in four states, and ditto for Dodge. And we can't leave out Auto, West Virginia.

Tale of a Tub

American humorist H.L. Mencken had great fun with a yarn about the original American bathtub, published in the *New York Evening Mail* on December 28, 1917. In the utterly fictitious story, Mencken described the supposedly first stationary tub in the United States with its own pump and drain, and narrated its purchase by one Adam Thompson of Cincinnati, in 1842, who installed the innovation in his mansion. As he went on with the saga, Mencken gave his fertile imagination free reign, and using the names of real persons and places, described how the bathtub had been outlawed as a menace by health departments, permitted by doctor's prescription only in Boston, subjected to outrageous installation taxes in Virginia, and other such nonsense. But the public believed every word of Mencken's hilarious account, which he "never thought would be taken seriously;" and despite his immediate disclaimer, excerpts of the account continued to be reprinted as fact. The story can be found in many periodicals, books, government publications, and even in reference encyclopedias.

Star Wars is now the all-time box-ofice champion among American films, having surpassed the former record-holder, *Jaws*. *The Godfather* remains in third place, followed by *The Exorcist* and *The Sound of Music*.

Gone with the Wind, which for many years ranked as the box-office champion, has now dropped to sixth place.

A group of sentimental surveyors set out to map the Gibson Desert of Australia in 1876, accompanied by a pet cow named Buzoe. Buzoe died of old age on the expedition and was buried with appropriate pomp and circumstance by her companions. But the map-makers felt that Buzoe deserved an even greater tribute, and so they commemorated her by marking the site of "Buzoe's Grave" on their map. Buzoe's Grave continued to be marked on maps of Australia for the next 59 years—as late as 1935!

A recent survey confirmed that regular aspirin users are less likely to suffer a heart attach than those who use aspirin infrequently or not at all. And surgeons at Case Western Reserve University have suggested that the little white tablet may even help prevent the spread of cancer!

Tennis Terms

The word "tennis" has been traced to literally dozens of sources. The most popular origin for the word is the French *tenez*, meaning "hold" or "ready," which French players presumably uttered before serving the ball. Another claim traces the word to the French *tente*, said to be the covered building where the game was originally played.

The word "duece," as used in tennis, comes from the French *à deux*, meaning "two to win." The word "court" itself is said to originate in the French *jeu de courte*, literally "short game," which was used to distinguish the indoor game of tennis from an outdoor game called *jeu de longue*.

The word "love," meaning "no score," has a number of reputed origins. Some say the word sprang from the French habit of drawing a zero on the scoresheet as an oval, which resembled *l'oeuf*, "egg." The English changed *l'oeuf* to "love", so the story goes.

It's a Bird!

There are some 8,600 individual species of birds in the world, including about 650 in the United States, and this leads to a serious problem in naming them all. As a result, birds probably have more names that people would find humorous than any other creature. The following are all names of birds found in the United States:

Wandering Tattler
Greater Yellowlegs
Ruddy Turnstone
Sandwich Tern
Laughing Gull
Buff-bellied Hummingbird
Chimney Swift
Flammulated Owl
Scissor-tailed Flycatcher
Easter Wood Pewee
Black-eared Bushtit
Tufted Titmouse
Brown Creeper
Pygmy Nuthatch
Blue-Gray Gnatcatcher
Bohemian Waxwing
Worm-eating Warbler
Boat-tailed Grackle
White-collared Seedeater
Marbled Godwit
Black-necked Stilt
Least Grebe
Common Loon
Flesh-footed Shearwater

Our favorites, however, are the Black-bellied Whistling-Duck, the Gray Jay, and the Blue-faced Booby.

The word "cellophane" is considered a brand name in England, France, and many other nations, where the term is traced legally to the La Cellophane firm, a French company that began making the product in 1920. But a court decision declared cellophane a generic term in the United States, the name of the substance rather than a particular product.

Nowadays, when a theater uses a prompter, he or she is hidden in a small black box underneath the front of the stage, so the audience doesn't realize when an actor needs assistance with his lines. But when the office of the prompter was created in 15th-century Europe, as a necessity in an era when new plays were presented in such quick succession that actors had little time to study the script, the prompter was very much in view during the performance. This bustling personage actually ran about the boards, script in hand, following the actors and feeding them their lines, in what we hope was not a "stage whisper."

Including amateur groups, there are now over 600 opera companies in the United States. And there are more than 1,300 symphony orchestras throughout the nation!

In 1977, phonograph and tape sales in this country reached the $3.5 billion mark, based on album and tape list prices. That's more than the total gate receipts for all sports events in America, and almost twice as much as the total gross for the film industry!

Aspirin was first marketed in 1899, and was originally available only on prescription. The first aspirin tablets did not appear until 1915.

Just a few decades ago, all the money in the world could not buy an electronic computer with half the speed and versatility of the pocket calculator any American can buy today for less than $20!

Old Bet

Perhaps the most impressive circus shrine in this country is the grave of Old Bet, the first circus elephant in America. Old Bet was brought to the United States in 1815, by Hachaliak Bailey of Somers, New York.

After six years of taking Old Bet on tour of the local villages, Bailey rented the elephant to Nathan Howes, who propelled her to fame as the star of the first tented traveling circus in America. Then, in 1927, while the circus was booked in a small town in Connecticut, Old Bet was shot to death by religious zealots, who mistook the elephant for the behemoth mentioned in the biblical Book of Job.

Bailey had Old Bet buried in Somers, with a memorial statue erected near the grave. The spot was soon overrun with circus performers and fans, who came to pay their respects to Old Bet. One of the most spectacular of these pilgramages occured in 1922, when Ringling Brothers sent their star elephant, Old John, on a 45-mile trek from Madison Square Garden in New York City to Somers. Trailed by a motorcade of journalists and photographers, Old John, approached Old Bet's grave and lowered a wreath of flowers on the spot with his trunk.

Prudery is generally associated with Victorian England, but 19th-century America was equally under Mrs. Grundy's thumb. In 1876, the American public was outraged by the announcement of a New York City dry goods firm—that they would henceforth carry a full line of ladies' undergarments. Hitherto, these "unmentionables" were always made in the home, as no lady would be caught asking for such intimate articles in a store. Moreover, when the ladies washed their lingerie, after hanging the garments on the clothesline, they covered them with a sheet, to protect their underthings from the gaze of male passersby.

In a recent year, copy machines throughout the world turned out some 225 billion copies, and businesses spent about $14 billion on copier services. About 105 billion copies were produced in the United States alone—that's about 485 copies per person! There are presently about four million copy machine in this country.

There are at least 1,116 individual brand names for the gasoline sold in this country. The names range from Ace, Age, and Archie's to Zip-N-Go and ZZYZX.

The word "diesel" was actually taken from the name of a man. Rudolf Diesel, a German engineer, invented an internal-combustion engine that would run on cheap crude oil.

Most people know that Lewis Carroll, George Eliot, O. Henry, and Mark Twain were pen names, not the real names of those authors. But among the pen names of famous authors we must also include George Orwell, Maxim Gorky, André Maurois, Knut Hamsun, and Voltaire.

In 18th-century Europe, courts often offered convicted felons an alternative to the death penalty. In France, the guilty could suffer deportation to French plantations in Guiana, called the "dry guillotine" because of the high death rate among deportees. And in England, convicted prisoners with enough money could choose a lesser form of punishment—deportation to the American colonies!

Black and White

Although vanilla and chocolate may be diametrically opposed on the color scale, they share more in common than you might imagine. Both cocoa and vanilla come from a bean. Both are natives of Mexico and Central America. Both are used primarily as a confectionery flavoring. In fact, for many years chocolate and vanilla were not thought of as opposites at all—they were almost always used *together!*

When cocoa from the New World first reached Spain, vanilla came with it, for the two beans do have one important difference: chocolate in its unadulterated form is bitter tasting; vanilla is sweet. Wealthy Spaniards began enjoying a chocolate beverage sweetened with vanilla, decades before coffee and tea became popular in Europe.

Three of this nation's Interstate Highways stretch from the Atlantic coast to the Pacific. The longest is I-90, which begins in Boston and ends in Seattle, covering a distance of 3,085 miles. The other coast-to-coast routes are I-10, between Jacksonville, Florida and Los Angeles, and I-80, between New York and San Francisco.

Route I-95 is the longest north-south Interstate in the nation, stretching for 1,867 miles between Houlton, Maine, and Miami, Florida. Six other Interstate routes run north-south from end of the country to the other.

"Sober Sue", exhibited during intermissions by Broadway's Hammerstein Victoria Theater in the summer of 1908, offered the greatest challenge ever to American comedians. The management of the theater offered $1,000 to anyone—patron or professional comic—who could make Sue laugh. All of New York City's leading comics rose to the bait. For weeks, they attempted to entertain Sue with gags, anecdotes, limericks, and funny stories. The theater audiences were rolling in the aisles, but Sober Sue never cracked a smile. Weeks later, when the poker-faced lady was well out of town, the actors discovered the reason for their failure. Sue's facial muscles were paralyzed, and she was physically incapable of even the slightest grin. The theater's management had thought up the gimmick as a means of luring audiencs into the house during the normally slow summer months, taking advantage of the free performances donated by the city's highest-priced comedians.

Alas! Alas! Alas!

Although no one can be absolutely sure of such things, many historians believe that Sir Isaac Newton, John Ruskin, and Immanuel Kant all died virgins.

The United States is the largest single contributor to the budget of the United Nations, chipping in a hefty 25 percent of the total U.N. budget. The Soviet Union contributes less than 13 percent, Japan and West Germany about seven percent each.

James Douglas, the earl of Morton, had the honor of introducing the "maiden," a guillotine-like device, into his homeland, Scotland. In 1581, Douglas was beheaded by that very same device.

Let It Rain!
Let It Pour!

As if there were any choice. This universal phenomenon carries with it beneficence or disaster. Many large populations pray for the blessing of rain, without which their food supply would parch and put their very existence in grave peril.

Rain, too, can bring floods and other unpleasantnesses.

The theme is so universal that mary artists have tried their hand at limning rain. Here follows some unusually drawings on the subject.

Woodblock print by noted Japanese artist Hiroshige.

Drawing by Crawford Young which first appeared in Caricature, *a magazine published in New York in the 1890s*

This magnificent drawing appeared in a most unexpected place, a humor magazine named Judge, which was published in the United States during the early part of the 20th century.

Drawing which originally appeared in Judge, a humor magazine which flourished in the United States in the 1920s

A painting by Anatoly L-vovich Kaplan, a great Soviet artist

From Punch, the great
English magazine of humor

Drawing by the great French artist, Honore Daumier (1808-1879), noted for his political caricatures, satirizing social inequity.

Pheidippides ran from Marathon to Athens

In September of 490 B.C., King Darius, the ruler of the powerful Persian Empire, sent his army to attack the city-state of Athens. His forces landed on the plain of Marathon, just a few miles from Athens.

Though greatly outnumbered, the Athenians marched out to meet the invaders, while sending a request for help to their allies in Sparta. The message was carried by Pheidippides, the best runner in Athens.

Racing out of the city on foot, he ran all that day and through the night, forging ahead across rough, rocky terrain in which the road was often barely suitable for mules and mountain goats. The next morning, having covered a distance of 140 miles, he arrived in Sparta. After delivering his message and getting the answer, he set out to rejoin the Athenian troops, once again covering the distance in a day and a night.

Just a few days later, the Athenian and Persian armies clashed in the now famous battle of Marathon. Though he'd had only a short time to rest up from his magnificent two-way run, Pheidippides participated in the battle as an infantryman.

Contrary to expectations, the Athenians decisively defeated the Persians. Like his fellow soldiers, who had fought so hard against the numerically superior enemy, Pheidippides was exhausted when the fighting came to an end. Nonetheless, he gamely accepted the Athenian commander's request to carry the news of the victory to the anxious inhabitants of the city. Casting off his heavy armor, the exhausted Pheidippides set out on his last and greatest run.

The distance from Marathon to Athens is 22 miles, 1,470 yards. Pheidippides covered it in just a few hours, but the ordeal was too much for his already overtaxed system. Shouting, "Victory, victory" with his last breaths, he staggered into the central marketplace of Athens, then dropped to the pavement—dead.

The Athenians never forgot this noble patriotic sacrifice; and in the years that followed, they established a series of memorial games, including running events of various kinds, in memory of Pheidippides. When the Olympic Games were revived in 1896, a road-race called the marathon was made a regular event. In 1924, its distance was standardized at 26 miles 385 yards.

Peanut butter is one peanut derivative we can't thank George Washington Carver for. That great favorite of the schoolboy was introduced by a St. Louis doctor in 1890 for patients who needed an easily digestible form of protein. Today, about half of the United States' annual peanut harvest of some four billion pounds is used for peanut butter, with the remainder going to salted nuts, candies, oil, and livestock fodder.

Only about ten percent of our crop is used to manufacture peanut oil; but throughout the rest of the peanut-growing world, the goober is grown almost exclusively for its oil.

Perhaps the world's most elaborate dollhouse is the palatial structure presented to Queen Mary of England in 1924. The structure is built on a scale of one inch to the foot, and is about nine feet long, five feet wide, and five feet high. The miniature marvel comprises over 50 rooms, and contains a working elevator, a real plumbing system, and its own electric generator. Actual cobwebs cover the doll-size bottles of authentic vintage wine in the wine cellar, and the model is adorned with diminutive oil paintings, sculptures, murals, and painted ceilings executed by famous artists. The library includes hundreds of miniature volumes, handwritten by 170 well-known authors, including Rudyard Kipling. This miniature mansion has been written up in an official description spanning a two-volume text.

Queen Victoria was wont to express her displeasure with the oft-quoted comment, "We are not amused." No doubt those were the words issued by the prudish monarch upon being presented with a singular music box in 1887. Some prankster, had a musical bustle constructed for the modest queen.

When the wearer of the bustle sat down, a mechanism played the British anthem, *God Save the Queen*.

It has often been claimed that the *Gettysburg Address* can be written on the head of a pin, but what do you make of a machine that can squeeze 400 novels onto a square inch of glass? The machine is the micropantograph, whose diamond point will produce writing, legible through a microscope, on the scale of 32 million words per square inch.

Crime does not pay—at least, it didn't for the nephew of a rich Frenchman in the 1940s. The youth had great expectations from his uncle, who lived near Boulogne. The wealthy uncle had many relatives, but only the nephew ever received any letters from him. The unscrupulous, greedy young man poisoned his uncle, and leaving nothing to chance, used the uncle's letters as a guide to forge a will declaring himself the sole beneficiary of the estate. But the uncle's housekeeper went to the authorities charging forgery. It seems that her employer was illiterate, and for nearly 50 years, the housekeeper had been ghosting all the man's correspondence and papers.

The first American to be executed for a crime was John Billington, a signer of the Pilgrims' compact, who was hanged for murder in Plymouth, Massachusetts, on September 30, 1630.

Modern electronic computers can accept up to 100 million instructions per second, retrieve any piece of information in just 250 billionths of a second, and print data at the top rate of 6,000 lines per minute. The world's most powerful computer, the Control Data Corporation's CDC 7600, can perform 36 million operations in one second. You can pick up a CDC 7600 for about $15 million the next time you need help balancing your checkbook.

The oldest tennis court in existence can be found in Paris, and dates from the year 1496.

The nation's first air-conditioned movie theater was the Metropolitan in—where else?—Los Angeles, which was fitted for an air distribution system in 1921.

Spifflicated!

Écarté, a play performed in London, circa 1875, had the shortest run in theater history—and probably also the wettest. The play closed after only one act, because the producer, a generous man, had ordered real champagne for the first act drinking scene—instead of the customary colored water or tea. The actors took full advantage of the indulgence, and many of them fell before the first curtain did—hence, the producer had to cancel the performance before the beginning of Act Two and give refunds to the entire audience. The poor man was so chagrined at the fiasco that he closed the theater for the rest of the season.

Leonardo da Vinci, Giovanni Boccaccio, Paul Cezanne, Alexandre Dumas *fils*, Erasmus, August Strindberg, Jack London, and Richard Wagner had more in common than their creative genius—all of these men were children of unmarried parents.

In 1931, the British novelist Arnold Bennett set out to prove that the drinking water of Paris was perfectly safe. He drank a glass of the water, contracted typhoid, and died.

According to the United Nations, the country in which the largest percentage of men and women live to be 85 years old is Puerto Rico, where 21 percent of men and 33 percent of women attain that age. In the United States, 30 percent of all women reach the age of 85, but less than 14 percent of men.

The nation with the lowest percentage of men and women reaching the age of 50 is the African country of Guinea, where only about one-quarter of the population lives to be 50 years old.

The tiny nation of Liechtenstein was the first country in Europe to abolish the death penalty, eliminating the practice *de facto* in 1798. By 1976, only France and Spain among all nations in Western Europe retained capital punishment for common criminals.

Did you ever wonder why compasses often employ a fleur-de-lys symbol to indicate north? Well, ancient sailing charts used the names of the eight winds for the eight points of the compass. The name of the north wind was Tramontano. By 1500, the arrowhead and letter "T" designating Tramontano had evolved into the fleur-de-lys.

John von Neumann, who played a major role in developing the modern computer, was a bit of a stored program computer himself. Friends claimed that Neumann could repeat verbatim any passage from any book he'd ever read.

In Japan, the bath was traditionally a large wooden tub placed outside in the garden and filled with very hot water. The entire family bathed together at the same time. In Japanese baths, both public and private, there is rarely an attempt to achieve privacy. Public baths often have large unprotected openings through which people passing in the street can observe the bathers. But nowadays, bathing in Japan—especially in the cities—is becoming westernized.

Cat-'o-nine Tales

The notion that a cat can fall from a great height and survive is not an old wives' tale, and may have contributed to the idea that a cat has nine lives. One cat fell from the 20th floor of a Montreal apartment building in 1973 and suffered only a pelvic fracture.

The story of a cat that fell from the Washington Monument and survived has been batted about for years. According to some, the facts are these: during construction of the Monument, workers came across a cat lurking in the framework near the top of the structure. The cat panicked, and leaped from the scaffolding. Incredibly enough, the cat survived the 500-foot-plus fall—but, even more amazingly, the stunned creature was pounced on and killed almost immediately by a wandering dog.

In past centuries, the Cossacks of Russia organized massive caviar-hunting expeditions twice each year, with every member of the community taking part in the two-week campaigns. Among other things, the Cossacks used cannons to stun the fish in the water.

The Russian Czar Alexander I is aften credited with introducing caviar to the social elite of Paris. The word "caviar," however, is not Russian in origin (the Russians call it *ikra*), but comes from the Italian *caviola*, derived from the Turkish word *khavyah*.

The cocktail known as the Manhattan was introduced by Lady Randolph Churchill, Winston's mother. The occasion was a party at New York's Manhattan Club, in honor of the newly elected Governor Samuel Tilden. The drink combined bourbon with sweet vermouth and a dash of bitters.

American presently consume over a billion gallons of ice cream, ices, and sherbet each year—enough to completely fill the Grand Canyon. Americans are, by far, the world's largest consumers of ice cream. The average person in this country puts away about 23 quarts each year—that's roughly equivalent to a cone per person every other day. Only Australians, Canadians, and New Zealanders eat even half that much. Compare that figure with the average yearly consumption of 100 years ago—about one teaspoon per person!

The oft-heard idea that caffeine is an effective antidote to inebriation is simply—er, without grounds. Time is the only remedy for excess alcohol in the bloodstream, so coffee is an aid to the intoxicated only insofar as it takes time to drink it.

In Western cultures, cattle became a favored standard of exchange at a very early date, since cattle, to a great extent, already formed the basis of wealth. Cattle were generally owned by rich and poor alike; land, only by the aristocracy. Our words "capital" and "chattel" come from the word "cattle," or rather from "head of cattle," based on the Latin *caput*, "head."

"Pecuniary" comes from the Latin *pecus*, which means "cattle." "Coin" comes from the Latin *cuneus*, which indicates "stamp" or "die"; and "fee" derives from the Anglo-Saxon *feoh*, or "cattle."

The world's greatest typing buff must certainly be Mrs. Marva Drew of Waterloo, Iowa. Over a six-year span, Marva exercised her skills by typing the numbers one to one million on a manual typewriter—a feat requiring 2,473 pages!

The Christmas card first appeared in the United States in 1874, brought out by Bavarian-born Boston lithographer Louis Prang. Prang's card was designed by Mrs. O.E. Whitney, and based on an English card signed *Charles Dickens* that Prang had brought back from Europe. At first, the cards were produced for export to England, since the custom of sending greeting cards at Christmas had yet to appear in America. But Prang's cards went on sale here the following year. Christmas-card fever soon became a permanent American ailment.

More people are trained for the operation of the typewriter than for any other machine on earth requiring specialized training.

The 10,000 golf courses in the United States occupy some 1,550 square miles of our nation—an area larger than the state of Rhode Island! An estimated 10 million Americans now play the game.

The English initially called the hamburger "Salisbury Steak" after Dr. James H. Salisbury, who in the 1880s recommended to his patients that they eat well-done beef patties three times daily, with hot water before and after, to relieve colitis, anemia, asthma, and other ailments. Today, the only ailment hamburger is thought capable of curing is severe hunger.

Polygamist Nonpareil

At the age of 24, Theresa Vaughn was put on trial for bigamy in Sheffield, England, on December 19, 1922. On the witness stand, Mrs. Vaughn confessed that she was not merely a bigamist, but a polygamist of unparalleled proportions. In the course of five years, the young woman had married 62 men in over 50 cities in Great Britain, Germany, and South Africa. In other words, Mrs. Vaughn had been acquiring a new husband every month.

"Camp" entertainment is hardly a modern discovery. In fact, one of the funkier phenomena of all time was a sister act that toured the American scene from 1893 to 1896, and had a seven-year Broadway run.

The four Cherry sisters, ages 17 to 22 at their debut, launched their incredible careers with a skit of their own invention, on an amateur program in Cedar Rapids. The sketch was so egregiously bad that the girls had to play behind a wire screen, to avoid the rotten tomatoes and other vegetables that rained down on them nightly as they performed their ludicrous routine.

Nevertheless, for three years, the Cherry sisters played to packed houses in the midwest, and they opened on Broadway at the then large salary of $1,000 a week.

Finally, in 1903, the girls went back to the farm—with a kitty of $200,000. They were convinced that they were the greatest actresses ever to appear on stage.

A latrine at the palace of Knossos, Crete, which dates from about 2000 B.C., had a wooden seat over an earthenware pan, and a reservoir and piping for flush water. With a few scattered exceptions, no such sanitary device was to appear in England until the 18th century.

Americans presently consume over one billion tubes of toothpaste each year. Yet caries, or tooth decay, is by far the most common disease in this country today, afflicting about 90 percent of all people. Ancient peoples had neither effective toothbrushes nor toothpastes of any seeming worth, but we have no proof that they suffered from tooth decay any more than we do today.

The Navahos are the most populous Indian tribe in America, numbering close to 100,000. The Navaho Indian Reservation, which occupies parts of Arizona, New Mexico, and Utah, is larger than a number of states.

Surprisingly, the Navahos are much more populous today than they were a century ago. In 1869, the Navahos numbered less than 10,000.

The world's record for watermelon bursting is an impressive 155 feet, seven inches, achieved by a California man who dropped a 15-pound melon from the roof of a seven-story building. That mark might have been significantly improved if the record-holder had dropped a melon found in Georgia in 1975—weighing 90 pounds!

Over 60 percent of all pinball machines manufactured in this country are exported, the majority to Western Europe.

Twenty-one million Americans—about one in every ten—now play the piano, more than the number who play all other musical instruments combined.

Throwing money around will usually make you quite popular. But not always. An old English law stipulates that a person swearing or tossing money at a tax collector should be fined according to his station. A tithe-tossing gentleman will have to cough up three to five shillings as a fine. Day laborers can be more careless—their fine for delivering their tax money through the air is but one shilling.

Americans are no longer surprised to learn that many major corporations are able to avoid paying any federal income taxes for a given year—even when they show a profit. But some corporations play the tax game even more skillfully than that. In 1974 and 1975, the Ford Motor Company used tax credits not only to avoid paying income taxes, but to earn a $189 million refund from Uncle Sam as well!

There are parts of China that are *west* of India. The westernmost corner of China's Sinkiang Province is closer to Europe than New Delhi or Calcutta, India.

The heaviest dog on record was a Wisconsin Saint Bernard who at age five weighed 295 pounds.

On the night of Napoleon's marriage to Josephine, her dog mistook his amorous assault as an attack, and promptly leapt into the bed and bit him.

WELCOME TO ACCIDENT

Appellation, U.S.A.

Among the curiously named towns and villages in the United States are such gems as:

Accident, Maryland
Ammunition Depot, Nevada
Anvil Location, Michigan
Aroma, Indiana
Assumption, Illinois
Bacon, Georgia
Battiest, Oklahoma
Bloomer, Wisconsin
Bountiful, Utah
Brilliant, Ohio
Burnt Corn, Alabama
Cocoa, Florida
Deadwood, South Dakota
Darling, Mississippi
Difficult, Tennessee
Dime Box, Texas
Frostproof, Florida
Hand, South Dakota
Intercourse, Pennsylvania
Ivy, Arkansas
King of Prussia, Pennsylvania
Kite, Georgia
Lemon, Mississippi
Licking, Ohio
Little Medicine, Wyoming
Magnet, Nebraska
Marked Tree, Arkansas
Mexican Hat, Utah
New Era, Michigan
New Limerick, Maine
Nine Times, South Carolina

Ninety-Six, South Carolina
Old Dock, North Carolina
Overpark, Mississippi
Painted Post, New York
Paint Bank, Virginia
Paisley, Oregon
Paradise, California
Parchment, Michigan
Petroleum, Kentucky
Polo, Missouri
Radium, Kansas
Reform, Alabama
Sleeper, Missouri
Sleepy Eye, Minnesota
Snowflake, Arizona
Social Circle, Georgia
Soso, Mississippi
Temperance, Michigan
Truth or Consequences, New Mexico
Whoopflearea, Kentucky
Young America, Minnesota

At the beginning of the 17th century, cinnamon thrived along the Malabar Coast of India, which was in the hands of the Portuguese. But in the middle of the century, the Dutch deviously took control of cinnamon commerce, buying the rights from Malabar kings to destroy all cinnamon plantations in the area to enhance the value of the new Dutch plantations on the island of Ceylon. Thus, when the English seized Ceylon in 1795, they inherited the Dutch monopoly.

Irish innkeepers of yore used the expression "kettle or screw?" when inquiring the favored liquid refreshment of their patrons. "Kettle" meant hot punch; "screw" meant wine.

Speaking of Ireland and liquid refreshment, the city and county of Cork have no etymological connection with the bottle stopper. The word *cork*—or *corcaigh* in Irish Gaelic—signifies a swamp, referring to the fen upon which part of the city was built.

Louis Cyr was the strongest man in the world

He stood only five feet, ten and one-half inches, but his huge chest, which bulged 60 inches in circumference, seemed like a barrel that had popped out of his 300-pound frame. His legs and his biceps were tremendous. The strength of the farm boy from St. Cyprein, Quebec, is the stuff that legends are made of.

But Louis Cyr was no legend. He really could lift a full barrel of cement with one arm, and he once pushed a freight car on the railroad tracks up an incline. On another occasion, 18 men who in the aggregate weighed 4,300 pounds stood on a platform. Louis Cyr lifted the platform. And to get tongues wagging, Cyr lifted 588 pounds off the floor—with one finger!

But undoubtedly, Cyr's most dramatic feat occurred on the day he was pitted against four workhorses. On December 20, 1891, standing before a crowd of 10,000, in Sohmer Park, Montreal, Louis Cyr was fitted with a special harness. Four draft horses were lined up opposite Cyr, a pair of them to his left, and a second pair to his right. Heavy leather straps encased his upper arms; sturdy hooks at the end of these straps were attached to whiffletrees which led to harnesses strapped to the four horses.

Cyr stood with his feet planted wide and placed his arms on his chest. As Louis gave the word, the grooms urged their horses to pull. The regulations of the contest ruled out any sudden jerk. The four horses pulled with all their might and main on the strong man, trying to dislodge Louis's arms from his chest. If Cyr lost his footing or either arm left his chest, he would lose the contest.

The grooms whipped the horses, and urged them in every way to pull harder and harder. But the horses slipped and slid, while Cyr didn't budge an inch. After a few minutes of tugging, it was obvious that Cyr was stronger than all four horses put together.

Linguists have estimated that just 4,000 words constitute 99 percent of all the English words used in common speech and writing—and just 300 words make up 75 percent!

Parts of the Irish Republic are *north* of Northern Ireland!

Classy Con Man

Swindlers have peddled everything to the unsuspecting from worthless desert real estate to the Brooklyn Bridge.

Hans Hermann Weyer, a window dresser in West Germany, offered his wealthy countrymen the one thing money presumably could not buy: a title of respect.

Beginning in the 1960s, Weyer offered his clients bogus certificates conferring on the holder any title that struck their fancy. For $2,500, Weyer would take his status-hungry victims to the Syracuse Cathedral in Sicily, and certify them as knights of the nonexistent Holy Order of Agatha.

For the academically minded, Weyer offered degrees from such fanciful institution as the National College of Toronto and the Sheffield Philosophical University, a document signed by the "Archbishop Professor Charles Brearley" himself.

In perhaps his best coup, Weyer sold the title of Knight of the Orthodox Church of Cyprus to one of Germany's largest mail-order furniture dealers, then sold a photograph of the ceremony to his client's major competitor for $40,000. The embarrassing photo eventually appeared in the competitor's company newspaper.

Before entering prison in 1978, Weyer amassed a fortune close to ten million marks. By his own count, he had peddled 350 doctoral degrees, 80 consular titles, 76 certificates of nobility, and 23 orders of distinction—every one of them bogus.

The term centipede means "hundred legs," but centipedes do not have a hundred legs, and millipedes do not have a thousand legs. A centipede has one pair of legs per body segment; only if it has exactly 50 segments will it have a hundred legs. Millipedes have two pairs of legs for each body segment.

There's another difference between the two creatures: Some centipedes are venomous, and can be dangerous. All millipedes are harmless.

A species of a fish called the goby is probably the smallest fish on earth. This diminutive creature lives in some lakes in the Philippines. Four of these fish in a line would measure less than an inch.

Traveling due south from Chicago, you would never touch South America. Chicago is actually west of every point on that continent.

Phony Figures

As of 1970, 120.2 million telephones were in use in the United States alone, considerably more than the combined number of phones in Japan, Great Britain, West Germany, Russia, and Canada. Out of 100 households in New York State, 95 had telephones. And Washington, D.C. averaged 102 telephones per hundred households!

The state that has been best able to resist the lure of electronic gab is Mississippi, which has only 75 phones per 100 households—still a fantastic proportion when compared to even the most technologically advanced nations of the world. For example, Japan has fewer than 40 phones per 100 households, and West Germany has fewer than 35 per 100.

Nineteenth-century French novelist Honore de Balzac was so fascinated by the handkerchief that he planned to write a book on the psychology of women based on "how they hold their handkerchief."

Cork comes from the bark of the cork oak, which contains a waxy substance that helps make the wood impervious to water and gases. A one-inch cube of cork contains some 200 million air-filled cells, so that captive air accounts for about half of a cork's volume. The air-filled cells are responsible for cork's bouyancy and elasticity, and contribute to its high degree of imperviousness to air and water.

Today, Spain leads the world in cork production, followed by Portugal and Algeria. The annual world production of about 300,000 tons now barely satisfies the demand for cork stoppers, suggesting that the cork may someday disappear from wine bottles altogether.

In medieval times, when handkerchiefs were rare, the finger and the sleeve were considered the proper implements for wiping the nose. At the time, forks were not used at the table, and food was eaten with the hands. So etiquette demanded that the cultured individual touch his food only with the right hand, and his nose only with the left. The medieval English *Boke of Curtasye* advised that it was proper to blow one's nose with a finger as long as the finger was then wiped on the sleeve or skirt.

Where can you find Rome, Naples, Athens, Berlin, Amsterdam, Madrid, Geneva, Turin, Antwerp, Hamburg, Cairo, and Bombay, all in one state? In New York. And let's not forget Babylon and Jericho.

Catgut strings are made from the intestines of sheep, horses, and other hooved animals— but never from cats.

Spain is the only country in which a wife does not take the name of her husband upon marriage. A Spanish wife retains her maiden name, while children may adopt either her name or her husband's, or both.

In ancient cultures, lightning was generally associated with the appearance of a god. The ancient Greeks thought that lightning and thunder were omens of Zeus, and considered any place that lightning struck to be sacred.

Salmoneus, the legendary king of Elis, Greece, attempted to imitate Zeus by driving his chariot over a bronze bridge to imitate thunder, while throwing torches in the air to represent lightning.

Amsterdam police have a special branch, called the *grachtenvissers*, whose only duty is to cope with motorists who drive into the canals.

Approximately 46,000 pounds of earth must be mined and sifted to produce a half-carat diamond. In an average year, diamond production for the entire world stands at about ten million carats—just four-and-a-half tons!

On December 20, 1938, 27-year-old Mary Joyce of Taku, Alaska, hitched a team of five huskies to a sled and left her snug hunting lodge, bound for Fairbanks, Alaska—1,000 miles away. Three months later, Mary and her dogs arrived safely in Fairbanks, completing the longest dog sled trip ever undertaken by a woman. Not once during her arduous trek did the temperature climb higher than a bitter 34 degrees below zero—and a number of times, the thermometer dropped to 60 degrees below!

In 1698, at the age of 22, Yuen Tong, a Chinese Buddhist holy man, assumed a squatting position prescribed for sustained meditation. When he died 62 years later, Yuen Tong had never once risen from that position.

At his own instructions, the ascetic was embalmed and prepared for display in the Pagoda of the Rocks in Kunming—still sitting!

The Rabbits' Wedding, a book for children up to seven years of age, contains a scene in which a white rabbit and a black rabbit are married in a forest. In 1959, the Alabama state senate charged that the book constituted an appeal for racial integration. The book was thereafter placed on the "reserved" shelves of the state libraries.

Daisy Ashford, born in England in 1891, won renown throughout the English-speaking world with her comic novel The Young Visitors—a book she wrote when she was only nine years old. Daisy's book, a deft portrait of Victorian society, scored an immediate success, and has since topped the 200,000-copy mark in sales. But despite her early literary triumph, Daisy Ashford never wrote another book.

The International Federation of Airline Pilots recently singled out Los Angeles International as the nation's most unsafe airport. Since the airport is located in a residential area, all night flights must approach from and take off toward the west, over the ocean, to reduce noise levels in the surrounding area. Pilots claim these restrictions make the airport particularly hazardous.

In 1974, the firefly was declared the "official insect" of the state of Pennsylvania.

Clam chowder was invented by a group of Breton sailors shipwrecked off the coast of Maine. The enterprising seamen gathered clams and mixed them with salvaged pork, crackers, and potatoes in a large cauldron, or chaudiere. Milk was added to the recipe later to produce New England clam chowder, and tomatoes to produce Manhattan chowder.

High Fashion

During the 17th century, high-heeled shoes became fashionable in Venice. Eventually, the heels became so high that women could not walk in them, and servants were hired so that the ladies could lean on them while getting in and out of a gondola.

Fleeting Fame

During the mid-19th century, a regular diner at the famous New York restaurant Delmonico's told the proprietor of a dish made with lobster and cream that he'd enjoyed in South America. The next night, the diner was presented with a lobster cooked in a chafing dish with sherry, thick cream, and egg yolks. The invention was promptly installed on Delmonico's menu, christened Lobster Wenburg after the diner, a shipping magnate.

But Wenburg's fame was indeed short-lived. Lobster Wenburg remained on Delmonico's menu until the night its namesake became embroiled in a drunken brawl that ravaged the restaurant. Wenburg was ejected from the restaurant, and from the menu as well—Lobster Wenburg became Lobster Newburgh forevermore.

Flash in the Pan

William Sidis, Jr., the son of an American psychiatrist, became his father's star pupil a short time after his birth in 1898. At the age of six months, William knew the alphabet. By the time he was two years old, the boy could read and write. Soon after his ninth birthday, having already completed 11 years of grammar school and high school, young Sidis entered Harvard University.

An 11-year-old student at Harvard, William amazed his teachers with a lecture displaying his knowledge of highly complicated mathematical concepts. At the age of 16 he was graduated with honors, and at 19 was made a full professor of mathematics.

Alas, Sidis' studies in mathematics need never have gone further than simple arithmetic. For at 26, the child prodigy was found operating an adding machine in a New York store. In 1943, the lonely ex-genius died in a rooming house.

There's more than one way to win an international sporting event. A defector from Czechoslovakia told a Senate subcommittee that on the eve of a championship hockey game between his country and Canada, the most attractive Czech female agents were dispatched to the hotel where the Canadian team was staying. The night of high jinx apparently took its toll on the Canadians, for the next day, the Czech team won handily.

A Brazilian palm species, the *Raphia taedigera*, can claim the largest leaves in the plant kingdom. The feather-like fronds of this short, stout tree are sometimes over 70 feet long and 19 feet broad. Imagine a leaf that could stand on its end to the height of a seven-story building!

Maroilles, a cheese first produced in 960 by monks at the abbey of Thierache, is bathed in beer during the ripening process. Frenchmen call it *vieux puant*—"old stinker."

Most cars today are equipped with either a four-, six-, or eight-cylinder engine. But a 1930 Cadillac was powered by a 16-cylinder engine! And speaking of Cadillacs, the largest automobile ever constructed was a special limousine built for King Khalid of Saudi Arabia in 1975, which measured 25 feet, two inches in length, and weighed 7,800 pounds.

Go fly a kite!—but not in Washington, D.C.—for Congress long ago decreed a $10 fine for kite-flying in the Capital.

And you might want to know that if you carry a woodcock in Washington, between January 1 and July 1—be it alive or dead—that's a fineable offense.

Sublimely Ridiculous

In all countries and climes, artists have tried to lend a little mirth to the earth by drawing pictures and cartoons which ridicule man and his ways. There follow a number of such drawings from all over the world which present some marvelous absurdities.

This mockery of human presumption, drawn by a Russian, appears in a book titled Fifty Years of Soviet Art.

From the British Punch, *a magazine of worldwide reputation.*

Grandville, one of the greatest of French satirists, flourished around 1840.

This delicious piece was wrought by Ronald Searle, a famous British artist.

This fantasy first appeared in Bizarre Magazine, *a Parisian publication which flourished around 1960.*

This drawing by Caran D'ache is to be found in a book called Les Courses dans L'antiguité.

From Lustige Blätter, *a world-renowned German publication.*

During the first century, a Roman glass-maker presented himself to the Emperor Tiberius and claimed he could manufacture unbreakable glass, proving his claim by dropping a glass vessel on the floor. The emperor promptly had the glass-maker beheaded and his shop demolished, fearing that glass of such quality could lessen the value of gold and silver—with which the Imperial treasury was quite well stocked.

Gladiators' Revolt

Though millions of people who have seen the 1960 movie *Spartacus* take the story to be a work of Hollywood imagination, the film is actually based on real events in the history of ancient Rome. In 73 B.C., a former soldier named Spartacus escaped from a gladiator training school and took refuge on Mt. Vesuvius, where he was joined by other escaped gladiators and slaves. Spartacus' army, ultimately 90,000 strong, defeated two Roman forces and overran southern Italy, then fought its way toward the Alps.

When many of Spartacus' men refused to leave Italy, he led them south to the toe of the Italian boot, hoping to escape to Sicily. But his army was defeated in 71 B.C. by a force of eight Roman legions.

There is one major inaccuracy in the film, however. Spartacus was not captured and crucified along with his men. He was slain in battle.

Of the almost four billion people in the world today, approximately a third eat with a knife and fork, a third with chopsticks, and a third with their fingers.

World production of paper and paperboard now stands at an astounding 140 million tons per year. How much paper is that? Well, if the entire supply were used to produce standard 20-pound bond typing paper, the yearly world production figure would exceed 40 trillion sheets—10,000 sheets for every person on earth!

A 1959 poll showed that crossword puzzles are the number one indoor game in the United States. An estimated 30 million Americans regularly wrack their brains for the name of "an East Indian shrub" or "an African antelope." And an even larger percentage of the population regularly accepts the crossword challenge in England.

The word "windfall" does not owe its origin to the idea of sudden good fortune blown across one's path as if by the wind. Its origin is rather more prosaic. Centuries ago in England, the tenant of an estate was forbidden to fell trees on his land, for the best timber was reserved for the Royal Navy. But the tenant could claim for his own any trees felled by the wind. The timber the tenant then sold indeed earned him a "windfall" profit.

During the 14th century, when public latrines generally emptied into urban streams, the London street Sherborne Lane became known as Shiteburn Lane in tribute to the pungent watercourse it ran parallel to. The London Bridge, which at the time carried over a hundred homes, could boast just one privy. Most bridge dwellers therefore opted for a more direct route to the River Thames, leading to a popular definition of London Bridge as a structure "wise men go over and fools go under."

Today, the custom of the Mussulman is to carry a comb with him to manicure his whiskers. He does so immediately after prayer, while still on his knees, and any strands of hair that fall out of his beard are carefully picked up and preserved for burial with the owner. Five hundred million Mohammedans still swear by the beard of the Prophet.

The longest jail sentence on record is 381 years, passed on a 16-year-old boy in Montreal in 1964. The youth had pleaded guilty to six counts of attempted murder and a series of armed robberies.

The world's first adhesive postage stamps were placed on sale in England on May 1, 1840, selling for one or two pence and bearing the image of Queen Victoria. The first U.S. government postage stamp appeared seven years later: a five-cent stamp bearing the picture of Benjamin Franklin, and a ten-cent stamp bearing George Washington's image.

The primary sewer main of Imperial Rome, called the *Cloaca Maxima*, continued to serve as a storm drain right into the 20th century.

The Noon Watch

In 1642, Rembrandt painted *The Shooting Company of Captain Frans Banning Cocq*, in which 29 life-sized civic guards are shown leaving their armory at high noon, with the sun shining brightly upon them.

Less than 200 years later, the picture had become so dingy and dark that someone facetiously called it *The Night Watch*, a nickname that has since supplanted its true title.

Nero has long had the reputation of being one of the most sadistic, blood-thirsty Roman emperors. Though cruel and ruthless, Nero actually detested bloody gladiatorial contests, preferring plays, concerts, and poetry readings, and himself played the lyre and wrote poetry. In those spectator games that Nero did provide, he often refused to allow any of the contestants to be killed.

Oddly enough, it was partly Nero's distaste for gore that turned the Roman populace against him, for music and poetry were not deemed fitting pastimes for a Roman emperor.

Oyster "Shells"

The famed Marennes oyster owes its origin to a peculiar incident that took place during the 17th-century religious wars. At the siege of La Rochelle, France, the Huguenot defenders began tossing oysters from the parapets of the city when they ran out of more potent ammunition. Some of the missiles landed in the nearby salt marshes. Peasants who later found the oysters discovered the meat had turned an odd green color. The characteristic Marennes green proved to be the result of diatoms (algae) living in the marsh water.

During the Nazi occupation of Czechoslovakia, the jeweled crown of Bohemia was hidden in an oven in a Prague castle. According to an ancient legend, any impostor who placed the crown upon his head would die shortly thereafter. But the Nazi governor of Czechoslovakia scoffed at the superstition, and placed the crown not only on his own head, but on the heads of his two sons as well.

Several weeks later, the Nazi governor was killed by a Czech patriot. Soon after, one of his sons died by falling from his horse, and the other son fell in battle.

How did America's favorite Thanksgiving Day fowl become known as a "turkey"? No, the bird is North American in origin, not Turkish. Early European settlers in America thought the bird looked like the guinea fowl, which was sometimes imported to Europe through Turkey. Thus, for a time the guinea fowl and the American bird were both known as the Turkey-cock.

Curiously, the word "assassin" is derived from the narcotic drug known as *hashish* in Arabic. In the early Middle Ages, a secret order of Moslems were sworn to murder Christian leaders of the Crusades and other enemies of the sect. They committed their murderous acts, supposedly, while under the influence of hashish, and were therefore known as *hashishin*, or "hashish users."

Egypt is not the most populous nation in Africa. That honor belongs to Nigeria, the tenth most populous nation in the world, with a population of over 63 million. Egypt's population is estimated at about 37 million.

In October, 1957, Mrs. Beverly Nina Avery, a 48-year-old barmaid from Los Angeles, obtained her 16th divorce, thus becoming the most married-and-divorced person in the world. Mrs. Avery reported that five of her former husbands had broken her nose.

Parting Ways

There are over 35 different legal grounds for divorce in the United States, but not one of these grounds is legal in all 50 states. A loathsome disease can result in a divorce in Kentucky and Illinois. Joining a religious sect which does not believe in marriage provides sufficient grounds in Kentucky and New Hampshire. But attempting to take the life of a spouse is grounds for divorce only in Tennessee and Illinois, and intolerable severity, only in Vermont. And in Virginia, the guilty party in a divorce granted on the grounds of adultery cannot remarry without the consent of the court.

A painting dating from ancient Rome suggests that the Romans used *tabulae*, a game similar to modern backgammon, to play a form of classical "strip poker."

The first automatic parking meter in the United States appeared in Oklahoma City, Oklahoma, in 1935. The coin slots accepted nickels.

How great a number is one trillion? Well, if you start counting now and continue counting for 24 hours each day, you'll reach that number in about 30,000 years.

Some 750,000 people in the United States are bitten by wild animals each year. About five percent must be treated for rabies.

The most common given name in the world is Muhammad.

There is enough stone in the Great Pyramid of Cheops, in Egypt, to build a wall around all of France. The construction of the massive tomb required the work of 100,000 men for 20 to 30 years.

In October 7, 1965, 16-year-old Charles Linster set a record for push-ups that will be hard to beat. Performing for three hours and 54 minutes, Linster executed 6,006 push-ups without stopping.

Highway Favorites

What's the most popular make of American car? Well, if we take the 1971 figures, it's the Chevrolet, with 2,320,777 in sales.

The next most favored car is the Ford, with 1,761,112 cars sold.

A distant third is the Oldsmobile, which sold 775,199 cars.

Did you know that you can sail from New England almost to the tip of Florida without once venturing out into the open seas? The Intracoastal Waterway will take you down the East Coast in protected waters, utilizing an intricate system of rivers, bays, estuaries, and canals. And when you reach Florida, you can start on another journey—along the shores of the Gulf of Mexico all the way to Brownsville, Texas, via another Intracoastal Waterway!

Skyscrapers are no threat to the landscape of Washington, D.C. A law forbids a builder to construct any building taller than the U.S. Capitol—which stands 287½ feet tall atop an 88-foot hill, with a statue atop its dome increasing its height by 19½ feet.

The largest outdoor ice-skating rink now stands, oddly enough, in Japan. Completed in 1967, the colossal 165,750-square-foot ice palace cost close to a million dollars to construct.

Mihara Yama, an active volcano on a small Japanese island not far from Tokyo Bay, is considered a sacred shrine, "God's Fire Stove." Unhappy Japanese by the hundreds have leapt into the volcano's crater in search of eternal peace.

Many people do not have the enzyme required to digest cow's milk. In these people, a glass of milk will induce diarrhea.

Attic Salt

Richard Brinsley Sheridan is best known to us as a dramatist, the author of *The School for Scandal* and other memorable works. But Sheridan also served as a member of the British Parliament for a number of years. One day a political opponent, Lord Belgrave, delivered a speech in the House of Commons that ended with a long Greek quotation.

"If the noble Lord had proceeded a little farther," Sheridan rose to reply, "he would have seen that the quotation applied the other way." Sheridan then delivered the remainder of Belgrave's quoted passage, in Greek, for the edification of his fellow legislators. Lord Belgrave acknowledged his oversight, and complimented Sheridan for his quick recollection.

When the parliamentary session was over, Sheridan admitted that the quote contained not a word of real Greek. Sheridan had merely made up the words he uttered to approximate the sound of Greek—which, apparently, was Greek to the other legislators as well.

Fancy Footwear

The earliest form of shoe was the sandal, worn in ancient Egypt, Greece, and Rome. Next came the boot, generally worn for hunting and traveling, until the Romans took to wearing boots for ordinary outdoor activity.

Though the sabot had been in use much earlier, by the 11th century wooden clogs became the standard footwear of the European peasant. In the 1400s, people began to mount their shoes on separate wooden blocks to protect their footwear from mud and water. Soon, both the platform and the shoe were combined, to become the forerunner of the heeled shoe.

It was not long before Europe's fashion designers went to work. Among the more bizarre footwear developed were shoes with points so long that they had to be fastened at the knee; platform shoes with soles a foot high; shoes which were extraordinarily wide at the toes; and boots faced with fur.

Yet shoes are more outrageously styled today than they have been in centuries. Witness silver lame shoes with Cuban heels for men; platform shoes with six-inch heels for women; and women's boots in every color of the rainbow. We've even been told of a pair of women's heels which are made of clear, hollowed-out plastic, and are filled with water and live goldfish—to create a walking aquarium.

Shoe of the 14th century

French 19th century creation

French gaiter

Elaborate buskin

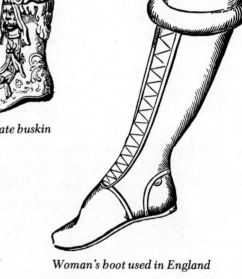

Woman's boot used in England

French clog

Fancy skate made of satinwood and gilded metalwork, made by Mr. Loy of London.

Ancient buskins

Fancy woman's shoe

THE AVON $1.98 SHOE

French laced boot

Duckbilled shoes of the 15th century

Queen Victoria's blue satin slipper

So-called Congress shoe of the 1890s

An ancient spiked shoe.

Ancient sandals

Incredibly enough, the largest advertising sign ever erected adorned—if that word might be used—the Eiffel Tower in Paris. The letters of the word *Citroen*, comprised of 250,000 bulbs and over 20 miles of electrical wires, were mounted vertically on the spire. In place from 1925 to 1936, the sign could be seen from 24 miles away.

Some feminists may be disturbed to learn that the word *lady* came from two Anglo-Saxon words meaning *loaf kneader*. But they can take solace in the fact that the word *lord* is derived from two Anglo-Saxon words meaning *loaf guardian*.

The Boeing 747, the largest jetliner in the world with a capacity of up to 500 persons, is a full 23 times as long as the smallest manned airplane ever to leave the ground, the Stits Skybaby. Flown in 1952, the midget craft measured just nine feet, ten inches in length, but achieved speeds of up to 185 miles per hour.

Where are there six republics, five nationalities, four languages, three religions, and two alphabets, all within one country about the size of Colorado?

The country of Yugoslavia is made up of six republics—Serbia, Croatia, Slovenia, Macedonia, Montenegro, and Bosnia-Hercegovina—with people of five nationalities (one for each of the six republics except Bosnia-Hercegovina, whose population is a mixture of the other nationalities).

There are four languages; Serbo-Croatian is the most widely spoken.

The three religions are Roman Catholic, Orthodox Christian, and Moslem. The two alphabets are the Latin and the Cyrillic which is used to write Serbo-Croatian.

Polyglot Prodigy

Jean Baratière, born in 1721 in Germany, could converse in French with his mother, Latin with his father, and German with the neighbors' children—by the time he was four years old!

At five, Jean had an excellent knowledge of Greek, and actually translated a Greek Bible into Latin. Already at home in four languages, he turned to Hebrew, which he mastered before his sixth birthday. To pass the time, Jean compiled a dictionary of rare and difficult Hebrew words.

Entranced with these ancient tongues, Master Jean then turned to Chaldaic, Syriac, and Arabic. At ten he entered the University of Altdorf. At the advanced age of 13 he received one of the highest academic honors in Germany, becoming a member of the Prussian Royal Academy. Unfortunately, the mental giant, physically frail, died before his 20th birthday.

Lawn bowls, commonly known as bowling on the green or lawn bowling in the United States, is the forerunner of ten-pin bowling, and dates back to at least the 12th century. King Richard II of England, concerned that his soldiers were spending their leisure time at bowls instead of the military sport, archery, outlawed the game in 1388. The next spoilsport was Henry VIII, who declared the game illegal except for the "wealthy and well-to-do." The two monarchs were equally ineffective in discouraging the sport in England, where lawn bowls is still widely played.

The cow, and to a lesser extent the goat and sheep, are by far the most common providers of milk for cheese. But the milk of the buffalo, camel, horse, llama, yak, reindeer, ass, and zebra have also been used to make cheese in various parts of the world.

Roller derby, though today predominantly a rough-and-tumble all-women's spectacle, actually originated as a marathon relay race. In 1935, 25 two-person teams met at the Chicago Coliseum to race on roller skates a distance equal to that between New York and California.

By law, spices imported by this country may be sold if they contain as much as one percent impurities by weight. The most common culprits are, regrettably, mold, insects, and rodent excreta.

In 1500 B.C., a Chinese minister prepared a list of the most delicious foods available in China. At the head of the list of meat dishes were orangutan lips and swallows' tails.

The Butler County Mushroom Farm in Pennsylvania is the largest mushroom farm in the world. The farm, which occupies an abandoned limestone quarry, includes over 100 miles of subterranean passageways, and produces some 40 million pounds of mushrooms each year.

Scientists in the Antarctic region are often amazed to find king penguins who—apparently even more amazed by the men—keel over backwards in surprise.

About 80 percent of all obese children grow up to be obese adults.

Keeping in Shape

Fred Plaisted was only 17 years old when he won his first professional rowing race. But it was his last professional race that earned Plaisted immortality—a race he won 56 years later, at the age of 74.

In 1924, the elderly champ took up the challenge of two other veteran oarsmen, Jim Riley and Jim Ten Eyck, in Saratoga, New York. He had no easy match on his hands, for Ten Eyck had been the U.S. amateur single sculls champion in 1899 and 1901. Each of the men bet $1,000. For three grueling miles, Fred kept the other oarsmen struggling in his backwash. At the finish, the 74-year-old was still well in the lead.

Plaisted never raced for money again, but he celebrated his 84th birthday by defeating an ex-Olympic champion in a rowing race in Philadelphia. And on his 91st birthday, Fred was still rowing three miles every other day, just to keep in shape!

Philatelist's Delight

The most valuable stamp in the world today is a nondescript one-cent stamp issued in 1856 by the colony of British Guiana. In 1873, the prize stamp—called "One-Penny Magenta"—was purchased from a schoolboy for 84¢. In 1940, the stamp brought $35,000 when sold by Mrs. Arthur Hind, the wife of a noted philatelist. Insured for $560,000 when exhibited in 1965, the stamp was sold five years later in New York for $280,000.

Since the stamp's only claim to fame was its rarity, Mr. Hind took no chances with his investment. In 1938, the philatelist allegedly bought the only other surviving copy of the stamp—and burned it!

Claude Seurat was the skinniest man who ever lived

Claude Ambroise Seurat, better known as "The Living Skeleton," was born at Troyes, France on April 10, 1797. His parents were poor but robust people, and their infant son seemed destined to follow in their footsteps— Claude was an apparently normal child of average size. But as he grew in stature, his weight did not increase correspondingly. Indeed, what little flesh he possessed as an infant seemed to wither away. At full maturity, Claude had a back-to-chest thickness of only *three inches*, one inch less than the measurement of his puny biceps.

In 1825, at the age of 28, Seurat agreed to exhibit himself in London. On the way northeast from his native Troyes, he stopped at Rouen, where no less than 1,500 people crowded around him one day. A contemporary account of Seurat's London premiere on August 9, 1825, is given by a Mr. Hone in the *Every Day Book*. Hone was "instantly riveted by [Seurat's] amazing emaciation; he seemed another 'Lazarus come forth' without his grave-clothes... My eye, then, first caught the arm as the most remarkable limb; from the shoulder to the elbow it is like an ivory German flute... not having a trace of muscle, it is as perfect a cylinder as a writing rule."

Seurat's head was the only part of his body that was not shrunken. Accordingly, neither were his faculties in any way diminished. Seurat was smart enough to extract a small fortune from this London exhibition, though he did not live long enough to enjoy it.

In 1640, Cervantes' *Don Quixote* was placed on the *Index* of forbidden books in Spain, due to one sentence it contained: "Works of charity negligently performed are of no worth."

The cicada lives longer than any other insect—some for as long as 17 years. Most of the cicada's life is spent underground, and some live for only a few weeks after emerging.

A Tall Story

Measured from its base rather than from sea level, the tallest mountain on earth is not Mt. Everest, but Mt. Kea on the island of Hawaii. The summit of Mt. Everest is 29,028 feet above sea level; the summit of Mount Kea, or Mauna Kea, is 13,796 above sea level. But the base of Mauna Kea lies 19,680 feet below the ocean, so that from base to summit Mauna Kea actually stands 33,476 feet tall!

Mauna Kea's twin peak, Mauna Loa, is also taller than Mount Everest when measured from its base on the Pacific floor. Mauna Loa rises to a height of 13,680 feet above sea level, but its summit is actually over 30,000 feet above its base. Mauna Loa is also the world's largest mountain in cubic content, and the world's largest volcano.

Even *Mickey Mouse* has not escaped the censor's hand. In 1937, the comic strip was banned in Yugoslavia because it ran a certain story considered anti-monarchical.

The next year, Italian censors ruled that Mickey was a poor model for children, and they banned the comic.

In 1954, authorities in East Berlin determined that the animated rodent was anti-communist, and they banned all *Mickey Mouse* comics.

Plant on the Roam

The resurrection plant, a desert growth found in arid regions of America and the Near East, owes its name to its extraordinary ability to come to life again from a seemingly dead and shriveled state. And unlike most other plants, which must wait for water, the resurrection plant can move over the land to search for needed moisture.

In the presence of water, a resurrection plant will flourish, sporting green fernlike leaves. But when moisture is scarce, the plant pulls up its roots and withers into a dry, ball-like mass of apparently dead matter. This withered mass is carried along the ground by the wind, and can remain in a dormant state for years if no water is found.

But once moisture is located, or after a rain, the plant sinks roots into the wet ground and springs to life again. The plant fares well until the moisture has evaporated, then curls up into a withered ball and roams again in search of water.

If you were to squash an insect and find that the crushed creature has secreted red blood, you can be sure the blood came not from the insect, but from an animal it had bitten. The blood of an insect is almost colorless.

The London Bridge that now resides in Lake Havasu, Arizona, is not the old London structure that was "falling down, falling down" in the familiar nursery rhyme. The bridge was actually built in 1832, as a replacement for the older storied bridge.

The continent of Antarctica covers about five million square miles. Of these, only a few hundred are free from a permanent covering of ice.

The world's largest flower is the rafflesia, a parasitic plant found in the forests of Sumatra, Indonesia. The rafflesia has no stem and no leaves—simply one enormous, fetid-smelling flower. The thick-pedaled growth often reaches a diameter of three feet and a weight of 15 pounds. And the nectary in the center of this giant is capable of holding as much as 12 pints of liquid!

In 1967, seeds of an Arctic tundra shrub, *Lupinus arcticus*, were found in a frozen lemming burrow with animal remains established to be at least 10,000 years old. When placed in conditions favorable to growth, the seeds germinated within 48 hours!

Dressing for Bed

Georges Clemenceau, twice the premier of France, had the peculiar habit of going to bed each night in a full dress suit: trousers, waistcoat, coat, and even gloves! The only concessions to comfort he allowed himself were the exchange of his starched shirt for an unstarched one, and the wearing of slippers instead of street shoes.

Clemenceau slept in this manner his whole life, but in his final days, he was thwarted in his intention of meeting his Maker fully prepared. In a half-conscious state, he could offer no resistance to the doctors who removed his formal clothes.

Bibliomancy, or divination by the Bible, entailed opening the Bible at random and taking the first passage the eye fell upon as a prediction of the future. This practice, also called Lots of the Saints, was so common by the fifth century that several Church councils expressly forbid it. In 793, Charlemagne condemned the practice in an edict.

In 1930, a Boston court condemned Theodore Dreiser's *An American Tragedy* and fined the author. Across the Charles River in Cambridge, the book was then required reading in some Harvard University courses.

The average pay phone in the United States handles about 18 calls per day. But a pay phone in a Chicago bus terminal, the busiest pay phone in the nation, averages 270 calls a day.

The next time you go camping in the woods and would like the weather forecast in the morning, don't turn on a radio—try to find a scarlet pimpernel. The scarlet, white, or purplish flowers of this herb will close up in the morning if rain or cloudy weather is in store, and expand if the weather will be fair. This prophetic property has earned the scarlet pimpernel the nickname of "poor man's weatherglass."

Ng *ka py* is how you order a shot in Peking. It's made from millet, with various aromatics added.

The growth of beards varies considerably among the peoples of the earth. The Celts and Slavs have the most luxurious appendages; the Chinese, but a few hairlets; the Ethiopians, a curly beard; and the American Indians, hardly any tuft at all.

You think traffic jams are a 20th-century phenomenon? Well, street traffic was so thick in ancient Rome that Julius Caesar forbid almost all wheeled vehicles to use the streets during the daytime. The nightly clatter of cartwheels kept many a light-sleeping Roman tossing in his bed.

The early Christians suffered greatly at the hands of the Romans—most notoriously, in the gladiatorial arenas. But the coming of Christian emperors did not stop the carnage in the Eternal City's amphitheatres. During the reign of the Christian emperors, many magicians and heretics were publicly tortured and slain in the same arenas where Christians had been fed to the lions.

Sixteenth-century Danish astronomer Tycho Brahe, for whom the moon's largest crater was named, had his nose cut off by a sword during a duel. Brahe replaced the lost appendage with a nose made of gold and silver.

Heron of Alexandria, an engineer who lived in the first century, devised what may have been the world's first vending machine. The device dispensed holy water only when a coin was introduced into the appropriate slot.

Certain orchids produce seeds so small that 35 million would weigh just an ounce. The seed of the Seychelles coconut can weigh 40 or 50 pounds!

Damascus, Syria, is the oldest city in the world still inhabited. The city is mentioned in the book of Genesis. Today, its inhabitants number close to a million.

Although Clark Gable, Humphrey Bogart, Gregory Peck, James Stewart, and John Wayne have all appeared in a number of classic films, each of these actors received the Academy Award for *Best Actor* only once. Do you know the name of the film that earned each thespian the Award?

No, Clark Gable did not win the Academy Award for *Gone with the Wind*—he won it for *It Happened One Night* filmed in 1934.

Humphrey Bogart failed to win the Award for *Casablanca* and *The Maltese Falcon*, but won the prize in 1951 for *The African Queen*.

Gregory Peck won—not for *Spellbound*, but for *To Kill a Mockingbird*.

James Stewart won for *The Philadelphia Story*, in 1940.

And it took John Wayne until 1969 to win the Award, for his performance in *True Grit*.

Odoriferous Assault

Any animal that tries to nibble on the fruits or leaves of the elephant tree is in for an unpleasant surprise. With the slightest tug on one of the elephant tree's leaves, a hungry herbivore will be inundated by a cloud of fetid-smelling oil as foul as a skunk's spray.

The elephant tree is a small shrub tree indigenous to northern Mexico. The mist it discharges consists of tiny particles shot in a jet from openings in the bark. The jet can reach up to three feet from the tree. Any bothersome animal disturbing this arboreal wonder will advertise its mistake for weeks to come.

There are 455 known active volcanoes in the world, 80 of which are under water. The great majority of the world's volcanoes are found in the Pacific Ocean and on bordering land masses.

It's been said that the Pyramids of Egypt owe their existence to the onion, since the workers who constructed them subsisted largely on the vegetable. The Greek historian Herodotus claimed to have seen an inscription on the Great Pyramid at Giza that listed the amounts of onions, garlic, and radishes eaten by the workers who built the monument. For some reason, Herodotus also maintained that the onion was good for sight, but bad for the body. Many a tearful chef might disagree.

In the United States, more bicycles are currently manufactured each year than automobiles. In the years ahead, the total number of bikes in use here, now estimated at 90 million, is expected to approach the number of passenger cars registered in the nation, which now stands at about 115 million.

The Arab states of the Mideast have in recent years produced close to 800 million metric tons of oil annually. Would you believe that an English firm is currently shipping some $100,000 of petroleum each year to the Arab states? The bizarre fact has a simple explanation: The petroleum imported by the Arab states is in the form of lighter fluid.

The most heavily consumed food item in the United States is milk. The average American consumes over 290 pounds of milk and cream each year, plus another five pounds of condensed and evaporated milk. Potatoes rank a distant second, at about 120 pounds per person, with beef third.

A newborn infant cannot shed tears. Normally, a baby begins to shed tears when crying at about three months of age.

Shuffleboard may strike you as a modern playground game. Actually, shuffleboard has been played in various forms since the 15th century, under such names as shovelboard, shoveboard, slide-groat, shovel-penny, and shovegroat. In England, the game was especially popular among the aristocracy.

The ancient Incas of Peru were masters at decorating their teeth. Unlike primitive tribesmen today who often grind their teeth down to fine points, the Incas inlaid their teeth with gold and semi-precious jewels. When an Inca maiden smiled, it was a very bright smile indeed. The custom was adopted briefly in the West; some wealthy women, who had more diamonds than they knew what to do with, inserted genuine sparklers in their front teeth.

What Price Genius?

Christian Heinrich Heinecken was born in Lubeck, Germany, in 1721. While still little more than an infant, Christian displayed an intellect of rare power. Before his third birthday, he had learned to read three languages. The king of Denmark was astounded by Christian's astute discussion of ancient history.

But while the boy wonder could read three languages, he could write in none of them—his fingers were so frail that he could not grip a pen! He had still not learned to eat solid food when he died at the age of four.

The 10th-century English King Edgar banned "warm baths and soft beds" as effeminate.

When 19th-century English advertisers began to peddle inventions we now call alarm clocks, the class-conscious Victorians preferred to call them "servant regulators."

Over 100 million Americans—including two-thirds of all adults—now wear eyeglasses. Close to ten million regularly don contact lenses.

Are you right-handed? Then the fingernails of your right hand grow more quickly than the nails of your left hand. If you're left-handed, your left fingernails are the faster-growing. And on either hand, the middle fingernails grow more quickly than any other.

No alphabetic language in existence today contains more than 72 letters, and most contain far less. Chinese writing, in contrast, contains close to 50,000 characters.

In the course of a single day, the average American suffers bombardment from 500 to 600 advertisements—including billboards, signs, and radio/TV commercials.

The Aztec king, Montezuma, consumed a golden goblet of chocolate beverage before he entered his harem, then tossed the cup into the lake beside his palace. Indians were still diving for the golden goblets years after the Spanish began to colonize the area.

There are perhaps a billion words in the world's three or four thousand languages, but there is only one word that has entered over 1,200 different languages without change—the Hebrew word *amen*. The word, which in Hebrew means "truly," was introduced to the Greek language by translators of the Old Testament, and in turn found its way into Latin. Ever since Classical times, translators of the Bible have chosen to use the Hebrew word instead of a translation. The Bible has been translated into over 1,200 languages—and every one of them now contains the word *amen*.

The Circus Maximus, the largest sports arena in ancient Rome, could dwarf even the largest of modern stadiums. The structure, used predominantly for chariot races, was 700 yards long and could seat some 250,000 spectators.

Super Horse

"De mostest hoss in de world"—that's how groom Will Harbut described his companion of 21 years, America's great racing horse Man O' War. Foaled on March 29, 1917, Man O' War was purchased by Samuel D. Riddle for $5,000, at a Saratoga auction in August 1918.

The legendary Man O' War, also known as Big Red, won 20 of the 21 races in which he started in his brief two-year career.

In 1921, Man O' War was retired because Riddle feared the horse would be injured by the excessive weight he would be forced to carry in the next Kentucky Derby. The handicap was imposed in order to give the other entries a chance to win. After his retirement, Man O' War sired 383 offspring, who were to win a total of $3,500,000 in racing purses. Man O' War himself earned approximately $2 million in prize money and stud fees. He died on November 1, 1947.

Frontinus, a first-century Roman soldier and administrator, wrote a book on military affairs in which he claimed he would ignore all new developments in war machinery. No, Frontinus was not a pacifist. He believed that the invention of engines of war had "long since reached its limit," and could not be improved upon.

The longest sermon on record was delivered by a minister in West Richland, Washington, in 1955. The declamation lasted 48 hours and 18 minutes. A congregation of eight was still present at the sermon's end.

Black may seem to us to be the natural color of mourning, but people around the world do not necessarily agree. White is the color of mourning in China and in much of the Moslem world. In Turkey, the color is violet.

Chocolate was popular in Spain for more than a century before it caught on elsewhere in Europe, for the Spanish carefully guarded the methods of manufacturing drinkable chocolate. Late in the 16th century, when the Dutch captured a Spanish ship laden with cacao beans, they considered the unfamiliar cargo so worthless that they tossed the beans into the sea.

Some foods are so low in calories that it takes more calories to chew and digest them than the foods contain in the first place. Celery is among the foods with "negative calories."

Moths do not eat wool. Moth larvae are the real culprits. Once the larva becomes an adult, it can't hurt your clothes.

George Washington grew marijuana on his Virginia plantation. Washington's crop raised no eyebrows—cannabis, or hemp, was used to make a number of commercial products at the time. In fact, Thomas Jefferson grew marijuana on *his* plantation, too.

The laws of colonial Connecticut forbade a mother to kiss her child on the sabbath. The Jane Law outlawed Christmas, dancing, playing cards, and mince pies.

The Longest Peel

The record for the longest unbroken apple peel now stands at 155 feet, 1¾ inches. The record-setting peel was removed—in 11 hours!—from an apple 18½ inches in diameter.

There is enough water in the seas and oceans of the world to completely cover the earth to a depth of two miles.

The apple-peeling feat, recorded by the Western New York Apple Growers Association in 1975, was the work of 16-year-old Kathy Wafler. Apple peeling must run in Kathy's family—her father, Fritz, is a former world champion.

Kamala and Amala, Indian girls, were raised by wolves

Throughout history, there have been many reports of human babies brought up by animals—wolves, apes, lions, and so on. But upon investigation, very few of such stories have turned out to be true. One case that has been authenticated is that of the Indian "wolf-girls."

In October, 1920, the Reverend J.L. Singh, who headed an orphanage in Midnapore, India, was asked by his neighbors to get rid of a "man ghost" which supposedly inhabited a large anthill nearby. Singh organized a party to keep close watch over the anthill. When darkness fell, he saw three full-grown wolves come out of a tunnel within the hill, followed by two cubs. Then, close behind, emerged two horrible-looking creatures with what appeared to be human bodies.

The following morning, the den was dug up. Huddled together were two wolf cubs and two young children, both girls—one about eight years old, the other about one-and-a-half. When captured, the children were even more ferocious than the cubs.

The task of weaning these "wolf children" back to human ways was formidable. The Reverend and his wife gave the girls the names of Amala and Kamala. The children refused to wear any clothing; long matted hair fell below their shoulders; their teeth were sharp and pointed. The girls refused all vegetable food—but could scent the odor of raw meat at a considerable distance. Though they were not able to stand erect, the girls could move along on all fours at an astounding speed. They slept through most of the day, but liked to prowl about at night. They avoided humans, while seeking the society of dogs and goats.

Little by little, however, the wolf-girls came to accept the kindness of the missionary and his wife. Then, after almost a year in the orphanage, Amala, the younger child, died.

Kamala wept—the first time she had ever shown human emotion.

For weeks, Kamala lingered over the places where Amala had sat and slept, sniffing anxiously like a dog, and uttering strange cries. After a while, Kamala drew closer to the missionary's wife and began to take greater interest in the other children. She stopped gulping down her food in wolf fashion. She

learned to drink out of a cup instead of lapping up her liquids. She even mastered some 40 words and began to wear clothing.

After some time had passed, Kamala learned to walk upright, but she still proceeded slowly and unstably. When she wanted to run, she reverted to moving along on all fours.

After nine years in a human environment, Kamala had lost most of her animal charac-teristics and had become a lovable, obedient child. Then, on November 14, 1929, she died.

One reason for her early death was explained by the physician attending her. He stated, "There was great difficulty in feeding the poor wolf-girls anything but meat and milk. If they could have been induced to take a balanced diet, they could have returned to an ordinary human condition from the state of an animal."

A Paris newspaper once printed two unrelated notices consecutively instead of separately, producing this gem of a paragraph:

"Doctor M. has been appointed head physician to the Hospital de la Charité. Orders have been issued by the authorities for the immediate extension of the Cemetery of Mont Parnasse."

The 50th anniversary of Mickey Mouse, observed in 1978, did not go unnoticed in the Soviet Union. A youth newspaper in Moscow reported that the occasion was being celebrated "on a grandiose scale" in the United States. "Unlike other movie stars," the article observed, "Mickey Mouse doesn't make any secrets about his date of birth."

A hangnail does not, of course, "hang" from the finger. The word *hangnail*, meaning a bit of torn skin at the base or side of a fingernail, comes in part from the Old English word *ang*, meaning "pain."

Many birds eat more than half of their weight each day, and young birds can eat even more. The bird's prodigious appetite keeps it busy through most of the day, especially when there's a brood of newly-hatched young to feed as well. A mother bird may bring food to its growing fledglings over 1,200 times in a day!

The first recorded instance of a suitor presenting his fiancée with a diamond ring occurred in 1477, when Maximillian, archduke of Austria, sealed his troth with a diamond. Today, 85 percent of all American couples choose diamonds for their engagement or wedding rings.

Haves and Have-nots

Economists at the University of Pennsylvania have developed a new method for determining the relative wealth of the world's nations. The method, which focuses on the worth of each country's currency in buying items in other nations, finds that the United States is the second-richest country in the world.

Using the wealth of the United States as a standard, with a rating of 100, the method assigns a rating of 78.2 to West Germany, 73.2 to France, 63.5 to Britain, and 59.2 to Japan. The only nation with a rating higher than 100 is the oil-producing sheikdom of Kuwait, which earned a rating of 161. But the economic study did not consider a number of small Arab nations, or most communist countries.

At the other end of the scale, Rwanda earned a rating of 3, Bangladesh 3.2, and Ethiopia 3.8.

A Roman glutton named Arpocras once devoured four tablecloths and a broken glass at one sitting.

Pink elephants are not necessarily creatures to be found only in dreams or in delirium. Albino elephants are, in fact, very rare! They appear in a pale yellowish-gray hue and they have pink spots!

In June, 1759, the great Mexican volcano Jorullo erupted for the first time, turning level farm land into a peak of volcanic discharge that now rises to a height of over 4,300 feet. The volcano's eruptions buried two rivers in the vicinity. When the rivers-turned-underground streams reappeared a considerable distance from Jorullo, their waters were so heated by the steaming volcanic rock that the rivers had been changed into hot springs, with temperatures over 125 degrees.

The highest number with a name is the centillion, which is 10 with 600 zeroes, or 10^{600}.

Inches and Ounces

It may strike you as odd that the word *ounce* was derived from a term meaning "one-twelfth," for there are 16 and not 12 ounces in a pound. This is how the word came into our language:

In the 12th century, the city of Troyes, France, was famous for its annual commercial fairs. Merchants from all parts of Europe came to Troyes with their wares. To keep business flowing smoothly, they needed a standard set of weights and measures. The unit of weight adopted was the pound, consisting of 12 ounces.

In Latin, *uncia* means one-twelfth. The word "ounce" was derived from *uncia*, and originally referred to one-twelfth of the pound originating in Troyes. The 12-ounce pound, still used today by jewelers and druggists, is thus known as a "pound troy," and the measuring system based on that pound is called "troy weight." The more familiar 16-ounce pound was developed later to accommodate bulkier, cheaper goods such as potatoes and coal.

The derivation of our word "inch" from *uncia* needs no similar explanation.

The number 999 is not the largest three-digit number. That honor goes to 9^{9^9} or 9 raised to the power of 9^9. How large is that number? If written out, the number would stretch from New York to Chicago.

A billiards room was considered *de rigueur* in fashionable Victorian homes. Architects of the era took great pains to design the room so that persons entering or sitting in the raised spectator section would not disturb the players. Even the fireplace was carefully positioned to avoid distraction. A billiards etiquette book from the period advised that persons about to enter a billiards room should listen through the door until they heard the balls click, so that their entrance would not disturb a player about to shoot.

During the 1890s, when a bicycle-riding craze swept America, bicycle paths began sprouting up in many cities. One of the oddest bikeways in the nation stretched between Pasadena and Los Angeles in Southern California. Called by some the predecessor of the modern superhighway, the Pasadena Cycleway consisted of a narrow elevated road, similar to a boardwalk, wending its way between houses and over empty fields. Lamps were provided for night riding. Bike rental and repair shops stood at each end of the cycleway, and toll booths appeared sporadically along the nine-mile route.

When Christopher Columbus set sail on his first trip to America, few people in Europe truly believed that the world was flat. As early as the second century B.C., an astronomer and mathematician named Hipparchos calculated the circumference of the earth to within a few hundred miles of its presently known dimensions.

William H. Harrison enjoyed the shortest tenure of all American Presidents. Harrison died barely a month after taking office in 1841, allegedly from the strain of an arduous campaign, and was succeeded by John Tyler.

Idols of the King

When King Farouk fled Egypt in 1952, a number of personal items were left behind in the monarch's luxurious palace, among them: a vast collection of American comic books; 50 walking sticks; a pocket radiation counter; 75 pairs of binoculars; 1,000 ties; a set of photographs depicting copulating elephants; and immense stamp collection; and a $20 double eagle which had vanished some years before from the Philadelphia Mint museum.

Thomas Hariot, an English mathematician sent to the colonies by Sir Walter Raleigh, is the first Englishman to have smoked tobacco, but his patron became the most famous smoker of Renaissance England. Raleigh acquired the taste readily, and became a passionate devotee. It is recorded that Raleigh even "tooke a pipe of tobacco a little before he went to the scaffolde."

The earliest mention of an inn is found in Aristophanes' *The Frogs*. In the play, a group of men enter an old tavern, where they devour 16 loaves of bread, 20 meat balls, garlic, fish, and cheese, and then make off without paying the bill.

In 1972, a judge in Los Angeles sentenced a man to a jail term for pickpocketing—and ordered the thief thereafter to wear mittens whenever he ventured out of doors. The thief promptly vanished.

Opinion differs about the moral value of coffee. Despite suppression on religious and political grounds, coffee became the universal beverage of Islam. It was then opposed by Italian churchmen as a drink of the infidel, but was Christianized by Pope Clement VIII. By 1650, coffee had reached most of Europe. Although introduced in North America about 20 years later, coffee became the staple American drink only after tea had been downgraded with the Boston Tea Party of 1773.

There is enough stone in the Great Wall of China to build an eight-foot wall around the earth at the equator.

The most long-lived animal is the giant tortoise of the Galapagos Islands. Specimens have been estimated to be as old as 190 years.

The Biggest Bergs

If you see an iceberg drifting lazily in the open seas, you can bet the berg is nine times as big as it looks. As a rule, only one-ninth of the mass of an iceberg is seen above water.

The life of an iceberg depends on its size and construction, but some of these huge ice mountains have been known to exist for centuries before completely melting.

Antarctic icebergs are generally larger than their Arctic cousins. Flat-topped icebergs breaking loose from the Antarctic ice pack have been as large as 60 miles long, 20 miles wide, and 300 feet high. The upper surface area of such a berg would thus measure 1,200 square miles—almost as large as the state of Rhode Island. And the largest iceberg on record, sighted in the South Pacific Ocean in 1956, stretched 208 miles long and covered more than 12,000 square miles—an area larger than New Jersey!

The tobacco plant was first brought to Europe for cultivation in 1558 by Francisco Fernandes, a physician whom Philip II had sent to the New World to report on its products. Jean Nicot, the French ambassador at Lisbon, sent some tobacco seeds to Catherine de Medici, queen of France, and was immortalized by the application of his name to tobacco's most baleful element, nicotine.

C. Arthur Thompson of Victoria, British Columbia, Canada, had played golf for many a year. It kept him so agile that he even was able to tour the links when he was past 100 years of age. On October 3, 1966, at the age of 97, he managed to shoot a round lower than his age. Thompson scored a 96 on the 6,215-yard Uplands course.

When the racehorse Mill Reef broke a leg, he received sympathy cards from his admirers at the rate of 30 a day.

Sarah Bernhardt, recognized as the greatest actress of the later 19th century, was as versatile as she was talented. On a number of occasions, Sarah won critical acclaim for her performance in a male role. In 1900, she acted the lead role in a French production of Shakespeare's *Hamlet!*

Talk about strokes of luck! In 1929, a Nebraskan named James Cash was playing golf on a course in Belmont, Massachusetts. He drove a ball from the tee to the edge of the cup, and started down the fairway toward the green. Then, an earth tremor shook the course—and dropped the ball into the cup for a hole-in-one!

The grouse, a common game bird, is known to dig its way into a snowdrift to escape freezing winds, and to remain there, buried alive, for days on end. Since the temperature inside a snowdrift on a wintry day is likely to be warmer than that of the surrounding air, the grouse thus escapes fatal exposure to sleet and frost.

The Greek Demosthenes, one of the most noted and quoted orators of all times, suffered a severe speech impediment as a young man! He overcame his handicap, in part, by putting pebbles in his mouth to practice enunciation, and shouting his speeches against the din of crashing ocean waves.

The ancient Greeks—who gave us the word "oyster" from their *ostreon*—feasted regularly on the mollusks. They also used oyster shells for casting votes, scratching the name of the chosen candidate on the inner shell—making Greek politics a real shell game. Greek juries also used the shells in recording their verdicts. Thus, a person condemned to exile was *ostracized.*

Eskimos wear sunglasses! For 2,000 years, Eskimo hunters in the Arctic have carved driftwood eye shields with narrow, glassless eye slits to ward off snow blindness.

The Dutch are probably the world's best ice skaters. Of 13 million Netherlanders, an estimated 25 percent are speed skaters. Some rural women are confident enough of their skating abilities to carry baskets filled with eggs on their heads!

A tin of rations dating from the Civil War was discovered recently, and its contents were fed to a dog. The pooch found the century-old victuals quite delicious!

At the beginning of the 19th century, over 20 percent of the population of the United States lived in the state of Virginia.

Always on Sunday

Do you feel like picking up the phone on March 17 and wishing your grandfather in Dublin a happy St. Patrick's Day? It will only cost you $4.50 for the initial three minutes; that is, if you dial directly yourself, and it's daytime. If you wait until night (after 6 PM), or if it happens to be Sunday, it would only be $3.60. If you don't know the number, and you need operator assistance, the fees go up to $5.40 during the day, and $4.05 at night or on Sunday. If you're afraid that your grandfather's buddy, or someone else, might pick up the phone and you want to put in a person-to-person call, the costs escalate to $9.60 during the day, and $7.20 at night or on Sunday.

In 1977, New York City alone paid some $2.5 million for copier services. Officials of the financially strapped city asked employees to cut copier use by 20 percent, claiming that the reduction would slice $500,000 from the city budget each year.

Have you ever wondered how much gasoline a car burns when it's idling? Well, it wastes more fuel than you might have imagined—1.6 ounces each minute! At that rate, you would burn a gallon of gasoline by idling for 80 minutes.

It's actually cheaper to turn the car off and start it again. A car requires, on the average, about a half-ounce of gasoline to start.

In Uruguay, duelling is legal as long as both parties in the dispute are registered blood donors.

The rapid transit system of London was and still is called the "underground." But when the first underground rail lines were constructed in the United States, American rapid transit pioneers had to search for an alternative term. "Underground Railroad" to most Americans suggested the network of secret way-stations that brought escaped slaves North before the Civil War. So, the word "subway" was born of necessity.

The word *phony* may or may not owe something to the telephone. A New York paper once reported that "phony implies that a thing so qualified has no more substance than a telephone talk with a supposititious friend." But most dictionaries trace the word to the expression "fawney rig," British slang for a valueless ring.

The King of Cool

The development of the modern air conditioner is usually credited to Dr. Willis H. Carrier, who accumulated more than 80 patents on various cooling devices. Carrier was a young man working for the Buffalo Forge Company, manufacturer of fans and heating coils, when he was presented with a humidity control problem at the Sackett-Wilhelm lithographing plant in Brooklyn, New York.

Since paper absorbs water, expanding or contracting according to its moisture content, color printing at the time was basically poor and unpredictable. Carrier designed an effective system for controlling the humidity inside the lithography plant, and thus succeeded in developing the world's first scientific airconditioning system.

A recent poll conducted in the United States confirmed that a fear of great heights and a fear of insects were two of the fears most commonly shared among Americans. But the most widely held fear is, surprisingly, speaking before a group! Forty-one percent of those polled reported that they were terrified of public speaking. Only 19 percent claimed a fear of death.

Incidentally, 18 percent reported a fear of flying.

The greatest load ever hauled by draught horses was reported in 1893, when two Clydesdales who together weighed 3,500 pounds carried a sled with fire logs weighing almost 144 tons!

The first lighthouse in the United States was the Boston Light, built by the Province of Massachusetts in 1716.

The highest city in the United States is Leadville, Colorado, an old mining town in the Rocky Mountains that is still home to some 4,300 people. Leadville is 10,200 feet above sea level!

Computer designers most often name their creations with acronyms—words made from the first letters of a series of words. Those who believe that scientists do not formulate their acronyms with an eye toward mirth might look at GOMIT, SNOBOL, LISP, SLIP, JOHNIAC, and JOVIAL—that's Jules's Own Version of the International Algorithmic Language.

The first zoo in this country was the Philadelphia Zoological Garden, which opened on July 1, 1874.

The bite of a poisonous snake is not necessarily fatal if untreated. About half of the people are bitten by such snakes in the United States survive without treatment.

About 83 percent of all Americans now live in a home with either a record player or a tape machine of some kind. Yet in a recent year, only 53 percent of Americans bought a single record or tape. Obviously, a lot of people are still listening to old records and tapes.

The term *air conditioning* was coined by textile engineer Stuart Cramer in 1907. Cramer had earlier designed equipment to atomize water into the air of cotton mills, since textile mills require high humidity. Cramer's equipment thus "conditioned" the moisture content of the yarn.

The Great Wall of China took 1,700 years to complete.

It has been said that of all the man-made structures on the face of the earth, the only one that could conceivably be visible from the moon is the Great Wall of China. Winding its way over more than 1/20 of the earth's circumference, the Wall is an unparalleled feat of engineering and human determination. In size, materials, and human labor, it is the largest construction project ever undertaken by man. Enough stone was used in the entire

project to build an eight-foot wall girdling the globe at the equator!

From its eastern end at Shanhaikuan on the Yellow Sea to its western end at Chaiyukuan in the Gobi Desert, the Wall stretches over mountains, deserts, and plains a distance of 1,500 miles. If the Wall were picked up and moved to the United States, it would stretch from New York to Topeka, Kansas! But with its numerous twists and turns, the Great Wall is actually 1,700 miles long—and including all its peripheral extensions and offshoots, the length is 2,500 miles. More than 24,000 gates and towers dot the Wall over its serpentine course.

In the eastern regions of China, the Wall is built of stone faced with brick, to an average height of 25 feet. Here the wall is generally 20 to 30 feet wide at the base, tapering to 15 feet at the top. Most portions of the

China, laborers were conscripted for the project; many died during the construction. The wall was continually augmented and improved over the centuries, with the major work being done during the Ming Dynasty (1368-1644).

Why such a gargantuan project was undertaken is not known for certain. Originally, the Wall was thought to have been built to provide a defense against Mongolian tribesmen to the north, but authorities point out that the height and the extent of the Wall made it undefendable against any army determined to invade China. Indeed, armies were successful in breaching the Wall many times throughout Chinese history. The Wall itself may have been a prime motive for some of the Mongolian invasions, for by enclosing many of the water sources in the outlying regions, the Chinese made it necessary for the

eastern Wall are wide enough to permit six horsemen to ride abreast along the top.

In the west, however, the Wall is constructed largely of earth faced with stone, or simply of earth piled into mounds. Today, this section of the Wall has fallen into ruin, and at points is almost obscured by drifting sands.

As the Wall stands today, it is an amalgamation of many walls built over a period of 1,700 years—making the Wall the longest continuous construction project in human history. The first emperor of China, Ch'in Shih Hwang-ti, from whose name the word *China* is derived, began building the Wall in the 3rd century B.C. Large portions of the eastern Wall were constructed during this 11-year reign. From all over the newly unified

tribesmen on the Mongolian plains to cross the Wall in search of water.

Some authorities maintain that the Wall was constructed solely to define the limits of Chinese sovereignty. (The Chinese penchant for walls is well demonstrated by the fortifications built around all old Chinese cities.) All land within the Wall was considered China; everything beyond, the wilderness. In fact, the Wall did serve for hundreds of years as the boundary between the Orient and the Occident.

Others maintain that the Wall was undertaken to provide employment for the Chinese masses in times of hardship and unrest. Whatever the reason for its construction, the Wall stands as one of the most incredible, and certainly the largest, construction feats ever accomplished by man.

Most people know that *The Jazz Singer* was the first "talkie," or movie with an accompanying dialogue soundtrack, to be filmed anywhere in the world. The film, which starred Al Jolson, was released in 1927. But do you know the name of the first full-length Technicolor movie? It was *Toll of the Sea*, which was released in 1922—17 years before *Gone With the Wind*.

The nation that annually receives the largest number of tourists is, at present, Spain. In 1974, over 30 million people visited that nation, more than twice as many as the second-ranking nation, West Germany. That same year, the United States received 14 million visitors. It's likely that the number of tourists coming to the U.S. will increase in coming years, due to the devaluation of the dollar.

About 11 percent of America's annual potato crop now goes to potato chips. Americans put away some 400,000 tons of chips each year—about four-and-a-half pounds per person!

Movies about jail breaks are notoriously exciting. But they can't hold a candle to real-life events. In the movies, one or two, or at most a handful of prisoners attempt to escape together. Compare that to what happened in Uruguay in 1971. Paoul Sendic and 105 other Tupamaro guerillas escaped from prison through a tunnel 298 feet long.

The greatest single snowstorm ever recorded in the United States inundated the Mount Shasta Ski Bowl, in California—189 inches of snow fell in that storm. The greatest accumulation of snow ever recorded in this country over a 24-hour period fell on Silver Lake, Colorado—76 inches! And the deepest snow ever to blanket a town in this country fell on Tamarack, California—an incredible 451 inches, or more than 37 feet.

Katharine Hepburn has been nominated for an Acacdemy Award more times than any other actress or actor in history, 11 times. She's won an award three times. Bette Davis was nominated ten times, and won twice. Tops among actors is Spencer Tracy, with nine nominations. Marlon Brando has been nominated seven times, and has won two Oscars—for *On the Waterfront* and *The Godfather*.

Most people could name the three races that comprise the Triple Crown of thoroughbred racing—The Kentucky Derby, the Preakness, and the Belmont Stakes. But can you name the three legs of harness racing's Triple Crown? They are, for trotters, the Hambletonian, in DuQuoin, Illinois; the Kentucky Futurity, in Lexington, Kentucky; and the Yonkers Futurity, in Yonkers, New York.

For pacers, the three big races are the Little Brown Jug, in Delaware, Ohio; the Messenger, in Westbury, New York, and the Cane Pace, in Yonkers, New York.

Due in part to inept French leadership and the superiority of English archers, the French forces that were defeated at the important Battle of Crecy, in 1346, suffered some 4,000 losses, or one-third of the entire French force. The English lost less than 100 men.

Many people believe that vast hordes of wild horses once roamed the North American plains, and that American Indians were skilled horsemen for thousands of years before the arrival of Europeans. The fact is, the Indians of the American Southwest obtained their domesticated horses directly from the Spanish. As late as 1700, there were still no reports of wild horse herds anywhere in North America.

The first nickelodeon in this country was established in neither New York City nor Southern California. It appeared in McKeesport, Pennsylvania, in 1905.

According to current United Nations projections, by the year 2000, Mexico City will be the most populous city on earth, with over 30 million inhabitants. Tokyo will rank second by that time, with 26 million people, followed by São Paulo, Brazil. The metropolitan area of New York will rank fourth, with a population of about 22 million.

And How Much Can A Fly Eat?

The next time you have a pesky fly in your house that simply refuses to be caught, take heart: A housefly lives only about 15 days.

The binary number system, which forms the basis of most computer languages, has only two digits, one and zero. If you don't already understand the binary system, you'll just have to take our word for it that this is the way a computer counts from one to ten: 1, 10, 11, 100, 101, 110, 111, 1000, 1001, 1010. That number actually reads one eight, no fours, one two, no units, for a total of ten.

The smallest county in the entire United States is also one of the most populous. New York County, which comprises Manhattan Island in New York City, is in size the smallest county in the nation, covering only 31.2 square miles. The other counties in New York City are Kings (Brooklyn), Queens, Bronx, and Richmond (Staten Island).

For the largest county in the nation, we must travel cross-country to California. San Bernadino County is the largest single county in the nation, taking in much of the Mohave Desert and reaching from the suburbs of Los Angeles all the way to Arizona border.

Few Americans today know a single word of the languages spoken by the people who inhabited our land before we arrived—the Indians. But quite a few English words have entered our language from the Indian languages. The list of words taken from Indian languages would include *skunk*, *pecan*, *chipmunk*, *bayou*, *woodchuck*, *tepee*, *igloo*, *toboggan*, *moose*, *totem*, *racoon*, *persimmon*, and *squaw*.

Streetcars, though dependable and inexpensive to build and clean, were not without disadvantages. Among these was the danger posed to idle strollers by a speeding trolley. The Brooklyn Dodgers of baseball fame were not so-named because of their agility on the playing field. Initially, the team was called the Trolley Dodgers, in tribute to the maze of trolley lines crisscrossing Brooklyn at the height of the streetcar era.

The dog and the cat have identical gestation periods of 64 days. While the dog on the average lives longer than the cat, the longest recorded lifespan of a cat is an amazing 34 years, against a dog's longest recorded lifespan of 27 years.

Tamerlane built pyramids from the skulls of his victims

In 1336, an obscure tribal chieftain, living near the Central Asian city of Samarkand, celebrated the birth of a son. The Mongol chieftain named his baby Timur. Later, when Timur was crippled by an arrow, he received his nickname, Timur-i-Leng, or Timur the Lame. To the Western world, he is more familiar as Tamerlane.

Making Samarkand his capital, Tamerlane set out on a decades-long campaign to subjugate the world to his rule. He created an empire that stretched from the Ganges River in India to the very gates of Europe. Much of present-day Russia, including Moscow, was incorporated into his domains.

Merciless to his enemies, Tamerlane ravaged huge areas, reduced great cities to rubble, and slaughtered hundreds of thousands. Indeed, he left cruel testimonials to his victories by building great pyramids from the skulls of his victims—70,000 at Isfahan, 90,000 in Baghdad, and 100,000 at Delhi. At Sebsewar in Persia, the merciless monarch enclosed 2,000 live people inside a brick and mortar tomb.

The nation from which the highest number of immigrants enters the United States is Mexico. In a recent year, over 62,000 Mexican immigrants legally entered the U.S., more than twice the number of the second-ranking nation, the Philippines. South Korea was third, Cuba fourth, and Taiwan was fifth.

TV KO

New television shows seem to fall by the wayside these days even before anyone knows they're on. Would you believe that a TV show once survived all of *one* day? Well, in 1969 a program called *Turn On* was cancelled after just one show, allegedly due not to poor ratings but to the censor's disapproval of the show's brand of humor.

A number of shows have bitten the dust after just two episodes, including the 1975 program *Adams of Eagle Lake*, a crime drama starring Andy Griffith.

Athenian women used long, daggerlike pins to fasten their chitons over their shoulders. According to the Greek historian Herodotus, when a group of angry women used the pins to stab to death an Athenian soldier, the city forbade the wearing of all but the Ionian tunic, which did not require pins. The law was later revoked; but by then, women were using buttons and safety pins.

The words *almanac*, *admiral*, *harem*, and *mattress* have all come into English from Arabic. Hungarian has given us *coach* and *paprika*. Chinese was the origin of our *catsup*, *tycoon*, and *silk*. *Yogurt* comes from Turkish, *sabbath* from Hebrew, *sauna* from Finnish, *bizarre* from Basque, and *kangaroo*, *boomerang*, and *koala* from Australian Aborigine.

The greatest English dictionary on either side of the Atlantic is the *Oxford English Dictionary*, conceived in the mid-19th century, but not completed until 1928. The *Oxford* lists almost all recorded English words, and their varying usages from the seventh century through the 20th century. Compiled with the aid of hundreds of research assistants in both England and America, the *Oxford* remains the largest dictionary in the world. Its 12 volumes contain about 415,000 words, almost two million illustrative quotations, and close to 228 million letters and figures!

During the Watergate crisis, the House Committee on Impeachment used a copy machine to duplicate an estimated 1.5 million pages.

Talk about confusing addresses! The towns of Ohio, Oregon, Tennessee, Virginia, Vermont, Kansas, and Wyoming are all in the state of Illinois. New York State can boast the towns of Alabama, Maryland, Maine, and Wyoming. There's a California in four states, a Delaware in five, and a Wyoming in nine states. The town of Nebraska is in Indiana, and the town of Virginia is in Nebraska!

The oldest free-running ferry in the United States is the Oxford-Bellevue ferry in Maryland. The ferry, which crosses the Tred Avon River, was in operation in 1760.

The Mississippi River now has 17 ferry routes. Only the Puget Sound in Washington has more.

The first golf course in the United States was probably the six-hole course in Yonkers, New York, laid out in 1888. The first 18-hole course did not appear in this country until 1893, in Wheaton, Illinois.

One of the most exciting events at Western rodeos is the last-horse-wins contest. For this race, jockeys do not ride their own horses, but are assigned to a strange animal just before going to the post. Thus, each jockey rides as fast as he can, to beat his own horse, which he hopes will win the race by finishing last.

Fancy Felines

"Ligers and tigons" may sound like a classic Spoonerism, but creatures of these names actually exist. They are the hybrid offspring of one of the rarest cross-matings of all—between a lion and a tiger. There are fewer than a dozen of these creatures in captivity today. When the father is a lion, the cub is called a liger; when the sire is a tiger, the animal is a tigon.

The first common unit of length was the *cubit*, used by the Egyptians and Babylonians thousands of years ago. Originally, the cubit was defined as the length of a man's arm from the elbow to the end of the middle finger, but the actual length of the cubit varied from place to place and from time to time. Through most of Egyptian history, the cubit was equivalent to about 20.6 inches.

One advantage of the cubit was that in the absence of a measuring device the unit could easily—handily, you might say—approximated. Presumably, long-armed merchants were quite popular in Egypt.

The Rich Get Richer

In 1975, the eight largest banks in the United States all showed a profit. None of these banks paid any federal income taxes that year. The same year, Northwest Airlines, Western Electric, Bethlehem Steel, Lockheed Aircraft, and National Steel all escaped federal income taxes, as well.

The first American to die in the electric chair was one William Kemmler, who was executed in Auburn, New York, in 1890. The first person to die in the gas chamber, a chinaman named Gee Jon, was executed in Nevada in 1924.

King Francis I of France, a tennis buff, constructed a huge floating court on a ship he called *La Grande Francoise*. The vessel was intended to outshine Henry VIII's *Great Harry*, but the French ship sunk in the harbor at Le Havre before the first tennis game could be called due to seasickness.

The original French guillotine, erected on the Place de Grève in 1792, went on to claim the heads of some 8,000 Frenchmen. Despite common belief, the great majority of people executed by the guillotine during the years following the French Revolution were not aristocrats, but common thieves and rebels.

Many people believe that the compass was indispensable to all ancient sea-going civilizations. Actually, the compass is a more recent invention than you might think, and the earliest compasses were so unreliable as to be virtually useless for long voyages. Ancient seamen for the most part relied on star positions to chart their courses.

In Transit

Move on, get going—no matter how! Artists from all over the world present movement in intriguing forms.

"A Moonbeam Tangle," a drawing published in London in 1881. The artist was Joseph Bligh.

A *little merriment, as portrayed in* Harper's Roundtable, *a magazine of the 1890s.*

The above drawing is by Kemble, who used to do pieces for the old Life Magazine.

Leslie's gives the swells of the day an idea of how to attract attention.

From the world famous Life Magazine, *an American humor publication of the early 1900s.*

From Harper's Roundtable, *a magazine published in New York in 1896.*

This drawing first appeared in Caricature and Other Comic Art *by James Parton, which was published in 1877 by Harper & Brothers of New York.*

From a German magazine named Gebrauchgraphik.

A *drawing from the* Pictorial Sunday Book *by Dr. John Kitto, published in London during the last century.*

A marauder with windsails hastening to his malefactions. *This drawing appeared in St. Nicholas Magazine in 1889.*

Flying machine invented by Signor Ignazio of Milan, Italy, from Leslie's Mazagine, *1883.*

From Life Magazine, *an American humorous publication of the early 1900s.*

These five drawings appeared in England's humorous magazine, Punch, sometime in the latter part of the 19th century.

The so-called "Three Wise Men" mentioned in the Bible's story of the Nativity were neither "kings" nor "wise men," The word used to describe them, *magi* is actually the plural of a Persian word meaning *wizard*. *Wizard* originally meant *magician*, without the implications of genius that the word has since acquired. In fact, our word *magic* is derived from the same word!

The tomato, a mainstay of modern Italian cuisine, was unknown in Italy until the 17th century.

Among the freakier identical-twins-separated-and-reunited stories is the one about a set of male twins in Nebraska. The boys were adopted by separate families living 50 miles apart a year after their birth, and did not meet again until they were 21 years old. At that time, they discovered that they were both repairmen for the same telephone company; both had married similar women in the same year, and both had one son. Moreover, the twins each had a fox terrier with the same name—"Trixie."

The Sahara Desert covers an area of about three-and-one-half million square miles. That wasteland is larger than Australia, and almost as large as the United States. In fact, the Sahara is larger than all of Europe, excluding European Russia!

Hollywood did not create the Frankenstein story. The movie was based, very loosely indeed, on a book written in 1818 by Mary Shelley, the wife of poet Percy Bysshe Shelley. She allegedly based her tale on the claim of earlier alchemists.

Unique in the annals of pugilism was the fight held in Bristol, England, in 1943, between two American soldiers, Louis Fetters and Carmine Milone.

As the gong announced the start of the first round, Milone rushed toward Fetters, leading with a haymaker. But Milone hurtled forward so fast that he lost his balance, and falling, struck his head against a ring post, lost consciousness, and was counted out. Thus, the fight ended without a single blow being struck by either participant.

The average business letter in this country costs $4.17 to send out. Included in this cost is secretarial and executive time for dicating and typing, as well as the cost of postage and stationery.

Lohengrin, or *Here Comes the Bride*, as the song is so often called, is played at weddings so often, that most people assume the music is the wedding march in Wagner's opera. But in the opera *Lohengrin*, the famous melody is played, not as the bride approaches the altar, but several hours later, when the wedded couple retire to the bridal chamber. Perhaps the tune should be retitled *A Little Night Music*.

In the 1920 Presidential election, Socialist candidate Eugene Debs received over 915,000 votes, or almost three-and-a-half percent of the popular vote, yet did not win a single electoral vote. Debs ran his entire campaign from jail.

Only seven of Emily Dickinson's poems were published during her lifetime. In all, she wrote about 1,000 poems.

Six hundred years ago, the few existing clocks were accurate to within only about an hour per day. Until 1582, even the calendar in use was ten days out of line with the seasons. In contrast, we now have atomic clocks—utilizing the oscillations of individual cessium atoms for time measurement—that are accurate to within one second every 60,000 years!

In the United States, it's almost impossible to survive without an income, in some form or another, of at least a few thousand dollars. Yet one-fourth of the world's population lives on a per capita income of less than $200 a year.

Playboy pads are not unique to human bachelors—but at least one bird has them, too. The male bower-bird of Australia seems to require—in addition to his home nest—a covered "love nest," where he entertains his lady friends. These bachelor bowers of the bird-world are often lavishly decorated, usually with stolen articles, all of one particular color. In the 1940s, a striking blue boudoir constructed by one of the birds was uncovered. The retreat contained, among other objects, a blue railroad ticket, a string of blue glass beads, a blue hair-ribbon, and 178 blue bags pilfered from a nearby laundry.

Charles Lindbergh refused to carry a radio receiver or transmitter on *The Spirit of St. Louis* when he completed man's first solo flight across the Atlantic Ocean. He did wear a wristwatch, however.

Prize Trophy

The most valuable sporting trophy in existence is Porter's Plate, a large silver plate given to the Duke of Portland by his horse trainer, John Porter, in 1900, and valued in excess of $25,000. The border of the platter contains 25 sunken, glass-covered wells, each of which hold tail hairs of a famous race horse of yesteryear. The classic horses represented in Porter's Plate include St. Simon, Diamond Jubilee, and Flying Fox.

The first seven presidents of the United States were not born as citizens of this nation. Martin Van Buren, the eighth president, was born in 1782, six years after the signing of the Declaration of Independence, and thus was the first president born a citizen of the United States.

When we look at distant objects in space, we're looking through time as well as space. If the object we are viewing is a billion light years away, then the light we are seeing left that object a billion years ago. Theoretically, at least, it's possible to look far enough into space to see the beginning of the universe!

The largest stained-glass window in the world is not to be found in any European cathedral. The 300-foot-by-23-foot window adorns the American Airlines terminal building at New York's Kennedy Airport.

The food or drink with the least amount of calories per 100 grams is coffee, with just one calorie per 100 grams. Tea has two calories. The least caloric food is a fresh Jerusalem artichoke, with seven calories per 100 grams. Cooked zucchini has 12 calories per 100 grams, and raw lettuce, 13.

At the other end of the scale, pure lard is the most caloric food, with 902 calories per 100 grams. Salad oil is next, with 884 calories, followed by butter, raw pork fat, and choice sirloin steak.

Until 1930, all meals served aboard airliners in this country were cold meals. That year saw the appearance of the first stewardess aboard a domestic airline, a registered nurse. Before then, the copilot had the job of serving meals to the passengers.

During World War II, the United States government ordered the removal of air-conditioning equipment from luxury stores, such as Tiffany's in New York, for use in war-related industrial plants. Little did the factory workers realize that they were toiling in air chilled by the same machines that had cooled the brows of America's social elite in the jewel-bedecked aisles of Tiffany's!

Don't be Taken in by the Wash

Keeping up with the Joneses takes a peculiar form among poor families on the Italian Riviera. There, an outside balcony is considered such a necessary part of a residence that families who can't afford to build a balcony have one painted on the side of the house. For the sake of realism, many of these paintings depict the family wash hung over the bars, just as on real railings.

The town of Bagdad, California, once went 767 days without receiving a single drop of rain. That's more than two years!

Surely few people in this country could claim they have never swallowed an aspirin. But did you ever stop to think about what you were swallowing? Well, aspirin—known medicinally as "acetylsalicylic acid"—is one of the salicylates, a family of drugs found naturally in many trees and shrubs. Willow trees and wintergreen berries are particularly rich in these substances. Salicylates have probably been in medicinal use for some 20,000 years!

A community with a population of 15,000 can be considered a small city. But all the people of a city that size could work comfortably each day in just one building—the size of the Empire State Building in New York.

The famous Macedonian phalanx employed a 24-foot-long pike called the sarissa, which permitted a warrior in the sixth fighting rank to extend his arm to the first. This weapon was not subsequently employed by other peoples.

The human heart beats about 36 million times a year, on the average. Thus in a 72-year lifetime, your heart will go thump-thump some two-and-a-half billion times!

To gridiron buffs, football is the most exciting sport ever invented, but actually, the game includes less action than most other sports. In the average college football game, the ball is in motion a mere 20 percent of the time. The remainder of the hour is consumed by huddles, formations, etc.

Hair-Raising Hobby

British poet Leigh Hunt, the friend of John Keats and other Romantic writers, made a hobby of collecting locks of hair from famous persons. Hunt's collection, now owned by the Lamar Library of the University of Texas, included the tresses of Napoleon, John Milton, Samuel Johnson, Elizabeth Barrett Browning, Edgar Allen Poe, and George Washington.

In 16th-century Holland, most town officials were zealous advocates of witch-burning, but in the Dutch hamlet of Oudewater, municipal authorities were tender-hearted. To save women accused of sorcery from immolation at the stake, the burghers of Oudewater constructed a scale, still on view in the public square, on which they would weigh the accused witch. Inevitably, the woman was declared too heavy to ride through the air on a broomstick—and so was vindicated of the charge of witchcraft.

Diehard Ditty

During the 19th century, the composition of one-finger piano pieces was a popular parlor game. Of the thousands of such pieces invented, the lone survivor is *Chopsticks.* This catchy ditty has become internationally popular, and its theme has been used to ornament the compositions of such musical greats as Franz Liszt and Nikolai Rimski-Korsakov.

It seems incredible, but one of the worst persecutions of an American was caused by a man's insistance on wearing a beard. Between 1830 and 1840, Joseph Palmer of Fitchburg, Massachusetts was rebuffed by friends, jeered at by local shopkeepers, and stoned by small children—all because his fellow townspeople did not approve of Palmer's beard. Finally, four Fitchburg men waylaid Palmer and tried to cut off the offensive whiskers by force. Palmer escaped with his beard intact, but was arrested for brawling. Refusing to pay the fine, the unshaven and unregenerate Palmer was imprisoned for over a year.

Among the antique novelties auctioned in London in 1932 was a certain armchair, dating from the 15th century and ornately carved. The chair's unique feature was a seat-operated mechanism that unleashed two curved iron bars from their hiding place in the arms. Within a second of a person's seating himself in the chair, the bars would lock over the thighs of the seated individual, who could not then free himself from the chair's iron grip.

Through most of the Middle Ages, decapitation was not a widely used method of execution in Europe. In a peculiar twist of the medieval mind, decapitation was held to be a "privilege" of the aristocratic classes. Members of the lower classes were dispatched by hanging—or a number of more gruesome means. Heretics and witches were burned.

In the world of gems, a number of organic substances are recognized as precious or semi-precious. Amber is a fossil resin. Coral is the skeleton of marine creatures. Pearl is formed within the shell of certain mollusks. And jet is lignite, which comes from decomposed wood.

The greatest wrestling champ in the world was Gama of India, who was 58 years old at his retirement in 1936. Standing a mere five feet, seven inches tall, and weighing 260 pounds, Gama sent terror into the souls of other wrestlers. In fact, as early as 1910, when Gama was in London, he could find no British wrestlers willing to accept his challenge that he could throw any 20 of them successively in an hour. Only two Westerners ever agreed to wrestle with Gama. They were the American, B.F. Roller, and the Pole, Stanislaus Zbyszko. Both men were thrown by the Indian champion in fewer than 30 seconds.

For Chess Buffs

More books and articles have been written about chess than about any other game. The John G. White Collection of chess literature, in the Cleveland Public Library, includes nearly 50,000 books, periodicals, brochures, and clippings about chess.

"Tennis, anyone?" Would you believe that the origin of this oft-quoted line has been attributed to none other than Humphrey Bogart, the late actor. Bartlett's Familiar Quotations claims that "tennis, anyone?" was the only line Bogart spoke in his first play—though Bogey himself later denied ever having uttered the line.

The ubiquitous red condiment known as catsup was reportedly based on an oriental invention, called "kaychup" in Malay, and was enjoyed in England for some 100 years before becoming popular in the United States.

Some dictionaries, by the way, will accept not only "catsup" and "ketchup," but "catchup" as well.

Fingal's Cave didn't need Mendelssohn's famous overture of that name—for centuries, the cavern had been making its own music. Located in the Hebrides, Fingal's Cave emits musical sounds produced by the wind blowing around its prism-shaped pillars.

Among the famous persons whose handwriting was considered illegible were James Joyce, whose manuscript of *Ulysses*, confiscated in the mails by an English censor during World War I, was a first suspected of being a spy's code.

Napoleon Bonaparte's letters were sometimes mistaken for maps of battlefields.

It Wasn't the Sandwich that Was the Hero!

If you ever have to make good on an offer to eat your shirt, you might was to emulate a certain chemistry professor from Harvard. Having lost a bet, the chemist set about to make his shirt palatable. First, he soaked the garment in acid, dissolving the fibers so they would be digestible. Then, he dipped the material in a base to neutralize the acid, and put the remaining filtered mass on a slice of bread. A little ketchup and a dash of relish completed our hero's sandwich.

The discovery of the X-ray in 1895 was not met with unmitigated joy. Indeed, the ladies of England were thrown into horrible consternation by reports that a British firm was prepared to market X-ray eyeglasses that would allow the wearer to penetrate through clothing and view another's private parts. No such item was ever marketed, but a certain manufacturer and a London department store cleaned up a sales of their "X-ray proof" undergarments.

There are about 98,000 postmen in Britain. Of these, 3,000 were bitten by dogs in 1968.

The average American three-year-old spends more time watching television than any other single activity—except sleeping, of course. A 1974 survey found that the three-year-old in this country spends an average of 30 hours a week—more than four hours a day—in front of the TV set.

No one has ever explained the disappearance of the 9,000 ton British liner, the *Waratah*. The *Waratah*, returning to London from its maiden voyage to South Africa, left Durban with 211 passengers and crew aboard in July 1909. The ship was traveling in a busy lane, and was within sight of land, yet it vanished without any distress signals having been seen either at sea or on shore. For weeks following the disappearance, five ships dragged the waters where the *Waratah* had last been seen, but nary a life preserver not a fragment of wreckage was ever found.

Daredevil acrobat Sigwart Bach of Germany performed one of the most breathtaking tightrope acts in history. In the summer of 1948, 19-year-old Bach strung a 490-foot wire between two Alpine peaks near Oberammergau. Then, scorning to use a safety net, Bach walked on the wire over a 9,000-foot ravine— and then walked back again.

In 1914, a wristwatch displayed at the Swiss National Exhibition at Bern was regarded by most viewers as merely a "passing fancy." Today, wristwatches make up about 80 percent of all Swiss watches, and the wristwatch has become the single most popular item of jewelry in the world.

If you're ever reading a Civil War novel and come across a reference to the Grand Canyon, you can be sure that the author didn't do his homework. No white man laid eyes on the Grand Canyon until John Wesley Powell reached it in 1869, four years after the end of the Civil War.

They Flew the Coop, Alright!

Pigeon racing was a popular sport in America in the 1920s. During a race from Havana, Cuba to Washington, D.C., which began on the fourth of July, 1928, 27 of the 28 homing pigeons entered n the race unaccountable disappeared. The lone survivor of the 1,175-mile race, *Eureka*, was declared the winner by default, and no trace of the other birds was ever found.

Perhaps the most powerful European dynasty of all time was that of the Hapsburgs. For 600 years, this family prospered in a dozen European nations, ending its official existence at the end of World War I. The Archduke Francis Ferdinand, whose assassination in 1914 precipitated the outbreak of the First World War, is an example of the pervasiveness of this First Family of Europe. Among his 2,047 ancestors, Francis Ferdinand counted 20 Englishmen, 47 Danes, 52 Poles, 82 Spaniards, 124 Frenchmen, 196 Italians, and 1,484 Germans and Austrians.

Beavers build dams, canals, and lodges

Busy as a beaver is one catchword that's really based on fact. Almost from the day he is born until the day he dies, the beaver simply never stops working!

The beaver's ingenuity and industry are astounding. This buck-toothed rodent spends his life constructing lodges, dams, and canals that are marvels of animal engineering. And his only tools are a set of powerful front teeth and a broad, flat tail!

When a young beaver has learned how to use these tools, he leaves his parents' lodge and begins constructing a home of his own. His first step is to select a good location for his dam. When he has found a quiet waterway where no other beaver has staked a claim, he sets to work at once, gnawing down trees and carrying the lumber back to his dam site. In one night, this bark-happy vegetarian can cut down an aspen six inches thick, chop it neatly into six-foot lengths, and drag the logs to the bank of the stream where he plans to build his dam.

If there are not enough trees near the site, the beaver will go further into the forest in search of lumber. But as eager as he is, the beaver doesn't believe in doing an ounce of unnecessary work. So, if the distance from the trees to the dam site becomes too great for him to drag the lumber, the beaver simply digs a canal! He then uses this canal—which may be over one thousand feet long—to float the lumber down to the construction site!

To build his dam, the beaver first lays a foundation of branches and leaves packed together with mud, then piles layer upon layer until a pond is formed on one side of the levee. While working, the beaver uses his

flat tail like a trowel, slinging mud and packing it tightly to waterproof his construction.

Next, the hardworking rodent gets busy building his house, a lodge constructed of wood and mud in the middle of the newly-formed pond. This house is actually a two-story log cabin, most of it below the surface of the water. This underwater fortress contains many rooms and passageways, and the only entrance is under the surface of the pond. The beaver's snug and comfortable living quarters are in a penthouse above the water.

By the time the dam and house are completed, summer has arrived. The young beaver then takes a break from his busy schedule to find a wife. And he's choosy, for once two beavers have mated, they stay mated for life!

Once mated, the beaver continues to work. He and his partner must chop down more trees to make the dam higher, so the pond behind the dam will grow bigger. They must also hurry to store up twigs and branches and pieces of bark for the coming winter. Year after year, Mr. and Mrs. Beaver continue their work.

Why does this clever creature insist on living in the middle of a pond? To make sure that no other animal can reach his lodge during the long periods the beaver spends inside his house. And there's another reason the beaver keeps so busy: His front teeth keep growing as long as he lives. If he doesn't grind them down with constant gnawing, those teeth will grow so large that the beaver won't be able to chew his food!

The great industry of this animal benefits other woodland creatures, too. The ponds and lakes that result from beaver dams provide perfect nurseries for fish and wild fowl. The beaver-made reservoirs make life possible for animals that might otherwise die of thirst in the dry summer months. And in parts of the country where beavers are left to build their dams unmolested, floods and soil erosion are practically unknown!

A record amount of milk was furnished to a human milk bureau by a Los Angeles woman in 1925. Over a period of 11 months, the young mother sold over 767 quarts of milk to the bureau, at the price of ten cents per ounce. The woman realized $2,456 from the sale.

She Drowned Her Sorrows!

There have been many cases of persons drinking themselves to death, but the case of the 12-year-old girl who drowned from drinking too much water is probably unique. The girl was playing "saloon" with her friends, and in the course of the game, she consumed three quarts of water in 20 minutes. Her bloodstream absorbed so much of the liquid that it filled her lungs, producing all the symptoms of drowning. The girl died within 12 hours of the fatal overdose of H_2O.

The Grand Canyon is the most popular natural attraction in the United States. Yellowstone National Park is second, followed by Niagara Falls, Mount McKinley, and California's sequoias and redwoods.

The most popular man-made attractions in this country are presently the Golden Gate Bridge, Mount Rushmore, the Houston Astrodome, and the Statue of Liberty, in that order.

Fish can get seasick if kept on board a ship.

Remember the days of the reasonable family doctor? Well, that personage still exists, in the form of Dr. Lydia Emery of Yoncall, Oregon. Dr. Emery charges a modest $1 for an office visit, and only $2 for a housecall. There's even a discount for sick children—their parents pay merely 25¢ for a consultation with Dr. Emery. The good physician has charged the same fees ever since opening her practice in the small mill town, and she anticipates no increases in the foreseeable future.

Shylock had nothing on a certain firm of loan sharks in Dallas, Texas, who operated during the 1930s. During an investigation in 1938, these shysters were found to be charging an interest rate of 585 percent annually. One victim, who borrowed $20 to pay a hospital bill, had been paying the firm $2.25 a week for nine years. Yet, although the man had paid $1,053 in interest, the firm still claimed he owed them the original $20.

A man is 70 times more likely to suffer from color blindness than a woman. Color blindness occurs once for every 14 men, and once for every 1,000 women.

The record for the highest reputed dive belongs to Alexander Wickham of the Solomon Islands. A swimming champion, Wickham accepted a challenge by bookmakers to dive off a 206-foot cliff in Melbourne, Australia. In 1919, Wickham accepted the dare without having seen the cliff, and the bookies offered 5-to-1 odds that he would not dive at all, and 10-to-1 odds that he would not survive the fall if he did. But Wickham both dove and lived to tell the tale, although he was black and blue for months afterward. The cliff was the height of a 17-story building.

Lowered speed limits result in better fuel mileage, but only to a point. A car actually operates at maximum fuel economy at speeds from 25 to 35 miles per hour.

The United States Census Bureau, which had predicted a world population of over six billion by the year 2000, projects that, by the turn of the century, the mortality rates in the poorer countries will fall below the rates in the richer, industrialized nations. The projections have nothing to do with improved health conditions in the poorer nations, however. The higher mortality rate predicted for the richer countries is based on their present low birth rates, which will result in a population topheavy with elderly people.

A survey, conducted in 1976, found that 30 percent of the leading executives in this country attended only 12 colleges. Those schools are, in order of their contributions to the business world's upper echelon: Harvard, New York University, Yale, University of Pennsylvania, University of Michigan, Columbia, Northwestern, City College of New York, Princeton, University of Wisconsin, MIT, and the University of Illinois.

The sun is over 330,000 times as large as the earth. And there are stars in the universe more than 60,000 times as large as the sun!

In the earliest church-tower clocks in Europe, there were no hands, merely a bell and striker to provide the hour. The word "clock" comes from the French cloche, "bell." Originally, the word was applied only to those time-keeping devices that struck the hours by a bell or a gong.

There's more than one way to win a race, and probably the most bizarre way ever was found by the thoroughbred Brampton, who finished first—but in an upside-down position. The race was run in Dargaville, New Zealand, on February 2, 1931. The jockey was Joe Parson, who got to within 40 feet of the finish line—when Brampton suddenly stumbled and fell, rolling over several times and then sliding across the line, with Parson hanging on for dear life, to finish a split second ahead of the second-place horse.

The annals of history show a case of a queen who was not crowned until after her death. The posthumous monarch was Inez de Castro, wife of Prince Don Pedro of Portugal. Inez was murdered two years prior to her spouse's coronation in 1357, but her body was exhumed and crowned when Don Pedro ascended the throne.

The human brain makes up only two percent of a person's total weight, but uses about 25 percent of the body's oxygen.

In 1865, Uranus H. Crosby built the Crosby Opera House in Chicago. Soon after the theater opened, Crosby realized that the business venture was doomed to bankruptcy. Not one to say die, Crosby devised a means of saving the Opera House. He held a raffle, with the theater as the prize, and sold 185,000 raffle tickets at $5 each. After the drawing, Crosby offered the winner $200,000 for the Opera House, and succeeded in buying it back at that price. The raffle created so much favorable publicity for Crosby, that the Opera House began to draw crowds, and eventually Crosby recouped the entire $1 million that he had originally put into the building's construction.

There is a city in the United States that is closer to Tokyo, Japan, than it is to Boston, Massachusetts. The city? Why, it's Honolulu, Hawaii, of course!

Americans are certainly not losing their taste for pizza. In 1978, the New York State Crop Reporting Service declared that, during the previous year, the state had set a new record for cheese production—407 million pounds—with the sharp rise in production most accounted for by the surge in mozzarella production. Mozzarella is, of course, one of the major ingredients in most pizzas.

We can't vouch for quality, but for quantity alone, California, New York, and Pennsylvania are the leading ice-cream producing states in the nation.

The increased appearance of male flight attendants is not the only change greeting air travelers today. In the 1960s, when girdles, white gloves, and a hat were required dress for stewardesses on many airlines, the average age of a flight attendant was in the low 20s. Today, that average hovers around age 30.

The relaxed regulations governing dress, marital status, and other personal affairs has resulted in a far lower attrition rate among flight attendants, too. One airline reported that its attrition rate had dropped from 36 percent in 1968 to just four percent today.

The earliest Kodak cameras were preloaded at the factory with film for 100 pictures—each round in shape, and just two-and-a-half inches in diameter. After the film was completely exposed, the camera itself was returned to the factory, where the film was developed and a new roll inserted in the camera.

The United States Census Bureau has estimated that, if the world's population continues to grow at its present rate, the number of people on this planet could reach 6.3 billion by the year 2000. The projected increase of 2.2 billion people between 1975 and 2000 would equal the entire world population increase from the time of Christ until the middle of this century!

Absolutely pure gold, which you may never have seen, is so soft that it could be molded like clay. Even so-called "pure" gold, dubbed "24 karat," contains a small amount of other metals.

The Parthenon in Athens, considered today the epitome of classical grace and simplicity in architecture, was originally painted in colors that we'd find quite gaudy.

King Prajadhipok, ruler of Siam from 1925 until 1935, took out unemployment insurance policies with European companies to insure himself against the loss of his throne. He was forced to abdicate in 1935 and lived comfortably on the insurance money until his death in 1941.

Train Time

Until time zones were standardized in the mid-19th century, each town had its own time, determined by the local jeweler. All clocks and watches for the community were set accordingly to jeweler's time.

Naturally, long-distance travel could be quite confusing. In the railroad terminal in Buffalo, New York, for instance, there were four clocks to consult when examining a railroad schedule: one showing Buffalo time, one showing the time in Portland, Maine, one showing New York Central Railroad time, and another showing Lake Shore Railway time. Each railroad then operated on a different time, which was usually determined by the time in the largest city the line served.

The drive-in movie theater had its humble beginnings in 1933, when Richard Hollingshead, Jr. set up a screen in front of his garage in Riverton, New Jersey. Later that year, Hollingshead opened the Camden Drive-in in a 400-car parking lot, and another American institution was founded.

The peak year for drive-in theaters was 1958, when there were 3,484 drive-ins from coast to coast. By now that number has dwindled. Texas has the most drive-ins of any state: 264. Alaska has but one.

On February 25, 1979, an unidentified auto enthusiast outbid all other comers and purchased a 1936 Mercedes Benz 500-K roadster at an auction in Los Angeles. The price? A neat $400,000, plus the auction house fee. That figure was more than double the previous record amount paid for an automobile at auction.

At the same auction, another bidder purchased a 1929 Mercedes for a paltry $320,000. And a 1955 Ford Thunderbird sold for $17,000!

A recent poll in a major American city found that only 59 percent of the people polled believed that the fire department would come to their aid at once if they were summoned, and barely half thought the police would respond at once if needed. The same poll discovered that a majority of these people believed that their neighbors would come to their aid in an emergency, but a minority thought that their children could receive a good education in the public schools.

The painting known to all Americans as *Whistler's Mother* was never given that title by its creator, James Whistler. The artist actually named his work *Arrangement in Black and Gray: The Artist's Mother*.

The painting, by the way, is the only work by an American artist presently exhibited at the Louvre, in Paris.

Only one United States president was married in the White House: Grover Cleveland. And only one president remained a bachelor throughout his life: James Buchanan.

Believe it or not, the Taj Mahal of India was once sold to an Englishman who planned to dismantle the structure for its marble! In 1830, a British merchant purchased the Taj, considered by some people to be the most beautiful building on earth, and laid plans to take it apart stone by stone, so that he could sell the marble in England. Fortunately, the plan was dropped before the wrecking crews could begin work.

On a similar note, an Arab leader who occupied Egypt, once attempted to dismantle the Great Pyramid at Giza. He abandoned the plan when he discovered that he could more easily obtain stone from a nearby quarry.

Extinct Animals

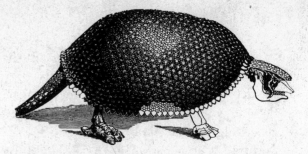

Though some of these creatures were extinct 300 million years ago, others did not die out completely until this century—and many other species are in danger of extinction today.

Here are just a few of the creatures that once roamed the earth, but live no more. Let's hope that animals such as the Mexican Grizzly Bear, Giant Otter, Javan Rhinoceros, and Blue Whale—all endangered today—do not soon join this list.

GLYPTODON   *The glyptodon was a gigantic mammal, related to the armadillo, that lived in South America more than a million years ago. Later, the glyptodon invaded North America and reached the southern United States.*

DODO   *The flightless, swan-sized bird known as the dodo lived on the Indian Ocean islands of Mauritius and Reunion, becoming extinct in 1681. The Dutch called the dodo the "nauseous bird," because cooking would not make it palatable.*

MAMMOTH   *This elephantlike creature has given us a word meaning "enormous," but the mammoth was probably no larger than the modern elephant. Remains of the mammoth have been found in many places in the Northern Hemisphere. The creature was hunted by stone-age man, and may have survived in Siberia until relatively recent times.*

STEGOSAURUS   *Stegosaurus means "plated lizard." These dinosaurs lived in North America some 150 million years ago. The spiked tail may look fearsome, but the stegosaurus was actually a harmless vegetarian. The largest were 30 feet long.*

TOXODON *These hoofed, herbivorous mammals were very numerous in South America before the Pleistocene Age, some 500,000 years ago. The largest toxodons were the size of a rhinoceros.*

ICHTHYOSAURUS *A marine reptile, the ichthyosaurus breathed by lungs but well adapted for life in the water. It flourished throughout the world, but was extinct before the Paleocene Era, 65 million years ago.*

PLESIOSAURUS *This marine reptile was well adapted for life in the open seas. Some measured over 30 feet in length. The plesiosaurus was extinct by the end of the Cretaceous period, 70 million years ago.*

DRACO *This small reptile used the winglike membranes on its sides to glide from tree to tree.*

PTERODACTYL *These winged reptiles lived in many parts of the world some 100 million years ago. The smaller species were the size of a sparrow. But other pterodactyls were the largest creatures ever to fly, with a head four feet long and a wingspan of 18 feet.*

IGUANODON *This amphibious reptile of the dinosaur age was named iguanodon because its teeth resembled those of the iguana lizard. The largest species measured 33 feet in length, and stood 13 feet tall on its hind legs. The thumb formed a spikelike weapon. The iguanodon ranged over Northern Europe and England during the Cretaceous period, more than 100 million years ago.*

MEGATHERIUM *This was the largest of the ancient ground sloths, a group of mammals related to the modern sloth. But the megatherium was much larger, equalling the elephant in bulk. It lived in North and South America during the Pleistocene age, which began 800,000 years ago.*

MESOPITHECUS *This ancient primate, an ancestor of the modern ape, lived more than 25 million years ago.*

RHAMPHORHYNCHUS *A small pterodactyl, or flying reptile, that lived some 100 million years ago. The body was about four inches long, but the tail grew up to 15 inches in length. The creature lived mainly on fish.*

ARCHAEOPTERYX *This is the most ancient bird of which fossil remains have been discovered. The archaeopteryx had a reptilelike head, teeth, and a lizardlike tail, but also had feathers and wings. About the size of a crow, the archaeopteryx flourished in Europe and other places during the Jurassic period, some 150 million years ago.*

CLAOSAUR *Most of what we know about extinct reptiles has been learned from skeletons such as this.*

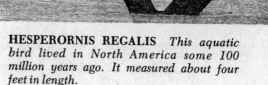

HESPERORNIS REGALIS *This aquatic bird lived in North America some 100 million years ago. It measured about four feet in length.*

In a bizarre combination of the old and the new, the Havasupai Indians, who live in isolation on the floor of the Grand Canyon, decided to use a copier machine to publish their tribal newspaper. The Indians then transported the machine into the canyon on the back of a mule!

The average journalist in the United States has a working vocabulary of about 20,000 words; the average lawyer, about 15,000 words. At the other end of the scale, the average farm worker has a vocabulary of about 1,600 words.

If valued separately, the raw materials that make up the body of a living 150-pound human being would bring just under six dollars. If you're thinking about selling a relative for scrap, you would do better to wait for his demise. A human skeleton may now bring over $500.

The legs of dancer Fred Astaire were insured for $650,000. For quite another reason, the legs of actress Betty Grable were insured for $250,000.

Most Americans would probably guess correctly as to the most common last name in this country: Smith. Would you like to try your hand at guessing the most common names in some other nations? Well, in Germany, it's Schultz or Schulz; in France, it's Martin; in Spain, Garcia; in Sweden, Johansson; in the Soviet Union, Ivanov; and in Great Britain, it's—yep, Smith.

The most common last name in China, by the way, is Chang, followed by Wang and Li.

There are actually only 16 minerals we value as gems. But many of these minerals are found in two or more colors, and a specific gem name is given to each variety. For instance, the ruby and the sapphire are in fact different forms of the same mineral, corundum. The emerald is green beryl, the aquamarine is blue beryl. The carbuncle is red garnet. And jasper, onyx, sard, sardonyx, cat's-eye, carnelian, bloodstone, and agate are all forms of quartz.

To commemorate his 700th parachute jump, British Army Sargeant Hector Macmillan made a leap in full Scottish national dress, including kilts, while playing *The Road to the Isles* on his bagpipes.

Put That In Your Pipe And Smoke It!

Among the more ingenious espionage agents was a British spy, who, after his retirement, revealed a device of his own construction for hiding secret papers in his pipe. The pipe bowl contained a hidden chamber between the inner and outer walls, in which the man secreted his tissue-paper notes. Had the spy, who smoked the pipe continuously, ever been apprehended, a slight twist of the pipe's overlapping rim would have caused the secret chamber to invisibly dump its contents into the bowl, where they would be burned along with the tobacco.

Credit for introducing tennis to America is usually given to Mary Ewing Outerbridge of New York. Miss Outerbridge saw a variation of the game being played by British soldiers during an 1874 visit to Bermuda, and brought back the rules and some pieces of tennis equipment to her brother, the director of the Staten Island Cricket and Baseball Club in Staten Island, New York.

Reportedly, customs officials were unable to decide under what section of the Tariff Act Mary's equipment belonged, and after a week of consideration decided to allow the equipment in duty free.

Rat-A-Tat-Tat

Believe it or not, until the year 1888, many Americans were convinced that rats could read English. In that year, there is a record of a man in Maine who wrote to the rodents occupying his basement, asking them to decamp, and even recommending new quarters in a building on the same street. The man placed his written request in one of the rodents' holes, and according to his report, the rats departed the next day. However, the man left no indication as to whether or not the rats followed his suggestion as to the nearby abode.

The first American publication that could justifiably be termed a newspaper was brought out in 1690 by Benjamin Harris, a bookseller who had been forced to flee England after publishing a seditious news pamphlet. Harris called his Boston paper *Publick Occurences Both Foreign and Domestick*, and promised it would be issued "once a moneth (or if any Glut of Occurences happen, oftener)." Harris's four-page paper was suppressed after only one issue for certain comments found distasteful by Massachusetts governor Simon Bradstreet.

How Do You Like These "Spudions"?

Comic Stan Laurel, of Laurel and Hardy fame, was an amateur horticulturalist, who dreamed of producing a hybrid between the onion and the potato. After many failures, Laurel finally succeeded in producing the hybrid, but not one of his friends would deign to taste it.

In France, between the 13th and 18th centuries, lawyers beefed up their business by duping peasants into suing animals and insects for property damage, and banishing the destructive creatures from the environs by court decree. To increase court costs and attorneys' fees, the trials were prolonged as long as possible. One case, brought in 1445 against a swarm of malevolent insects by the citizens of St. Julian, dragged on for 50 years before the plaintiffs finally dropped the suit. The peasants collected nothing from the insects—but the peasants' lawyers collected plenty!

The horse certainly hasn't disappeared in the United States since the onset of the automobile. The current horse population of this country is estimated at 72 million!

In 1978, bidders shelled out $6 million for half a share in Triple Crown winner, Seattle Slew, making him the most valuable single animal specimen in man's history.

A modest modern air-conditioning system has a cooling effect equivalent to the melting of 2.4 million pounds of ice in 24 hours! The air-conditioning system of the Pentagon cools 12 million cubic feet of air *per minute!*

Man has devised some rather exotic ways to make a living, and in many cases has come up with equally exotic words to identify these professions. Here's a sampling of some less familiar terms: a *puffer* is an auction booster; an *abigail* is a lady's maid; a *boniface* is an innkeeper; a *couturier* is a dressmaker; a *tonsorialist* is a barber; a *factotum* is a jack-of-all-trades; a *grifter* is a circus concessionaire; a *costermonger* is a fruit peddler; and a *croupier* is a gambling-house employee.

You've no doubt enjoyed the dessert treat tapioca pudding. But did you ever wonder what tapioca is made from? Oddly enough, it's made from a starch taken from the root of the cassava, or manioc plant. Tapioca pudding may be popular in the United States, but the cassava plant is found only in South America and other tropical areas.

The first record of the use of spices dates from the age of the pyramids in Egypt—approximately 4,600 years ago. Onions and garlic were fed to the 100,000 laborers who toiled in the construction work under Cheops. These vegetables were administered as medicinal herbs to preserve the health of the laborers.

Playing Possum

When in mortal danger, many animals feign death. But none do this as convincingly as the American opossum and the dingo, a wild dog of Australia. The dingo will allow its captor to beat it unmercifully until the chance to escape presents itself. The entrapped oppossum will assume its famous "possum" pose, which is to lie limp with its tongue hanging out of its mouth and its eyes open and rolled back.

The saltiest lake in the world is the Dead Sea, which is so full of chemicals that it is really difficult for anyone to drown, or even remain fully submerged in it for any length of time. The chemicals make the water so heavy that it is also hard to swim. Each stroke you take makes you feel as if you're pushing away a ton of bricks. Of course, it's so easy to float in the Dead Sea that the thing to do is to get out there under an umbrella, hold a book in hand and simply lie on your back and read in comfort. But when you get out of the water, you'll find yourself covered with an oily film which is rather difficult to remove.

Warm ocean currents make Europe significantly warmer than North America at corresponding latitudes. Paris is as far north as Grand Falls, Newfoundland, while Oslo, Norway, is farther north than Juneau, Alaska. Traveling due east from Cape Hatteras, North Carolina, you would not reach Europe, but Morocco, North Africa.

The most poisonous substance yet discovered is the toxin of the *Clostridium botulinum* bacteria. Just 1/3000 of an ounce of this toxin could poison the entire human population of the earth.

The toucan's bill, which is bigger than its body, gives it an ungainly, comical appearance. But in spite of its large size, the thin-walled bill is lightweight and easy to carry.

Gustatory Gymnastics

The next time you're thinking about setting a record, try your hand at one of the following gastronomic achievements. The records for consuming various items are:

Raw eggs: 56 in 2 minutes
Potato chips: 30 bags in 29 minutes
Sausages: 17 in 90 seconds
Oysters: 480 in 60 minutes
Prunes: 100 in 12 minutes
Beer: 2½ pints in 10 seconds

Bon appetit!

There is only one case on record of a country being moved from one continent to another— at least on maps. Before Panama gained its independence from Colombia in 1903, the nation was considered a part of South America. After independence, the Isthmus was regarded as a part of Central America—which belongs to North America.

On the average, a city dog lives longer than a country dog—11 years compared to eight.

The stupidest creature ever to inhabit the earth was the *Stegosaurus*, a six and one-half ton creature with a brain weighing only two and one-half ounces.

The planet Venus takes 247 earth days to spin around on its axis, and 224.7 earth days to orbit the sun. Thus, the Venusian day is longer than the Venusian year.

Surprisingly enough, Jupiter—the largest planet in our solar system—has the shortest day. The massive planet requires only 9 hours and 50 minutes to make a complete rotation on its axis.

In just over 150 years of independence, the Central American nation of Honduras has endured 139 coups and revolutions.

The late Grantland Rice is recognized not only as one of the great sports writers of all time, but also as the most prolific American writer on record. His stories of athletes and athletic events comprised an estimated 67 million words—the equivalent of almost a thousand 300-page books!

The sheep population of Australia is estimated at over 145 million—ten times the size of the human population. And the sheep population of the world tops the one billion mark!

Long Live the König

George I, who ascended the throne of England in 1714 at the age of 54, never learned to write or speak the English language.

The new monarch of the British people was a German by birth, but as the descendant of James I of England, he was also heir to the English crown. The "foreign" king was not at all interested in learning the tongue of his British subjects, being much more concerned with his smaller holdings in Germany than in the far-flung British Empire.

Since the king's English ministers never bothered to learn German, George could not participate in the meetings of his own cabinet.

If the entire population of the earth were crammed within the boundaries of the United States, the population density of our nation would still not reach that of Belgium or the Netherlands.

The Panama Canal connects two oceans

The Panama Canal is neither the longest, the widest, the deepest, nor the oldest canal in the world. Yet, as the only canal which connects two oceans, and the canal whose construction presented the most difficult challenges, the Panama Canal is the greatest man-made waterway in the world.

The initial attempt to build a canal across the narrow isthmus of Panama in Central America resulted in one of the most tragic engineering failures in history. In 1881, a French firm headed by Ferdinand de Lesseps—who had earlier constructed the Suez Canal—began to dig a canal across the isthmus. While de Lesseps was able to conquer the desert of Suez, he could not overcome the mosquito of Panama. Within eight years, close to 20,000 men died of malaria while working on the ill-fated project. The French company went bankrupt after suffering losses totaling $325 million, and de Lesseps left Panama.

In 1907, an American construction crew headed by G.W. Goethals journeyed to Panama to try their luck where the French had failed. Panama leased the United States a strip of land 10 miles wide for the canal. A massive project to wipe out the malaria-carrying mosquito was successful, and work proceeded without the hazard of disease that doomed the French venture.

Construction began at both ends of the projected canal and progressed inland through a dense tropical jungle. An artificial lake was formed; locks were constructed; the famed Gaillard Cut, for years the largest ditch in the world, was dug through 660-foot Gold Hill. At the peak of construction, 300 railroad cars—each carrying 400 tons of dirt—left the site daily. A total of 10 billion tons of earth were moved for the canal—a figure greater than the total weight of the

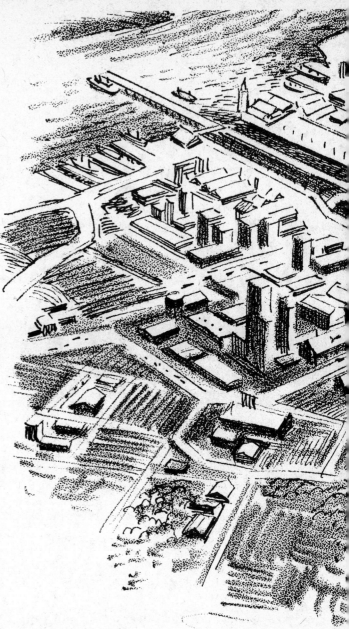

Great Pyramid of Cheops! In 1914, the canal was completed.

To navigate the canal, a ship must rise or fall a total of 85 feet. To accomplish this, massive locks were constructed which raise a westbound ship first to the level of the artificial lake—Lake Gatun—then to the level of a second lake—Miraflores—and, at the Pacific end of the canal, lower the ship back to sea level. For eastbound ships, the procedure is reversed.

The locks at Miraflores comprise the largest lock system in the world. The largest Miraflores lock is over 1,000 feet long, with gates seven feet thick and as high as a seven-story building. Electric cars, or "mules," on the side of the canal pull the ship through the locks, and water empties in and out of the lock through tubes as large as railroad tunnels.

The St. Lawrence Seaway between Canada and the United States extends over 2,300 miles from Duluth, Minnesota, to Belle Isle, Quebec, and hence is more than 45 times as long as the Panama Canal. But the St. Lawrence waterway was built by deepening and widening rivers, and utilizes the Great Lakes for much of its length. The Panama Canal, on the other hand, was carved out of virgin jungle. In addition, the time saved by a seven-hour trip through the canal is a saving unmatched by any other canal in the world, with the possible exception of the Suez (a 9,000-mile journey around South America requires at least two weeks). Each year, over 15,000 ships take advantage of the Panama shortcut.

An interesting footnote to the Panama Canal story: due to the curve of the isthmus, the Pacific end of the canal actually lies 27 miles *east* of the Atlantic end! Also, the canal has provided the world with perhaps its most clever palindrome (a line that can be read in either direction):

A man, a plan, a canal—Panama!

Cock-a-doodle-doo!

The chicken population of this country now stands at close to 380 million. That means there's more than a chicken in this nation for every pot—there's almost two!

The chicken was probably not domesticated much earlier than 1500 B.C., in Southeast Asia. Domestic breeds of the chicken descended from fowl that lived in the jungles of India.

There are more than a hundred breeds and varieties of chicken, but only a few are raised on a large scale for their meat or eggs. Some breeds provide excellent layers, while others are valued for their meat.

Here are some creatures—all males—that strut about and declare, "I am cock of the walk!"

DOMINIQUE MALE *An American breed with yellow legs and gray plumage.*

BANTAM COCK *A bantam is a small domesticated fowl, often a dwarf variety of a standard breed.*

SILVER GRAY DORKING MALE *The Dorking is an English breed raised primarily for its meat. The Silver Gray Dorking is the most common. All Dorkings have five toes, while most other breeds of chicken have four toes.*

SINGLE-COMB WHITE LEGHORN *This is the most common variety of the Leghorn breed, and is widely used for egg production in the United States.*

BLACK JAVA MALE *Other Java chickens may have mottled plumage.*

SILVER WYANDOTTE *The Wyandotte is an American breed suitable for both egg and meat production. The White Wyandotte is the most common variety.*

BLACK-TAILED JAPANESE BANTAM MALE *Bantams are often raised by poultrymen as novelties.*

Don't Catch A Falling Star!

On June 30, 1908, a 49,000-ton meteorite crashed into a forest in Central Siberia, felling about 80 million trees in a 35-mile radius. The landing of the Tunguska Meteorite, the largest falling star in history, caused a depression containing 200 small craters, and produced an airwave recorded on a barometer 800 miles away! Fortunately, the Tunguska area of Siberia is completely uninhabited, so no lives were lost. In fact, Tunguska is so inaccessible, that it was not until 1927—nearly two decades after the disaster—that an expedition could be sent to the area to report on the damage.

Want to enjoy a long life? Maybe you'd better move to Hawaii. With an average life expectancy of 73,6 years, the Hawaiians live longer than the residents of any other state in the United States.

The term "foolscap," which refers to the dimensions of a sheet of paper, may be derived from the Italian *foglia*, "leaves." But a more interesting derivation traces the term to the period of the English Civil War. Charles I declared that all paper manufactured in England should bear the royal arms as a watermark. When Oliver Cromwell toppled the monarchy in 1649, he ordered that a fool's cap and bells be substituted for the royal arms on all English paper.

In 1927, the *New York Times* reported with front-page headlines the first public demonstration of long-distance TV transmission. The newspaper commented that the image was "like a photo come to life," but added that the medium's "commercial use is in doubt."

In recognition of the secret-message capabilities of the crossword puzzle, the Hungarian government ordered, in 1925, that all newspaper crosswords first be submitted to official censors for approval.

One crossword not submitted for government approval was the work of a Budapest man who left a suicide note in the form of a crossword puzzle, with the reasons for his act, and the persons to be contacted, cleverly incorporated into the puzzle.

High Society

Social climbers might take a tip from the tale of "Princess Caraboo of Javasu." On the night of April 3, 1817, a young woman was found wandering about in a daze by a rich family in Almondsbury, England. The family took in the wanderer, and set about trying to establish her identity. The mysterious stranger wore Eastern dress, and had many Oriental mannerisms. She spoke no English, talking only in an apparently Asiatic tongue, unknown to the foremost linguists of the day. Finally, a sailor appeared claiming that he knew the woman's language and would volunteer to translate her story. The sailor conversed with the young woman and related that she was Princess Caraboo of Javasu, an island near Sumatra. The princess had been kidnapped from her native land and sold to pirates, who were then shipwrecked off the coast of England. The princess immediately became an idol of British Society, because of her royal status. However, a newspaper article mentioning a peculiar scar on the princess's back led to an acquaintance recognizing the impostor as one Mary Baker of Devonshire, a servant girl. Miss Baker and her sailor friend had decided to hoax British Society and had succeeded—to the embarrassment not only of the plutocrats, but also of the many British philologists who had failed to realize that the princess was talking mere gibberish to them for over a year.

Modern multi-millionaires include John D. Rockefeller, who left a fortune of $26,273,845 at his death in 1937; H.L. Hunt, whose revenue from his oil wells accumulated to an estimated $2-3 billion before he died in 1974; insurance magnate John D. MacArthur, whose demise in 1978 enriched his heirs by some $1-5 billion; and Howard Hughes, the eccentric hermit whose estate was estimated by the *New York Times* at $1.5 billion upon Hughes's death in 1976. Aristotle Onassis, "The Golden Greek" who died in 1975, amassed $500 million in his lifetime, while Brazilian Jorge Wolne Atalla and his brothers, coffee magnates with lucrative side ventures in cattle, sugar, and other commodities, are said to be worth about $1.3 billion in toto.

The Houston Astrodome, the home of baseball's Houston Astros, is covered with a domed roof—but that hasn't stopped the Astros from recording at least one rained-out game. On June 16, 1976, rain fell so hard on the city of Houston that the grounds surrounding the domed stadium were completely flooded. Players and umpires were prevented from reaching the ballpark, and the game was called.

Jokesters referred to the event as baseball's first "rain-in."

Wealthy men have bought their way into office at least since the days of the Holy Roman Empire, when Charles V purchased the emperor's throne for 544,000 guilders. The loser of the election, France's Francois Premier, could put up only 310,000 guilders in payoff money. Charles's chief fund-raiser was usurer Jacob Fugger, nicknamed "The Rich," who lived by the shibboleth, "I want to gain while I can." When Fugger died, in 1525, he had gained over 3 million gold florins.

One American dies in an automobile accident for every 541 reported accidents in this country. In a typical recent year, nationwide, about 46,000 persons died in auto accidents.

It Takes a Shark To Beat a Shark

Strange are the aids that come to the law in the prosecution of justice. And one of the strangest cases on record is that of *The Shark's Papers*.

In 1799, off the coast of Jamaica, the *Nancy*, an American ship suspected of smuggling, was seized by an English revenue cutter, and steered into Port Royal. However, before being boarded by the British, the crew of the American vessel threw overboard the contraband cargo, as well as the ship's papers. The *Nancy's* captain duly produced a set of fake papers, which he had prepared for such a contingency, and presented the forgeries to his captors.

A few days later, the trial was held, and the officers of the *Nancy* were about to be acquitted for lack of evidence of the smuggling charge, when the captain of another English ship dramatically entered the courtroom with the *Nancy's* original papers. The papers had been discovered in the stomach of a shark harpooned by the British vessel's crew that morning. The Americans were convicted. *The Shark's Papers* are currently on display at the Institute of Jamaica in Kingston, and the head of the telltale shark has been preserved by the Royal United Service Institution in London.

Oysters are an expensive delicacy today, but in times past they were one of the cheapest foods available. In medieval England, an entire bushel could be bought for about four pence, and as late as the 19th century, oystermen peddled their wares from wheelbarrows on the streets of London, for about four pence a dozen. In fact, oysters were so cheap that the saying arose: "Poverty and oysters always seem to go together." How times do change!

Schooldays

What do Mae West, Bobby Fischer, Dorothy Kilgallin, Bernard Malamud, Barbara Stanwyk and Beverly Sills have in common? All these famous individuals graduated from Erasmus High School in Brooklyn, New York.

Divorce, Cowboy Style

In the days of the Wild West, divorce papers were dispensed by slot machine. In the early 1870s, a law firm in Corinne, Utah was so swamped with divorce cases, that they had a machine constructed to issue the required documents at $2.50 per set. Utah was then a territory requiring no grounds for divorce, and the only thing necessary for validation of the papers were the signatures of the couple involved.

The Romance of Chocolate

Early in the eighteenth century, an Austrian nobleman named Prince Dietrichstein ordered a chocolate beverage in a Vienna chocolate house and was so enraptured by the waitress who served him that he wooed and eventually married her. The Prince commissioned the noted Swiss portraitist Jean-Etienne Leotard to paint a portrait of his wife, Anna Beltauf, in her waitress garb. Titled *La Belle Chocolatiere*, the painting soon found its way to a museum.

In 1872, an American executive of the Walter Baker Chocolate Company saw the painting during a trip to Europe, and purchased it for use as the firm's emblem. Baker chocolate products still bear a reproduction of the Leotard portrait.

The onion is the most widely used vegetable in the world. In total production both the potato and tomato surpass the onion, but neither is used in such a wide variety of dishes and in such a wide variety of cuisines as the onion.

Among the many names applied to the toilet, "crapper" is probably considered to be one of the more vulgar. But the term is actually derived, in the most curiously coincidental linking of an inventor with his invention, from Thomas Crapper, a 19th-century English sanitary engineer.

Crapper's major innovation was a mechanism that shut off the flow of clean water when the toilet's reservoir was filled.

This century, bedtime comfort has been extended as far as the family dog. A 1938 advertisement for a "hygienic" dog bed boasted that the bed came in sizes "to fit all dogs."

The year 1979 marked the 100th anniversary of the famous "5 & 10 Cent" store. Frank Winfield Woolworth opened the first one in Utica, New York in 1879. It failed. But that didn't make him give up the idea. He opened one in Lancaster, Pennsylvania, and this time it worked. Today, there are 1,419 Woolworth stores throughout the United States. Of course, finding items that can be bought for five or 10 cents might be a little problematic.

Aid for the Eyes

Before the invention of eyeglasses, man had to rely on medicinal remedies of a rather dubious value to improve his vision. Fourth-century Romans believed that a person seeing a falling star should quickly begin counting. The viewer would be free from eye inflammations for as many years as he could count before the star disappeared.

For those too slow to catch a falling star, another ancient antidote to eye inflammation required that the sufferer tie a piece of linen around his neck with as many knots as there were letters in his name. White spots before your eyes? Simply catch a fox, cut out his tongue, tie it in a red rag, and hang it from your neck. And if you have something in your eye, just touch your lid, say "I buss the Gorgon's mouth," and spit three times.

Ho! Hum!

Yawning is commonly caused by temporary deficiency of the air supply in the lung. When the body is wearied and in a sleepy condition, the process of respiration is sometimes involuntarily suspended for a few seconds. Nature at once, however, comes to the rescue, and by setting up a spasmodic action in the muscles of the mouth, throat, and chest, produces a deep inspiration, which compensates for the stoppage of breathing. This is known as a yawn.

Not to be confused with Croesus is Crassus, a Roman citizen born around 115 B.C., who was one of the richest men who ever lived. However, Crassus' gains were ill-gotten, the result of "fire and rapine," Plutarch tells us. An example of Crassus' unscrupulousness was his establishment of Rome's first fire department.

At the sound of a fire alarm, Crassus and his myrmidons, 500 strong, would rush to the scene of the blaze, but they would do nothing to quench the flames until Crassus had obtained his price from the owner of the burning building. If the victim of the fire could not—or would not—meet Crassus' sum, the firemen would stand by idly, watching the structure burn to the ground.

Crassus also trafficked in slaves, whom he bought unskilled, trained himself, and then sold for enormous profits. Crassus' greed was such that although, as a lieutenant in the Roman army he was allowed to buy captured enemy lands for a pittance, he often preferred to seize whatever property he wanted, killing the hapless owners.

Sometimes, machines seem to carry a jinx. Such was the case with the "Death Car of Sarajevo," in which Austrian Archduke Francis Ferdinand and his wife were riding when they met their untimely death at the hands of an assassin in Sarajevo, Bosnia, on June 28, 1914. This incident caused the outbreak of World War I.

The automobile also spelled disaster for scores of other individuals. In the 12 years following the assassination, the car had 15 different owners, and was involved in six terrible accidents. Thirteen persons were killed, and many more injured, in these mishaps. The last of the wrecks occurred in Cluj, Rumania, in 1926. The death car was so badly damaged, that it was never again restored to working order. However, the outside of the car was refurbished, and the machine has been preserved in Vienna, Austria.

Behemoths of the Seas

"This is the sea, broad and wide," said the Psalmist. "There go the ships, and this leviathon which Thou has created to disport himself therein."

Since then, and long before, the whale has been a subject of enormous curiosity to man, and myriads of legends and fantasties have grown about this huge beast. There are many species of whales extant, and they differ in interesting ways. Here are a number of these behemoths of the seas:

COMMON WHALE *Like all members of the whale family, this sea creature is warm-blooded and breathes with lungs. The flippers are actually mammalian hands, not fins.*

BLUNT-HEADED CACHALOT *Cachalot is another name for the sperm whale, the largest of all toothed whales. All sperm whales are in fact "blunt-headed."*

WHITE WHALE *The adult of this species is pure white all over, while the young are brown or gray. Most adults measure about 18 feet in length.*

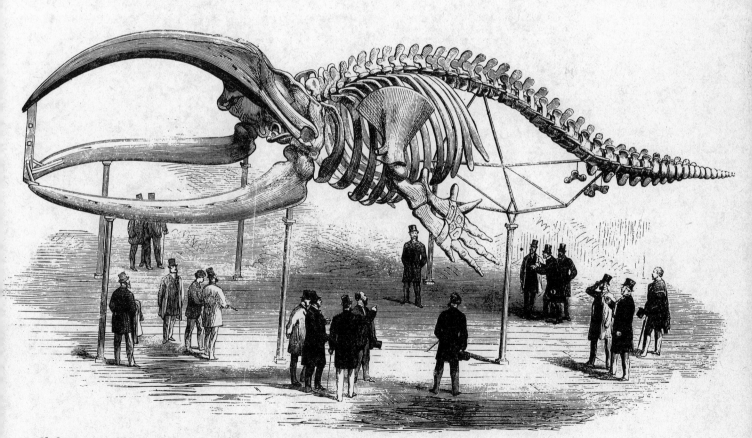

Skeleton of a whale, as depicted in the Illustrated London News.

BOTTLE-NOSED WHALE *This toothed inhabitant of the North Atlantic prefers cuttlefish as its food. The largest males may measure over 30 feet in length.*

SPERM WHALE *The male sperm whale may measure over 60 feet in length, but the female rarely exceeds 35 feet. The sperm whale lives primarily in tropical waters, unlike most whales, and may descend up to 10,000 feet in search of food.*

ATLANTIC RIGHT WHALE *Also called the Biscay whale, this toothless creature averages about 60 feet in length. It lives in the Atlantic near northern Europe, and visits the eastern United States.*

HUMPBACK WHALE *This mammal is found in all the world's seas. The average length is 50 to 60 feet. Humpback whales can communicate with each other from hundreds of miles apart by means of a low-pitched cry.*

The cochineal insects furnish a great many of the very fine colors. Among them are the gorgeous carmine, crimson, scarlet, and purple lakes.

The cuttlefish gives us sepia, the inky fluid which the fish discharges in order to render the water opaque when attacked.

Indian yellow comes from the camel. Ivory chips produce ivory black and bone black.

The exquisite Prussian blue is made by fusing horses' hoofs and other refuse animal matter with impure potassium carbonate. This color was discovered accidentally.

Blue-black comes from the charcoal of the vine stalk. Lamp black is soot from certain resinous substances.

Turkey red is made from the madder plant, which grows in Hindostan, and mastic is made from the gum of the mastic tree which grows in the Grecian archipelago.

The yellow sap tree in Siam produces gamboge; the natives catch the sap in cocoanut shells. Raw sienna is the natural earth from the neighborhood of Sienna, Italy. Raw umber is also an earth found near Umbria and burned.

Bistre is the soot of wood ashes; ultramarine is obtained from the precious lapis-lazuli; and India ink is made from burned camphor.

Chinese white is zinc; scarlet is iodide of mercury; and vermillion comes from the quicksilver ore called cinnabar.

Forbidden Fruit

Despite traditional belief, the Bible nowhere states that the apple was the fruit which the Mother of Mankind induced her mate to share with her. Genesis says only that Adam and Eve partook of the fruit of "the tree of knowledge of good and evil, which had been placed off bounds by divine prohibition. Although Western Judaeo-Christian tradition names the fruit as the apple, in the East, the belief prevails that the forbidden fruit was a banana.

Twinkle, Twinkle Little Star

Amateur astronomers can tell a star from a planet because only stars twinkle. The twinkling is due to irregularities in the density of the air through which the stars' light passes. As stars are much further from the earth than planets, they are perceived as twinkling points, while the planets are clearly perceived as disks.

Porcupines do not "shoot" their quills at an enemy when under attack. Actually, the quills, or spines, of the spiked animals are only loosely attached to their bodies, and are shed upon contact with any object. During battle, the porcupine thrashes about wildly with his tail, and thus, the quills are likely to be dislodged and become embedded in the flesh of the attacker.

The highest payoff odds ever recorded for a horse race were a nifty 396-1, paid on a horse named Waverly Steps, whose steps were far from waverly on June 24, 1968, at the Woodbine track. On December 11, 1964, a horse named Wilson Hill Doll was indeed a doll to the few bettors who wagered on her. The horse came in at 279-1 and paid off a neat $559.60 on a two-dollar bet.

The highest payoff on a daily double wager was recorded at a Detroit race course in 1973—a whopping $19,909 on a two-dollar bet!

The term *cracker* for a poor white Southern, especially someone from Georgia, dates back to the American Revolution. The term is believed to be an abbreviation of *corn-cracker*, bestowed upon the humble Georgians because their staple food was cracked corn.

Crazy Contests

The list of bizarre contests and celebrations held annually in this country includes these monumental events:

The World Championship Duck Calling Contest, held in Stuttgart, Arkansas, in late November.

The World Wrist-Wrestling Championship, held in Petaluma, California, in early October.

The Rattlesnake Festival and International Championship Gopher Race, held in Dade City, Florida, every October.

The World Championship Watermelon Seed Spittin' Contest, which is the talk of the town in Pauls Valley, Oklahoma, every June.

The International Chicken Flying Meet, a major annual even in Gallipolis, Ohio.

The National Cow Chip Throwing Contest, held in Beaver, Oklahoma, in late April.

The International Brick and Rolling Pin Throwing Contest, a mid-July event in Stroud, Oklahoma.

And let's not forget the World's Championship Armadillo Races, which sets the town of Uvalde, Texas, abuzz every October.

The word *tabloid*, now used to mean a newspaper heavily illustrated with pictures, and generally sensationalist both in text and illustration, originally referred to a condensed preparation of drugs. The word, which is the copyrighted trademark of Burroughs, Wellcome, and Company of London, was applied to tabloid newspapers because of the condensed form of such journals.

The elephant has more muscles in its trunk than any other creature possesses in its entire body, their number being no less than 40,000; while the whole of a man's muscles only number 527. The proboscis, or trunk, of the elephant, which contains this vast quantity of small muscles, variously interlaced, is extremely flexible, endowed with the most exquisite sensibility, and the utmost diversity of motion.

The appellation Eternal City, for Rome, Italy, originated with the poet Virgil. In the *Aeniad*, Jupiter tells Venus that he will bestow eternal empire on the Romans.

The Wicked Witch of the East

The richest woman in the United States—and perhaps the world—was Hetty Green, "the witch of Wall Street." Born Henrietta Robinson, in 1835, Hetty was heir to her family's vast shipping and whaling fortune, worth approximately $10 million. Hetty increased her holdings through shrewd investments and loans, and in 1867 married millionaire Edward H. Green, the executor of her father's will. In the marriage contract, Hetty stipulated that her husband was to have no control over her own fortune. The marriage lasted only a few years, perhaps because of Hetty's now-legendary avarice. "The witch of Wall Street" commuted to her office every day by ferry, from her tumbledown living quarters in Hoboken, New Jersey. She dressed in rags, and when her son's knee became infected, Hetty took the boy to Bellevue as a charity patient. When the hospital discovered her identity and demanded payment, Hetty refused, and removed her son from treatment, necessitating the amputation of the leg several years later. When Hetty Green died, in 1916, her estate was worth over $100 million.

The Incas built the first highways in America

Today's sprawling superhighways may seem to be the ultimate in road construction, but more than 350 years ago, the Inca Indians of South America built a system of roads through the Andes Mountains that would astound even modern engineers.

At its peak, the Inca Empire extended almost 2,500 miles from Colombia to Chile, and through this mountain country the Incas strung a network of roads to unite their vast domain. As the most important element of the Incas' imperial organization, the road system was built to speed communication and to provide for the efficient movement of men and supplies. The land the Incas ruled was as treacherous as it was vast, and their roads had to cut through marshes, jungles, and soaring mountains. These arteries often climbed heights of over 10,000 feet, and some roads were as long as virtually any modern highway!

Stone-retaining walls bordered the roads along much of their length. Enclosed way stations along the route provided for a messenger relay system, and offered protection against sudden mountain storms. Some roads tunneled through mountain cliffs—one such tunnel is almost 750 feet long! At other points, the Incas built causeways over wide marshlands and spanned raging rivers with bridges constructed of twisted rope cables.

The longest of the Inca bridges was immortalized by Thornton Wilder's novel *The Bridge of San Luis Rey*. This 148-foot suspension span crossed a deep ravine of the Apurimac River, swinging precariously in the mountain winds 118 feet above the waters. Until the bridge fell earlier in this century, it was in use longer than any other bridge in America.

All the roads of the Inca Empire met in their mountain capital of Cuzco, Peru, which is today the oldest continually inhabited city in America. Before moving to Cuzco, however, the center of the Inca empire had been another Andes city, but it wasn't until 1911 that this "lost city" was discovered.

Machu Picchu, 50 miles north of Cuzco, is one of the few urban centers of pre-Columbian America that survives virtually intact. The city straddles a narrow saddle between two peaks, 2,000 feet above a river. Paved stairway streets—stepped because of the slope of the city—weave between stone houses and military fortifications. Hundreds of agricultural terraces give the city the appearance of a gigantic stairway climbing the side of a mountain.

Even today, archaeologists admit the possibility that other Inca roads and cities may still be lost in the Andes, but to this point Machu Picchu is their greatest find.

Your Billions of Ancestors

Did you ever think how many male and female ancestors were required to bring you into the world? First, you have a father and mother. That makes two human beings. Each of them had a father and mother. That makes four more human beings. Again, each grandparent had a father and mother, making eight more human beings. So, on we go back to the time of Jesus Christ, 56 generations. The calculation indicated 139,235,017,489,-534,976 births must have taken place to bring you into this world. All this only since the birth of Christ—*not* since the beginning of time!

So, if from a single pair, for 5,000 years, each husband and wife had married at 21 years of age and there had been no deaths, the population of the earth would be 2,199,915 followed by 144 ciphers.

Panama hats, made of the tender leaves of the jijippa plant, are not manufactured in Panama, but in Equador and Peru. The hats were mislabeled because they were first introduced into general commerce through Panama, where many of the hats were sold.

Lobster Lesson

If you discover *langouste* on the menu of a French restaurant, then find the word translated as "lobster" in your pocket dictionary, you're in for a surprise when the dish arrives. *Langouste* is the French word for the sea crawfish, or rock lobster, and not the crustacean we commonly enjoy in America. *Langoustine*, meanwhile, is the French word for the large prawn often used in the Italian dish *Scampi*. *Ecrevisse* refers to the crayfish, or fresh-water lobster. Then how do you say "lobster" in French? Only the word *homard* refers to the creature we commonly know as the lobster.

The saying, "You can fool some of the people all of the time, and all of the people some of the time, but you can't fool all of the people all of the time" is popularly attributed to Abraham Lincoln, in a speech made at Clifton, Illinois on September 8, 1858. However, there is no extant copy of the Clifton speech, and some people claim that not Lincoln, but circus impresario P.T. Barnum first made the statement.

Ancient Advertising

In Greece, it was the public crier who announced sales, bid the people to come to the theatre, or to visit the public baths.

The Egyptians, Greeks, and the Romans knew something about advertising, and accomplished results through posters stuck on the wall of dwellings.

In medieval times, it was the public crier who went throughout the streets, enumerating the goods that a certain merchant had for sale.

In England, the first printed advertisement was set up by Caxton, the celebrated printer, who announced the completion of *The Pyes of Salisbury*, a book containing a collection of rules for the guidance of priests in the celebration of Easter.

The first newspaper advertisement appeared in 1642, during the civil war in Great Britain.

In the year 1657, a weekly newspaper, devoted to the interests of advertisers, made its appearance in London. But it was not until the 18th century, that newspaper advertising became the recognized medium between manufacturer and buyer.

The tabby cat, who is distinguished by a striped or brindled coat, was named for Attabiah, Bagdad, where a richly-colored watered or moire silk, resembling the tabby's fur, was manufactured.

Have you ever wondered why the little red schoolhouse was painted red? The custom originated in the Northeastern United States, where red paint was cheaper than any other color.

To put another feather in one's cap now refers to any creditable exploit or acquired honor. The phrase comes from a custom in ancient Lycia, where a feather was added to the hat of a warrior each time he killed an enemy.

Tobias Hobson, an innkeeper in Cambridge, England, under Charles I, is responsible for the term *Hobson's Choice.* When a guest at Hobson's inn asked for a horse, he was escorted to the inn's stable by Hobson himself, who told the traveler that he could choose any horse he wanted—except that he must choose the horse standing nearest the door! So, today, we call a choice that offers no alternative *Hobson's Choice.*

Salmon have leaped as high as six feet in ascending waterfalls. Some species of trout can also swim up waterfalls, against the current.

Rats are natives of Asia, and their raids westward belong to comparatively modern times. The little animal was unknown in ancient Europe. The black rat first came to Europe from Asia in the 16th century; and about the beginning of the 17th or the ending of the 16th century the rat arrived in America.

The grey rat came to Europe from India, by way of Russia, and is now known as the Norway rat from a mistaken tradition that it came from Norway to England, and form England to America.

Four-Ton Fantasy

An Indian maharajah of recent times boasted a one-ton bed complete with four life-sized nude statues that automatically began fanning and playing music the moment the monarch put his weight on the mattress.

Somewhere Over the Moonbow

Some night, when the moon is bright and it has been raining, go outside and look for a moonbow. This unusual phenomenon is rarely noticed, except by scientists, because the faintness of the moon's light makes the colors of the moonbow less visible than those of the rainbow.

Stay away from tornadoes! Ranging in forward speed from five to 139 miles per hour, and ranging in distance traveled from 100 feet to 219 miles, and ranging in width of path from six to 5,500 feet, tornadoes have caused property damage from one dollar to the $26 million hococaust that ravaged St. Louis on September 29, 1927. This multimillion-dollar disaster occured within a mere five minutes!

The largest bell in the world is in the Kremlin, in Moscow. The *Tsar Kolokol*, or "king of bells," was cast circa 1735, at the command of the Czarina Anna. The bell, which is 26 feet high, 66 feet in circumference, and 400,000 pounds in weight, has never been rung, because its excessive weight caused it to crack as it was being erected.

The fondness for big bells must be part of the Russian mystique, for another mammoth bell in Moscow, presented to St. John's Cathedral by Czar Boris Goudenov, weighs 250,000 pounds.

Surfers: Take Note

The highest wave in history is estimated at 112 feet. The wave was encountered by the U.S.S. *Ramapo*, on February 6, 1933, during a hurricane.

How sweet it was *not* for the 21 persons killed and 50 injured in the Boston Molasses Bath of January 15, 1919. This singular disaster occurred when a tank containing two million gallons of molasses exploded, crushing ten buildings, and causing over $1 million in property damage. The victims of the accident were either trapped in collapsing buildings or drowned by the sticky deluge, which flooded into the streets. About 50 horses were also trapped by the sudden flood, and since they could not be rescued, were shot to end their suffering.

The military custom of sounding taps before bedtime originated in public houses, where a signal known as "taps-up" alerted drinkers that the tap room was about to close for the night.

Ulysses S. Grant was actually christened Hiram Ulysses Grant. The name change occurred when the Congressman who nominated Grant for West Point erroneously wrote the youth's name as Ulysses Simpson Grant on the application form. Simpson was the maiden name of Grant's mother. The young cadet took advantage of the error as an excuse to get rid of the name Hiram, which he considered too old-fashioned.

The term *entangling alliances* was coined by Thomas Jefferson, not as is popularly supposed, by George Washington. In Jefferson's first inaugural address, delivered on March 4, 1801, he said, "Peace, commerce, and honest friendship with all nations—*entangling alliances* with none." However, Jefferson may have been deliberately echoing Washington's farewell speech of September 17, 1796, which concluded, "...Why, by interweaving our dealing with that of any part of Europe, entangle our peace and prosperity in the toils of European ambition, rivalship, interest, humor, or caprice?"

The term *red tape*, as a synonym for bureaucracy, originated in 18th-century England, where official and legal documents were tied up with red tape.

If you are too tender-hearted to shoot a deer, you can still find yourself an antler trophy—on the ground. Deer shed their horns once a year, during the breeding season.

Do You See the Light?

In terms of daylight, in London and Bremen, Germany, the longest day has 16½ hours. At Stockholm, Sweden, it is 18½ hours in length. At Hamburg, Germany, and Danzig, Poland, the longest day has 17 hours. At Leningrad, Russia, and Tobolsk, Siberia, the longest is 19 hours and the shortest five hours.

At Tornea, Finland, June 21 brings a day nearly 22 hours long, and Christmas one less than three hours in length. At Wardbury, Norway, the longest day lasts from May 21 to July 22 without interruption, and in Spitzbergen, Norway, the longest day is three-and-one-half months. At St. Louis, Missouri, the longest day is somewhat less than 15 hours, and at Montreal, Canada, it is 16 hours.

The phrase *to the manner born*, meaning to be habituated to from birth, was first written by William Shakespeare, in his tragedy *Hamlet*. The Danish prince tells his friend Horatio, "that to my mind, though I am native here and to the manner born, it [carousing] is a custom more honored in the breach than in the observance." Because of Hamlet's royal heritage, the phrase has sometimes been misinterpreted as "to the *manor* born." This erroneous spelling is still occasionally used today.

The figure of *John Bull* as the personification of England comes from a treatise by John Arbuthnot, a Scots satirist, published in 1712. Actually, the title character in the *History of John Bull* was intended to parody the bull-headedness of the Duke of Marlborough during the War of Spanish Succession. But John Bull is also portrayed as a good-natured, hearty, bluff country gentleman, and the English found their Scots neighbor's lampoon so attractive, that they adopted the character as their national image.

Phenomenal Card Hand

The phenomenon of holding 13 cards in one suit occurred in the United Service Club at Calcutta, on January 9, 1888. A judge and three physicians were the players, and they and the witnesses made due record of it. The pack had been perfectly shuffled and cut. It was the dealer who held the hand. It has been calculated that the chance of this occurring is one in 158,750,000,000.

Animal Peculiarities

Tortoises and turtles have no teeth, the horse has no eyebrows, and all animals which chew the cud have cloven feet.

Both mandibles of the parrot's beak are movable; but most birds are able to move only one.

The frog, owing to its peculiar structure, cannot breathe with the mouth open, and if it were forcibly kept open the animal would die of suffocation.

Pigs are poor swimmers, because their forelegs are set too closely under them, and when they fall into the water, they sometimes cut their throats with the sharp points of their cloven feet.

The eyes of hares are never closed, as they are unprovided with eyelids. Instead, they have a thin membrane, which covers the eye when asleep, and probably when at rest.

The deer is furnished with supplementary breathing places in addition to the nostrils, an extraordinary provision of nature, which gives the beast of the chase a freer respiration.

The owl has no motion in the eye, the globe of which is immovably fixed in its socket by a strong, elastic, hard, cartilaginous case, in the form of a truncated cone; but in order to compensate for this absence of motion in the eye, the owl is able to turn its head around in almost a complete circle without moving its body.

Sheep have no teeth in the upper jaw.

Women's Apparel

Oh, my goodness gracious! What they used to wear!

Today, some of these things seem absolutely absurd, as probably our vestments of today will appear to be 100 years from now.

Here are a few of the eccentricities of a former age.

In days when it was extremely stylish for a gal to have a very thin waist, the shirtwaist came into vogue.

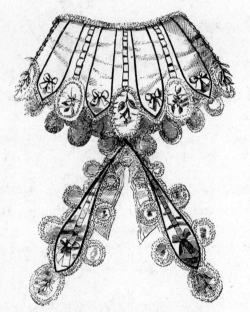

This is a fichu, a kind of decorative collar, as advertised in the London News *of the 19th century.*

Back a hundred years or so, bonnets were the rage.

Here are some very stylish hats of the 1890s.

ENTIRELY ELASTIC.

FITS LIKE A GLOVE.

Today's transparent and peekaboo lingerie wouldn't have proven very acceptable to women who wore the union suits of the 19th century.

The corset, of course, was a bulwark of feminine propriety. This picture derives from the London News.

Capes were greatly in vogue in the 19th century and the early 20th century. This is a creation in fur which merited an advertisement in the London News.

This bustle was standard underpinning which made skirts billow out in an attractive manner.

Oceans occupy three-fourths of the earth's surface. At the depth of 3,500 feet, waves are not felt. The temperature of the ocean is the same, varying only a trifle, from the poles to the equator.

A mile down, the water has a pressure of a ton on every square inch.

If a box, six feet deep, were filled with sea water and allowed to evaporate, there would be two inches of salt left on the bottom of the box. The average depth of the oceans of the world is three miles, and there would be a layer of salt 230 feet thick over the entire bed, should the water evaporate.

The water of the ocean is colder at the bottom than at the surface. In many places, especially in the bays on the coast of Norway, the water freezes at the bottom before it does above.

Waves are very deceptive. To look at them in a storm, one would think all the water travelled. The water stays in the same place, but the motion goes on. Sometimes in storms, these waves are 40 feet high, and travel 50 miles per hour. The force of waves breaking on the shore is 17 tons to the square yard.

Christians differ widely in their concepts of the afterlife, but the Koran tells Moslems exactly what to expect in Heaven. After a 300-course banquet, the right-living Mohammedan male will be given eternal youth and vitality, and will be presented with a palace, 80,000 servants, and 72 beautiful wives, whose youth and pulchritude will endure forever. Amen.

Early Rising Birds

The thrush is audible about half-past four in the morning.

The quail's whistling is heard in the woods about three o'clock.

The blackcap turns up at half-past two on a summer morning.

By four, the blackbird makes the woods resound with his melody. The house sparrow and tomtit come last in the list as early rising birds.

At short intervals after half-past four, the voices of the robin and wren are heard in the land.

The greenfinch is the first to rise, and sings as early as half-past one on a summer evening.

The lark does not rise until after the chaffinch, linnet, and a number of other hedgerow fold have been merrily piping for a good while.

Colorful Signposts for Streets

Formerly, all the streets in Merida were distinguished in a manner peculiar to Yucatan, by images of people, birds, or beasts set up at the corners. Many still retain the ancient signs.

There is a street called La Calle del Flamingo, because of a huge red flamingo painted on the corner house. Another is known as the street of the Elephant, and the representation of it is an exaggerated animal, with curved trunk, and a body as big as a barrel. There is the street of the Old Woman, and on its corner is the caricature of an aged female, with huge spectacles astride her nose. The street of the Two Faces has a double-faced human head, and there are others equally striking.

The reason for this ideographic sort of nomenclature was because when the streets were named, the great mass of inhabitants were Indians who could not read, and therefore printed signs would have been no use to them, but a picture of a bull, a flamingo, or an elephant could be understood.

If permitted, hogs will live from 15 to 20 years of age. They commence breeding when they are from nine to 12 months old. From one pair only, in 10 years, allowing only six to a litter, upwards of 6,434,838 pigs would be obtained. That is to say that, if instead of three acres and a cow, a farmer started with some acres and a pair of pigs, he might, in the course of 10 years, count their progeny by the millions. One sow can actually produce 355 pigs in 20 litters; while a boar only 20 months old, was already the father of 1,466 hogs.

It's a Matter of Taste

From some experiments made at the University of Kansas, it appears that the average person can taste the bitter of quinine when one part is dissolved in 152,000 parts of water. Salt was detected in water when one part to 640 of the liquid was used. Sugar could be tasted in 228 parts of water, and common soda in 48. In nearly all cases, women could detect a smaller quantity than men.

North Dakota is called the Flickertail State because the region abounds with Richarson ground squirrels, popularly known as flickertails.

It has been computed that the average growth of the fingernail is 1/32 of an inch per week, or a little more than an inch-and-a-half per year. The growth, however, depends to a great extent upon nutrition, and during periods of sickness or of abstinence, the growth is retarded.

Growth is faster in the summer than in winter, and differs for different fingers, being most rapid in the middle finger and slowest in the thumb. The average time taken for each fingernail to grow its full length is about four-and-a-half months.

Monkey Business

In 1705, while the French and English were at war with one another, a small ship was dashed to pieces off the coast of the English fishing village of West Hartlepool. The only survivor of the wreck was the crew's pet ape, who was captured by fishermen as he held fast to a floating plank from the wreckage. The denizens of Hartlepool, unfamiliar with the hairier members of the primate family, did not at first know what to make of the strange creature. But when they heard the monkey chattering in some foreign tongue, they guessed at once that he was a French spy in disguise—and the poor ape was court-martialled and hanged for espionage.

Names of Fabrics

Muslin is named from Mosul, in Asia; taffeta from a street in Bagdad; drugget from a city of Ireland, Drogheda; and cambric from Cambrai, France.

Gauze gets its name from Gaza, Palestine; dimity from Damietta, Egypt. Damask originally comes from the city of Damascus, Syria; satins from Zaytown, in China; and velvet is either from the Italian word *vellute* (woolly), or the Latin word *vellus* (a hide or pelt).

Serge derives its name from Xerga, a Spanish name for a peculiar woolen blanket. Shawl is the Sanscrit *sala* (floor), for shawls were first used as carpets and tapestry. Bandanna is from an Indian word meaning to bind or tie, because it is tied in knots before dyeing.

Alpaca is from an animal in Peru, of the llama species, from whose wool the fabric is woven. Calico from Calicut, a town in India, formerly celebrated for its cotton cloth, and where calico was also printed. Blanket is called after Thomas Blanket, a famous clothier, connected with the introduction of woolens into England about 1340.

Eleven states in all have been named after people:

Delaware—Sir Thomas West, Lord De La Warr

Georgia—George II of England

Louisiana—Louis XIV of France

Maryland—Henrietta Maria, Queen of Charles I of England

New York—Duke of York (England)

North and South Carolina—Charles I of England

Pennsylvania—Sir William Penn, father of William Penn

Virginia and West Virginia—Elizabeth, "Virgin Queen" of England

Washington—George Washington

Four state capitals are named after presidents: Jackson, Mississippi; Lincoln, Nebraska; Jefferson City, Missouri; and Madison, Wisconsin.

No less than 25 states took their names from Indian tribes or words: Alabama, Arizona, Arkansas, Connecticut, Idaho, Illinois, Indiana, Iowa, Kansas, Kentucky, Massachusetts, Michigan, Minnesota, Mississippi, Missouri, Nebraska, North and South Dakota, Ohio, Oklahoma, Tennessee, Texas, Utah, Wisconsin, and Wyoming.

Icebergs, Icebergs Everywhere, Nor Yet a Ship Did Sink!

Talk about miracles, there was the famous mass collision of ships off Newfoundland on May 27, 1945, involving 22 vessels, yet resulting in no lost lives or sunken vessels. The disaster occured when a westbound convoy of 76 allied ships were ploughing through a dense fog. One of the boats struck an iceberg, and, discovering eight other icebergs in the vicinity, sounded the alarm. All the ships in the convoy tried to change course immediately, and in the next 10 minutes, the 22 collisions took place. Fortunately, the human toll was nil. But never since have ships traversing the Atlantic been required to sail in convoy.

Rice, is no doubt, the most extensively used article of food the world over. Hundreds of millions of people chiefly subsist on it, and its consumption is constantly increasing. It is the principal diet of at least one-third of the human race, forming the chief food of the native populations of India, China, Japan, Madagascar, many parts of Africa, and, in fact, of almost all Eastern nations. The Burmese and Siamese are the greatest consumers of it. A Malay laborer gets through 56 pounds monthly; a Burmese or Siamese 46 pounds in the same period.

The Eastern nations also chiefly obtain their beverages from rice, which is the principal grain distilled in Thailand, Japan, and China. Saki, or rice beer, is produced in Japan. Although rice is such a universal article of food, it is not as nourishing as wheat or some other grains. More than nine-tenths of it substance consists of starch and water; consequently it forms more fat than muscle.

Punctuation Marks

It is strange that the use of points for purposes of punctuation should be such a comparatively modern invention. Of the four generally used points, only the period (.) dates earlier than the 15th century. The colon (:) is said to have first been introduced about 1485; the comma (,) some 35 years later; and the semi-colon (;) about 1570. It is difficult to understand how the literary world dispensed for so many centuries with the useful points, and their lack must have added to the toil of the decipherer of written documents.

When we remember what curious inversions of meaning may be caused by the misplacing of a comma, we marvel how early authors contrived to escape strange misreadings of their works, in which no points guided the students. Dickens' printer took his sentence, "Woman: without her, man is a brute," and misplaced the important comma to come up with: "Woman: without her man, is a brute."

Zoological Enigma

The axolotl, an amphibian which provides a part of the food supply of Mexico, is a very singular creature. It grows to a length of about a foot, and has four legs, and a newt-like tail surmounted by lungs and gills. While it seems to be more fish than reptile, some naturalists have supposed it to be the larva or tadpole of a gigantic batrachian that has never been seen in the adult state. The animal is capable of living entirely in water or entirely on land.

Not By His Spots!

There's no such species as the black panther—at least not in the animal kingdom. The animal known by that name is actually a member of the leopard family, rather than a distinct species of the cat family. But because you can, supposedly, "tell a leopard by his spots," the belief has arisen that the black panther is a species in itself, like the lion or the tiger.

In the golden days of Roman literature, to be a successful author was to be as great as a king, for kings looked to their poets for immortality, as Augustus Caesar did to Horace. Thus, it was to be expected that authors would feel their importance and display more or less vanity.

One of their weaknesses was to see their portraits painted in artistic fashion in their parchment books. This work was entrusted to artists called "miniatores," that is, artists whose work was largely done in vermilion, a color extracted from cinnabar, and called by the Romans "minimum." Those "miniatores" chose the oval form for their beautifully brilliant portraits on the parchment books, and hence, the origin of the term "miniature," a small hand-painted oval or round portrait.

The wealthiest man in 17th-century France was Nicholas Fouquet, minister of finance under Louis XIV. Fouquet acquired his immense fortune by dipping into the royal treasury, and through his marriage to the wealthy Marie Madelaine de Castille. When Fouquet's peculations came to light, he was tried, convicted, and banished by court decree, but the Sun King had his former minister's sentence commuted to life imprisonment. Meanwhile, Louis confiscated Fouquet's magnificent chateau just south of Paris, Vaux-le-Vicomte, and hired the architects and landscape artists who had created that residence to plan the Palace of Versailles.

Would you believe in a tree that produced baked apples, or a pet squirrel who shined its master's shoes with its tail every morning? Louis Stone, a cub reporter from Winsted, Connecticut, published reports of such "freaks of nature" in the local papers in 1895, and everyone believed them. For the next two decades, Stone built up a national reputation as a journalist with interesting stories, invented by himself and unchecked by editors who cared nothing for veracity so long as their papers sold well. Eventually, Stone was found out, and acquired the nickname "The Winsted Liar."

O'Higgins won a battle with an army of animals

In 1814, Bernardo O'Higgins headed a small army of Chilean patriots who had been trying to free their country from Spanish rule since 1810. Though they had few arms, the Chileans often managed to give the Spaniards a bad time.

The Spanish king sent boatloads of soldiers to wipe out O'Higgins and his patriot army. But the Chileans fought with such courage and skill that, weak and outnumbered though they were, they could not be vanquished. Nevertheless, under this constant onslaught,

O'Higgins' ragged men were being forced to retreat, day by day. It seemed only a matter of time until their backs would be up against a wall.

Just outside the Chilean city of Santiago lay the small town of Rancagua. Here, on October 1 and 2, O'Higgins and his army made a desperate stand. Worn out by days of fighting, tortured by thirst and merciless heat, the Chileans stood surrounded.

Then came a terrible blow. O'Higgins himself was struck by an enemy bullet.

The Chilean patriots seemed doomed to defeat, when the wounded O'Higgins conceived a plan. He ordered his men to round up as many mules, cows, sheep, and dogs as possible. Barns, stables, and pastures were emptied of their livestock, and all the animals were quickly mustered before the commander.

With the vast herd of animals assembled before him, O'Higgins was lifted to his horse. Then, with a shout and a lash of his whip, O'Higgins sent his steed charging ahead. The frightened animals began to run. Soon they became a stampeding, bellowing mass. O'Higgins drove them on and on—straight for the Spanish lines. Maddened by fear, the animals paid little heed to the formidable array of soldiers before them.

The Spanish veterans had never seen such a thundering horde. Terrified, they broke ranks and ran!

Close on the heels of the charging beasts came O'Higgins and his men. They galloped through the path which the animals had made for them. Slashing with their swords, they sped through the Spanish lines.

Helpless and stunned, the Spaniards watched the Chileans escape. Before the Spaniards could reorganize their forces for pursuit, the Chileans were safe in the mountains. There they recuperated, enlisted new recruits, and gathered arms.

Three years later, at the head of an army of 4,000 men, Bernardo O'Higgins returned to destroy the Spanish battalions. In 1818, O'Higgins proudly proclaimed Chile's independence from Spain, and became the first ruler of the new nation.

Yellow ants are eaten in Brazil, mixed with resin as sauce. Locusts are eaten in the Crimea, Greece, India, Arabia, Persia, Africa, and Madagascar. The aborigines of Australia make a cake of the pounded bodies of a night-flying moth. Not contented with the honey and bees wax which the bees yield, the Singalese eat the insects themselves.

White ants are much prized as food in various parts of Africa. The Hottentots eat them both raw and cooked, and thrive wonderfully on them. In India and the East Indies, the natives mix white ants with flour, and make them into pastry, which is considered to be highly nutritive.

The wire worm, the larvae of a small beetle, is eaten by some Turks, and some Chinese eat some species of worms. Spiders, nearly an inch in length, are roasted over the fire and eaten by the natives of New Caledonia.

The cicadae, loudly humming, four-winged insects, were largely eaten by the Greeks, and their delicate flavor was commented on by many writers.

Snails have been used as food from very ancient times. Pliny, a famous Roman naturalist and writer, states that they were much appreciated in Rome, and were fattened on meal until they attained great size and excellent flavor.

Pliny says that cossi were held in high esteem among the Roman Patricians, and were fattened upon flour and wine. These insects are supposed to be grubs of a large beetle.

The Chinese eat the chrysalis of the silkworms, after the silk has been unwound from the cocoons. They fry them in butter or lard, add the yolks of eggs, and then season them with pepper, salt, and vinegar.

The number of backgammon players in the United States has soared from 200,000 in 1969 to more than two million today. In 1973, game producers sold more backgammon sets than they had sold in the previous 20 years combined.

India ink has never come from India. The French are correct in calling it China ink.

Baseball originated more as an offshoot of rounders, an old English sport, than of cricket, as many people believe. Rounders in past centuries was played similarly to baseball, with the important difference that a player put out a baserunner by hitting him with a thrown ball instead of tagging him out. The tag-out was instituted in 1840, and modern baseball was born.

The Homing Faculty

Many animals are endowed with senses which remain quite mysterious to our understanding, and all we know is that these senses exist. There is the homing faculty, well known to occur in many animals, such as the bee, many migratory animals, many fishes, the horse, dog, etc.

Many bee hunters find their prey by catching bees and letting them free at different points. Each bee strikes home immediately, and so, to find the bee hive, one only needs to follow the bee line of two or three bees, as they point to one and the same spot, where the hive is to be found.

Eels and fishes often go from one pond to another, very distantly located, or from a pond to the sea, in a quite straight line, without any mistake. A young alligator which has just got out of its egg will immediately head for the direction in which water is close by.

A falcon, sent from Teneriffe to Lerme, in southern Spain, managed to escape, and 16 hours later returned, quite exhausted, to Teneriffe. A dog, carried from Mentone, in the south of France, to Vienna, came back to Mentone. A donkey of Gibralar, which was shipwrecked 200 miles away on the Spanish coast, also managed to get to his home in Gibraltar.

The youngest player ever to don a major-league baseball uniform was Joe Nuxhall of the Cincinnati Reds. Nuxhall was a tender 15 years, ten months when he suffered a six-run, one-inning shellacking at the hands of the St. Louis Cardinals on June 10, 1944.

Though Greek and Roman gods were generally thought capable of flight, only one god—Mercury, the messenger—was depicted with wings in classical art.

The word "kerchief" comes to us from the French *couvrir,* "to cover," and *chef,* "head," since at one time the hanky was used chiefly to cover the head. Later, the prefix "hand-" was added to differentiate the kerchief carried in the hand or pocket from the neckerchief usually worn around the throat.

Bullfighting, the most popular sport in Spanish-speaking countries, once almost gained ground in the United States. In 1880, a bullfighting promoter built an arena at 116th Street and Sixth Avenue in New York City, and staged a maiden U.S. fight with famous Spanish matadors on July 31. Two thousand Americans attended the bullfight, but due to the objections of the ASPCA, the sport was immediately outlawed, and there has never been another bullfight in this country.

A Tree that Yields Milk

The cow tree, that botanical curiosity of South America, grows on the broad, barren plateaus of Venezuela, where it would be next to impossible to find fluid sufficient to slack one's thirst were it not for this wise provision of nature.

The sap of the cow tree, as its name implies, resembles milk, both in look and taste. A slight balsamic taste has been reported by some naturalists who have drank the strange liquid; otherwise it was said to "have the flavor of rich cream, and to be very wholesome and nourishing."

The tree frequently attains a height of 100 to 125 feet, and it is not unusual to see a trunk of this species 70 to 80 feet, perfectly smooth, and without a limb. A hole bored into, or a wound made in the bark of this wonderful tree is almost immediately filled with a lacteal-like fluid, which continues to flow for some days, or until it coagulates at the mouth of the wound and forms a waxy mass, which stops further flow.

A tombstone in Florence credits one Armato degli Armati, who died in 1317, as the "inventor of spectacles." But the tombstone has been found to be of relatively recent origin; the claim is a complete fabrication. Historians have tried for centuries to trace the true inventor of eyeglasses, but all we know for certain is that they first appeared in the area of Pisa, in Italy, late in the 1280s.

You might think that commercial air service began with the airplane. But by 1914, the Zeppelin Company was offering the first regularly scheduled air flights between German cities, in rigid-framed, hydrogen-filled airships. Despite the dangerously volatile nature of hydrogen, Zeppelin's airships achieved a remarkable safety record on their commercial flights.

Each of our calendar days begins and ends first in the Kingdom of Tonga, a 220-mile-long, 150-island chain in the South Packific. Tonga lies just west of the International Date Line.

Originally, Tonga was in the same time zone as the nearby Fiji Islands, but Tongan King Taufa-ahau Tupou IV established a unique time zone for his kingdom—Tongan Standard Time. Thus, the day begins one hour earlier in Tonga than in the Fiji Islands.

Seward's Bargain

When the United States purchased Alaska from Russia in 1867, the selling price was $7.2 million, or about two cents an acre. Yet most people of the time regarded Alaska as no more than a frozen wasteland, and dubbed it "Seward's Folly" or "Seward's Icebox," in dubious honor of Secretary of State William Seward who had arranged the purchase.

In 1896, "Seward's Folly" became "Seward's Bargain," when gold was discovered in the Klondike. In 1969, some $900 million were bid for oil leases in Alaska.

It's possible to write an entire book with just one pencil! The average lead pencil will write some 50,000 words, which is equivalent to about 200 pages.

Julius Caesar and Alexander the Great were both epileptics.

Contrary to popular belief, a person does not become less vulnerable to infectious disease the older he or she is. The mortality rate from infectious disease is actually the lowest before a person reaches the age of 15.

You may need a magnifying glass to verify it, but there are exactly 118 grooves on the circumference of a dime.

The film *Quo Vadis*, a spectacle set in ancient Rome, employed some 30,000 extras.

George Custer, the officer who led his troops into the massacre at Little Big Horn, was the youngest American Army general in history. He became a general at the age of 23.

Custer also had the dubious honor of finishing last in his graduating class at West Point. In 1861, when West Point graduated 35 students, Custer ranked 35th.

Lettuce is the world's most popular green vegetable—and the only vegetable or fruit that is never sold frozen, canned, processed, or in any other form but fresh.

The Curse That Worked

Those who believe in the efficacy of curses often cite the Tichborne curse as a case in point. In 1150, Mrs. Mabella Tichborne of Alrerford, England, revenged herself on her wealthy but tightfisted husband by placing his family under a deathbed curse. The moribund Mrs. Tichborne decreed that unless the Tichbornes annually presented the villagers with a supply of flour on Lady Day (March 25), the family line and name would be extinguished by the birth of nothing but daughters for a generation. Between 1796 and 1830, an unsuperstitious Tichborne defied his ancestor's curse, and discontinued the act of charity, but after becoming the father of seven girls and no boys, the man resumed the "cursed" custom.

If that bottle of your favorite whiskey is marked "Seven Years Old," you can be sure that the whiskey has not been aging in that bottle for seven years. The age of a whiskey refers to the time it was aged *before* being bottled. Liquor does not improve in any way once it has been bottled, although it can deteriorate under certain conditions.

Americans are not the world's biggest meat eaters. The people of Argentina eat more meat than any other people on earth—about ten ounces daily.

Siberia is sparsely populated, but it's far from a wasteland. In fact, about one-quarer of all the world's trees grow in Siberia!

Fortune 500

Fortune magazine regularly ranks all American corporations in terms of sales volume, publishing a list that is known as the "Fortune 500." In 1978, General Motors headed that list, followed by, in order: Exxon, Ford Motor, Mobil Oil, Texaco, Standard Oil of California, IBM, Gulf Oil, General Electric, and Chrysler.

Have you ever wondered what corporations are at the *bottom* of that list? In 1978, the corporations ranking 495 through 500 were: Idle Wild Foods, Koehring, Buttler Manufacturing, Economics Laboratory, Dennison Manufacturing, and McCormick.

Fortune also publishes lists of the second 500 top-ranking corporations, and the top 50 non-industrial corporations. And then there's a list of the top 500 corporations outside the United States.

Of all the companies on Fortune's 1978 lists, as many as 242 reported sales of more than a billion dollars.

No British monarch ever set foot in America while it was a colony of England—or long afterwards, for that matter. The first British monarch to reach America was George VI, who came to visit the New York World's Fair in 1939!

Topsy Turvy

On October 18, 1961, an abstract painting by Henri Matisse entitled *Le Bateau* was inadvertently hung upside down in the Museum of Modern Art in New York. The mistake went unnoticed for 47 days, during which time more than 100,000 people viewed the painting, apparently without noticing the error.

A hecklephone may indeed sound like an instrument designed for razzing a public speaker. Actually, the hecklephone is a woodwind instrument. And so is the tenoroon, bombardon, contrafagotto!

The Bajus, a Malayan tribe whose members live their entire lives aboard small ships in the Sulu Sea, become so used to the motion of their floating homes that when they go ashore and walk on dry land, they become dizzy and "landsick."

There are now an estimated 20 million ice skaters in the United States, and the U.S. Figure Skating Association can boast over 30,000 of them as its members. In 1950, there were but 120 indoor ice rinks in this country. Today, American ice skating rinks number over a thousand, logging about 20 million admissions annually.

Unlike most other fruits, bananas are picked green and allowed to ripen later. If the fruits are allowed to ripen on the plant, they split open and lose much of the sweet flavor.

The hanging Betty lamp was one of the first lighting devices of Pilgrim America. The metal lamp contained a wick set in a slot and a reservoir filled with fish oil. The term Betty owes nothing to a woman of that name—the word was probably derived either from the German *besser,* "better," or the French *petit,* "small."

Lobsters reach full maturity after about eight years. An adult lobster usually measures from 12 to 14 inches in length and rarely weighs more than ten pounds. But the largest lobster on record measured three feet from mouth to tail, and tipped the scales at 42 pounds! This giant crustacean is now on exhibit at the Museum of Science in Boston.

Lobsters are so small at birth that hundreds could fit in the palm of your hand. As the creature grows, it must continually shed its shell and replace it with a new one to fit the enlarging body. After molting, the lobster will remain unprotected for months until its new shell has formed, during which time the defenseless lobster must indeed "lay low."

We all recognize such phrases as *plastered, under the table, soused, tipsy,* and *bombed* as slang synonyms of *drunk,* but many more colorful terms for insobriety have been lost from the language. Of the over 400 terms for inebriation that have been coined since Colonial days, *bungey, nimptopsical, cherry-merry,* and *as stiff as a ringbolt* have all fallen into disuse.

When the firing on Ft. Sumter began the American Civil War, the Confederacy officially included only seven states. South Carolina had been the first to secede, in December, 1860, and six other states seceded before the war began in April of the following year. Soon later, Virginia, Arkansas, North Carolina, and Tennessee joined the Confederacy.

Although Oslo was the traditional capital of Norway, for many centuries the city was named Christiana. The change was made in 1624, after the original Oslo burned down and was rebuilt, on the opposite side of the Aker River, by King Christian IV. Then, after World War I, Norwegians petitioned their legislature to restore the ancient name of their main city. On July 11, 1924, a law was passed stating, that as of January 1, 1925, the capital would again be called Oslo.

During the 1880s, an American doctor named Willoughby Miller proved that tooth decay was due in part to bacteria in the mouth. These microorganisms produce substances that combine with carbohydrates to form organic acids. The acids then dissolve the calcium salts that make up most of the tooth.

The first toilet paper manufactured in the United States was unbleached pearl-colored manila hemp paper made in 1857 by a New Yorker named Joseph Gayetty. Gayetty's name was watermarked on each sheet. The paper, which sold for 50¢ per 500 sheets, was called "Gayetty's Medicated Paper," and billed as a "perfectly pure article for the toilet and for the prevention of piles."

Basketball, now the third largest sport worldwide, is the only widely played game with an exclusively American origin.

The first successful design for a heavier-than-air, gasoline-powered aircraft was not the work of the Wright Brothers, but of Samuel Pierpont Langley and his assistant, Charles Manley. But Langley's test vehicle, launched from a boat in the Potomac River, plunged immediately into the water upon takeoff—just nine days before the Wright Brothers' first successful flight.

Chocolate was so highly prized in pre-Columbian America that both the Aztecs and the Mayans used cacao beans as currency. At the market in the Mayan city of Chichen Itza, ten beans could purchase a rabbit, four beans a pumpkin. A slave was real steal at just 100 cacao beans.

In 1952, an entire program of television's Arthur Godfrey Show was presented on *ice skates.*

The ancient Romans were the first to attach a postmark to letters, indicating the hour at which they were received, and the first to establish a system truly speedy by modern standards. On the average, the mails moved through Italy at a rate of about five miles an hour, traveling 30 to 50 miles per day. At one point, letters could reach Reims from Rome in but nine days, more quickly than many letters sent between those cities today!

The Gibson, a martini with a pearl onion instead of an olive, is named after New York artist Charles Dana Gibson. But the drink was actually invented not by Gibson, but by his bartender.

After the death of her husband, Prince Albert, Queen Victoria continued to sleep in a double bed, and had her servants lay out the deceased prince's bedclothes each night. A picture of Albert's corpse hung continually above her bed.

Early American inns certainly didn't share our idea of hotel privacy. An innkeeper of the period would think nothing of asking a guest to share his bed with a stranger when accommodations became scarce.

The grandest grand piano of all times was manufactured by Challen of London in 1935, and measured 11 feet, eight inches in length and weighed over 2,500 pounds. The longest string of this piano was nearly ten feet long!

The oldest surviving watermark, a circle surmounted by a cross, dates from the year 1302. Watermarks are formed by pieces of wire or wax set in the frame in which the paper pulp dries. Since less pulp can settle along the outlines of the watermark figure, the paper will be thinner along those lines, and the figure visible.

The first watermark in the United States, the word "company," appeared on paper produced by a mill near Germantown, Pennsylvania, the first paper mill in America.

In 1948, the game of ice hockey was virtually unknown in the Soviet Union. It now ranks as one of that nation's most popular games. Around the time, there were but 1,500 hockey players in Sweden, and only one rink with artificial ice. Since then, the number of registered Swedish players has soared to over 160,000.

During the 17th and 18th centuries, most city dwellers in Europe emptied their chamber pots directly out their window. Residents customarily emptied the pots in the evening, shout out "gardy-loo," a corruption of the French *gardez l'eau*, "watch the water," to warn passersby below.

The longer a cork has been in the bottle, the more likely it is to stick. But the temperature of the wine cellar influences the ease of cork removal as well.

As much as 300 pounds of force are required to dislodge the most stubborn corks.

A poll taken in the United States in 1929 found that 53 percent of all persons who wear glasses found them "more or less becoming."

The lightbulbs we use today are far less costly to operate than any of the light sources used by our ancestors. A 100-watt bulb requires less than one cent of electricity per hour to operate, and costs less than a dollar. To produce by candle the light provided by a single bulb would cost over $400!

The basket used in the game of basketball was originally constructed without a hole at the bottom. Later, a small hole was cut in the bottom of the basket—not for the ball, but for a pole the referee used to dislodge the ball. Incredibly enough, it wasn't until 1912—some 20 years after the game was invented—that open-bottomed baskets were placed into official service on the basketball court.

Oyster gathering was once declared illegal in France from May to October. The law, coupled with the false rumor that a breeding oyster is inedible, may have led to the belief that oysters are taboo in any month without an "r" (May, June, July, August). Actually, oysters may be eaten at any time of the year.

An estimated 20 million Americans now play pool each year. And over a half-million homes in North America are equipped with a billiard table of some kind.

After his journey to the East in the 13th century, Marco Polo declared the Chinese postal system superior to any in Europe, describing a network of 10,000 courier stations and a force of 300,000 post horses. The Venetian traveler claimed that Chinese foot couriers ran with bell-studded belts so that couriers waiting at the next station would be made aware of their approach.

The chocolate bar first appeared on a large scale during World War I, when chocolatiers shipped blocks of solid chocolate to GI's in training camps around the nation. Since the weighing and cutting of smaller blocks became too time consuming, manufacturers began to individually wrap chocolate "bars" for shipment to the soldiers, and the chocolate bar, as we know it, was born.

Thirteen aqueducts brought water to Rome during ancient times. But contrary to general belief, most of these aqueducts were underground. Of the 220-mile total length of Rome's eight main aqueducts, only 30 miles were constructed above ground.

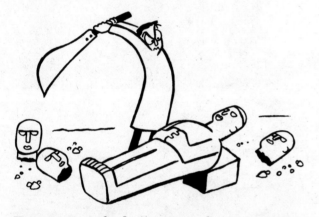

Even an icon had to account for its actions in Foochow, China, in 1900. In that year, a wooden Buddhist statue slipped off a temple shelf and killed a man who had gone to the temple to pray. The man's family accused—not only the culpable statue, but also the 15 other statues that occupied the same shelf—of murder, and the case went to trial. The Chinese court declared the statues guilty, and sentenced them to death. The idols were publicly beheaded, as major criminals.

The oldest surviving ice skate, made in Sweden sometime between the eighth and tenth centuries, consisted of a piece of cow rib fastened to the foot with leather thongs.

During the crossword-puzzle craze of the 1920s, the London Zoo was so deluged with questions that they announced they would no longer answer inquiries pertaining to the names of unusual animals. Libraries in England began to black out the crosswords in all their newspapers to prevent puzzlers from monopolizing the papers. And one Liverpool crossword buff went to far as to black out, in the library's dictionary, a key word needed to complete a puzzle contest that the puzzler was intent on winning for himself!

Little League baseball began in 1939, with three teams in Williamsport, Pennsylvania. Today, the Little League has well over 60,000 teams and one million players from one end of the globe to the other.

Most of the diamonds of antiquity were found in rivers and streams in India. But since the 18th century, most diamonds have come from South America or Africa.

In 1740, the discovery of diamonds in Brazil shifted the mining industry from India to South America. But since the discovery of rich diamond supplies in South Africa, that nation has become the center of diamond mining. Africa now produces 80 percent of the world's gem diamonds, and 73 percent of all industrial diamonds.

After the invention of binoculars in 1823, single and double-lens opera glasses became so popular that a contemporary writer advised: "A bunch of violets, an embroidered handkerchief, a large opera glass, and a bottle of smelling salts—these are the four things a lady of fashion must have at the theater."

In addition to carrying opera glasses, fainting at the theater seemed to be quite the thing to do.

The Earl of Bridgewater used to dine with a dozen dogs

The Rev. Francis Henry Egerton, earl of Bridgewater, was a prince of the Holy Roman Empire, a scholar, and a patron of the arts. In addition, he was enormously wealthy. During the last few years before his death in February, 1829, Lord Egerton took to heart the adage that a man's best friend is his dog.

Lord Egerton was a permanent resident of the prestigious Hôtel de Noailles in Paris. Each night, he would sit down to a formal dinner with a dozen guests—all of them canine. In a Parisian journal of 1826, there is this account of a typical evening with the earl:

would do more than honor to a party of gentlemen; but if, by any chance, one of them should, without due consideration, obey the natural instinct of his appetite, and transgress any of the rules of good manners, his punishment is at hand. The day following the offense, the dog dines, and even dines well; but not at milord's table; banished to the antechamber, and dressed in livery, he eats in sorrow the bread of shame, and picks the bones of mortification, while his place at

"No less than a dozen favorite dogs . . . daily partake of milord's dinner, seated very gravely in armchairs, each with a napkin round his neck, and a servant behind to attend to his wants. These honorable quadrupeds, as if grateful for such delicate attentions, comport themselves during the time of repast with a decency and decorum which table remains vacant till his repentance has merited a generous pardon!"

After dinner, Lord Egerton liked to take a fast turn about town in his elegant carriage. For company, he would bring along a pack of his pampered pooches, each outfitted with four tiny boots to protect its paws from the mud of the Paris roadways.

The first basket in the history of basketball was scored by a youngster named William R. Chase, at a YMCA in Springfield, Massachusetts, in 1891. Chase's team won that maiden game, 1-0.

New pinball games are being invented continually. Each of the four major pinball machine manufacturers now brings out from six to 12 new games every year. Designers say they aim for a game that demands about 75 percent skill, but allows for 25 percent luck so that unskilled players can enjoy playing as well.

Poor Little Rich Man

In 1885, when James Henry Paine died at the age of 80 in his two-dollars-a-week hovel on Bleecker Street, New York City, his neighbors thought he would be tossed into a pauper's grave. For nearly three years, Paine had been a familiar Greenwich Village figure, foraging through trash cans for food and picking up cigar butts in the street. But it seems that Paine had been a miser whose estate was valued at $391,200.

The earliest prototypes of the bicycle of which we have a record appeared in France and England late in the 18th century. These simple vehicles consisted of two wheels linked by a wooden "backbone" upon which the rider sat, propelling the machine by pushing with his feet against the ground.

But these vehicles were virtually useless until 1816, when Baron von Drais of Karslruhe, Germany, introduced a pivoted front wheel that could be turned by a handle, enabling a rider to steer his "hobby horse" for the first time.

Well, chocolate contains drugs. In addition to caffeine, the delectable sweet contains *theobromine*, a mild stimulant.

Drawn butter is not simply melted butter. Melted butter is prepared over a flame; drawn butter is melted over hot water. Drawn butter, unlike melted butter, won't burn.

Many Americans caught their first glimpse of the banana at the 1876 Centennial Exposition in Philadelphia. The fruit sold there for ten cents apiece, a high price at the time. Despite the banana's skin, each was wrapped in tin foil. Bananas were still unfamiliar to most Americans that the fruit and the telephone became the two most curious items at the Exposition!

The French long considered oysters a brain food. In the 15th century, King Louis XI feted the Sorbonne professors on oysters once each year "lest their scholarship become deficient."

Aspirin is today the most widely used medicinal drug in the world. Americans alone swallow about 22 billion tablets each year—close to 100 pills annually for each person!

The brilliance of a diamond is due to its high refractive powers. Much of the light reaching a diamond is reflected back into the stone rather than through it. The best diamonds are transparent and colorless, but diamonds actually range in color from clear to black.

The first public demonstration of a complete incandescent lighting system was held at Menlo Park, New Jersey, on December 31, 1879. The inventor? Thomas Edison, of course. That date marked the end of a decade and the beginning of a new age.

Adjusting for inflation, the highest paid classical pianist of all time was probably I.J. Paderewski, who amassed a fortune of some five million dollars for displaying his keyboard wizardry in concert. Around 1920, Paderewski had another job to keep him busy when he wasn't practicing the piano—he was prime minister of Poland.

Candles were little used for lighting in Classical times, and came into general popularity during the Middle Ages, when lamps became a luxury. The oil-burning lamps the ancient Greeks used were evidently quite smoky, for one writer complained that it was impossible to enjoy a meal indoors until "wine made the guests indifferent to the smoking lamps."

Gems are weighed by the *carat* rather than the grain or gram. The word comes from *carob*, a bean once used to weigh gems on a balance scale because of its uniform size.

An English carat is equivalent to 3.168 grains, or 205.3 milligrams, but in most places the metric carat, equivalent to 200 milligrams, is the standard.

A *word square* is a set of three or more words arranged in the form of a square so that the words read across the same as they read down. For example, the words *peat*, *each*, *ache*, and *they* will form a word square if set one atop the other in that order. Though word squares most often include just four-letter or five-letter words, word squares with as many as nine letters have been constructed. But if you can construct a word square with ten letters on a side, yours will be the first!

The record time for a cross-country bicycle trip was established in 1973, when Paul Cornish pedaled from coast to coast in just 13 days, five hours, averaging 225 miles per day.

In 1970, the first annual crossword puzzle championships were held in England, sponsored by the Cutty Sark Distlling Company. Puzzle buffs were asked to complete five puzzles and send them to the contest organizers. Over 20,000 persons successfully completed the puzzles!

The finals were held in a television studio, with a 43-year-old diplomat named Roy Dean taking first prize—the Cutty Sark trophy, a silver cube mounted on a stand.

Easy Does It!

In 1966, a woman wrote to the London *Times* to announce that she had just completed a crossword puzzle published in the paper's April 4, 1932 issue.

Each major league baseball team has under contract—in addition to the players on the parent team—about 200 players in its farm system.

Cheese-making remained basically a family industry in Europe until the 15th and 16th centuries, when cheese-makers began joining together to form cooperatives. Road taxes actually played a part in the change to community cheese-making. At the time, carts were assessed a tax for using a highway according to the number of cheeses they carried, rather than the total weight of the cheese. Thus, cheese-makers who joined together to produce large cheeses could transport their product much more cheaply.

During World War II, the Germans recognized the English penchant for the crossword puzzle by showering England with leaflets containing crossword puzzles with propaganda messages. A typical clue might be *warmonger*, with "Churchill" or "Roosevelt" the answer.

Many First Ladies have smoked a cigarette now and then, but only two have smoked a pipe. The wife of Andrew Jackson, the country's seventh President, was a habitual pipe smoker, but she never got a chance to preside over the White House, briar in hand, for she died shortly after Jackson's election.

Mrs. Zachary Taylor, however, was reported to have often smoked a pipe in her days in the White House, though always in private. Shocking as this may seem today, pipe-smoking was a common enjoyment among American women at the time, especially in the Southwest.

Dolly Madison, wife of the fourth President, took her tobacco in the form of snuff.

King Richard III of England customarily traveled through his domain with his mattress, blankets, and heavy wooden bedstead. After his death, the bedstead remained in the inn where he'd last slept. A century later, the landlord of the inn took apart the bedstead and found a double bottom filled with Richard's stash of gold coins.

In the city-state of Sparta in ancient Greece, young men were required to sleep in a tent along with 15 other men, while their wives remained at home. Even married men were not permitted to sleep away from their communal tent until the age of 30!

An estimated one million bicycling injuries and one thousand cycling deaths occur yearly in this country. A great many of these accidents involve an automobile.

Englishmen of the Elizabethan era attached great ceremony to the marriage bed. Often an entire wedding party accompanied the bride and groom to their bedroom for music, games, and the official blessing of the bed by a cleric. When the bride began to remove her wedding dress, she customarily tossed one of her stockings to the revelers, and the person who caught the garment was deemed the next in the room to marry.

Sunglasses are nothing new in optometry, for tinted lenses were already common by the 16th century. A century later, amber or mica lenses in several colors were available. Samuel Pepys bought a pair of green spectacles in London during the 1660s, and reported them quite popular. It wasn't until around 1885, though, that tinted glass spectacles began to appear.

During World War II, American soldiers in their foxholes taunted their Japanese adversaries with indelicate references to the Emperor Hirohito. The Japanese frequently replied with what they considered the only fitting retort: "To hell with Babe Ruth!"

Proctor & Gamble is the single leading television advertiser, with a $261 million volume in 1975—almost twice the amount spent by its nearest rival, the General Foods Corporation.

Spermaceti, which came into common use for candle making during the 18th century, is a translucent wax made from whale oil. Spermaceti vaporizes easily and therefore leaves little liquid residue. Spermaceti candles became the first standard measure for artificial light. One "candle power" was initially designated as the light given off by a spermaceti candle weighing one-sixth of a pound and burning at the rate of 120 grains per hour.

The Birth of Billiards

It's possible that billiards developed from the game of bowls, or lawn bowling, which was quite popular in England during the late Middle Ages. According to some accounts, avid English bowlers became so fed up with rainy weather and wet grass that they took their game indoors. But the size of the indoor bowling "alley" was limited by the size of the rooms in which the game was played. The smaller courts were less challenging.

To make the game more difficult, bowlers began propelling their bowls with sticks instead of rolling them. Gradually, hoops and other obstacles were added to the alley. Then at some unknown date, the court was raised to a table top, and *voilà*!—billiards was born.

The marriage bed of Philip, duke of Burgundy, and Princess Isabella of Portugal was probably the largest bed of all time, measuring 19 feet by 12½ feet. Constructed in 1430 in Bruges, Belgium, the bed has long since been dismantled.

The largest bed now on the market measures about nine feet square.

During the 1920s, when a crossword puzzle craze swept America, a pollster found that 60 percent of all passengers riding the trains passed their time battling crosswords. The B & O Railroad went so far as to place dictionaries on all its main-line trains, and the Pennsylvania Railroad printed crosswords on the back of its diner car menus!

In 1897, before the invention of the airplane, August André and two companions attempted a daring flight over the North Pole in a gas-filled airship. But the three men vanished in the frozen Arctic. In 1930, their bodies and equipment were found by explorers—and some 33-year-old photographic plates left by the tragic mission provided excellent pictures when developed.

Spices cost but a fraction of their worth just a few centuries ago, but international spice trade still totals over $200 million a year. Pepper accounts for about a quarter of the total.

Plastic contact lenses began to replace the earlier glass contacts around 1938. Until 1950, contact lenses were made to fit over almost the entire eye. Today's contacts fit only over the cornea.

Incidentally, 65 percent of all American contact lens wearers currently are women.

About 80 million watches and an equal number of clocks are produced annually throughout the world. Swiss manufacturers account for about half of the production. The United States, Japan, and the Soviet Union each produce about 35 million clocks and watches a year, with the American figure consisting mostly of clocks, the Japanese mostly of watches.

The organization that was to become baseball's National League was founded in 1876, with teams from New York, Philadelphia, Boston, Chicago, St. Louis, Cincinnati, Louisville, and Hartford. The American League, meanwhile, was founded in 1901, with teams in Baltimore, Washington, Philadelphia, Boston, Chicago, Detroit, Cleveland, and Milwaukee.

The Milwaukee club moved the next year to St. Louis, and in 1903, the Baltimore team moved to New York. It was this team that went on to become the Yankees.

Honesty Pays

What would you do if you found a billfold containing $225. Well, Joan Campaign played it straight, and turned the wallet into the police. Two weeks later, the wallet was claimed, and the owner sent Ms. Campaign a lottery ticket worth 55¢ in gratitude for her action. A poor return for Ms. Campaign's honesty? Not so—the following week that lottery ticket won Ms. Campaign a car, a boat, a mobile home, and a trailer—worth a grand total of $45,000!

The largest arc lamp ever constructed measured over six feet in diameter, and produced a light equivalent to two billion candles. At 20 miles above earth, the lamp would produce the illumination of a full moon.

Postage stamps have ranged in size from a 1913 Express Delivery issue in China, nine-and-three-quarters inches long and two-and-three-quarters inches wide, to midget stamps, issued in Colombia during the 1860s, that measured just eight by nine-and-a-half millimeters.

The highest nominally valued stamp ever released was issued in Germany during the inflation of 1923—one stamp cost 50 billion marks!

Skateboard Surge

Skateboards first reached the public eye in 1962, when the proprietors of the Val Surf Shop in North Hollywood, California, began attaching roller skate wheel trucks to boards. But in the mid-1960s, cities from San Diego to Providence, Rhode Island, began to outlaw skateboards on public streets. The bans were due mainly to the loud noise made by the clay composition wheels, and the dangers posed by the boards to the skateboarder himself.

Then in 1973, a California surfer named Frank Nasworthy devised the first skateboard with urethan wheels, which provided more traction and a quieter ride than the earlier wheels. Skateboarding soon became safe and acceptable, and the sport took off again.

The familiar lullabye *Rock-a-bye-Baby* is at least as old as the Elizabethan period. The lyrics may harken back to an earlier period when a mother might place her cradle in the branches of a tree to be rocked gently by the wind.

At one time, the natives of Ceylon placed their teeth on an altar when they had fallen out, beseeching the gods to spare those teeth remaining.

Fluorescent lights work on a principle similar to the one that makes fireflies and certain other animals and fungi glow. These creatures absorb ultraviolet light and emit it at a longer, and therefore visible, wavelength.

The glass tube of the flourescent light is coated on the inside with flourescent mineral salts called "phospors," and filled with mercury and argon vapor. When electricity flows through the tube, ultraviolet radiation emitted by the mercury excites the chemical, which then radiates visible light. Flourescent lights are more efficient than any other practical light source, and produce almost no heat.

The organ is about 2,000 years older than the piano! In the third century B.C., Ctesibius of Alexandria built a hydraulic pipe organ activated by a keyboard. The piano was not invented until the 1690s.

The ancient Romans were prouder of their achievements in civil engineering—bridges, roads, baths, aqueducts—than they were of their temples and tombs. Frontinus, the water commissioner of the Imperial City for part of the second century, went so far as to boast: "With such an array of indispensable structures . . . compare, if you will, the idle Pyramids or the useless, though famous, works of the Greeks."

The chamber pot was often called a *jerry pot* in England. But there's probably no connection between that term and the expression *jerry-built*, which means cheaply, shabbily constructed. *Jerry-built* is usually traced either to the city of Jericho, jelly, the French world *jour* ("day"), or a presumably disreputable Liverpool contracting firm known as Jerry Brothers. But it may be related to the gypsy term for excrement.

Tungsten, the element commonly used for the filaments of incandescent lightbulbs, has the highest melting point of any metal—6,100 degrees.

The Crossing of the Bar

For those who cannot swim the English Channel, there are more ingenious modes of crossing that body of water, and attracting the attendant publicity. For example, one man rowed across the Channel in a coffin, while another man walked across it shod in wooden boots in the shape of flatboats. Still another enterprising individual traversed the Channel in an inflated rubber suit sporting a sail the size of a bath towel.

A list of all the pinball machine games designed in this country would include well over 1,500 entries. Only the most dedicated pinballer might claim to have played even half the games now in existence.

In 1842, a British Royal Commission appointed to improve the sanitation system of London turned to the sewers of Imperial Rome for their model. The sewers of ancient Rome were not only superior to anything London could boast at the time, they were better than anything that had been seen in Europe since the decline of the Roman Empire!

Unbuttoning the Truth

During 1977, readers of the London newspaper *The Guardian* were engaged in an intense debate in the paper's correspondence column concerning a question that must surely have entered every person's mind: Why do men's garments have buttons on the right side, and women's on the left?

One reader suggested that a man traditionally needed buttons on the right side so that he could fend off an assailant's sword with his right hand while buttoning his coat with the left. Another reader pointed out that "if there were buttons on both sides of the garment there would be no room for buttonholes." And yet another reader answered the question with a question of her own: "Why are shirt buttonholes vertical and pajama jacket buttonholes horizontal?"

The controversy continues.

The Old Testament contains 39 books, 929 chapters, 23,214 verses, 592,439 words, and 2,738,100 letters. The New Testament has 27 books, 270 chapters, 7,967 verses, 132,253 words, and 933,380 letters.

The Bible, the Old and the New Testament, collectively, has 66 books, 1,199 chapters, 31,181 verses, 724,692 words, and 3,471,480 letters.

The word *Lord,* or its equivalent, *Jehovah,* occurs 7,698 times in the Old Testament; or, to be more exact, the word *Lord* occurs 1,853 times, and the word *Jehovah* 5,845 times.

Four verses of the 107th Psalm—the 8th, 15th, 21st, and 31st—are exactly alike, and the 36th chapter of Isaiah and the 19th chapter of Kings II are alike.

These facts were ascertained by the prince of Granada, heir to the Spanish throne, who was for 33 years a prisoner in the Palace of Skulls, Madrid, with no companion except his Bible, which he faithfully perused and dissected for the benefit of more fortunate humanity.

In each respiration, an adult inhales one pint of air. A man respires 16 to 20 times a minute, or 20,000 times a day; a child 25 to 35 times a minute. While standing, the adult respiration is 22; while lying, 13. An adult takes in at least 360 litres of air an hour. The amount of air inspired in 24 hours is 10,000 litres (about 10,000 quarts).

The superficial surface of the lungs, *i.e.,* of their alveolar spaces, is 200 square yards.

The amount of oxygen absorbed in 24 hours is 500 litres, and the amount of carbonic acid expired in the same time, 400 litres. Two-thirds of the oxygen absorbed in 24 hours is absorbed during the night hours from 6 P.M. to 6 A.M. Three-fifths of the total carbonic acid is thrown off in the daytime.

The heart sends through the lungs 800 litres of blood hourly, and 20,000 litres, or 5,000 gallons, daily. The duration of inspiration is five-twelfths; of expiration seven-twelfths of the whole respiratory act; but during sleep, inspiration occupies ten-twelfths of the respiratory period.

The first dining establishment to print a menu offering a variety of foods and liquors was Boulanger's Restaurant, which opened in Paris in 1765. Previously, coffee houses and taverns served "Ordinaries," regular meals at a common table at a fixed time and price. Parisians so enjoyed eating when and what they liked that, 50 years later, the city had more than 125 restaurants—one of which served 197 differently prepared meat dishes!

The Buried Forests of New Jersey

In the early 1800s, an industry, the like of which did not exist anywhere else in the world at that time, furnished scores of people in Cape May County, New Jersey, with remunerative employment, and had made comfortable fortunes for many citizens. It was the novel business of mining cedar trees—digging from far beneath the surface—immense logs of cedar. The submerged forest of southern New Jersey was discovered first beneath the Dennisville swamps, and have been a source of interest to geologist and scientist ever since.

Thomas Jefferson was the father of the American patent system; he drew up the earliest patent laws, and while he was secretary of state under Washington, he gave his personal consideration to every application that was made for a patent.

When the Bank of England moved into new quarters in London, in 1800, bank officials boasted of the impregnability of their bullion vault. Imagine, then, the bank president's surprise, when he was visited by a workman claiming to know a secret means of entering the vault undetected. The president scoffed, and the laborer offered to prove his claim, making a $4,000 wager with the president that he would be in the vault at midnight and explain his secret.

Sure enough, when bank officials went down to the vault on the stroke of twelve, the workman was there. After collecting his $4,000, he explained that one day, while engaged in sewer repairs, he had crawled into an unused drainpipe, discovered and climbed a ladder, and found himself under a trap door. Opening the door, he found himself gazing at the gold of England—so much for "the world's most impregnable bank vault."

If you think ducks absorb water like other creatures, you're all wet! During a rainfall, or while paddling about on the water, ducks rub themselves with oil secreted from glands near the tail. As oil repels water, the ducks never get wet. Thus, the saying "to run off like water from a duck's back" is based on a very real phenomenon.

Full of Hot Air

Electric fans actually increase, rather than decrease, the temperature of a room. The fans heat the air by setting it into rapid motion. But the air emitted by the fan is still cooler than human skin, and the fan's gusts absorb the heat and moisture of the skin they touch, making the person feel more comfortable.

Although many states have official flowers, there is not national flower of the United States, for Congress has never been able to agree on which flower should be so honored. Many schools and societies have designated the goldenrod as our national flower—but it is doubtful that sufferers from hay fever and sinus trouble would concur in this choice.

Variations of the Game

Every man, when he takes up his cards at a game of bridge, holds one out of 635,013,-559,600 possible hands. The total number of variations possible among all four players, is so enormous as to almost exceed belief. It has been calculated that if 1,000,000 men were to be engaged dealing cards at the rate of one deal every minute, day and night, for 100 million years, they would not have exhausted all the possible variations of the cards; only 100,000th part of them.

Dig these Initials!

It took mankind a long, long time to convert spoken language into written form. Even today, there are more languages which exist only in spoken form than there are languages with a written form.

The first writings of man consisted of pictures, which gradually became conventionalized. This kind of ideographic writing still exists in our numerals, and in Chinese and Japanese writing.

The alphabet was the last stage in the development of writing. The term *alphabet* comes from the first two letters of Greek—*alpha* and *beta*.

The Roman alphabet, which is used for most European languages, and also for the newly-written languages of Africa, consists of 26 letters.

Other alphabets are the Greek alphabet (on which the Roman alphabet was originally based) which contains 24 letters; the Cyrillic alphabet used for the Russian, Serbian, and Bulgarian languages, which contains 32 letters; the Hebrew alphabet which contains 27 letters; the Arabic alphabet which contains 28 letters.

Indian languages, such as Sanskrit, use the Bevanjari alphabet, while other Oriental languages use a system of characters devised from the Chinese characters.

For centuries, fancy letters have been devised to lend interest to stories and titles. Some of the more remarkable effusions of the 19th century follow. These pieces of art are now in the public domain, and may be used freely by anyone.

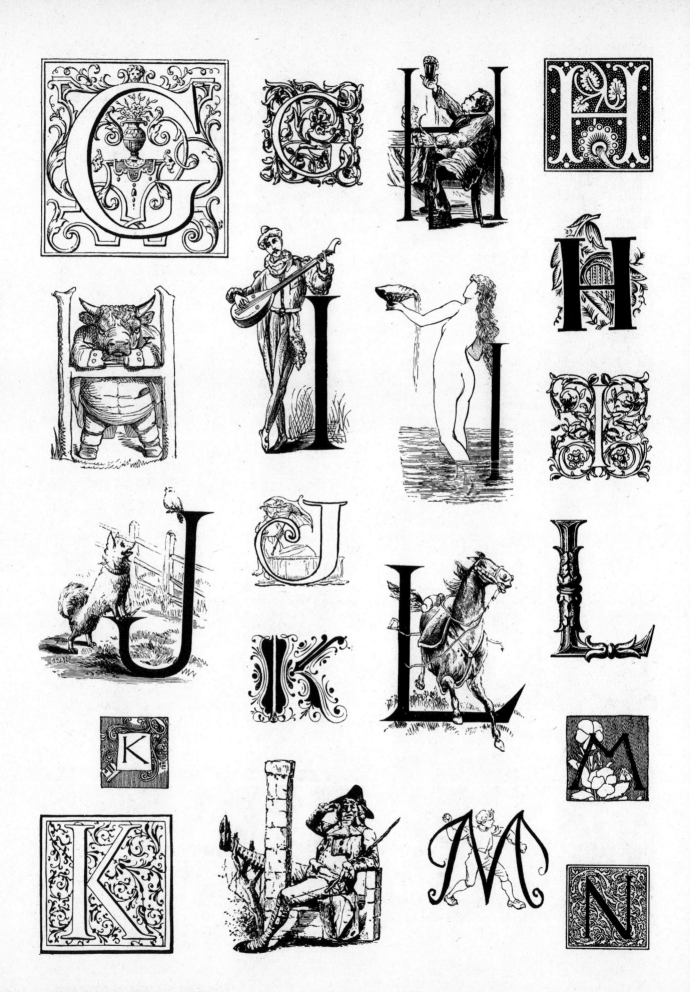

Charlie Knew Best

On clocks with Roman numerals on the dial face, the number four is generally shown as IIII rather than IV. No one knows exactly why this is so, but a clockmakers' tradition tells the following story.

Around 1370, a French clockmaker named Henry de Vick made a clock for King Charles V, and submitted it to the monarch to be approved. Charles prided himself on his critical acuity, and unable to find anything wrong with the workmanship of the clock, was nevertheless determined to point out an error. So, he told de Vick that he had incorrectly shown the number IIII as IV. De Vick snorted and boldly told the king that he was wrong, but Charles silenced the clockmaker with a menacing shout of "I am *never* wrong!"

Apparently, none of the other clockmakers dared brave Charles's displeasure, and so, from the 14th century on, IV was always depicted on clock faces as IIII.

Around the middle of the 19th century, the bicycle in common use—called a high-wheeler—consisted of an extremely large front wheel turned by the pedals, and a very small rear wheel. Front wheels with 54-inch or even 64-inch diameters were common, while the rear wheel sometimes measured no more than 12 inches across!

The term *passing the buck* came to us from gamblers' argot. In certain card games, a marker is placed on the table before the player whose turn as dealer will come on the next round. This marker, called the *buck*, is passed among the players with the rotation of the deal.

Unconscious Hostility Par Excellence

The newspaper Vecerny Pravda, reported that Vera Czermak jumped out of her third story window when she learned her husband had betrayed her. Mrs. Czermak recovered in the hospital after landing on her husband, who was killed.

Sardanapalus, the last great king of Assyria, had quite a thing for beds, right to the end. According to a Greek tale, the monarch committed suicide, along with his wives and concubines, on a pyre fueled by his 150 beds.

That the Dutch people were not well-thought of by the English in the 18th century is shown by a number of disparaging phrases—containing the word Dutch—which came into our language under the reign of Charles II. False courage, especially if produced from excessive consumption of alcohol, is called *Dutch courage*; telling a person in distress to remember that things might have been worse is called *Dutch comfort*; a cowardly surrender is called a *Dutch defense*; and an outing on which the invited party must pay his own way is called a *Dutch treat*. Perhaps the most pejorative term is a *Dutch bargain*, a deal made while the buyer is in his cups. The most flattering term is *to talk like a Dutch uncle*, which means to criticize or reprove someone—severely, but kindly.

The Plains of Abraham, in Quebec, were not named for the Biblical patriarch, but for one of his namesakes, Canadian pioneer Abraham Martin. Known as Maitre Abraham, Martin applied to the founder of Quebec, Samuel de Champlain, for a homesteader's deed on the famous heights. The deed was granted, and Maitre Abraham was so often seen on the heights with his cattle and sheep, that the other residents of the St. Lawrence River Valley named the heights the Plains of Abraham.

King of Keyboards

Would you like to venture a guess as to the world's largest manufacturer of pianos? Steinway? Baldwin? An old, distinguished European firm? Well, only about 60,000 pianos are currently produced in Europe each year—plus some 170,000 manufactured in the Soviet Union. As of 1960, the largest piano manufacturer in the world was Yamaha, a Japanese firm that was turning out close to 190,000 pianos a year!

Japan is presently the largest piano producer, manufacturing over 280,000 annually. Even more surprising, most of those pianos are sold in Japan, which by and large, was not introduced to the instrument until this century.

In 1909, the peak year for American piano sales, over 364,000 new pianos were purchased in this country. Sales have since steadily decreased.

Most television commercials, movies, and adventure, western, police, and drama programs are shot on film with a movie camera, then transferred to electronic tape for television transmission. News broadcasts, soap operas, and situation comedies are usually recorded directly on videotape. That's why the half-hour situation comedy has a different "look" from, say, the hour-long police drama.

The story of the courtship of John Alden and Priscilla Mullins is well known. A similar, though less familiar incident occurred in Virginia, with a minister named John Camm in the John Alden role.

The reverend Mr. Camm, who later became President of the College of William and Mary, was 51 years old when romance entered his life in the form of Miss Betsy Hanford, who was considerably younger than Camm. One of Camm's male parishioners asked the minister to aid him in wooing Miss Hanford, who had repeatedly refused the young man's offers of marriage. Camm duly called on the young woman, who insisted that her decision was irrevocable, and told Camm that by reading Samuel II, 12:7, he would find out why.

Camm returned home, and took his Bible from his shelf. There he found the pertinent passage, which read, "And Nathan said to David: Thou art the man." Soon afterward, Miss Hanford became Mrs. Camm.

Leonardo da Vinci, the epitome of the renaissance man, even designed a latrine with a flush toilet, ventilation shaft, and a door that would close automatically in the event the previous user was negligent. But Leonardo's suggestions went unheeded for centuries.

During the Middle Ages, almost all of London's waste matter was channelled directly into the River Thames. Medieval monks complained that the stench of the river overcame their incense and "caused the death of many brethren." And as late as the 1850s, the Thames was sufficiently rank to prompt talk of moving Parliament from its building on the river. One parliament member delivered a speech in the House of Commons protesting that he and his colleagues were "utterly unable to remain there in consequence of the stench which arose from the river."

In 17th-century Spain, spectacles were considered so chic that no fashionable man or woman would be seen without them—whether the glasses were needed for vision or not!

The one letter of the alphabet used neither to designate U.S. army companies nor a street in Washington, D.C. is *J*. This is not because of any superstitions about ill-luck attached to the 10th letter of the alphabet, but because in the 19th century, the letters *I* and *J* were identical in appearance, and confusion was feared if both letters were used in the above instances.

Four Flags of the South

The familiar "Rebel Flag" was actually only one of four flags raised by the Confederate States of America during the Civil War. The first flag, consisting of one horizontal white bar between two red bars, and a field of seven white stars, was raised in March, 1861. But during the Battle of Manassas, in July of that year, the Confederate forces had difficulty distinguishing their flag from that of the Union forces, and a new flag, the "Battle Flag," was raised shortly thereafter. This was the familiar flag, with a red field crossed diagonally by blue bars with 13 white stars.

In 1863, a third flag was raised, a plain white flag with the "Battle Flag" in the upper left corner. But it was found that when this flag was hanging limp it looked like a white flag of truce. So the fourth Confederate flag was raised—identical to the third—except for a red bar down the right edge.

Naval cadets are called midshipmen because, in the 17th century, British cadets enrolled in officer training programs were assigned quarters *amidships,* on the lower deck.

Modern pencils are made from a combination of graphite and clay. The two substances are ground together, pressed into thin sticks, and baked. The proportions of graphite and clay will determine the hardness of the lead.

Then why is the writing substance called "lead"? Before graphite's chemical nature was determined late in the 18th century, graphite was called "black lead" due to its resemblance to that material.

At its peak, the aqueduct system of ancient Rome brought 300 million gallons of fresh water to the capital daily.

Modern New York, with a population close to eight times that of ancient Rome, brings in one-and-a-half billion gallons of water each day.

The record for oyster devouring was set in 1975, when a 48-year old Florida man gulped down 588 in just 17½ minutes. And clam-eaters, take heart: the same year, a Washington man slid 424 of the slimy critters down his gullet in just eight minutes.

Technically, the military term *Absent Without Leave* should be abbreviated A.W.L. But the U.S. War Department, apprehensive that A.W.L. would be misconstrued as *Absent With Leave,* inserted the *O.,* despite the fact that *without* is one word.

The term *bootlegging,* meaning the illegal sale of liquor, originated in the days of the Wild West, when whiskey was sold to the Indians illegally by peddlers, who carried the unlawful flasks of booze in the legs of their boots to hide them from government authorities.

During the World War I, German and Austrian submarines were called *Untersee Boats*, or undersea boats, and were designated by *U* followed by a number. Eventually, German submarines came to be known as U-boats.

The monkey wrench does not owe its name to our endearing fellow-primate. Rather, the term is a corruption of Moncke wrench, after a London blacksmith, Charles Moncke, who invented the implement.

By the end of 1861, the paper dollar issued by the Confederate States of America was worth only 90¢ in gold. By 1863, it was worth but 6¢ in gold.

In 1865, a bushel of potatoes sold in Richmond, Virginia for $100, and a pound of coffee, for $40! But this was actually less than the price of the items in most Northern cities.

The original peeping Tom was the only man to view the naked Lady Godiva on her famous ride. The legend of Lady Godiva is that her husband, Leofric, Lord of Coventry, imposed steep taxes on his subjects, which led his wife to protest against the hardship. Leofric met Godiva's complaints with the answer that he would remit the harsh taxes only if she would ride naked through the town.

The charitable beauty issued a proclamation explaining the purpose of her riding in the raw, and requesting all the townspeople to remain indoors with their shutters closed during the performance. The good lady's appeal was honored by everyone except Tom the tailor, who bore a hole in his shutter in order to get a glimpse of the naked woman. Tradition has it that Tom was struck blind for his impertinence. In any case, Lord Leofric did rescind the burdensome taxes.

George Washington was the father of our country, but he was not, strictly speaking, the first American president. That honor belongs to John Hanson of Maryland, who was chosen *President of the United States in Congress Assembled* in 1781, before the executive branch of government had been established as a separate entity by the Constitution. Hanson was succeeded in the post by Elias Boudnot, Thomas Mifflin, Richard Henry Lee, Nathan Gorhan, Arthur St. Clair, and Cyrus Griffin. So, George Washington, the first chief executive elected under our present Constitution, was actually the eighth president of the United States.

The Yale lock has nothing to do with the famous university in New Haven, but is named for its inventor, Linus Yale, a Middletown, Connecticut, lockmaker who was born in 1797.

The first widely-known professional basketball team was the Original Celtics, founded in 1915 by a group of New York City youngsters. The squad disbanded in 1928, then regrouped in the 1930s as the New York Celtics, before permanently disbanding in 1936. At the height of their popularity, the Celtics played a game every night and two on Sunday, and were almost continually on the road. Yet during the 1922-1923 season, the Celtics amassed a whopping 204 wins against just 11 defeats!

Who was the man in the "iron" mask?

In 17th-century France, when Louis XIV proclaimed, "*l'état c'est moi!*"—"I am the State!"—the glutted prisons were France's busiest institutions. Louis could ruin a life with a carefree flourish of the royal quill. But though the "Sun King" chose his victims indiscriminately, there were at least *apparent* reasons why a poor wretch might have incurred the king's displeasure.

But not so for The Man in the Mask. Why he lingered "in durance vile" no one knew. No one knew *then*—no one knows *now!*

In 1669, a tall, well-dressed man of courtly bearing was turned over to Monsieur Saint-Mars, governor of the fortress of Piguerol. Monsieur Saint-Mars treated his prisoner with great respect, permitting him such privileges as books and the comfort of a priest. But there was one thing Monsieur Saint-Mars would *not* allow: the prisoner was never permitted to show his face. For 34 long years, the prisoner wore a mask of black velvet—wore it because to take it off meant death; wore it, perhaps, to hide a face whose agony might shame the king.

Alexander Dumas romanticized this story in his great novel *The Man in the Iron Mask.* But it is a well-authenticated fact that the mask was fastened to the prisoner's face not by rivets of steel, but by rivets of fear.

Why did Louis XIV condemn this man to a living death? Why did he go to such extremes to hide this man's identity? Why did he spare this man at all? These are questions which historians, after centuries of research, have been powerless to answer.

Some have suggested that the prisoner was an illegitimate son of Louis XIV, and was jailed because he represented a threat to his half-brother, the dauphin, heir to the throne.

Others maintain that the prisoner was Eustache d'Auger, a young participant in the Black Masses conducted by the notorious poisoner, Madame de Brinvilliers. Supposedly, of the several participating ladies who later became royal mistresses, one saved d'Auger from the guillotine by begging mercy from Louis XIV.

Still another view is that the prisoner was a twin brother of Louis XIV, imprisoned to avoid a contest for the throne. Because of his royal blood, he was treated with the dignity due his station. His face was covered to avoid identification.

Intriguing possibilities, all—but whether any of these postulations are true, no one can say with certainty.

Every year, after their long migration, the swallows return to San Juan, Capistrano in California. The usual date is March 19th, and the swallows have missed the date only once in 1935, when they were delayed three days by a storm. The birds travel 6,000 miles from South America to their summer home in southern California.

The airplane was not the first vessel to take a man into the air. Long before the first airplane flight, hot-air balloons had taken hundreds of men into the realm of the birds.

Though other inventors had earlier risen above the ground in a balloon, it was the work of Joseph and Etienne Montgolfier who first turned the attention of the world toward manned balloon flight. In 1783, the brothers constructed a bag 30 feet in diameter, held it over a fire until it had inflated with smoke, and watched it rise high into the air above Annonay, France. Later that year, the first manned balloon climbed 3,000 feet into the air above Paris.

The terms *oculist* and *optometrist* are virtually interchangeable. An *oculist* is an eye-care professional, without a medical school degree. An *optician* is a technician who grinds and sells optical lenses. However, an *ophthalmologist* is a medical doctor with specialized training in eye care. (An occultist, in case you wondered, sees what's not there.)

About 75 percent of the world's supply of raw cacao beans now comes from Africa. The nation of Ghana, which did not begin cacao cultivation on a large scale until 1879, presently accounts for about 30 percent of the African crop. The annual worldwide production figure now tops the million-ton mark—that's over two billion pounds of cacao each year!

Many kinds of oyster actually change sex four times a year, alternating between male and female. Each full or part-time female will release two million eggs in the summer, of which only about 50 will survive.

Despite the popularity of school, professional, and international basketball, the honor of playing before the largest crowd in basketball history belongs to the Harlem Globetrotters. The wizards of basketball high jinks drew 75,000 people to a Berlin stadium in 1951.

The club, formed in 1927, now plays before two to three million fans each year!

The first game of baseball with rules similar to the modern was played in 1846, in Hoboken, New Jersey.

The world's longest scheduled nonstop airplane flight is Pan American's New York-to-Tokyo service, inaugurated in 1976. The thrice-weekly flight covers 6,754 miles in less than 14 hours.

A 60-watt light bulb contains a tungsten wire filament .0019 inches in diameter and about three-and-a-half inches long, coiled 1,200 times. About 50,000 filaments can be produced just one pound of tungsten.

The onion was depicted on a number of Egyptian monuments as a symbol of eternity, due to its layer-upon-layer formation within the shape of a sphere. Similarly, our word "onion" comes from the Latin term *unio*, which has also given us "union" and "united."

Private Words

Medieval monks usually referred to the latrine with the euphemism *necessarium*. But the most common name for the latrine during the Middle Ages was *garderobe*, or *wardrobe*, a term euphemistically comparable to the modern *rest room, water closet, comfort station,* or *john*.

The word *john* probably comes form an older term for the latrine, *jakes*, which in turn, may be derived from the common French name Jacques. The word *privy*, of course, comes from "private." Even our word *toilet* is a euphemism, adapted from the French *toilette*, a woman's dressing table or room, in turn derived from *toile*, a kind of cloth.

Eyeglasses are considered so vital today that it's hard to imagine a world without them. Yet eyeglasses were not commonplace anywhere in the world until about 450 years ago. And precision, individualized lenses date back no further than the 18th century!

The Cincinnati Red Stockings were America's first fully professional baseball team, beginning their play in 1869. In their first year of play, the Red Stockings played 66 games without a defeat.

The earliest known treatise on medicine was a 2700 B.C. Chinese work entitled *The Classic Herbal.*

The largest stone of true gem quality ever exploited was a Brazilian aquamarine that tipped the scales at 229 pounds. Found in 1910, the hefty stone yielded over 200,000 carats of quality aquamarines!

In 1941, the Federal government forced the National Broadcasting Company (NBC) to divest itself of one of its two component networks. One of the networks was sold to Edward Noble, of Life-Saver candy fame, and went on to become the American Broadcasting Company (ABC). The network that Noble purchased for $8 million now boasts an annual TV advertising volume of well over a half-*billion* dollars!

The first black baseball player to make the major leagues was Jackie Robinson, who made his debut for the Brooklyn Dodgers on April 11, 1947. Seven years later, the first team on which the majority of players were black took the field for the Dodgers. The players were Robinson, Don Newcombe, Jim Gilliam, Sandy Amoros, and Roy Campanella.

Nice Try

In an attempt to extract a confession from an arrested suspect, the police in a Pennsylvania town set a collander on his head with a wire attached to a copier machine, claiming the device was a lie detector. When the prisoner was asked a question, a policeman pressed a button on the copier and out came a slip of paper reading "He's lying." The suspect confessed.

Alas, a judge threw the confession out of court.

The first person ever to appear on television was one William Tayton, an office boy in the building where TV pioneer J.L. Baird carried out his experiments. Baird is the Britisher credited with demonstrating the first true television system, in 1926. Tayton received one crown, roughly $1.25, for his role as TV's first model.

The first play-by-play radio broadcast of a baseball game was aired from Pittsburgh on August 5, 1921.

Generally, it's cheaper to haul freight in the United States by railroad than by any other form of transportation. At the beginning of 1979, it cost about 2.2 cents to move a ton of freight one mile by railroad. The rate for truck transportation was 11 cents per ton/mile, and for shipment by air carrier, about 33 cents per ton/mile.

Sixteenth-century Aztec Indians in Mexico played a game called *tlachtli*, which they developed from an earlier Mayan game. The object of the game—similar to modern basketball—was to propel a ball through vertical stone rings.

Spectators at *tlachtli* matches frequently took to their heels the moment a player scored a goal, since a goal earned the scoring player the right to collect clothing and jewelry from the crowd.

And talk about pressure to win games—the captain of the losing team was often beheaded!

American marines came to be known as leathernecks because their uniforms originally included leather-lined collars, not worn by any other branch of the military.

There are now an estimated half-million licensed airplane pilots in this country. Only one in five owns his own plane.

When you watch television you're actually looking at a rapidly changing pattern of dots, with only one dot among thousands illuminated at any one time. But the brain retains the impression of illumination for about a tenth of a second after the light is removed. So, the eye is unaware that the picture is being assembled piecemeal in dots, and the whole surface of the viewing screen appears continuously illuminated.

This pattern of dots, by the way, changes much faster than once every tenth of a second—about four million individual details of an image are transmitted every second!

Basketball! Basketball! Basketball!

During the 1950s, the combined attendance at all basketball games played in the United States was larger than the combined annual attendance totals of baseball, football, hockey, and six other major sports!

Have you ever wondered who was daring—and crazy—enough to test the world's first parachute? Actually, the honor goes to a sheep, which was dropped from a tower in Avignon, France, buoyed by a seven-foot parasol. Shortly later, in 1797, Andre Garnerin rose above Paris in a balloon basket attached to an umbrella-like parachute and, at more than 2,000 feet above earth, undauntedly cut the basket loose from the balloon. Garnerin survived one of the most daring feats in aviation history, and went on to give a number of parachuting exhibitions from even greater heights.

Among the many activites that kept the prolific Thomas Jefferson busy, was the compilation of a unique Bible. About 1804, during his first term as president, Jefferson put together a 46-page New Testament, consisting of excerpts from the four gospels, arranged according to a scheme of Jefferson's own invention. *The Jefferson Bible*, composed primarily of Jesus' actual words, was originally intended to teach Christianity to the Indians. But Jefferson was so pleased with the work that he used the book for his own bedtime reading.

Tests have been conducted to determine the more humane way to prepare a lobster for human consumption. In the test, one lobster was plunged alive into boiling water, while another was submerged in cold water that was then slowly brought to a boil. The lobster plunged rudely into boiling water perished within a minute, squeaking and moving about the pot in apparent pain. But the second lobster remained quite passive as the water heated up, eventually swooning and passing on gracefully—without squawking.

The tests are of interest to the diner as well as to the lobster, for lobsters boiled slowly were found to have tenderer, tastier flesh than those put to a speedy death.

The word *bride* is derived from an ancient Teutonic word meaning "to cook."

The backgammon craze is certainly not new. During the Third Crusade in the 12th century, backgammon-like games were so popular among the Crusaders that kings Richard I of England and Philip II of France issued a joint edict prohibiting all gambling games among their troops.

The greatest enemy of the banana is the wind. Due to the weak, leafy stem of the banana plant, winds of just 20 to 30 miles per hour can devastate an entire banana plantation in minutes.

James A. Naismith, the inventor of basketball, originally planned to use square boxes as his targets. When square boxes were unavailable, Naismith substituted two half-bushel peach baskets, and the new game immediately became known as basketball.

Ah! Le Fromage!

The French are the world's greatest cheese eaters. Although the United States is the world's biggest cheese producer, the average American consumes from ten to 12 pounds of cheese annually, including about four pounds of cottage cheese. The average Frenchman, on the other hand, consumes some 30 pounds of *fromage* each year.

The first pencil factory in America was established in Concord, Massachusetts, in 1812, when William Monroe made 30 cedar pencils and sold them to a Boston hardware dealer.

But it was in the City of Brotherly Love that the first American pencil with an eraser was produced. In 1858, Philadelphian Hyman Lipman was granted a patent for a pencil with a piece of rubber glued into a groove at the end.

You Are My Sunshine!

The earth in circumference measures less than 25,000 miles. A single sunspot on the surface of our nearest spectral neighbor can extend more than 185,000 miles. Yet even that is no more than—well, a spot compared to the size of the sun over 864,000 miles in diameter, with a mass 330,000 times that of the earth.

We're hurtling through space at about 66,620 miles per hour as we circle the sun, 93 million miles away in the center of our solar system. Our planet is literally bathing in the sunshine of the sun's energy, which is fueled by 4.5 million tons of gas each second! Temperatures on the surface of the sun approach 11,000 degrees F.; temperatures at the core, an unfathomable 36 million degrees F. Sunspots, which appear dark on the sun, are actually blazing away at about 7,200 degrees F.

But sometimes, neither the size nor power of the sun can be as breathtaking as the kind of perfect sunscopes illustrated here.

Published in Moscow in 1967, The Art of the Book *contained hundreds of premier pieces of Soviet art. Here are two which depict a burst of sun through the clouds.*

A Russian drawing which first appeared in a book entitled Graphic Arts of Lvov, *published in Kiev in 1975.*

This excellent drawing of the sun on hills first appeared in a book entitled Modern Woodcuts and Lithographs *by Jeoffrey Holme, which was published in London by The Studio in 1901.*

From an album called Fifty Years of Soviet Art, *published in the Soviet Union under the editorship of A. Kupetsian of Graphic Arts.*

"The Last Furrow," a drawing from Modern Pen Drawings: European and American *by Charles Holme, published in London in 1901.*

This delightful drawing derives from a publication entitled Grandfather's Money-box, *which was published in Moscow in 1972.*

A charming drawing found in a collection called Russian Book Plates, *published in the U.S.S.R. in the 1970s.*

This drawing comes from Art of the Book, *a Moscow publication of 1967.*

This drawing derives from a book called Pictures and Stories from Forgotten Children's Books, *published in 1969 by Dover Publications, Inc., of New York.*

One Thousand Quaint Cuts from Books of Other Days, *was published in London by the Leadenhall Press. Here is one of the many fine statements from that book.*

This charming headpiece comes from Century Illustrated Monthly Magazine, *which was published in the 1880s and 1890s in New York City.*

This drawing, by the great French caricaturist known as Grandville, first appeared in Un Autre Monde, published in Paris around 1860. Grandville was born in 1803, and died in 1847. Grandville's real name was Jean Gerard. His illustrations for classics; such as La Fontaine's Fables are classic, as are his humorous drawings of human beings with animals' heads.

In 1955, the General Electric Company reported that scientists in their laboratories had succeeded in manufacturing a synthetic diamond by subjecting carbonaceous material to pressures of one-and-a-half million pounds per square inch, and temperatures over 5,000 degrees. The synthetic diamonds, the largest of which was a mere one-tenth of a carat, were of industrial quality only.

Backgammon is the oldest board game still played today. Archaeologists, excavating the ancient Sumerian city of Ur, found five game boards in the royal cemetery that bore a resemblance to backgammon boards. The 5,000-year-old Sumerian game was played on a board of 20 squares, with six dice and seven pieces for each player.

Women's basketball has been around since the 1890's, when Clara Baer introduced the game at a New Orleans college, using the rules published by basketball inventor James A. Naismith. But Clara misinterpreted some of Naismith's diagrams, assuming that certain dotted lines Naismith had drawn, to indicate the best area for team play, were actually restraining lines to be drawn on the court. Thus, for many years, women's basketball was played under different rules than the men's game, with each player limited to movement only within certain parts of the court.

Today, the women's game is played under the same rules as the men's games, and the former women's game is called "rover" or "netball."

Billionaire Howard Hughes designed a bed for himself which was equipped with piped-in music and hot and cold running water! It employed 30 electric motors to move himself and various parts of the bed!

Fifteenth-century Chinese scholars compiled an encyclopedia consisting of over 11,000 volumes.

During the Renaissance, cheese eating fell out of fashion among the upper classes in Europe, partly as a result of the warnings of physicians that it was an unhealthy, undigestible food. A writer of the time named Thomas Muffet wrote that cheese "lieth long in the stomach undigested, procureth thirst, maketh a stinking breath and a scurvy skin."

Mozart's piano pieces, as well as Beethoven's first piano sonatas, were composed for pianos with only five octaves.

P*hantom of the Opera* and other works may have contributed to the popular misconception that the city of Paris is built over a vast maze of ancient sewers and catacombs. While it is true that a network of caverns lies under Paris, these caverns are neither ancient nor catacombs. Most of the present sewer system was constructed during the mid-19th century, by Georges Haussmann. The older caverns were not used for burial until 1787, and prior to that were actually stone quarries.

Only one college basketball team has ever won the NCAA and NIT championships—the two major post-season tournaments—in the same year. In the 1949-1950 season, the team from the City College of New York finished their schedule without ranking among the top 20 teams, and was the last squad to be invited to both the NCAA and NIT tourneys. Yet CCNY went on to victory in both competitions, in the process defeating the teams ranked one, two, three, five, and six!

Mounted Mailmen

The Pony Express in America was actually more renowned in legend than in deed, enjoying but a brief life before disappearing into the annals of Western lore. In 1860, a private company set up a network of relay stations, each 10 to 15 miles apart, to carry United States mail by horseback between California and St. Joseph, Missouri. The mail was transferred to a fresh horse at each station, and a courier rode three horses successively before passing the mail pouches to the next rider. Ponies were never used.

The scheduled delivery time was eight days, although the fastest trip was seven days, 17 hours, when Lincoln's first inaugural address was brought to California. The service was expensive, initially costing five dollars for delivery of a half-ounce parcel, but the rates were lowered sharply soon after. Soon indeed, for the Pony Express system survived but 18 months, made obsolete by the completion of the first transcontinental telegraph line.

A newspaper crossword puzzle compiler once misread a word in a puzzle diagram and devised the clue "Catholic chief" for what he thought was "pope." The published answer was "dope," promoting a deluge of letters from Catholic readers.

Bicycle racers of the 1890s achieved speed records that would startle the modern cyclist. In 1899, Charles "Mile-a-Minute" Murphy earned his nickname by covering a mile in just under 60 seconds on a board track laid over the tracks of the Long Island Railroad. Murphy pedaled behind a train which was fitted with an enormous windshield, so that the cyclist was riding in a near vacuum.

In 1973, Dr. Allan Abbott pedaled in a near vacuum when he set the modern record for bicycle velocity, 140.5 miles per hour, racing behind a windshield-mounted car over the Bonneville Salt Flats in Utah.

Scrabble, one of the most popular games in America, was invented in 1948, and the present rules were formalized in 1953. If you're a Scrabble fan, read this and weep: During the 1970 national Scrabble championships, the woman who was to become the eventual winner amassed an eye-popping 1,266 points in a single game!

Baseball's American League was only three years old when its Boston team met the Pittsburgh Pirates in the first World Series. The National League had been in existence for more than 25 years by that time, but the American League club triumphed, five games to three.

The Chinese practiced the art of paper-making for many centuries before paper became known in the West. In 751, Arabs who had occupied the city of Samarkand in Central Asia were attacked by a Chinese army. The Arabs repelled the attack, and captured a number of Chinese skilled in paper-making. The use of paper then spread throughout the Arab world, and by the 12th century, reached Europe.

An enterprising inventor from Germany once constructed a bicycle that ran on dog power! Two pooches ran on treadmills fitted to the bicycle frame, and the treadmills turned the wheels.

In 1920, the year after baseball's Black Sox game-fixing scandal had exposed a number of players on the Chicago White Sox, an overwrought citizen of Joliet, Illinois, accosted Buck Herzog and accused him of being "one of those crooked Chicago players," then slashed him with a knife. Herzog was indeed a Chicago player—a Chicago Cub.

Americans shopping for bicycles are increasingly turning to lightweight 10-speed models. A decade ago, the sale of 10-speed bikes stood at just five percent of total bike sales, with an overwhelming 73 percent of the market garnered by single-speed, coaster-brake models. By 1977, 10-speeds accounted for 36 percent of the market and three speeds for just 11 percent.

Single speed bikes remain the favorite of about half of new-bike buyers.

Men's bikes outsell women's models by about two-to-one.

The people of ancient Rome rarely had anything more for breakfast than plain water.

Dawn was the normal waking time, and bedtime usually came between seven and nine o'clock in the evening.

Saanen, a cheese made in Switzerland, is the world's hardest cheese, requiring about seven years to fully ripen.

Baseball was *not* invented, as you may have heard, by West Point Cadet Abner Doubleday in 1839, in Cooperstown, New York. The game of "rounders," from which baseball evolved, and games called "base ball" or just "base" were played in England for many years before baseball supposedly began in America.

The journal of an American soldier at Valley Forge in 1778 told of the soldiers "playing at base." And it was reported that boys "playing at base" in the Wall Street area of Manhattan left their game to join in one of the riots that preceded the American Revolution.

The aircraft carrier is a good deal older than you might imagine. In 1918, the British constructed the world's first aircraft-carrying naval vessel, the 560-foot-long *Argus*. The United States first aircraft carrier appeared four years later, and was named after aviation pioneer S.P. Langley.

In 1942, a Russian pilot fell from his airplane and plunged 21,980 feet to earth, without a parachute—and survived!

The highest charge ever levied an advertiser for a television commercial was $350,000 per minute, during the 1978 CBS broadcast of the *Super Bowl*.

"Maine lobster" is not necessarily from the state of Maine. Though Maine now accounts for about 25 million pounds of lobster yearly, the term "Maine lobster" is also applied to much of the shellfish caught off the Maritime Provinces of Canada. Much of the Canadian catch, of course, ends up on American dinner plates.

The first neon-tube advertising sign in the United States was installed in 1923, on marquee of the Cosmopolitan Theater in New York. The sign beckoned playgoers to a production of *Little Old New York*.

When chocolate first reached Europe in the 16th century, the clergy declared it "the beverage of Satan" and "a provocative of immorality," since it was thought that chocolate was an aphrodisiac. The idea did not die easily. As late as 1712, the English magazine *The Spectator* warned that men "be careful how they meddle with romance, chocolate, novels, and the like inflamers."

Until the 19th century, most paper was made from substances derived from old linen and cotton rags, or from straw. Then papermakers found out how to make paper from wood pulp. At last there was an inexpensive, seemingly inexhaustible supply of raw material for paper—and the forest fire became the single most dangerous threat to world literacy.

Ebony, long used for the black keys of the piano, was originally chosen for that job, according to some historians, because it best showed off feminine white hands. Many of today's pianos use black plastic instead.

The word "clam" is actually a generic term used to designate some 12,000 species of bivalves. In Scotland, the word refers to the scallop. In the United States, "clam" usually refers to the quahog, or hard-shelled clam, and the steamer, or soft-shelled clam, though the two sea creatures belong to two entirely different genera of bivalves.

In 1840, English cheese makers probably thought they'd established the all-time record for cheese size when they delivered a half-ton Cheddar as a bridal gift for Queen Victoria. Little did they suspect that, 124 years later, the Wisconsin Cheese Foundation would produce a mammoth Cheddar tipping the scales at 34,591 pounds! The Cheddar was delivered for exhibition at the 1964 World's Fair in New York City aboard a specially designed, 45-foot-long refrigerated trailer called the "Cheese-Mobile."

There are presently an estimated 363 million television sets in use throughout the world, with the United States the leader by far with 120 million receivers, Japan 25 million, and England 18 million. And yes, there are still some countries that have no television at all.

Figure skating was first included in the Olympic Games in 1908, reappeared in 1920, and became part of the Winter Games when they were instituted four years later. Norwegian Sonja Henie was the most noted figure skater of that period, winning the Norwegian championships at age nine, and the world title at age 13! She captured gold medals at the Winter Olympics in 1928, 1932, and 1936, then went to Hollywood to star in a number of movies. Among other innovations, Sonja was the first woman skater to wear the short skating skirt.

In 1891, 30-year-old William Wrigley, Jr., moved to Chicago and set up the Wrigley Company with just $32 of his own money and a $5,000 loan. The firm initially sold soap, then branched out into baking powder. In 1892, Wrigley ordered some chewing gum to offer jobbers as an inducement to buy his baking powder. Wrigley's salesmen dispensed two packs of gum with each ten-cent package of baking powder, and the jobbers soon reported that they found it much easier to sell the gum than peddle the powder.

It didn't take Wrigley long to see the possibilities. By the turn of the century, Wrigley's gum was being sold coast to coast in stores and vending machines. By the end of World War II, the taste for Wrigley's product in America, Europe, and Asia was so great that his factories could barely keep pace with the demand.

The record-setting feat in the sport of bed pushing was achieved in 1975, when a dozen young people in Greensburg, Pennsylvania, wheeled a hospital bed a total of 1,776 miles in 17 days.

A group of students attempting to match that feat once fitted a wheeled bed with a 198 cc. engine, and then accumulated 52 traffic summonses during the bed's maiden voyage.

Seventeenth-century doctors prescribed tobacco as a cure-all, fashioning the leaf into pills, plasters, poultices, oils, salts, tinctures, and balms. Some physicians even recommended a tobacco-smoke enema for various ailments. The enema—administered with a device known as the Clyster pipe—was said by one doctor to be "excellent good against colic." And James I of England proclaimed that the Clyster pipe was the only way to take one's tobacco.

Well, different smokes for different folks.

In 1879, a business census conducted in the mining boomtown of Leadville, Colorado, reported four banks, four churches, ten dry-goods stores, and 31 restaurants. In contrast, Leadville then boasted 139 saloons and beer halls, and 228 gambling houses and private clubs.

The slang expression *in the clink* comes from an actual jail, Clink Prison in London, where chronic debtors served their terms in 17th-century England.

The euphemism Sanitary Engineer for garbage man is only the latest misuse of the term engineer to add cachet to unprestigious employments. In former times, sleepwear manufacturers were known as Pajama Engineers; rat-catchers as Exterminating Engineers; and beauty parlor operators as Appearance Engineers.

Grecian Cocktail

In America, the world *cocktail* may mean either a mixed drink, as opposed to straight spirits, or any alcoholic beverage sipped before lunch or dinner.

In the second sense, the cocktail has been with us for thousands of years. The ancient Greeks had a cocktail hour in the late afternoon or evening, complete with hors d'oeuvres. An Athenian gentleman would drop by a neighbor's house during the "happy hour" with a goatskin of wine, and expect to be treated to an outlay of appetizers—the Greeks called them "provocatives to drinking"—that might include caviar, oysters, nuts, olives, shrimp, and pate. Compare that spread to today's bar fare of peanuts, cheese, and crackers and you'll agree that in some ways we haven't come very far in the last 2,500 years.

The Orient has produced many picturesque names for more mundanely-titled Western inventions. For instance, the Chinese for *locomotive* is *fire wagon*; for *telephone*, *electricity talk*; for *safety razor*, *gentleman instrument*; for *movie theater*, *electricity shadow hall*; and for *life insurance*, *man old-age guarantee to feel at ease.*

Pin $

For centuries, metal pins were rare and costly items reserved for the rich. You've heard the expression *pin money*, meaning a small sum allotted by a husband for his wife's use, or money for incidental expenses. Well, when the term originated in the 14th century, *pin money* was just that, for at the time, pins were expensive enough to be real items in the budget. By custom, a husband would present his wife on the first or second of January with enough money to buy her pins for the year.

Pin money went by the boards in the 19th century, when mass production made pins the inexpensive purchase they are today.

If the air-conditioning were turned off in the Houston Astrodome, the entrance of warm humid air could cause it to rain in the stadium.

On the morning of February 9, 1855, strange hoofprints were seen about in the snow in Devonshire, England. The oval impressions, about the size of donkey hoofprints, were eight inches apart in a straight line, as if the mysterious animal had been walking a tightrope, and covered a distance of 98 miles, passing through 15 towns and a river. But the weirdest thing was that the tracks ran up and down the sides and roofs of barns and houses, continuing on the ground on the other side of these structures. The scientists who examined the tracks claimed they were made by no living creature, and many of the residents of Devon, declaring the abominable snowman must be the Devil himself, refused to leave their houses at night for many months thereafter.

The first metal coins were minted in the kingdom of Lydia, in Asia Minor, around the year 650 B.C., although there is evidence of silver money in Persia as early as 760 B.C.

The coffee plant is a tropical evergreen shrub indigenous to the eastern hemisphere; 25 species grow wild in Africa, Asia, and the Near East. Oh, there is some coffee grown in the United States—but only in Hawaii.

Two species of the coffee plant are far and away the most common. *Coffea arabica*, the oldest known variety, hails originally from Arabia or Ethiopia, and is now grown extensively in South America. *Coffea robusta* originated in East and Central Africa and is still the major coffee plant of the continent. *Robusta* is not—well—more "robusta" than *arabica*. Actually, it's milder in taste and aroma, and is less favored by Westerners.

Brazil once accounted for 66 percent of all coffee exports, but as Africa production has continued to rise, that figure has dropped to 40 percent. Today, about 30 percent of all coffee comes from Africa.

And It's Music!
Music! Music!

The world is full of music. Everybody loves music and many people play instruments. Here are two pages of musicians as depicted in the world's great humor magazines and publications.

Art Nouveau, U.S.A.

Harper's, U.S.A.

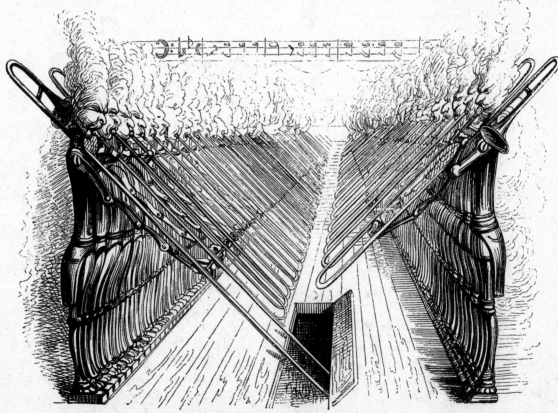

Grandville in *Un Autre Monde, France*

Gebrauchgraphik, Germany

Wilhelm Butch Album, Germany

Comic Almanac, England

Harper's, U.S.A.

Quaint Cuts, U.S.A.

Grandfather's Moneybox, U.S.S.R.

All hunting is divided into three parts: trapping and snaring; coursing and falconry; and hunting with implements (firearms, bow and arrow, boomerang, sling). For hunting novices, snaring differs from trapping in that the hunter uses a running noose of wire or cord to entangle his prey. Coursing is the pursuit of game with hounds.

Early methods of trapping involved primarily the pitfall and the deadfall. The pitfall was a pit covered with some flimsy material that would not bear weight; the deadfall consisted of a pit plus a weight (a log or stone) which would fall on the trapped animal. But modern trappers rely almost exclusively on spring-snapped, steel-jawed traps.

Falconry is a mode of bird-hunting that was known in ancient China, Persia, and Egypt. It attained its greatest popularity in Europe during the Middle Ages, and went into serious decline after the 17th century. This explains why the sport never caught on in the Americas.

In Great Britain and Western Europe, the sport of hunting often takes the form of the chase. The hunters pursue the game on horseback with the aid of hounds that have a keen sense of smell. In the United States, however, hunting almost always means the field sport of shooting small and large game caught unawares. During the 19th century, big-game hunting in Africa and India became a popular sport among wealthy Westerners.

An irreverent wag has pointed out that two drinks are mentioned in the Bible—Wine: *which gladdeneth the heart of man*, and Water: *which quencheth the thirst of the jackasses.*

Although it sounds like an apocryphal tale, it appears to be true: The great Greek dramatist Aeschylus was killed when a bird dropped a tortoise on his head from a great height.

Charles Steinmetz, the electrical wizard, was an inveterate smoker. Although a notice forbidding smoking was posted in the General Electric plant where Steinmetz worked, the great man ignored it until one day an executive asked him rather pointedly if he was not aware of the rule. Steinmetz answered with a cold stare.

The next day, Steinmetz didn't show up for work; and for two days thereafter, no one heard from him. The laboratory of the General Electric plant was practically at a standstill. Without Steinmetz, they just couldn't go ahead.

So the management ordered that a serious search be made throughout the city to locate their genius. After a while, they found him in the lobby of a Buffalo hotel. He was seated in a huge chair, puffing away nonchalantly at a huge cigar. When he was told that the whole company was out looking for him, and was asked why he had, without so much as a goodbye, left his office without notice, he calmly replied, "Well, I just came up here to have a good smoke."

After that, there was never a word mentioned to him about the no smoking rule.

How many drops are there in a pint? Well, there are two cups in a pint, and eight ounces in a cup. An ounce contains two tablespoons, and a tablespoon is equal to three teaspoons. Finally, a teaspoon contains 120 drops. So one pint contains 11,520 drops.

At a certain dinner party, Daniel Webster found himself the prey of a hostess who endlessly and mercilessly worried her guests. They were not eating enough, possibly they did not like this or that, and wouldn't they have more, and so forth.

"You're hardly eating a thing, Mr. Webster," she protested for the umpteenth time.

"Madam," said Webster solemnly, "permit me to assure you that I sometimes eat more than at other times, but never less."

There was the Montreal drunk who kept muttering, "It can't be done! It can't be done! It can't be done!' as he stood looking up at a big electric sign that read, "Drink Canada Dry."

Named by the Spaniards who first observed its practice in the New World, elevated to artistic and mythological fame by Charles Lamb's Dissertation, and raised to pre-eminence on a prestigious social occasion by Lyndon B. Johnson, the barbecue is so well established today it's now even built *inside* many homes.

Cooking with hot embers is one of the oldest of culinary methods; and to a hungry group at the beach, it sometimes seems like the longest. Particularly when the first delicious-smelling sizzlings have begun to waft your way.

While waiting for the charcoal to turn white in your transistor-sized hibachi, it may be some consolation to consider the backyard parties of certain tribes in New Guinea. They dig a pit, 20 feet long, 15 feet deep, and 10 feet wide, burn logs in it till it's half-filled with glowing coals, and then toss in wet leaves, followed by upwards of 50 whole pigs. They cover the whole shebang with sand, and go away and dance for two days, until they hear the words so dear to all barbecue standbys: "C'mon and get it."

Lew Worsham leaned over his putter on the 18th green of the Jacksonville Country Club. He needed to sink the ball in 2 to win the 1948 Jacksonville Open Championship, a $10,000 feature. He moved his putter carefully behind the ball. Suddenly, he straightened, dropped his club, and went to the side of the green.

"I touched the ball," he told the tournament official. "Call a penalty stroke."

Worsham then returned to take the 2 putts that would have won, the 2 putts that now gave him only a tie.

The next day, Lew lost the playoff to Clayton Haefner on the 21st green.

But even in defeat Worsham was marked as a great champion—a champion in sportsmanship. Not even his victory in the 1947 National Open earned him the respect he won by calling against himself a penalty nobody else had seen.

From Riches to Rags

Remember the Green Hornet from radio? Remember Captain Video from TV? Both these intrepid heroes were played by Al Hodge. Practically a national hero, this handsome actor was seen and heard in many an American household.

On March 19, 1979, this once famous man was found dead in his single room in a run-down New York City hotel. He was 66 years old. *Sic transit gloria mundi.*

One day, Dr. Creighton, Bishop of London, was riding on a train with a meek curate. The Bishop, who ardently loved his tobacco, took out his cigar case, turned to his companion, and said with a smile, "You don't mind my smoking, do you?"

The curate bowed, and answered humbly, "Not if Your Lordship doesn't mind my being sick."

Superstitious Stars

Performers are notorious believers in astrology, but did you know about the idiosyncratic superstitions of the following actors?

BOB HOPE has been wearing the same pair of cufflinks on stage for over 20 years. The cufflinks bear the engraved face of St. Genesius, the patron saint of actors.

PETER O'TOOLE swears by a pair of green socks when he's filming a movie—and if the socks don't match the outfit O'Toole is wearing in the film, he stuffs them in a pocket and carries them on the set that way!

GLEN FORD's talisman is a blue and white tie that he bought in 1931, at the age of 14, from his first paycheck. The actor wears the lucky tie during performances whenever he can.

ROBERT MORLEY's good-luck charm takes the shape of a teddy bear. Morley has carried the stuffed animal with him for nearly 50 years, ever since he first entered the world of show business.

James Thompson of Fairmont, Indiana, claims to be the oldest bicyclist in the United States. At the age of 105, Mr. Thompson still rides his bicycle over hill and dale, whenever weather permits.

Don't Be Shocked

Now we've heard everything—shock absorbers for horses! "The Supershoe," invented by farmer Ron Saffron and vetinarian Bill Blanshard of Wiltshire, England, contains a built-in shock absorber for hard ground.

In the 14th century, attack dogs with spears and buckets of fire harnessed to their backs were used in battle to upset cavalry horses.

The longest married couple in this country may be Joseph and Elisa Caroti of New Haven, Connecticut, who recently celebrated their 74th wedding anniversary. Mr. Caroti is 94 years old, Mrs. Caroti 92. The couple has six children, 12 grandchildren, 16 great-grandchildren, and one great-great grandchild.

Cold climates seem to result in longevity for the denizens, while hot weather seems to affect life-expectancy adversely. At least we might form this conclusion from the fact that the five countries with the highest life expectancy—Sweden, Holland, Iceland, Norway, and Denmark—are all in northerly locations, while the five countries with the lowest life expectancies—Guinea, Upper Volta, Chad, Angola, and Guinea-Bissau—are all located in torrid Africa.

The word *diamond* actually comes from a Greek word meaning "invincible." The Greek word, *adamas*, was originally applied to all hard metals, then to corundum and certain other hard stones. By the first century B.C., the word came to mean "diamond" in Greek and Latin. From *adamad* came the later Latin *diamas*, than the Middle English *diamaunt*, and our words *diamond* and *adamant*—adamant because the diamond is so hard and unyielding.

As Sam Lujack, a bank courier in Glendale, California, was leaving the bank one day, he was accosted by a hold-up man. The thief tried to grab Sam's briefcase, which contained $700 in cash. Sam resisted, and the thief shot Sam point-blank in the stomach. But Sam emerged from the fray unwounded—the bullet was found buried in a $500 wad of $20 bills that Sam had strapped to his stomach in a money pouch.

When Bobby Fischer threw a tantrum in Reykjavik, and then arrogantly ceded two games to Spassky before his blew Boris off the board, he performed a commercial alchemy. Thousands of chess books that had been gathering dust in the publishers' bins for many years suddenly became prime property, and chess sets—old or new—were transmitted overnight into pure gold.

The boom is still on, and the variety of chess sets is still proliferating. Today, the game—who'd have thunk it?—is the rage of cops, hardhats, and John Wayne.

Mangia! Mangia!

Lest anyone doubt that Americans are, on the whole, well fed, the U.S. Department of Agriculture has published statistics on the amount of food we consume in a year. The average American gulps down 1,154 pounds of vegetables, 1,136 pounds of dairy food, 694 pounds of meat and fish, 598 pounds of fruit, and 34 pounds of poultry—for a whopping total of two-and-a-half tons of food per person annually.

In 1877, a Dodge county, Wisconsin, cheesemaker named John Jossi set out to make Limburger cheese and instead ended up with a savory, semisoft product we now call Brick cheese. Brick cheese and Liederkranz cheese are the only cheeses invented by Americans.

Cocoa and chocolate are virtually unknown as a popular food outside Europe and the United States. Just five nations—the United States, England, West Germany, the Netherlands, and France—now account for four-fifths of all world chocolate imports, and ten nations account for over 95 percent of chocolate consumption.

Culture Vultures

Whether it's the impact of *Live from Lincoln Center* and *Masterpiece Theater*, or something else, Americans are going in for high culture as never before. In 1977-1978, a record 112 million Americans turned out for live cultural performances—62 million to the theater, 25 million to symphony concerts, 15 million to the ballet, and 10 million to the opera. Compare this figure to the audience of 70 million for professional sports events: 39 million to baseball games, 11 million to football games, 10 million to basketball games, and nine million to hockey games.

Skateboard Surge

Skateboards first reached the public eye in 1962, when the proprietors of the Val Surf Shop in North Hollywood, California, began attaching roller skate wheel trucks to boards. But in the mid-1960s, cities from San Diego, California, to Providence, Rhode Island, began to outlaw skateboards on public streets. The bans were due mainly to the loud noise made by the clay composition wheels, and the dangers posed by the boards to the skateboarder himself.

Then in 1973, a California surfer, named Frank Nasworthy, devised the first skateboard with urethane wheels, which provided more traction and a quieter ride than the earlier wheels. Skateboarding soon became safe and acceptable, and the sport took off again.

The leotard, a close-fitting garment worn by dancers, and sometimes by actors and acrobats, is named for its creator, Jules Leotard, a famous French aerialist of the 19th century. Although today the leotard is worn by performers of both sexes, Monsieur Leotard originally designed the costume to enhance male sex appeal. At the close of his memoirs, the celebrated daredevil addressed his masculine readers thus: "Do you want to be adored by the ladies? [Then] put on a more natural garb, which does not hide your best features."

Leotard's leotard was a one-piece elastic garment, with ankle-length tights and no sleeves. Today, the leotard usually covers both arms and legs, although legless and sleeveless varieties are available.

Altar Addicts

The most-married man in history has got to be King Mongut of Siam, on whose life the book and movie *The King and I* were based. Mongut had 9,000 wives and concubines. Other spectacular polygamists include King Solomon, with 700 wives, and Queen Kahena of the Bergers, with 400 husbands.

About 19 percent of all the paper manufactured in the United States is made from wastepaper. In West Germany, where the supply of pulpwood is more limited, 45 percent of all paper is made from waste; in forest-rich Finland, only three percent.

The idea of identifying the various throws of the dice with names such as *snake eyes* and *boxcars* is hardly new. The ancient Greeks also had names for the dice throws. A six was known as *Aphrodite*, and a one was called a *dog*.

Annette van Dorp was a 23-year-old student in Bonn, Germany, when she conceived the idea of how to make some money to pay her way through college. She realized what a chore it was for people to cut and trim large lawns. So she bought some sheep and rented them out for lawn cropping.

Her business thrived—in fact, became so good that now she owns over 100 of these animals. Her clients, residents of the city of Bonn, like the arrangement very much. They say that it costs $15.00 an hour to employ a person with a mowing machine, and that one sheep, at a cost of only $10.00 for the entire summer, will keep something like 150 square yards of grass short and nice.

Girl Scout Troop 12 of Great Falls, Montana is unique in the annals of scouting. Every member of the troop is a grandmother—and the 13 scouts have a total of 119 grandchildren. The youngest member of Troop 12 is 56; the oldest, 90.

Save Your Pennies!

Norman Rondeau, of Pawtucket, Rhode Island, bought himself a new car for pennies. For 433,000 pennies, that is, tied up in 86 sacks weighing a ton-and-a-half, which Mr. Rondeau delivered to his local car dealer in a pick-up truck.

The oldest city in the world is Gazientep, Turkey, which originated around 3650 B.C. Tied for second place are Jerusalem, Israel; Kirkuk, Iraq; and Zurich, Switzerland, all of which were founded around 3000 B.C.

Maybe They Forgot the Salt and Pepper

In the days when the U.S. Department of the Interior tagged migratory birds with metal strips engraved WASH. BIOL. SURV. (Washington Biology Survey), the Department received the following letter from a disgruntled farmer in Arkansas: "Dear Sirs: I shot one of your crows the other day. My wife followed the cooking instructions on the leg tag, and I want to tell you that the bird tasted just terrible."

New pinball games are being invented continually. Each of the four major pinball machine manufacturers now bring out from six to 12 new games every year. Designers say they aim for a game that demands about 75 percent skill, but allows for 25 percent luck, so that unskilled players can enjoy playing as well.

French noblemen at the court of Louis XIV often enjoyed perfumed foods. Meats were sprinkled with rose water, eggs were flavored with muck, and cream was mixed with ambergris.

During the American Civil War, four slave states declined to join the Confederacy, and remained nominally a part of the Union. The four states were Delaware, Maryland, Kentucky, and Missouri.

The largest live multiple birth was of octuplets (four boys and four girls) who were born to a Mexican woman, Maria de Sepulveda, on March 10, 1967. All eight babies died within 14 hours. The first survival of the largest group of multiple births was that of the sextuplets (three boys and three girls) born to Sue Rosenkowitz of South Africa, on January 11, 1974. The sextuplets were the result of a fertility drug, HCG, taken by the mother.

Why are British policemen called *bobbies*? The nickname originated with Sir Robert Peel, who in 1829 founded the organization on which the British Metropolitan Police System is based. The bobbies were also known as *peelers* at that time.

He didn't mean it as a joke, but a few years back, a parliamentarian from the north of England hurled a smile-provoking insult at one of his colleagues. The statesman's boner was: "That allegation is false, and the alligator knows it!"

Every High School Latin student knows Caesar's famous boast, *Veni, vidi, vici*—"I came, I saw, I overcame." Less well-known is the motto Queen Elizabeth I of England had inscribed on a medal depicting the British defeat of the Spanish Armada in 1588. The inscription read: *Venit, vidit, fugit*—"It came, it saw, it ran away."

One of the wittier epitaphs was composed by writer Hilaire Belloc (1870-1953) for himself. The two lines read:

"When I am dead, I hope it may be said—
'His sins were scarlet, but his books were
    read.'"

In 1949, the hair of Swami Pandarasannadhi of India was reported to be 26 feet in length—the longest human hair on record.

To Catch a Thief. . .

The French detective Eugene François Vidocq, who served as the head of Paris' famed *Service de Sûrete,* did not learn about crime and the ways of the underworld in any French police academy. Before becoming the most outstanding sleuth of his time, Vidocq was himself a jailbird. Born in 1775, Vidocq was a soldier, deserter, hardened criminal, master of escapes and disguises, and police spy before moving to the right side of the law.

After serving for 23 years in the *Sûrete,* the famed sleuth was removed as its head in 1832, charged with instigating a crime so that he might gain praise for uncovering it. For the remaining 25 years of his life, Vidocq ran a paper mill, employing ex-criminals for his work force.

In Illinois in 1954, copies of Hans Christian Andersen's *Wonder Stories* were stamped "For Adult Readers" to prevent children from obtaining "smut." And in 1876, Mark Twain's *The Adventures of Tom Sawyer* were excluded from the children's room in the Brooklyn Public Library.

A Most Unusual Escape

In 1899, Pearl Hart became a folk hero when she and an accomplice robbed one of the last Western stagecoaches. Sentenced to five years in prison for her part in the crime, Pearl was isolated from the men prisoners in the Yuma, Arizona, jail for fear she'd "corrupt their morals."

But after six months in jail, Pearl appeared to turn over a new leaf. She began reading books and writing poetry. The varden and the prison chaplain visited her often in her cell, and the governor himself once came to Yuma to see the "new" Pearl Hart.

One day, Pearl began complaining of illness. A nurse examined the jail's only woman inmate, and declared her pregnant. The warden was aghast. There were only two keys to Pearl's cell: his own and his wife's. Only two other men had ever been alone with Pearl in her cell: the prison chaplain and the governor of the Arizona Territory.

Pearl was conditionally pardoned in 1902 because of a "lack of accommodations for women prisoners."

If you're searching for a word that can be typed using only the top row of the letter keyboard, you won't have to look further than *typewriter.*

Productions of Shakespeare's *King Lear* were prohibited in England from 1788 to 1820, in deference to King George III's acknowledged insanity.

In 1925, a large crowd filled a hall in New York's Hotel Roosevelt to watch Yale defeat Harvard in the first intercollegiate crossword puzzle tournament.

In April, 1895, Captain Joshua Slocum boarded his 36-foot yawl *The Spray* in Newport, Rhode Island, and set sail on a voyage around the world—alone. More than three years later, in July, 1898, he arrived back in Newport. The 51-year-old Slocum had sailed a total of 46,000 miles all by himself, without crew or companion. And Slocum could not swim!

Apian Onslaught

The scourge of the so-called "killer bees" that have been traveling northward through South America is only in part the work of nature. The killer bees are actually natives of Africa, and were brought to South America by a geneticist during the 1950s. About two dozen of the lethal stingers escaped from the scientist's laboratory, and began breeding with South American bees. Millions of African killer bees are now drifting northward toward Central America at the rate of 200 miles a year.

American officials are presently considering plans to "cut them off at the pass." The pass is the isthmus of Panama.

Dick Allen of Happy, Texas, came into the world deaf, lacking ears or even ear holes. But Dick soon discovered that he had the happy facility of hearing through his open mouth. In fact, his aural sense was so acute that he was able to become a musician!

Late in the 1950s, officials of the Ford Motor Company rejected some 18,000 names for a new model car before settling on "Edsel." Only 109,466 Edsels were sold before the car was abandoned, a little more than two years after its debut. The Ford Company lost about $350 million on the car.

Flea-catching contests were once a popular amusement in China. In 1928, a nimble Chinaman became the world's flea-catching champion by snaring 21,000 of the leaping mites in four hours.

The victor was no stranger to fleas—he was a dog-catcher by trade!

In 1939, a novel called *Gadsby* was published in Los Angeles. Though the work contained 50,000 words, the letter "e" appears only three times in the entire book—in the name of its author, Ernest Vincent Wright.

The shortest English word containing all five vowels is *eunoia*, meaning "alertness." Considering the letter *y* to be a vowel, you might ask if there is an English word that contains all six vowels. The answer is *unquestionably*.

To *eat humble pie* means to admit error and apologize, a meaning you might correctly guess even if you had never heard the expression before. But the phrase's origin owes nothing to the eating of a symbolic pie of humility. The expression actually comes from *umble pie*, a dish made from the *umbles*, or entrails, of an animal, especially a deer. Since pies for household servants were formerly made from entrails, to "eat umble pie" figuratively meant to suffer a humiliating drop in social standing.

The regulations of Wells Fargo Express, governing the firm's stagecoach operations in the old West, absolved the company from responsibility for loss or damage of merchandise "by fire, the acts of God, or of Indians, or any other public enemies of the government."

The Temple of Borobudar depicts the life of Buddha in sculpture

The Temple of Siva at Borobudar, Java, is one of the largest and, to Western eyes, most peculiar Buddhist shrines in the world. By following a circular route to the top of the pyramidal structure, a visitor can study the life of Buddha and an elaboration of Buddhist religious doctrine—all told in finely carved relief sculpture!

This reliquary mound was built during the ninth century but lay overgrown with dense jungle for 900 years until its restoration early in this century. The monument consists of seven square terraces of gradating size, surrounded by a high wall and surmounted by three circular terraces or platforms. On these platforms rest 72 small bell-shaped stupas, or reliquary housings; each contains a sculptured Buddha visible through the stupa's perforated stonework. At the pinnacle, one large stupa encloses a large, unfinished Buddha.

Although four stairways—one on each side—rise across the terraces and platforms toward the topmost stupa, the builders of the Temple of Borobudar did not intend that pilgrims climb to the top of the shrine so simply. Rather, they planned a circuitous route lined with teeming relief sculpture. A pilgrim began his visit by walking around the high outer walls, examining the story in sculpture of the Buddha and the various moral doctrines of Buddhism. As he rose from terrace to terrace, the pilgrim inspected the pavilions, the statue-crammed niches, the carved waterspouts, and the relief sculpture that filled the terrace walls.

When read in a circular ascent to the shrine, these reliefs demonstrate, in pro-gressive fashion, ever more profound moral doctrines. The high walls of the terraces prevent a pilgrim from viewing a higher level than the one he is on.

The pilgrim's winding route does not stop when he reaches the circular platforms. Only after he has passed the 72 small stupas is he ready to view the great Buddha that crowns this marvelously ingenious structure.

What do the words *millinery, palace, meander*, and *tawdry* have in common? They all owe their origin to a place name.

Women's hats of striking beauty were made in the city of Milan, Italy; *millinery* became the word for women's hats. Wealthy Romans built large, luxurious homes, or *palaces*, on the Palatine Hill in Rome. In ancient Greece, a winding, wandering river was called the Menderes, which spawned the word *meander*. And St. Audrey's fair in Norwich, England, became famous for the cheap, low-quality jewelry that was sold there. *Tawdry* now describes any cheap, shoddy goods.

French artist Paul Cezanne, much noted for his still lifes, worked so slowly at his craft that he often had to use wax fruit as still life models. Real fruit would have rotted before Cezanne could finish his painting.

Americans are the most avid bowlers on earth—an estimated 65 million people bowl in this country. But the largest bowling alley in the world is to be found, surprisingly, in Japan. The Tokyo World Lanes Bowling Center boasts 252 lanes.

If you're traveling in Europe, don't ask an Albanian for directions to Albania. The name of that nation in its native tongue is Shqiperia.

There is a source of light energy right here on earth that is far more powerful than the sun. A laser beam, produced by energizing an artificial ruby in a certain way, emits the equivalent of 10,000 watts of light energy per square centimeter. The light energy emitted by our sun over the same area is six watts.

It's commonly believed that the city of Rome was founded by the Etruscans, and that the language the Etruscans spoke formed the basis of Latin. Actually, the Etruscans warred continually with other peoples on the Italian peninsula, and were more often an enemy than an ally of the early Romans.

The Etruscan language, meanwhile, is totally unrelated to Latin—unrelated, in fact, to any other known language. Even today it remains only partly deciphered. And no one is sure where the Etruscans lived before they reached Italy.

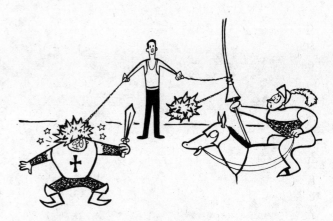

A Deadly Device

The mace is a shafted weapon held in one hand. It employs a flail at the end of a chain. The flail, or spiked ball, is linked to a wooden handle by the chain. While it cannot be snapped like a whip, the mace is wielded in much the same fashion. It was possible to envelop the opponent's sword blade with the chain, and thus to pull his weapon from his hand, or to knock the enemy senseless within his armor with the mace. One could even crush his skull.

In England, this weapon was called a *Morning Star*. In Spain, it was called a *mate suegra* or "mother-in-law killer." Originally a farmer's thresher, the mace became, as so many tools did, a peasant's weapon. Spikes were added to the ball to make it more effective. The length of chain made it easier to swing it about, and clear a path through a wall of armor.

As Lazy as a Bee

Male bees, called drones, cannot sting. The word *drone* has become a synonym for lazy because the male bee does no work at all. The drone is not equipped to gather pollen, make honey, or defend the hive. The male bees must actually be fed by the worker bees, which are undeveloped females.

The drone's sole function is reproduction, but normally only one drone mates with each queen. The others are driven from the hive to starve when nectar is in short supply. And the drone that does win the queen dies in mating.

The queen bee, on the other hand, is quite busy. At the height of the egg-laying season, she may lay as many as 1,800 eggs each day!

Everyone knows that the weather can get mighty chilly up in Alaska—a low of 80 degrees below zero has been recorded. But it can also get very hot in Alaska in the summer, when the sun is shining 20 hours a day. Temperatures over 85 degrees are common. In 1915, the U.S. weather station at Fort Yukon recorded a temperature of 100 degrees—and Fort Yukon lies almost directly on the Arctic Circle!

The word *stink* certainly has unpleasant connotations to our ears—and our noses. But originally, *to stink* meant merely "to smell." A line written by the 14th-century English poet Chaucer reads "The rose stinks sweetly."

There are normally some 50,000 earthworms in each acre of soil. In one year, the worms carry about 20 tons of earth to the surface; in 20 years, they replace the topsoil with a new layer of soil three inches thick.

The reign of Pepi II, pharoah of Egypt, was the longest of any monarch in history. Pepi II gained the Egyptian throne at the age of six, and ruled until his death in 2475 B.C.—a period of 91 years! By comparison, Louis XIV of France, the longest-reigning monarch in European recorded history, reigned for 72 years.

Incidentally, the senility that Pepi II suffered during the latter years of his life hastened the fall of his dynasty.

The area of the earth north of 60 degrees North latitude includes all of Greenland and Iceland, and most of Siberia, Alaska, Scandinavia, and northern Canada. Yet the area south of 60 degrees South latitude contains no trees, very few plants, and not one single permanent human inhabitant. The only industries in the area, which includes the continent of Antarctica, are sealing and whaling.

Even today, the British eat almost eight ounces of sweets per person per week, more than any other people.

The Twain Meets

Owing to the twist of the Isthmus of Panama, the Atlantic Ocean is, in some places on the Isthmus, actually west of the Pacific. Thus, there is a point in North America at which the sun rises in the Pacific and sets in the Atlantic. In fact, a boat in the Panama Canal runs northwest to southeast in passing from the Atlantic to the Pacific.

A 23-foot iron pillar in Delhi has not rusted in 1,500 years—and no one has figured out why.

The comic character Superman made his first appearance in June, 1938, in one of four stories presented in *Action Comics*, Number One. A copy of this comic is now valued by collectors at over $4,000!

Superman merited his own comic book in the summer of the following year. A copy of *Superman* Number One is now worth over $2,000.

Among other nicknames, New York City is sometimes known as "Gotham." Washington Irving first used the term, around 1805, to refer to "The Big Apple," since the residents of Gotham, England, were long regarded as fools.

But there is another side to the story. The residents of Gotham, England, were said by some to have purposefully played the fool in order to discourage royal visits. In that way they would avoid the expense of entertaining the king. An old saying from the English town goes something like this: "More fools pass through Gotham than remain in it."

A Kentucky law still on the books makes it illegal for a married man to buy a hat unless his wife is along to assist in the selection.

In 1914, as the United States prepared to open the Panama Canal, Secretary of State William Jennings Bryan sent invitations to the opening to the navies of a number of countries, including Switzerland. A land-locked nation, Switzerland never had a navy.

The word "uncopyrightable" contains 15 letters, none of which is used more than once. And the nine-letter word "strengths" contains but one vowel.

Jackhammer Blues

Even the largest, most well-equipped symphony orchestra in the world could not perform John Cage's *First Construction in Metal* without first scouting around for a number of additional instruments. The score for this avant-garde piece calls for, among other things, a piano with a metal rod strung across the strings, 12 oxen bells, eight cow bells, four brake drums, five thunder sheets, four Turkish cymbals, four Chinese cymbals, three Japanese temple gongs, tubular bells, sleigh bells, a tom-tom, and—from the blacksmith's shop—four muted anvils.

In 1975, voters in Philadelphia reelected Francis O'Donnell to the City Council. By election day, O'Donnell had been dead almost a week, but election officials had not had time to remove his name from the voting machines.

A recent survey revealed that more than half of all adults in France have not read a single book since childhood.

The members of some insect species are so short-lived that they have no way of eating. Some completely lack a mouth!

The United States can now boast over 125,000 registered dentists, more than any other country on earth. But two out of three Americans rarely or never call on their services.

Before Tennessee was granted statehood in 1796, the territory was known as both Franklin and Frankland.

A day on the planet Venus is longer than its year. Venus circles the sun in just over 224 earth days; it completes one rotation on its axis every 243 earth days.

In 1941, Governor Eugene Talmadge of Georgia ordered school libraries to remove from their shelves all books unfavorable to the South, the Bible, or the state of Georgia.

Ganymede, one of Jupiter's moons, is larger than the planet Mercury. Ganymede's diameter is 3,120 miles, compared to Mercury's 3,000 miles.

Camel's-hair brushes are made not from camel's hair, but from squirrels' tails. The hair of the one-humped camel, or dromedary, is too short to be used for brushes.

The abacus is considered by most people to be a calculating device of strictly Oriental origin and use. In fact, the abacus was widely used by the Greeks, Romans, and other peoples of the ancient Mediterranean.

The world's shortest scheduled flight takes passengers between two neighboring Orkney Islands in Scotland. The scheduled flight time is two minutes, although with a good wind the trip has been made in as little as 69 seconds. Fare on the twin-engine eight-seater is about ten dollars, but neither movies nor food is offered aboard.

Cheese making began well before recorded history, possibly among shepherds in the Indus Valley or in Mesopotamia. But most of the cheeses produced today were developed only within the last few centuries.

There are 773,692 words in the King James Bible (excluding Apocrypha), and 3,566,480 letters. For proof, any Doubting Thomas may simply count the letters for himself.

American Indians were the first to enjoy a clambake, burying clams along with lobsters and corn in sand pits lined with seaweed and hot coals. New England colonists quickly made the clambake a culinary custom in that part of the country. And settlers moving from New England to Ohio were not inclined to surrender the custom simply because there were no clams in Ohio. They buried chickens along with corn instead, but continued to call the feast a clambake. "Chickenbake" just doesn't have the same ring.

The sewers of London were not cleaned regularly until the late nineteenth century. One of the brave band of workers who toiled in the depths of the sewers accepted his job because he "didn't like the confinement or the close air in the factories."

Caricatures

Lampooning has always been a favored pastime of mankind, and some gifted artists have turned out some mighty clever caricatures. Here follow some of the best.

Impressions of movie greats by Jack Monte:

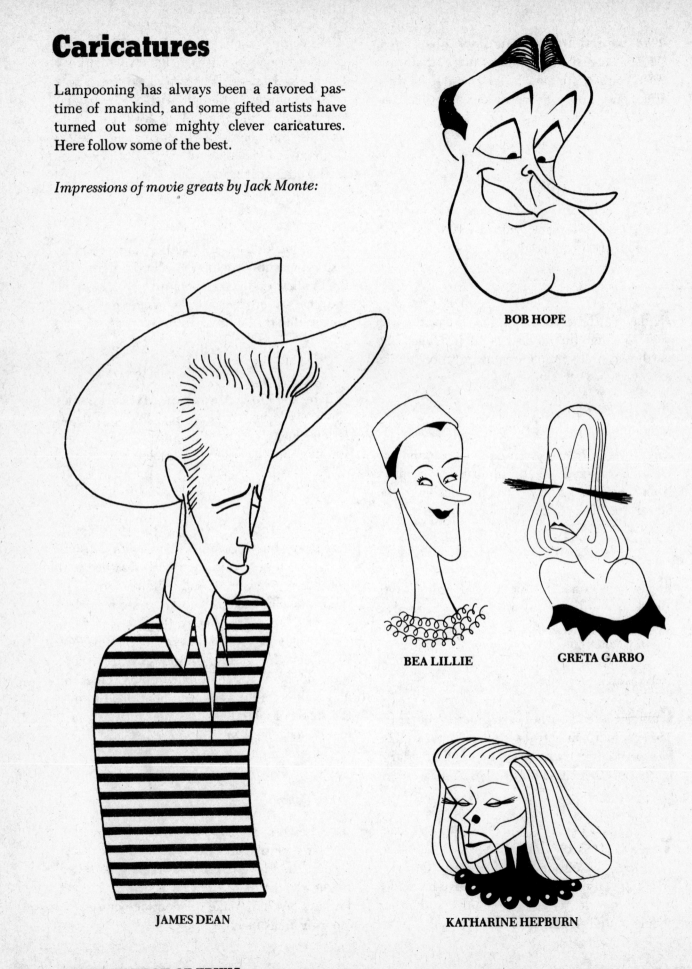

BOB HOPE

BEA LILLIE

GRETA GARBO

JAMES DEAN

KATHARINE HEPBURN

Some of Enrico Caruso's Best *Yes, that's right, the great operatic star, Enrico Caruso, was one of the most gifted caricaturists of our era.*

GUSTAV MAHLER

ARTURO TOSCANINI

ENRICO CARUSO, by himself

GIULIO GATTI-CASAZZA

ALFONSO XII, Spain

The longest shadow on earth is believed to be the one cast by El Pitron Peak on Tenerife, one of the Canary Islands. The mountain rises 12,200 feet above the Atlantic Ocean, and at sunrise and sunset casts a shadow nearly 150 miles long.

The Statue of Liberty in New York City was paid for by donations from French citizens. American donations paid only for the concrete pedestal of the statue.

The record for non-stop Charleston dancing is 22½ hours, set by 23-year-old John Giola in 1926. But what's that compared to the record set by 35-year-old Cathie Connelly in 1969? Cathie did the twist for 101 consecutive hours—more than four days!

Word Play

Is a *skilligalee* something you might cook in, or a bacteria that causes a common disease? Would you buy *calibogus* in the lumberyard, or in a department store? Even if you're a crossword puzzle aficionado, these unusual English words may have you stumped. The answer to both questions is: neither. *Skilligalee* is a kind of soup, although you'd probably never come across any, as it's given mainly to sailors or prisoners; *calibogus* is a concoction made of spruce beer and rum.

Want some more? What's a *cothamore*? A *jobbernowl*? *Rumblegumption*? (Answers: an Irish overcoat; a dunce; a Scottish word for common sense.)

The longest and heaviest of all snakes is the anaconda of South America. Specimens have been reliably reported to be as heavy as 950 pounds, and as long as 37½ feet.

The flying squirrel does not have wings, and, strictly speaking, it cannot fly but only glides from tree to tree. No mammal except the bat is capable of true flight.

King Richard II of England was so careless with royal funds that the monarch once had to pawn his crown to make ends meet.

A statue in the plaza of Guayaquil, Ecuador, bears the name of José Olmedo, that nation's most famous poet. But the figure is actually a representation of Lord Byron, bought by the Ecuadorians in a London junk shop to save money.

A law in Siena, Italy, forbids a woman named Mary to work as a prostitute.

The Dry Liquid

Liquid and *wet* are virtually synonymous, but in fact not all liquids are wet. At room temperature, mercury runs like water and changes its shape according to the container in which it is placed, making it a bona fide liquid. But mercury will not wet your fingers when you touch it.

Saffron, from Spain, enjoys the distinction of being far and away the world's costliest spice. Its average import price in the United States, between 1967 and 1968, exceeded $100.00 per pound, while Portuguese rosemary and Canadian mustard seed have been the least expensive of all spices and herbs. Between 1967 and 1968, the price for these last two has averaged somewhere between 7¢ and 8¢ per pound.

The world's largest ship model—a reproduction of the whaling bark *Lagoda* on exhibit at the Bourne Whaling Museum in New Bedford, Massachusetts—is three-quarters the size of the *Santa Maria* in which Columbus first sailed to America.

Bloodhounds can detect a scent up to 10 days old.

The frog fish catches its prey with a built-in rod and reel. Strands of thin fleshy material are rooted to the top of the fish's head, and these dangling strands attract smaller fish—who are quickly gobbled up by the frog fish.

The Gaboon viper has the longest fangs of any snake. The specimen kept in the Philadelphia Zoo in 1963 was a little careless and bit itself to death.

A certain Ceylonese insect so resembles a leaf that the creature is impossible to detect in a tree. The insect not only looks like a leaf in shape and coloration, but also sways in the wind to imitate perfectly the movements of wind-shaken leaves.

Table knives are a rather late innovation. Until about 1600, diners brought to the table their own knives, which, between meals, served as daggers.

High Spirits

It was Louis Pasteur's research, in the 1850s, into the actions of yeasts and molds, that resulted in the development of controlled fermentation that makes for a consistently good alcoholic product.

Freshly distilled spirits are stored in wooden casks for a minimum of two years to age and mature, during which time, the bite of the tannin is lost. In the United States, spirits are aged at 103 proof (51½% alcohol); in Scotland, the alcoholic content is 124 proof (62% alcohol). Cognac is aged to 140 proof pure, which means 70% alcohol.

The casks in which the spirits are stored are made of American white oak; but French cognac is aged in Limousin oak and black oak. The casks are then stored in draft-free surroundings.

Dorothy Parker named her parrot Onan because the bird spilled its seed upon the ground.

Which Way Is It to "Where Am I?"

When Spanish explorers first reached the Yucatan Peninsula in Mexico and asked the Indians what their homeland was called, they were answered with the word "Yucatan." The Spaniards then promptly gave the peninsula the name it bears today. But what does the word actually mean? Not understanding the explorers' question, the Indians had merely responded: *"Yucatan"*—"What do you want?"

A crossword addict made up what he termed was the largest crossword puzzle in history to be published. It consisted of 25,000 squares, and almost 8,000 definitions. The constructor, Henri Blaise, admitted that his puzzle took him eight years to construct. He estimated it would take the average crossword worker somewhere between three and four months to complete.

The puzzle won't be that easy to market, for it measures no less than three feet in one dimension, and five-and-one-half feet in the other. Furthermore, the definitions fill a book of 170 pages.

A Los Angeles man, named Robert Stilgenbauer, once compiled, but did not publish, a crossword with 3,149 clues across and 3,185 clues down. Stilgenbauer sent out 125,000 copies of the puzzle—which required 11 years to compile—but none was returned correctly completed.

A Gem of a Bet

Among the cleverest historical wagers was that made by Cleopatra of Egypt, with her lover Marc Antony. The crafty "serpent of the Nile" bet the Roman general that she could drink 10 million sistertia ($500,000) worth of wine before leaving the table. Antony rose to the bait, losing the wager when Cleopatra dropped two pearls, valued at the agreed-upon sum, into a glass of wine, which she then drained.

The General Was a Lady!

One of the most astonishing cases of successful masquerade on record was the woman who rose to the rank of inspector surgeon general of the British army disguised as a man. The woman, who called herself "Dr. James Barry," and was probably the first woman to attend the University of Edinburgh Medical School, served as a colonial medical inspector in South Africa and elsewhere in the British Empire for over 40 years. Dr. Barry was not suspected of being a woman until her death, in 1865. Then, a charwoman called in to lay out the general's body declared the sex of the corpse as female. Dr. Barry had achieved a reputation of extraordinary surgical skill (she performed one of the first successful Caesarian sections of modern times in 1826), and was also renowned as a duellist.

The American President who fathered the greatest number of children was John Tyler. Tyler was the father of 14 children by two marriages. Tyler's immediate predecessor, William Henry Harrison, was the second most fertile father among U.S. Presidents. Harrison had 10 children. Curiously, both Presidents were born in Charles City County, Virginia.

Talk about bouncing babies! The heaviest normal newborn infant was a Turkish boy weighing 24 pounds, four ounces, born on June 3, 1961. The lowest birth weight of a surviving baby was a 10-ounce girl. The tiny infant was born in England on June 5, 1938.

In 1976, 134,400 arrests were made for vehicle thefts. In the same year, 1,029,300 people were arrested for driving under the influence of alcohol.

If you're a student having trouble with your homework, take heart. Galileo was a college dropout; Pizarro was illiterate; and Louis Pasteur's university record was mediocre. Even Albert Einstein had trouble finding his first college teaching position.

Jean-Jacques Rousseau wrote a renowned treatise on the education of children, *Emile*. But the French philosopher abandoned his own five children who were brought up in an orphanage!

In the early days of the railroad, disgruntled British railway passengers gave some humorous nicknames to the least efficient lines. The old London, Brighton, and South Coast Railway was not-so-affectionately dubbed "The London, Brighton, and *Slow* Coach Line." The Lancashire and Yorkshire was re-christened "The Languid and Yawning." The Midland and Great Northern became "The Muddle and Get Nowhere."

Not to be outdone, the Americans renamed The Delaware, Lackawana, and Western Railroad "The Delay, Linger, and Wait," while The Chicago, Blufton, and Cincinnati was known as "The Corned Beed and Cabbage Railroad." The Leavenworth, Kansas, and Western achieved notoriety as "The Leave Kansas and Walk." But the most abused line was the Minneapolis and St. Louis, which was variously called "The Misery and Short Life," "The Maimed and Still Limping," and "The Midnight and Still Later."

Everyone knows that Idaho is the largest producer of potatoes in the United States. But did you know that (in 1977) North Carolina was the largest tobacco grower, Texas the largest producer of cotton, Illinois the largest for corn, and Kansas the largest for wheat.

Is bird's nest soup, the Chinese delicacy, really made with birds' nests? Yes, it is! Certain species of the swift—which are found in Asia, the Phillipines, and some islands in the Indian and Pacific oceans—build edible nests, which are sought out by Chinese epicures. It may quench your appetite for this exotic fare, however, to learn that the nests are made of dried mucus, secreted by the swifts' salivary glands.

The cigarette with the highest tar content on the market has 64 times as much tar as the cigarette with the lowest tar content. According to a Federal Trade Commission report, a regular-sized Carlton 70 filter cigarette contains less than one-half milligram of tar. A Players regular non-filter, from the hard pack, contains 32 milligrams tar.

Namesakes

These units of measurement, among others, were named after scientists: the ohm, the volt, coulomb, ampere, hertz, and joule.

The unit of electrical resistance known as the *ohm* was named after the German physicist Georg Simon Ohm, who died in 1854.

The *volt*, unit of electromotor force, was named after Alessandro Volta, the Italian pioneer of electrical science.

The *coulomb*, a unit of electric charge, can claim French physicist Charles de Coulomb as its namesake. Coulomb worked with electricity and magnetism.

The *ampere* was named after Andre-Marie Ampere, the French physicist who developed the science of electro-magnetism.

The *hertz*, a unit of electromatic or radio waves, was named after Heinrich Hertz, a 19th-century German physicist.

And the *joule*, a unit of work or energy, takes its name from James Prescott Joule, an English physicist of the 19th century who made discoveries in thermodynamics.

Watch the Birdie

Watch all the metamorphoses and the styles that artists have devised to portray a bird. On these pages, you will find eight drawings, and each one of them is drawn in a highly different style. Artist's license, of course.

From Mark Twain's Library of Humor, *illustrated by* E.W. Kemble.

From Quaint Cuts in the Chap Book Style *by* Joseph Crawhall, *published by Dover in New York in 1974.*

From London's Punch.

From Satire in the Fight for Peace, *published in Moscow in 1972.*

From the Wilhelm Butch Album, *published in New York, presumably in the 1890s.*

From Curious Woodcuts of Fanciful and Real Beasts *by Konrad Gesner, published in 1971 by Dover Publishing in New York City.*

From Calligraphy *by Johann Georg Schwander, published in 1958 by Dover Publications.*

Scene de la Vie Privee et Publique des Animaux, *published in Paris in 1842. The drawing is by the renowned Grandville.*

He Got It for Peanuts

The first American to be honored by a commemorative statue in India was George Washington Carver, whose numerous discoveries of industrial uses for farm products included a large variety of peanut products. In 1947, five years after Carver's death, the peanut growers of India erected a monument to the black inventor in Bombay. The peanut wizard was also honored by the American Congress, which made Carver's Missouri birthplace a national monument in 1943.

Upon assuming the consulship in 60 B.C., one of Julius Caesar's first acts was to establish a daily bulletin of government announcements, the *Acta Diurna,* to post in the forum. Posted proclamations and the announcements of town criers—and the grapevine—provided the news to many city residents for centuries, but it wasn't until the 17th century that newspapers proper began to spring up around Europe on a regular basis.

In the late 17th century, the German monarch Frederick William decided that the potato could solve his nation's food shortage, and decreed that all peasants should plant spuds. Those who refused would have their noses and ears cut off! It's unknown how many farmers lost their facial features because of the bog apple, but Frederick's decree may help explain why potatoes have become so popular in Germany.

To settle an oft-heard dispute: no, the sweet potato and the yam are not the same vegetable. The yam is, in fact, almost never seen in this country—no matter what food packagers claim to the countrary!

During the 19th century, some umbrellas were designed with one protruding side to offer protection for the bustle that most women wore in those days.

Delaware was the first state admitted to the Union. The last of the 13 original colonies to be admitted was Rhode Island, which joined on May 29, 1790, over two years after Delaware had ratified the Constitution.

West Point, the U.S. Military Academy, was established in 1802, when the academy graduated but two of its 10 students. There are now five military service academies in this country. Besides West Point and the U.S. Naval Academy in Annapolis, Maryland, the other service academies are: the U.S. Air Force Academy, Colorado Springs, Colorado; the U.S. Coast Guard Academy, New London, Connecticut; and the U.S. Merchant Marine Academy, Kings Point, New York.

Amor, Amor

John Barrymore was indubitably the most amourous actor in Hollywood. In the title role in the film *Don Juan,* which premiered at Warner's Theatre in New York on August 6, 1926, Barrymore kissed his various leading ladies a total of 191 times in the two hour and 47 minute duration of the picture. That was an average of one kiss every 53 seconds!

A Canadian by the name of John Wilson holds the record for the greatest number of stories in a house of cards—39 stories in a tower of 1,240 cards. Joe E. Whitlam of England bettered that feat by building a house of 73 stories—a stupendous 13 feet, 10¼ inches—but Joe cheated a bit by bending some cards into angle supports.

Fireworks

American audiences of the 1950s expected musical concerts to be enlivened with all manner of circus-like pyrotechnics. To please the crowds, an idiosyncratic French conductor named Louis Julien staged a special performance of *The Fireman's Quadrille* at the Crystal Palace in New York, on June 15, 1854.

Without warning the spectators what was to come, Julien arranged, at the climax of the piece, for fire engine bells to clang in the streets; the hall's windows to be smashed, and flames to burst through the roof. Then, firemen rushed into the auditorium and turned their hoses on the blaze. The audience was so taken in by "Crazy Julien's" realism, that when the piece was finished, a few minutes after the conflagration had been extinguished, many of the ladies were in a swoon, and other auditors were crowding each other to the exits.

Ironically, four years later, the Crystal Palace burned to the ground. Two years later, "Crazy Julien" literally went insane, and died.

When Lizzie Borden took her famous ax (if she did, that is), she not only undid her mother and father, but close to 2,000 American marriages. According to the *New York Times*, the controversy about Miss Borden's guilt or innocence—a question still unsettled today—was cited as the cause of 1,900 marital disputes that ended in divorce.

Culinary Stardom

The last word in gastronomic excellence today is the guide published by the Michelin Corporation, a French tire firm. Michelin annually rates restaurants in thousands of towns and cities, awarding each from zero to three stars accoring to culinary quality. One star indicates good quality in its class; two stars suggests the restaurant is well worth a detour; and three ranks the establishment among the best in the world.

In a recent year, Michelin rated a total of 3,036 restaurants in France: 2,382 were rated by unstarred; 581 received one star; 62 received two stars; and only 11 restaurants earned the highest Michelin compliment of three stars. Five of these gastronomic palaces were in Paris.

The rose has been a symbol of secrecy since classical times. In 16th century England, a rose was sometimes worn behind the ear by servants, tavern workers, and others to indicate that the wearer heard all and told nothing. In Germany, roses in a dining room suggested that diners could speak freely without fear that their secrets would travel beyond the room. The expression *sub rosa*, "under the rose," is thought to originate in the custom of carving a rose over the door of the confessional in a Catholic church.

If you ever send a letter to someone who lives in a city or town with the name of Franklin, you'd better be sure to write the name of the state carefully. There are 28 states in the nation with a city or town named Franklin!

Other city names that appear in many states include Washington, Clinton, Fairfield, Arlington, Ashland, Chester, Burlington, Georgetown, Greenville, Jefferson, Jackson, Kingston, Madison, Princeton, Oxford, Springfield, and Troy.

The Kremlin is the largest fortress in Europe

Today, Moscow's Kremlin is synonymous with the government of the Soviet Union. But the Kremlin is also a construction of extraordinary beauty and size. In fact, this age-old complex is the largest fortress in all Europe.

In medieval Russia, a kremlin was a walled bastion within a city which provided protection for the rulers who resided there, and served as the administrative and religious center of the surrounding district. A kremlin customarily included palaces, churches, barracks, storehouses, and markets, and hence, was a small city in itself.

The kremlin at Moscow, now known simply as the Kremlin, was the seat of the Czarist government until 1712, when the Russian capital was moved to St. Petersburg (now Leningrad). In 1918, after the Bolshevik Revolution, the capital was relocated in Moscow, and the Kremlin became the center of administration for the Soviet Union.

This massive city-within-a-city was built in stages over a period of six centuries. The first stone structures were erected in 1365, facets that adorn its facades. The Grand Palace, built in the 19th century, is the largest building within the Kremlin, and today houses the Supreme Soviet, the parliament of the Soviet Union.

The Spasskaya Tower, one of the Kremlin's 20 gate towers, is the most famous tower in all Russia. Nearby, the 270-foot Ivan the Great Bell Tower—the highest structure in the Kremlin—rises to a golden onion-shaped dome.

The renowned King of Bells, the largest bell in the world, is on display near the Bell

and the Czar Ivan III rebuilt the entire complex a century later. Over the years, the Kremlin has many times survived the destruction of Moscow itself. In 1812, during Napoleon's occupation, the Kremlin alone withstood the inferno that burned almost the entire city to the ground.

The Kremlin is situated on a small hill overlooking the Moscow River. The fortress consists of a complex of varied buildings surrounded by a triangular wall one-and-one-quarter miles around. In all, the Kremlin extends over an area of 90 acres.

Many of the structures comprised in the Kremlin are world-famous in themselves. The Palace of Facets, built by Italian architects in the late 15th century, is a charming milk-white palace noted for the diamond-shaped

Tower. This gigantic instrument, cast in 1733, weighs 216 tons and is over 20 feet high. Twenty-four men were required to swing its clapper. Unfortunately, the bell fell to the ground after only three years of use, and has not been tolled since.

The Kremlin also contains the largest cannon in the world, a gun so huge it has never been fired.

On the eastern side of the Kremlin lies the famed Red Square, the site of the incredibly beautiful cathedral of St. Basil. This ornate church, built in the later 16th century, is remarkable for its multi-colored onion-shaped domes. Another feature of Red Square is the black marble tomb of Lenin.

The diligence and fortitude of miner W.H. Schmidt have probably never been surpassed. From 1906 to 1938, Schmidt worked alone, tunneling 2,000 feet through a granite mountain in Kern County, California. Schmidt had staked a claim on the mountain, but being too poor to buy modern tools or hire assistants, he had to dig and transport the ore singlehandedly. His only tools were a modest jack-hammer, a lantern, and a truck, which Schmidt pushed himself by hand, to remove the loosened granite.

A tragic miscarriage of justice occurred in the plagiarism suit brought against playwright Richard Tully in 1912, by a woman who claimed that Tully's *The Bird of Paradise* was an imitation of a play she had written. Oddly enough, the woman could produce no manuscript of her own play for twelve years, but when she finally came up with a script, in 1924, the case was reopened, and the woman was awarded $781,990 in damages.

Tully appealed; and in 1930, the New York State Court of Appeals reversed the decision, finding no similarity whatsoever between the two dramas. But it was a pyrrhic victory for Tully, who had been wiped out financially by the court costs, and was so traumatized by the suit that he could not write another word for the remaining 15 years of his life.

The colloquial saying, "not worth a tinker's damn" has nothing to do with the value of a plumber's oath. The phrase is a corruption of "not worth a tinker's *dam*," a dam being the small piece of clay placed around a leak to hold the melted solder in place until it hardened around the hole. The soft clay could be used only once; then it was thrown away. Therefore, something of little value was said to be "not worth a tinker's dam."

One of the most oft-moved corpses in history was that of Abraham Lincoln, whose body was moved 17 times following his burial in 1865. The tranfers were motivated primarily to prevent theft of the body for purposes of ransom. Indeed, the fear was well-founded, for in 1876, six men actually succeeded in pilfering the former President's remains, although the graverobbers were discovered by the nightwatchman as they were lifting the coffin out of its tomb. The casket was then hidden under a pile of scrap lumber in a cellar, where it remained for two years. Since 1901, Lincoln's coffin has resided in a locked steel cage buried in solid cement 10 feet under the floor of Lincoln's mausoleum in Oak Ridge Cemetery, Springfield, Illinois.

Big-Time Game Hunter

The Marquess of Ripon, a late 18-century British statesman, was also an unsurpassed big-game hunter. Between 1867 and 1900, the Marquess bagged 370,728 game animals, including tigers, buffalo, deer, and rhinoceroses. That's an average of 216 animals a week. But the Marquess actually shot over 500,000 animals in his lifetime, although only about ⅗ of his kills were recorded by his secretary. The hardy hunter died in 1909, at the age of 82, while shooting birds on his estate.

The restaurant is such a seemingly natural and necessary institution that you'd suspect it's been with us for as long as man has lived in cities. But the restaurant, as we know it today, is a surprisingly recent development. That's not to say there weren't any commercial eating places before our time. But the menu, with its choice of dishes, is only about 200 years old. The fact is that the diner or coffee shop in which you may have lunch today offers more of a menu selection than the best restaurants of the world did just a few centuries back.

Compared to modern footwear, the shoes of earlier centuries were, for the most part, highly uncomfortable. It wasn't until the invention in 1818 of the left-shoe last and the right-shoe last that the left shoe was constructed differently from the right shoe. Prior to that, either shoe could be worn on either foot with equal discomfort!

Mission Impossible

Evangelist John Alexander Dowie, who at the turn of the century succeeded in establishing a new religion and buying and constructing Zion City, Illinois as the official dwelling place of his converts, set out, in 1903, "to save sinful New York." Dowie, who called himself "Elijah the Restorer," brought 3,000 of his followers along to Madison Square Garden, where in the midst of the evangelist's first sermon, the entire audience walked out in disgust. After a month of failing to convert New Yorkers to Zionism—either by small daily meetings or the distribution of Zionist literature—Elijah and his "angels" departed, having spend $300,000 on their vain effort to convert New Yorkers from vanity.

If ever a man tried to get to Heaven it was Ignatious Trebitsch of Hungary. Born a Jew in 1789, Trebitsch went to Germany at the age of 18, and was baptized in the Lutheran faith. Later, he removed to England, where he became a Quaker and a member of Parliament, then an Anglican curate, a German spy, and a Presbyterian missionary to Canada. After returning to Germany for awhile following World War I, Trebitsch spent the last 17 years of his life as a Buddhist monk, and died in a Shanghai monastery in 1943. Considering how much time he spent as a man of the cloth—albeit his coat was of many colors—it is hoped that Trebitsch was forgiven by God for his brief stint as a forger and convict durng his sojourn in England.

The first Sunday Schools had nothing to do with the propogation of religious teachings, and were, in fact, frowned on by many religious denominations as a desecration of the Sabbath. In 1780, in the slums of Gloucester, England, classes were held on Sunday to teach the three Rs to illiterate child laborers, who worked the other six days of the week from sunup to sundown. Because the classes were held on the Sabbath, the schools came to be known as Sunday Schools.

Tilt!

On June 19, 1939, the city of Atlanta enacted the first pinball legislation in the United States. The bill prohibited the use of the machines and provided for a $20 fine and a 30-day work sentence for violators.

Until the early 1930s, the natives of a community on the Danish island of Jutland always bowed before a white wall outside the door of their church when entering or leaving the house of worship. Questioned as to the reason for their homage to the blank wall, the Jutland worshipers were unable to give the cause. A historian from Copenhagen made an investigation, and discovered, under the wall's coats of paint, a picture of the Virgin Mary, painted over during the 16th century Reformation as idolotrous. Thus; for four centuries, custom alone had been responsible for the parishoners' genuflections to the wall.

There's been no peace for the residents of Aurora, Texas since April 19, 1897. On that day, a cigar-shaped vehicle, believed to be a ship from outer space, crashed through the window of Judge J.S. Proctor, killing its only passenger. The extra-terrestrial visitor—if such he was—was given a Christian burial in the cemetery at Aurora, but ever since, U.F.O. watchers have been besieging the small cow-community of 273 inhabitants with demands that the body of the outerspaceman be exhumed for examination. Unfortunately, the mysterious visitor's grave-marker was stolen a few years ago, and now no one knows exactly were to dig.

Pinball Wizard

In these days when golfers, tennis players, and other sportsmen are bringing home huge checks for tournament victories, can pinball players be far behind? The first annual Maryland Pinball Championship, held in June, 1979, drew 25,000 participants to more than 100 tournament locations throughout the state. Winners in various categories shared a $25,000 purse, and the top finisher also brought home his choice of any pinball game used in the tournament. Gary Wease, a 26-year-old sales manager, was crowned Grand Pinball Wizard for his victory in the Class A finals.

There's more to come, too. Promoters of the tourney are now thinking about a Mid-Atlantic tournament in the near future, set at up to 500 locations around the world.

John Heidegger, master of the king's revels in 18th-century England, was reputedly the ugliest man of his day—and was proud of the fact. Weary of Heidegger's boasts, British statesman Lord Chesterfield declared that he had seen many a visage more hideous than Heidegger's. The Swiss-born impressario promptly disputed Chesterfield's claim, and the upshot was a 50-guinea wager that Chesterfield could not produce, within a week, anyone uglier than Heidegger.

The English nobleman set out for the seamier sections of London, and there he found a woman whose grotesque features delighted his eyes. Chesterfield escorted the loathly lady in triumph to his friends. But Heidegger, refusing to yield the palm of repulsiveness, removed the hag's hat and set it on his own head. The woman took one look at the wearer of her hat and nearly swooned—so Heidegger won the wager.

Laconic—or pithy—speech, originated in Laconia, the ancient Greek country of which Sparta (Lacedaemon) was the capital. The Laconians were famous for their economical way with words. Julius Caesar's *Veni, vidi, vici* ("I came, I saw, I overcame") is classic laconic speech. But even terser was the reply sent by the Spartans to Philip of Macedon, who boasted, "If I enter Laconia, I will level Lacedaemon to the ground." The Laconic response was one word: *If.*

A marble slab used as a game board in the early days of Christian Rome bears a cross and the inscription: "Christ grants aid and victory to dicers if they write His Name when they roll. Amen."

The banana, whose prevalence in Central America has given rise to the phrase "Banana Republic," is actually a native of Asia.

A Slothful Creature

You probably know that the cheetah is the fastest animal on earth. But do you know the slowest-moving land mammal? It's the ai, or three-toed sloth. This South American mammal spends almost his entire life clinging to the trunk of a tree or hanging upside down from a branch. The ai cannot walk—if he ever moves along the ground, he does so by pulling his body along with his claws. And since it may take the ai a month to digest his food, his belly is almost continually filled!

Should some rude creature on the ground below disturb a slumbering ai, the lazy fellow can investigate the noise-maker with a minimum of effort—due to an unusual arrangement of neck vertebrae, an ai can turn his head through a 270-degree angle!

One of the most misquoted lines of English poetry is from Thomas Grey's *Elegy in a Country Churchyard*. The line, which reads, "Far from the madding crowd's ignoble strife," if often quoted as "Far from the *maddening* crowd's ignoble strife." The word *maddening* means wild, raving, or mad. Despite Thomas Hardy's popularization of the phrase by entitling one of his novels *Far From the Madding Crowd*, the misconception that the word is *maddening* persists.

Panorama of the Mississippi may not be the best picture ever painted, but it is certainly the longest. Completed by John Banvard in 1846, the painting was 12 feet wide and actually more than three miles in length. The *Panorama*, which required two hours to be shown, was exhibited by being gradually unfurled between two upright revolving cylinders on the stages of large auditoriums throughout the world. The picture's world tour earned about $200,000, a huge sum at the time.

Today, talking dolls and mechanical men abound, but perhaps the most fascinating automaton ever devised was built by Frenchman Jean Maillardet in 1842. It was given to the Franklin Institute in Philadelphia in the 1920s. The robot is the figure of a small girl, who draws pictures and writes poetry in French and English with pen and ink in a notebook placed on a desk before which she kneels. Since 1920 when the *Wunderstuk* first went on view, visitors to the museum have been allowed to take home one of the mechanicacl girl's compositions as a souvenir. The automaton was presented to the Institute after being discovered in a fire, and arrived in complete disarray, with all its wires and wheels twisted, and with many parts missing. But the Institute's technicians were able to restore the machine to working order, and over the years, the resurrected robot has delighted scores of visitors to the museum.

The smallest painting ever produced is probably a winter landscape painted by an unknown Amrican in the 1940s, measuring one 65th a square inch in area. The artist, having little room to maneuver, painted the landscape, in oils, with a brush composed of one single human hair.

Knot Bad!

Intricate tapestries adorn the walls of many of the world's museums, but the Ardebil Carpet, which hangs in the Victoria and Albert Museum in London, is probably the most astonishing rug in history. Completed in 1540, in Ardebil, Persia, the carpet, which measures 34.5 feet by 17.5 feet, contains 29,600,000 knots, or 340 knots per square inch. After hanging in the Mosque at Ardebil for three-and-a-half centuries, the carpet was sold to the Victoria and Albert Museum in 1893. It has been valued at $500,000.

Today, most jewelry adorns the hands, faces, and necks of women. But in ancient Rome, men sported more baubles and bangles than their mates. In fact, unmarried Roman girls were actually prohibited by law from wearing pearls. The pearls were worn instead by young men, who placed the pearls in tiny bells which, hanging from their ears, tinkled gaily.

Now You See It, Now You Don't

Falcon Island, 2,000 miles east of Australia, has been putting on a disappearing act for the last sixty years. In 1913, the tiny island—which was actually the peak of a submarine volcano—disappeared without warning under the sea. Thirteen years later, after a series of volcanic eruptions, the island reappeared and remained a tiny part of the British Empire until 1949, when the island suddenly disappeared again.

Five golf partners teed off at the Ithaca Country Club one fine summer day in 1938, and achieved one of the most remarkable scores in the entire history of golf. Playing a short par-three hole, the five golfers posted respective scores of 1, 2, 3, 4, and 5.

Track star Glenn Cunningham, for years the record-holder for the indoor mile, had a toeless left foot.

Among the many things that have been manufactured to coddle the owners of pets are a pair of doggie sunglasses, doggie pajamas, and for the Hassidic canine, a dog yarmulka.

What country boasts the safest drivers? Surprisingly, the Philippines have the lowest traffic fatality rate of any nation, 1.5 deaths per 100,000 population. Though you might guess that the United States is plagued with the most reckless drivers in the world, four other countries show a worse record. Who these are is likely to surprise you—Canada, Australia, West Germany, and Austria. Austria, at the bottom of the barrel, has a rate of 31.9 traffic deaths per 100,000 population. The United States averages 26.7.

Before eating anything, a raccoon will first wash the food in the nearest available water. Some raccoons will go hungry rather than eat unwashed food; others will go through the motions of washing when there is no water around.

The enchanting island village of Mont-St.-Michel, a popular tourist attraction off the coast of Normandy, was actually part of the mainland of France until 725. In that year, a tremendous earthquake shook the coast and left the city surrounded by water.

As Black As Snow?

We say "as white as snow," but the Japanese, repeating the phrase on January 31, 1925, laughed; and, on December 6, 1926, the French thought of the expression and howled. For on the first date, snow fell on Japan and it was *gray;* and at the later date, snow fell in France and it was *black!*

Dr. Fujiwara, of Japan's Tokyo Observatory, explained that the odd event was due to a mixture of snow and ashes from nearby volcanoes. On the other hand, the French could offer no explanation. They just looked at the snow and shrugged their shoulders.

Sidney Bechet was the first man to play a number of musical instruments in recording a song. He used six in making *The Sheik of Araby,* released in 1941. The feat was accomplished by recording the first instrument, re-recording it while the second was played in the studio, and so on until the disc contained the parts of all six instruments—soprano sax, clarinet, tenor sax, piano, bass fiddle, and drums.

Leafing Through History

Although it was Sir Walter Raleigh who smoked a bowl of tobacco before the Queen and was promptly rewarded with a dousing by a member of the court who thought Walter was burning, it was the Spanish explorers who discovered the Aztecs smoking crushed tobacco leaves in corn husks some 100 years earlier. Cigarette smoking spread rapidly to Spain, with the beggars of Seville getting credit for the first paper-wrapped variety.

Smoking didn't become popular in Northern Europe until the 1850s, when British soldiers brought Russian cigarettes back from the Crimean War. At the same time, cigarette manufacture and tobacco cultivation spread to the United States, where machinery was developed to replace the tedious hand-rolled technique.

Bats are not blind, but their vision is extremely poor. These winged mammals actually fly by radar, emitting high-pitched sounds from their throats and picking up the echoes with their super-sensitive ears.

In 1946, casting for distance, Wilbur Brooks of Indianapolis set his toe in the dirt, took a deep breath, and sent ⅝ of an ounce of bait 427 feet for a world's record. Out Wilbur's way the fish never knew what hit them!

Young puffins are fed and fed until they grow larger than their overworked parents. Then their parents fly away. The youngsters are too fat to start food-searching on their own, but well larded as they are, they don't starve. They live off their stored fat, gradually getting thin enough to go out on their own.

The total cost of constructing the Eiffel Tower in Paris was recovered from sightseers' fees during the first year after the Tower's completion.

Three thousand feet below the sea's surface, its waters are pitch black. Not even a tiny bit of the sun's light can penetrate down more than half a mile. Sea creatures that live at depths below 3,000 feet have been found to be blind or to possess their own phosphorescent "lighting system."

Through the centuries, man has made a great to-do about his hair. Some of the ancients went to great extremes in caring for their beards. The Lords of Nineveh oiled and curled their beards. The Kings of Persia plaited their hirsutulous draperies with golden thread. Early French kings daintily tied their whiskers with silken ribbons. Even today, the Sikhs of India dye their beards, for it is only a flaming red patch that will establish a Sikh as a man among men.

The cockroach is one of the hardiest, simplest, and most pesky creatures on earth—and also one of the oldest. The cockroach has existed on earth, in its modern form, for some 250 million years!

Figure this one out: In *Gulliver's Travels*, Jonathan Swift claimed that Mars had two moons, and described both their size and the time each required to turn once on its axis. More than a century was to pass before scientists discovered either moon. When they did, it was found that Swift's descriptions were uncannily accurate!

The names of the cards in a deck of playing cards—ace, king, queen, jack, ten, nine, etc.—contain a total of precisely 52 letters, the same number as there are cards in the deck!

A research company recently reported that the largest single cause of error in business systems was illegible handwriting! According to the report, more than $100 million is lost each year by American businesses due to mistakes traced to poor writing. The most common culprits are billing errors, illegibly written orders, and garbled records.

Georges Braque is the only artist whose works have been exhibited at the Louvre, in Paris, within 60 years of the artist's death.

Of all woodwind instruments, the oboe is considered the hardest to master. Of all brass instruments, the French horn is generally considered the most difficult to play correctly.

The Best Batters

A glance at baseball's all-time record holders will demonstrate that, in terms of endurance and versatility, Babe Ruth was not the most dominant hitter in the sport's history. In fact, Ruth leads all batters in only one major category: bases on balls.

Hank Aaron leads all batters in games played, at bats, extra-base hits, runs batted in, and total bases, in addition to home runs. Ty Cobb leads in batting average, runs, hits, and stolen bases.

Mickey Mantle is presently the leader in strikeouts, with 1,710, but either Lou Brock or Willie Stargell may soon break Mick's record.

You think you're pretty good at ping pong, eh? Well listen to this: In a 1936 table tennis tournament, two European players volleyed the opening serve for two hours, 12 minutes before the first point of the game was recorded!

The last surviving participant of the Boston Tea Party did not die until 1851, at the age of 115. The last surviving signer of the Declaration of Independence, Charles Carroll, died in 1832, at age 95.

The Mexican jumping bean is not a bean, but a seed. And it does not "jump," but rolls and tumbles due to tiny moth larvae that live part of their lives inside the beans.

The movement of the bean results from the larva's attempts to escape direct sunlight, which would render the inside of the seed too hot for comfort. The larva shifts about inside its temporary home, turning and tumbling the seed until it finds a patch of shady ground.

Only four gems are considered precious in today's jewelry market. The four gems are diamond, emerald, corundum in two forms (ruby and sapphire), and chrysoberyl. Pearl, which is an organic substance rather than a mineral, is also considered precious.

There are over 20,000 slot machines in the casinos of Las Vegas, Nevada—and in the city's supermarkets, drugstores, liquor stores, and restaurants. The average resident of the city spends about $800 a year in gambling casinos.

The French horn is a brass instrument; the English horn is a woodwind, while the trumpet marine is the name of a stringed instrument, and is not a horn at all.

The Board of Councilmen in Canton, Mississippi, once passed a resolution that stipulated:

"1. We shall build a new jail.

2. The new jail will be built out of the materials of the old jail.

3. The old jail will be used until the new jail is finished."

About 70 people are shot to death with a handgun in the United States *each day!* About 75 percent of these shootings take place between family members or close friends.

An annual growth rate in the world's population of just two percent would result in a doubling of the population every 35 years! The present birth rate is about 1.8 percent.

Architecture is often a thankless job. We have no idea today who designed and built many of the most notable structures on earth, including the Taj Mahal, the Pyramid at Giza, and most medieval cathedrals.

The 11th-century Pope Benedict IX was 23 years old when he *died!* He had reigned for 12 years, after becoming pope at the age of 11!

Under Cover

The English didn't invent the umbrella, but they did develop the first practical waterproof bumbershoot, late in the 17th century. The man usually credited with popularizing the umbrella in London was one John Hanway, a 17th-century traveler who brought the brolly to England from Portugal. Hanway created quite a stir by strolling through London under the strange contraption in all kinds of weather, and was often greeted by jokes from passersby. He was especially likely to suffer abuse from coachmen, who feared the popularity of such a device would cut into their trade.

Religious Londoners objected to the umbrella on moral grounds—after all, the purpose of heavenly rain was to make people wet. But despite these objections, the use of the umbrella spread steadily in the showery city. For some time, they were called Hanways in honor of their eccentric pioneer.

Strange Musical Instruments

Throughout the centuries, man has attempted to make better and newer and weirder musical instruments, the better to celebrate his joy.

The *Appolonicon* was a gigantic instrument which could be made to sound like a symphony orchestra. First played publicly in London in 1817, the Appolonicon was played automatically or manually. The brilliant arrangement of its five keyboards enabled five persons to play a composition together.

The largest stringed instrument ever constructed for a single player was a *pantaleon* played by George Noel in England in 1767. Played with wooden mallets like a xylophone, the instrument consisted of 276 gut and metal strings stretched over a horizontal soundboard which was 11 feet long by five feet wide.

Since the violin was introduced in the 1600s, several devices have been invented for playing the instrument automatically. But the only one to vibrate the strings with a bow was the *violonista*, which could be found in penny arcades in the early 1920s. The machine was about three feet long, two feet high, and two feet wide, It was electrically operated and controlled by air flowing through the perforations of a music roll.

A certain Austrian by the name of Karl Waetzel, who lived during the last century, had a particularly inventive turn of mind. He built a fabulous conglomeration of musical instruments which he called the *panomonico*, an instrument which could be played by a single person. The panomonico included 150 flageolets, 150 flutes, 50 oboes, 18 trumpets, five fanfares, three drums, and two kettledrums. The whole thing totaled 378 instruments. Waetzel's fantastic invention was purchased by Archduke Charles of Austria. The irony was that the Duke used the panomonico not to produce beautiful music, but for the purpose of annoying noisy courtiers of his royal household.

Playing the Sang, *a Chinese musical instrument.*

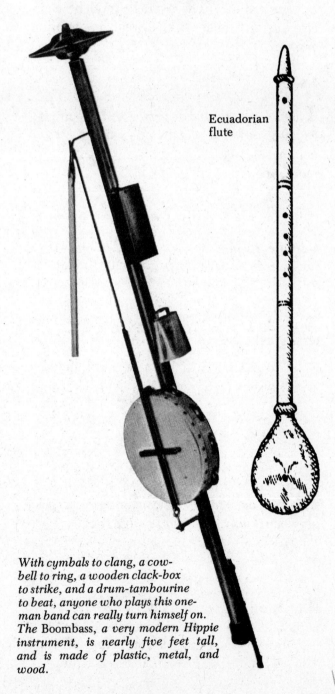

Ecuadorian flute

With cymbals to clang, a cowbell to ring, a wooden clack-box to strike, and a drum-tambourine to beat, anyone who plays this one-man band can really turn himself on. The Boombass, a very modern Hippie instrument, is nearly five feet tall, and is made of plastic, metal, and wood.

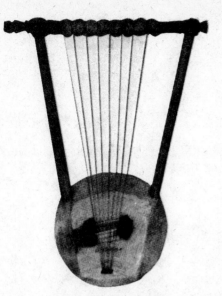

Around 1850, Don Jose Gallegos, of Malaga, invented a musical instrument which he called the Guitarpa. It combined a harp, a guitar, and a violin-cello, and had 35 strings. Twenty-six strings and 21 pegs acted upon the harp. Six strings belonged to the Spanish guitar, while three silver strings and 18 pegs managed the violincello. The pedestal by which the instrument was supported was so constructed that the Guitarpa could be either elevated or lowered at the musician's pleasure

The nyatiti is made of wood, string, beeswax, and pieces of reed. This eight-string Luo harp is a traditional musical instrument of a major tribe in Kenya.

A Chinese Gong, or—as one might say today—a super gong.

The 300-year-old secret of Stradivarius remains unsolved

Antonius Stradivarius was born in 1644. Initially a woodcarver, he learned to play the violin and consequently became interested in the making of violins. At 18, he became an apprentice to Niccolo Amati, the famous violinmaker of Cremona.

In 1680, Stradivarius left Amati's shop and began to work for himself. He experimented with his violins, giving them many different shapes. He was obsessed with the desire to make his violin sound as lovely as a beautiful human voice. He decorated his violins so exquisitely—inlaying them with mother of pearl and ivory and ebony—that not only are they the world's most wonderful violins because of their exquisite tone, but they are also the most beautiful violins ever created.

By the time he was 40 years old, Stradivarius was a renowned and extremely wealthy man. He kept his notes safely locked up. Not even his two sons, who labored with him in his workshop, knew his secrets. During his long life of 94 years, he made at least 1,116 instruments.

The hunt for the secret of Stradivarius has been carried on ever since his death in 1737. His violins have been carefully measured and copied in every detail, and some very fine violins have been made; but they have never attained the perfection of the master's instruments. Vuillane, a famous French violinmaker of the early 1800s, spent all his life searching for the secrets of the great Stradivarius. At last, he finally got in touch with Giacomo Stradivarius, the great grandson of the master. Giacomo told Vuillane that he had discovered in an old family Bible a formula for varnish which he believed to have been Antonius Stradivarius's own special formula. Giacomo said he had told no one about it and, even though he was sorely tempted during financial straits to sell it, he had made the decision that he would give nobody the priceless prescription except a member of the family, should any one of them decide to pursue the trade of violinmaker.

Diverse suppositions have been made about what makes the violins of Stradivarius supreme. Some have attributed the characteristic sound of his violins to the physical properties of the wood, or to the shape of the instruments; others maintain that the secret lay in the interrelation of the various parts of the instruments. Still others regard the answer as the special pitch which Stradivarius derived from the sap of trees then growing in Italy which have since disappeared. But the most widely believed theory is that Stradivarius's secret lies in the special composition of the varnish with which he coated his violins. Chemists have attempted to analyze the composition, and indeed, some violinmakers have greatly improved the tone of their violins by imitating as closely as possible the composition of Stradivarius's varnish. Nevertheless, no one has been able to discover his secret. It is as much a mystery today as it was nearly 250 years ago.

On April 14, 1910, a record 12,226 paid customers attended the opening-day ceremonies of the baseball season in Washington, D.C., and saw President William H. Taft throw out the first ball. Taft was the first President to perform the honored task, and the baseball season has traditionally begun the same way ever since.

In this century, more than 1,600 people have been publicly whipped in Delaware, where an old law provides this form of outdated punishment for the perpetrators of 24 minor crimes.

Sheer Coincidence

In 1925, a staff composer for Witmark, the New York music publisher, wrote a song called "Me Neenyah." The company printed and copyrighted it at once. Soon after, copies were sent to Europe, and a music publisher in Germany informed Witmark that the song was an infringement on one which had been copyrighted in Germany in 1924. Witmark and his composer compared the two pieces and found them identical, note for note, with the exception of one half-tone. Clearly, it was a coincidence—a composer might steal a few bars but not an entire melody. The German publisher and Witmark agreed on this point, and the matter was dropped.

To date, we have had only one lefthanded President, James A. Garfield, and even he was subjected to the conversion attempts of his parents. Though eventually he learned how to write with his right hand, he did not abandon the use of his naturally dominant left. Legend has it that our 20th President once demonstrated his ambidextrous powers by writing Latin with one hand while he wrote in Greek with the other.

Did you know that when you eat tapioca pudding, you're eating a dish made from the starch of the Brazilian cassava root?

In 17th-century America, "trials by touch" were held in which the defendant in a murder case was forced to touch the body of the victim to see if the corpse "gave a sign." The belief was that if the murderer touched the body of the victim, the corpse would move or somehow indicate the individual's guilt.

The letter used most in the English language is *e*, followed by *t, a, i, s, o, n, h, r,* and *d*, in that order. But the letter *s* begins more English words than any other letter, far surpassing its nearest rival, the letter *c*.

The avocado has three singular features: (1) its protein content is greater than that of any other fruit; (2) its ripeness can be determined only by a laboratory test of its oil content; and (3) its growth is sometimes so prolific that trees have collapsed under the weight of their fruit.

The U.S. Patent Office has on file a patent for boots with pockets for use by nudists.

What a Card

Most authorities agree that the earliest use of cards was as much for divination as for gaming. Hindu playing cards, for instance, used 10 suits respresenting the 10 incarnations of Vishnu. To this day, cards remain connected with many religious rites.

How were cards introduced to Europe? Some authorities credit the Crusaders, others the Saracens, some the gypsies, and still others point to the Tartars. More than likely, all of these sources are in some part responsible, since cards appeared in many different countries during the late 14th century.

It is the Italians who are credited with the introduction of those picture cards called the Tarot. This deck consists of 22 pictorial representations of material forces, elements, virtues, and vices, one of which was the forerunner of our modern-day joker. For centuries, gypsies have been reputed to foretell the future based on the interpretation of Tarot cards, which use characters and dress strikingly similar to those of the Romany tribe.

At some point the two types of cards—the Tarot and the playing deck—were combined, resulting in a 78-card deck composed of the 56 cards of the oriental variety and the 22 of the Tarot. The game derived is still popular in several countries. Further combinations of numbers and pictures resulted in decks of 40 cards (Italy and Spain), 32 cards or 36 cards (Germany), and 52 cards (France). This last deck became the standard in all English-speaking countries. The English retained the French symbols for the suits, but gave them English names. Today, if you want to call a spade a spade in France, you would say *pique*. In German, a spade is a *grun;* and in Italian, a *spada*. The costumes worn by the jack, queen, and king are of the time of Henry VII and Henry VIII.

The Soviet government attempted to substitute revolutionary figures for those of the corrupt monarchy, but the card tradition was so well entrenched that they finally had to give up.

The number of decks in circulation, long limited by the expense of hand-painting, rose dramatically with the invention of wood engraving and block printing. Today, there are more than 70 million decks sold per year in the United States alone.

The heaviest organ in the human body is the liver, which weighs an average of 3½ pounds. This is more than five times the weight of the heart.

For great occasions, nomadic Arab tribes usually prepare a feast whose main dish is, at least in size, without equal. This dish consists of eggs which are stuffed in fish, the fish then stuffed in chickens, and the chickens then stuffed in sheep, and the sheep finally stuffed in a whole roasted camel.

The longest throw in baseball history was the achievement of one Sheldon Lejeunne, who on October 12, 1910, threw a baseball a distance of 426 feet, 9½ inches. This is well over the average distance from the centerfield fence to home plate!

The highest mountain peak in California—the 14,494-foot peak of Mount Whitney—can be seen from the lowest point in the United States, which lies 282 feet below sea level in Death Valley, California. The two extremes are within 100 miles of each other.

On July 31, 1964, Alvin Parker flew a single-seat glider over a distance of 644 miles—the longest single-seat glider flight on record. Not bad for a plane without a motor!

Octopi and Squids

The octopus and squid belong to a class of sea creatures, called Cephalopods, that are found in almost all the world's waters. The octopus alone comprises some 140 species, ranging in size from just an inch to 28 feet in diameter.

The word "octopus" means "eight legs," but the tentacles of this creature might just as easily be called "arms." Each of the octopus' arms contains rows of suckers with which the octopus can grip its prey. But before killing a victim, the octopus paralyzes it with a secretion from its salivary glands. Octopi have been known to capture men with their tight-gripping tentacles, and are among the more ferocious creatures to be found in the deep.

The octopus also uses its tentacles to crawl along the ocean floor. Most live in shallow coastal waters, while others have been found in the deep sea. They prefer crabs or other crustaceans as their meal, but an octopus in captivity may devour its own arms—even if other food is available!

The squid has ten legs—or arms—equipped with suckers. Two of these tentacles are longer than the other eight. The squid uses the shorter arms to capture its prey, then transfers the catch to its mouth with the longer, more mobile arms. Squids range in size from just an inch or so to 52 feet in length, and the larger squids are the biggest invertebrate creaturs on earth.

Some squids are equipped with light organs in various regions of their body that make the creature phosphorescent. Others "fly" by leaping across the surface of the water, and can occasionally leap right onto the deck of a ship.

The most distinguishing feature of the squid, however, is its ability to squirt an inky substance into the water when set upon by a predator. The ink, or sepia, forms a screen to hide the squid, and also a dark "dummy" shape that the predator often attacks in place of the squid. After squirting its sepia, the squid becomes transparent and slips away in the darkness of the deep.

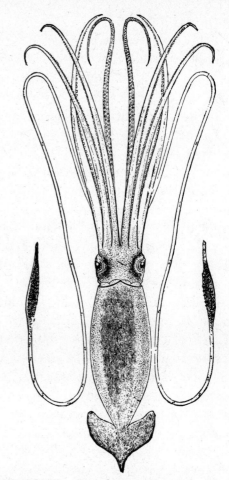

GIANT SQUID *Found primarily in the North Atlantic, this is the largest invertebrate creature on earth, growing up to 52 feet in length. Most are only seven feet long.*

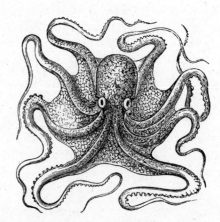

OCTOPUS VULGARIS *This is the common octopus, found in all the seas of the world. It may span over six feet with its tentacles.*

MUSK OCTOPUS *Like all octopi, this creature uses its tentacles as both arms and legs.*

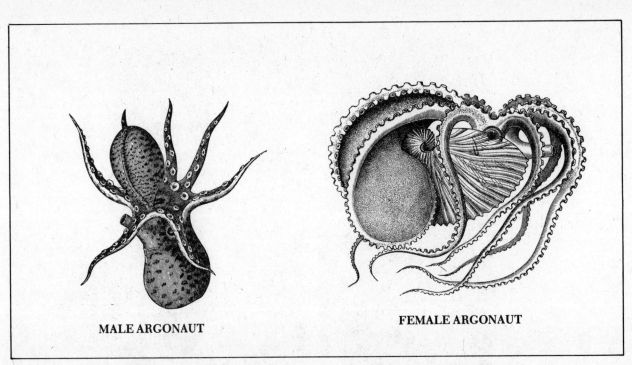

MALE ARGONAUT

FEMALE ARGONAUT

ARGONAUT   *Also called the paper nautilus, this Mediterranean denizen usually measures just an inch in length. The young develop in the female's spiral shell.*

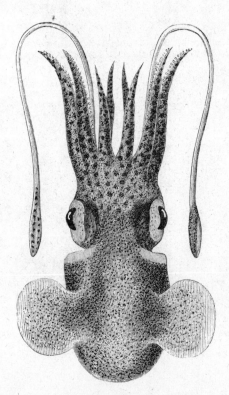

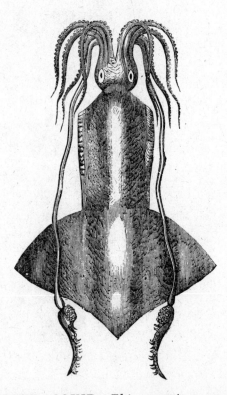

SEPIOLA   *Some members of this genus bear phosphorescent light organs. The creature takes its name from sepia, the inky protective fluid it secretes when attacked.*

HOOKED SQUID   *This carnivorous marine cephalopod has a long, tapered body, with tapered fins on either side. A horny plate is buried under the mantle of the squid. In the United States, this creature is used for fish bait, while in Mediterranean and Oriental countries, the squid is eaten as a delicacy.*

GIGANTIC CUTTLE-FISH *This cuttle-fish was caught by the French Corvette Alectaon near Tenerife.*

Houdini stayed underwater in a sealed coffin an hour and a half

No locks, no chains, no manacles could hold Harry Houdini, the greatest escape artist of all time. Born as Erich Weiss in 1874, this boy from Appleton, Wisconsin, did not take long to make headlines.

His handcuff act became so famous that he was invited to "escape" from London's Scotland Yard. Superintendent Melville, chief of this, the most famous police force in the world, placed Houdini's arms around a pillar and then handcuffed him. Before Melville was out of the building, Houdini had freed himself and caught up to the chief!

Houdini could open any lock in the world in a few minutes. Once, on a tour through Europe, the Continent's most famous locksmiths presented him with what they considered foolproof locks, the result of countless years of work. Houdini opened the locks so astonishingly fast that the master mechanics hardly knew what was happening.

During his European tour, Houdini escaped from jails in the cities of Liverpool, Amsterdam, Moscow, and The Hague. He duplicated these feats in almost every large city in the United States. The plain fact was that Houdini could enter or leave virtually any room, building, or cell at will.

His repertoire of escape acts fascinated millions all over the world. So uncanny were his performances that many believed Houdini possessed supernatural powers. Though Houdini vociferously denied being gifted with anything more than human attributes, his performances were so baffling that even his stout denials failed to squelch the talk. No one could fathom just how his stunts were accomplished; and it was not until after his death that his notebooks revealed how he contrived to do things which seemed beyond the powers of mortals.

One of his favorite stunts was to have himself bound by the police in a straitjacket used for the violently insane. No one, the police averred, could break out of this. But, in addition to the straitjacket, Harry had the police load him with iron shackles and ropes. Houdini was turned upside down, and hauled aloft in mid-air by means of a block and pulley. Then, in full sight of an astounded audience and an absolutely dumbfounded police detail, the incredible man would wriggle free.

How did he do it?

Houdini was one of the greatest athletes that ever lived. From his early youth on, he had practiced body control. He could flex virtually every muscle in his body. His fingers had the strength of pliers; and his teeth were so strong that they could be used like a can opener. His strength was so great that he could bend iron bars, and his tactile sensibility so fantastic that while blindfolded he could tell the exact number of toothpicks he was kneeling on.

Still, how did Houdini get out of that straitjacket? Answer: He contracted his muscles in such a way that he could slip one hand out of its bonds. By similar contractions and maneuverings, he would set his limbs free. Then the great locksmith would free himself from his iron fetters.

Houdini left explicit directions as to just how the stunt could be accomplsihed, but so far no athlete has come along with enough physical dexterity to perform the feat.

Unsurpassed as a magician, Houdini displayed courage and daring equally unmatched. In the days when the airplane was still a new and unproved machine, Houdini jumped from one airplane to another—3,000 feet above the earth—*while handcuffed!*

On August 26, 1907, Houdini leaped off a bridge in San Francisco Bay with his hands tied behind his back and 75 pounds of ball and chain attached to his body. He came up out of the water unharmed.

On another occasion, Houdini was thrown

into the East River in New York city, handcuffed inside a box to which 200 pounds of iron had been attached. But what were handcuffs, irons, and a river to Harry? He emerged within two minutes.

And then, on August 5, 1926, as if to cap all his former feats, he allowed himself to be sealed in a coffin which was then lowered into the waters of a swimming pool. Before a whole deputation of doctors and newsmen, he remained in the coffin under water *a full hour and a half!*

Immediately upon emerging, he was examined by physicians who all agreed that he had suffered no ill effects. Houdini contended that it was panic, not lack of air, which usually caused suffocation. His own muscle control was so phenomenal that he may have accomplished this stunt by means of suspended animation.

Yet despite the fact that the physicians gave Houdini a clean bill of health on August 5, 1926, the great magician and athlete did not live to see 1927.

Fantasy

Most artists have drawn their fantasies and recorded them for posterity. Some of these depictions are really great. There follow a few from notable magazines by noted artists.

A drawing which titillated the readers of Punch some hundred years ago

A drawing by Aubrey Vincent Beardsley (1872-1898). Beardsley defied all accepted conventions to originate a new method of illustration in black and white that was highly imaginative and decorative.

This is a drawing by Grand-ville, which first appeared in La Vie des Animaux

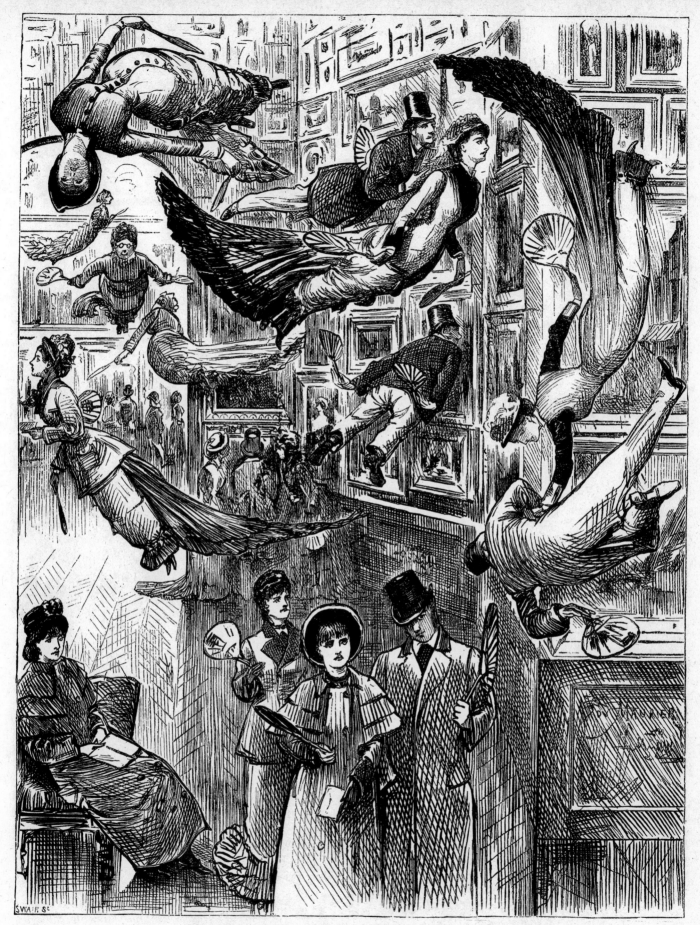

This imaginative drawing can mean or depict anything you want it to.
It first appeared in the internationally renowned Punch of London

Drawing which first appeared in Fifty Years of Soviet Art, *published in Moscow.*

A *delicious fantasy which appeared in an 1887 edition of* Youth's Companion, *a magazine published in Boston.*

Drawing by Grandville *which first appeared in* Un Autre Monde

Drawing by E. Wyttenbach, used for a cigar box cover around 1857

A woman's dream of peace, from the Comic Almanac, *or "How to handle your husband and children," authored by Albert Thackeray, printed in London between 1844 and 1853*

The first electronic digital computer was the ENIAC (Electronic Numerical Integrator and Computer), built by J. Presper Eckert and John Mauchly at the University of Pennsylvania. Completed in 1946, the ENIAC was a thousand times faster than any earlier computer. But the ENIAC was a huge machine by modern standards, a U-shaped assemblage of 40 panels occupying some 3,000 square feet, with 70,000 resistors, 18,000 vacuum tubes, and 6,000 switches!

The earth's surface holds 324 million cubic miles of water. Another 2 million cubic miles of H_2O lie underground, and 3,000 cubic miles are suspended in the atmosphere.

The words *laser, radar, scuba, snafu,* and *sonar* may look like ordinary words, but in fact each began as an acronym, a word formed by joining together the first letters of the words of a phrase. The phrases represented by these acronyms are:

Laser—Light Amplification by Stimulated Emission of Radiation
Radar—Radio Detecting and Ranging
Scuba—Self-contained Underwater Breathing Apparatus
Snafu—Situation Normal All Fouled Up
Sonar—Sound Navigation Ranging

James W. Zaharee of North Dakota, using a fine pen and a microscope, printed Lincoln's Gettysburg Address on a human hair less than three inches long.

The long-distance swimming record holder must be Mihir Sen of India. In recent years, he has swum from India to Ceylon, across the Dardanelles, across the Strait of Gibralter, and the length of the Panama Canal.

The construction of the ancient megalithic formation at Stonehenge, England, required an estimated 1.5 million man-hours of labor.

Biographical Balderdash

For the 1886 and 1888 editions of Appleton's Cyclopedia of American Biography, the policy of the editors was to accept all material received by mail. Their trusting nature made them the unwitting prey of some practical joker who sent them at least 84 biographies of fictitious persons. These phoney bios were all published, and went unnoticed until 1919, when 14 of the frauds were discovered by a librarian. This led to a search that brought to light 70 more by 1936.

The Hoang typewriter, a device for typing in Chinese characters, has 5,700 characters on a keyboard 2 feet wide and 17 inches high.

A two-day-old gazelle can outrun a full-grown horse.

In 1968, Mrs. Emma Smith, a 38-year-old housewife from Nottinghamshire, England, was buried in a coffin for 101 days as a stunt at the Skegness Amusement Park. Her feat is still unmatched—by any living human being, that is.

You won't find the world's largest Gothic cathedral in any European city. An American church, the Cathedral of St. John the Divine in New York City, is the world's largest place of worship built in the Gothic style. The church is 601 feet long and 320 feet across at its widest point.

Rainbows may be seen at night. Lunar rainbows were observed and recorded in ancient times and are not uncommon. When the sun shines through a sheet of falling rain, it is very apt to form a rainbow. The same effect is caused, now and then, by moonlight. Even strong electric lights shining through rain and mist have caused this phenomenon.

Prince Wenzel von Kaunitz-Rietburg, an 18th century Austrian statesman, changed his clothes no less than 30 times daily. This obsession occupied about four hours a day.

A Spicy Story

Columbus made his journey to America seeking a short way to India in order to import spices. The spices were extremely important to Europe at a time when refrigeration was not known.

Nowadays, international trade in spices amounts to something over $170 million a year. Pepper alone normally accounts for over one-fourth of the world's total trade in spices.

Honolulu, Hawaii, is the American city with the highest median family income—$12,539 in 1970. The city's nearest competitors were: San Jose, California; Seattle, Washington; and Indianapolis, Indiana. At the other end of the scale were New Orleans and Miami, where median family incomes were below $7,500.

There is a difference of 65,226 feet—approximately 12.35 miles—between the highest and lowest points on the earth. Mount Everest, the highest peak, rises 29,028 feet. The Mariana Trench in the Pacific, the lowest point on earth, is 36,198 feet below sea level.

A car runs more smoothly at night or in damp weather simply because the air is cooler, not because it contains more oxygen; the amount of oxygen in the air is a constant. Cool air is more dense than warm air; and therefore, an engine takes in a greater weight of air when it is damp and chilly. This accounts for the increased power and the freedom from engine knock which so many motorists notice when they drive at night or in the rain.

The first attempt to devise a "Tilt" mechanism for pinball machines was crude indeed. Nails were hammered into the underside of the machines to provide a painful surprise to players attempting to slap the board from underneath.

The Golden Touch

You've heard the phrase, "rich as Croesus"—ever wonder how rich the last king of Lydia actually was? We don't know exactly how much Croesus, who reigned from 560 B.C. to 546 B.C., was worth in dollars and cents, but the remains of an elaborate gold-refining works, uncovered by archaeologists digging at Sardis, suggest that Croesus minted his own pure gold coins. Before Croesus' time, coins were made of electrum, an alloy containing 20-35 percent silver, so Croesus' discovery of a purification process made possible the first standardization of currency.

The Ubiquitous Weasel Tribe

Should we see some small animal running in the woods, we might guess that it was a woodchuck or a skunk, or perhaps a raccoon. Most of us do not know that there are many, many small animals which, because of their size, look alike, but which are, each one of them, a distinct species. Here are some beasties you are likely to confuse:

PARADOXURUS *Also known as the palm civet, this cat-sized Asian native feeds on fruit and vegetation as well as small animals.*

ZIBETH *A close Asian relative of the civet.*

RACCOON *A strictly nocturnal, omnivorous creature common in North America. Before eating anything, the raccoon first washes its food in the nearest available water.*

ERMINE *Some ermines are brown in summer and white in winter. All are sought for their luxurious fur.*

SKUNK *This fearless American native is most noted for the fetid-smelling secretion it squirts to ward off would-be attackers. Skunks prefer insects, but also eat small rodents, frogs, and eggs.*

WOODCHUCK *This burrowing North American native is also known as the ground hog and American marmot. The woodchuck feeds mainly on grass and other vegetation.*

POLECAT *Americans use the word "polecat" to refer to the skunk, but in Europe, the polecat is a blood-thirsty, ferretlike night hunter.*

RATEL *A clumsy-looking native of Africa and India that is often called the honey badger. Ratels live in pairs, hunting small rodents, birds, and insects.*

MONGOOSE *A small Indian native long used to control rodents. The mongoose is noted for its ability to battle the feared cobra.*

MINK *A small, slim carnivore prized for its fur. The mink has partly webbed feet, and spends much of its time in the water.*

POTOMOGALE *An arboreal native of the Americas.*

COATI *Also known as the coatimundi, this American tree-dweller is sometimes tamed as a pet.*

ZORIL *This African native closely resembles the skunk in both appearance and odor.*

WOLVERINE *Also known as the glutton due to its voracious eating habits. The cunning, stealthy wolverine lives chiefly in the colder regions of North America.*

MANGUE *Also known as the kusimansel, the mangue is a native of West Africa. This dark-brown coated, burrowing animal is closey allied to the mongoose.*

CIVET *A catlike carnivore from Africa and Asia, the civet is noted for a musky secretion used to make perfume.*

BADGER *A sharp-clawed burrower found in many northern climes, and is the namesake of the state of Wisconsin.*

GENET *The spotted, catlike genet hunts along stream banks in Africa, Europe, and the Near East.*

SABLE *This Siberian native is famous for its fur.*

MARTEN *There are a number of marten species, including the sable. Many live in trees. The fisher is a large marten.*

GLUTTON *A carnivorous mammal named for its gluttonous habits. A relative of the marten and the sable, the glutton is about two-and-a-half feet long and lives in Northern Europe and in Asia.*

TAYRA *An otter-sized, long-tailed South American native often confused with the grison.*

WEASEL *A courageous hunter, the weasel can pursue its prey up a tree or in water. Some weasels turn white in winter.*

FERRET *The ferret is actually a domesticated breed of the polecat, used since ancient Roman times to hunt rabbits and to "ferret out" rats from their holes.*

CACOMISTLE *A raccoonlike native of the United States and Mexico.*

The Verrazano-Narrows Bridge is the longest span in the world

For many years, the entrance to New York Harbor through the Narrows Strait was considered too wide to be spanned with a bridge. Due to the depth of the Strait and its heavy ocean-going traffic—all ships entering the port of New York must pass through this channel—the use of a causeway, cantilever, or any other kind of bridge calling for the placing of pillars in the Strait was ruled out.

The construction of the Brooklyn Bridge in 1883 demonstrated that a suspension bridge could span a sizable distance without pillars obstructing the passage underneath. But the Brooklyn Bridge spanned only 486 feet, a distance hardly comparable to the 4,000-foot-plus width of the Narrows. Then, in 1937, came the completion of the Golden Gate Bridge in San Francisco, with its unbroken span of 4,200 feet. This achievement confirmed the capabilities of the suspension bridge, and plans for a bridge across the Narrows were begun in earnest.

A visitor to New York sailing through the Narrows in 1959 would have observed the bridge taking shape on the shores of Brooklyn and Staten Island. In that year, two steel towers began rising near the sites of Fort Hamilton and Fort Wadsworth, the old fortresses that had guarded the entrance to New York Harbor.

Two years later, a visitor would have found the tall gray towers completed, and thick steel cables strung above him across the busy Strait. By early 1962, a small segment of the roadway structure was suspended from the cables in the very middle of the Strait—for the construction of the roadway began in the center of the span and proceeded toward the two towers.

In 1964, after five years of work and $325 million in construction costs, the longest span in the world was opened to traffic. The bridge was named the Verrazano-Narrows after the Strait it spanned and the Italian explorer who was the first European to sail into the harbor.

From tower to tower, the span extends 4,260 feet, 60 feet more than the Golden

Gate span. The two towers—as tall as 70-story buildings—are so far apart that they were constructed five inches out of parallel to allow for the curvature of the earth! The highest point of the roadway is 228 feet above the water and extends between its two anchorages a distance of 6,690 feet!

One year after the opening of the Verrazano-Narrows Bridge, a second roadway level—which had been almost completely constructed but had not been intended for use for at least another ten years—was quickly put into operation as traffic on the bridge far surpassed all expectations. The two roadways provide for 12 lanes of traffic and weigh more than 60,000 tons!

INDEX

A

B

C

D

Dynamos
    Lightning produced by, 161

E

Eagle, bald
    Weight of nest, 163
Earl of Bridgewater
    Francis H. Egerton, 332
Earthquake
    Caused hole-in-one, 261
    Charleston, South Carolina, 59
    Greatest, 85
    Greatest in U.S., 59
    Incidence, 85
    Intensity, 85
    Montana, 11
    Most deadly, 79
    Pompeii, 135
Earth
    Amount moved for Panama Canal, 296
    Circumference, 55, 356
    Circumnavigation, 107
    Highest point, 41
    Lowest point, 41
    Moisture, 43
    Oceans, 318
    Oldest living thing, 79
    Relative size, 285
    Revolution and orbit around sun, 87, 88
    Satellites, 6
    Speed, 356
    Tallest living thing, 69
    Unexplored regions, 118
    Water, 418
    Weight, 56
    Year, 45, 87
Earthquake Lake
    Madison River, 11
Earthworms
    Number and habits, 379
East Hampton, Long Island, New York
    John Howard Payne, 84
East Pakistan
    Now Bangladesh, 88
Eating
    See CULINARY
Ecárté
    Drunken performance, 227
Ebony
    Piano keys, 363
Eckert, J. Presper
    ENIAC, 418
Ecuador
    Guayaquil, 384
    Poet, 384
Eddine, Helim
    Albanian ruler, 24
Edgar, King of England
    Banned warm baths and soft beds, 254

Edison, Thomas A.
    Telephone, 197
    Invented first typewriter which became
        ticker-tape machine, 186
    Invented light bulb, 94
    Invented talking doll, 105
Edsel
    Fiasco, 375
Edward II, King of England
    Measured inches with barleycorns, 155
Eel
    Electric, 75
    Roe used to fatten Christians, 186
Egerton, Francis H., Earl of Bridgewater
    Dined with dogs, 332
Egg
    French menu boners, 132
    Ostrich, 54
    Record consumption of raw, 132
    Whale, 28
Eggplant
    Dish, *Imam Bayaldi*, made with, 173
    Fourth most popular "vegetable" in Japan, 195
    Love apple, 85
    Mad apple, 85
    Name and color, 201
Egypt
    Labyrinth, 17
    Longest-reigning monarch, 379
    Population, 242
    Ptolemaic queens, 8
    Pyramid, 287
Eiffel Tower, The
    Elevators, 194
    Largest advertisement, 246
    Paid for by sight-seers, 399
Einstein, Albert
    Absentminded, 135
    Left-handed, 33
    Teaching, 387
Eisenhower, Dwight
    At West Point, 210
Elderberry
    Poisonous leaves, 133
Elderly
    Birthday, 68
    Proportion, 285
    Working, 73
Elegy in a Country Churchyard
    By Thomas Grey, 397
Electric
    Eel, 75
    Measurement, 387
    Shock, 35
Electronic computer, 40
Electrum
    For coins, 419
Elektro
    Mechanical man, 35
Elephant
    Born in U.S., 89
    Capacity of trunk, 89
    Fodder consumption, 153
    Gestation period, 140, 215
    Jumbo, 98

H

I

K

L

M

N

O

P

Q

R

S

Sign
    Neon, 166, 363
    Unusual, 86
Sikh
    Beard, 399
Silhouette, Etienne de
    French Finance Minister, 12
    Silhouettes, 12-15
Silkworm
    Length of thread, 167
    Smell, 48
Sills, Beverly
    Erasmus H.S., 302
Silver
    Coins minted at St. Joachimsthal, 186
    Coins minted in Persia, 365
    Foundation in Sri Lanka, 87
    Use as money, 152
Silverfish
    Insect, 22
Silver Gray Dorking
    English chicken, 298
Simon, Neil
    Barefoot in The Park, 73
Simplicissimus
    Drawing of skates, 41
Sinatra, Frank
    Golden records, 171
Single-Comb White Leghorn
    Egg breeder, 299
Sirloin steak
    Calories, 278
Sit-ups
    Record, 75
Siva
    Buddhist temple, Java, 324
    Hindu temple, India, 58
Skateboards
    History, 338, 371
Skating
    Ice, 161, 299, 243, 262, 328, 329, 331, 363
    Most unusual, 89
    Picture, 41
    Roller, 161, 211, 247
Skegness Amusement Park
    Burial stunt, 418
Skeleton
    Value, 292
Skhou
    Origin, 86
Skin
    Amount in human body, 26
    Shedding of human, 94
    Used for writing materials, 64
Skunk
    Habits, 420
    Smell, 207
Sky-diving
    Champion, 115
Skyscraper
    Banned in Washington, D.C., 243
    First U.S., 214
    See also individual buildings
Slaves
    Crassus, 303

George Washington, 64
    Martha Washington, 64
Sleep
    Dolphin, 48
    Dreams, 49
    Patterns, 20
    Pills, 49
    Warhol movie, 67
Sloan, Harry
    Stilt-walking, 204
Slocum, Joshua, Captain
    Sailed around world on yacht, 375
Slot machine
    Las Vegas, 401
    Selling divorces, 166
    Selling holy water, 252
Smell
    Silkworm, 49
Smile
    Unique to humans, 163
Smith
    Most common name in U.S., 89, 292
Smith, Emma
    Stunt burial, 418
Smith, Frances Octavia
    Known as Dale Evans, 125
Smith, John
    Most common name in U.S., 111
Smoking
    Anecdote, 369
    Aztecs, 399
    Charles Steinmetz, 368
    China, 32
    England, 32
    Espionage device, 292
    Habits, 50
    Largest cigar, 68
    Raleigh, 399
    Also see CIGAR, CIGARETTE, PIPE
Smuggling
    Narcotics, 65
    The Shark's Papers, 301
Snafu
    Acronym, 418
Snail
    As food, 324
    Kissing, 166
Snake
    Anaconda, 384
    As food, 51
    Fangs, 385
    Gaboon viper, 385
    Longest, 384
    Places without, 55, 160
    Poisonous, 263
    Rattlesnake, 26
    Venom, 26
Snake eyes
    Dice throw, 372
Snaring
    Hunting, 368
Snow
    California record, 99
    Deepest, 266
    Flakes, 80, 166

T

U

V

W

X

Y

Z

HART PUBLISHING COMPANY, INC.
NEW YORK CITY

511

TH BOOK OF TRIVIA